Coercive Control in Children's and Mothers' Lives

INTERPERSONAL VIOLENCE SERIES

SERIES EDITORS

Claire Renzetti, Ph.D.
Jeffrey L. Edleson, Ph.D.

*Parenting by Men Who Batter:
New Directions for Assessment and
Intervention*
Edited by Jeffrey L. Edleson and
Oliver J. Williams

*Coercive Control: How Men Entrap
Women in Personal Life*
Evan Stark

*Childhood Victimization: Violence, Crime,
and Abuse in the Lives of Young People*
David Finkelhor

*Restorative Justice and Violence
Against Women*
Edited by James Ptacek

*Familicidal Hearts: The Emotional
Styles of 211 Killers*
Neil Websdale

*Violence in Context: Current Evidence on
Risk, Protection, and Prevention*
Edited by Todd I. Herrenkohl,
Eugene Aisenberg, James Herbert
Williams, and Jeffrey M. Jenson

*Poverty, Battered Women, and Work in
U.S. Public Policy*
Lisa D. Brush

*Child Victims and Restorative Justice:
A Needs-Rights Model*
Tali Gal

Battered Women's Protective Strategies
Sherry Hamby

Men Who Batter
Nancy Nason-Clark and
Barbara Fisher-Townsend

When Men Murder Women
R. Emerson Dobash and
Russell P. Dobash

*Comparative Perspectives on Gender
Violence: Lessons From Efforts Worldwide*
Edited by Rashmi Goel and
Leigh Goodmark

*Religion and Intimate Partner
Violence: Understanding the Challenges
and Proposing Solutions*
Nancy Nason-Clark, Barbara
Fisher-Townsend, Catherine Holtmann,
Stephen McMullin

*Violence Against Women in the 21st
Century: Transnational Perspectives of
Empowerment and Subjugation*
Edited by Kristen Zaleski, Annalisa
Enrile, Eugenia Weiss, Xiying Wang

*State Sanctioned Violence:
Advancing a Social Work
Social Justice Agenda*
Melvin Delgado

*Collaborating for Change
Transforming Cultures to End Gender-
Based Violence in Higher Education*
Edited by Susan B. Marine and
Ruth Lewis

*Women, Intimate Partner Violence, and
the Law*
Heather Douglas

*Urban Gun Violence
Self-Help Organizations as Healing Sites,
Catalysts for Change, and Collaborative
Partners*
Melvin Delgado

Islamophobia and Acts of Violence
Carolyn Turpin-Petrosino

*Coercive Control in Children's and
Mothers' Lives*
Emma Katz

Coercive Control in Children's and Mothers' Lives

EMMA KATZ

OXFORD
UNIVERSITY PRESS

Oxford University Press is a department of the University of Oxford. It furthers
the University's objective of excellence in research, scholarship, and education
by publishing worldwide. Oxford is a registered trade mark of Oxford University
Press in the UK and certain other countries.

Published in the United States of America by Oxford University Press
198 Madison Avenue, New York, NY 10016, United States of America.

© Oxford University Press 2022

All rights reserved. No part of this publication may be reproduced, stored in
a retrieval system, or transmitted, in any form or by any means, without the
prior permission in writing of Oxford University Press, or as expressly permitted
by law, by license, or under terms agreed with the appropriate reproduction
rights organization. Inquiries concerning reproduction outside the scope of the
above should be sent to the Rights Department, Oxford University Press, at the
address above.

You must not circulate this work in any other form
and you must impose this same condition on any acquirer.

Library of Congress Cataloging-in-Publication Data
Names: Katz, Emma, author.
Title: Coercive control in children's and mothers' lives / Emma Katz.
Description: New York, NY : Oxford University Press, [2022] |
Series: Interpersonal violence series | Includes bibliographical references and index.
Identifiers: LCCN 2021059464 (print) | LCCN 2021059465 (ebook) |
ISBN 9780190922214 (hardback) | ISBN 9780190922238 (epub) | ISBN 9780190922245
Subjects: LCSH: Family violence. | Domestic relations. |
Control (Psychology) | Women—Abuse of. | Child abuse.
Classification: LCC HV6626 .K356 2022 (print) | LCC HV6626 (ebook) |
DDC 362.82/92—dc23/eng/20220413
LC record available at https://lccn.loc.gov/2021059464
LC ebook record available at https://lccn.loc.gov/2021059465

DOI: 10.1093/oso/9780190922214.001.0001

The manufacturer's authorised representative in the EU for product
safety is Oxford University Press España S.A. of El Parque Empresarial
San Fernando de Henares, Avenida de Castilla, 2 – 28830 Madrid
(www.oup.es/en or product.safety@oup.com). OUP España S.A. also
acts as importer into Spain of products made by the manufacturer.

CONTENTS

Preface vii
Acknowledgments xv

1. Understanding coercive control 1

2. Coercive control and the agentic child 39

3. Interviewing children and mothers about coercive control 56

4. Coercive control: Harms to children 78

5. Mother–child relationships under coercive control 125

6. Ready to recover? Challenges faced when breaking free of coercive control 183

7. Helping each other to recover: Mothers' and children's strategies 214

8. And they lived happily ever after? Outcomes for mother–child relationships after coercive control 246

9. A new way of life: Mutuality and closeness between mothers and children 306

10. Ways ahead 323

References 347
Index 371

PREFACE

Seven-year-old Roxie hugs her mother as she cries. Dad has locked them in the house and stormed off again, and they can't get out until he returns. How long will he be gone this time? Roxie is upset—Dad is always doing horrible things like this. The first time he hit her, a couple of years ago, he said that she was just like her mum because she answered him back like Mum did. He said that he would beat it out of her, just like he beats it out of her mum. Since then, Roxie has felt scared at home. She's stayed quiet and been more careful around Dad. Dad often says nasty things to Mum in front of her. He calls Mum bad names like "fat slag." He tells Roxie and her little brothers that they don't have to listen to Mum, that they can eat whatever they want, never mind what Mum has cooked them. Dad doesn't like Mum to go out, so Roxie and her mum and her brothers stay at home a lot. Roxie wants things to get better, but she doesn't see what could stop Dad from behaving the way he does.

Childhood should be a time of nurturance and growing independence. The intrepid child, supported by loving, empathetic, consistent, and boundary-setting caregivers, should be able to explore their world. As they learn new skills and tackle new situations, the inevitable mistakes they make should be used positively as opportunities for growth. As children get to know themselves and their preferences, their rights as enshrined in the United Nations Convention on the Rights of the Child should be respected, including their right to have a say in matters that affect them, and for their views to be given due weight.

Yet perpetrators of coercive control such as Roxie's father are catastrophically unequipped to give children the childhood experiences they need. A perpetrator of coercive control (usually, though not always, a child's father or father-figure) is singularly focused on one thing: their campaign to control their target or targets (usually the child's mother, and sometimes also the child themselves). To control their targets, coercively controlling fathers deploy an arsenal of harmful tactics: psychological abuse; manipulation; financial impoverishment; restriction of time, space, and activities; isolation; constant monitoring; and threats. Some perpetrators are also physically violent and sexually abusive. Overall, coercive control perpetrators are the most harmful and dangerous kind of domestic violence perpetrators, and tend to harm their partners and children in multiple ways.

We don't yet know how many children worldwide experience coercive control (when an incident of violence occurs in an intimate relationship, this doesn't necessarily mean a campaign of coercive control is happening, so our statistics on domestic violence are not ideal for understanding the true scale of coercive control). However, given what we know about the frequency of domestic violence, it is likely that millions of children globally are having their childhoods blighted by coercive control right now.

Mothers and children who are subjected to coercive control feel trapped. The perpetrator has made it clear that they must meet his expectations and obey his commands, or face awful punishments. Over a long period of abuse, he will have made every effort to cut off the escape routes—psychological and practical—that mothers and children would need to leave him. He may have told the mother that if she tries to leave he will kill her, or will make sure that she and the children never see each other again. He will have made it clear that he can get away with doing the things he threatens.

His chief demand is that family life revolves around meeting his needs and keeping him happy. He has little empathy for his children or his partner: From his point of view, their needs and rights do not exist. Sometimes he may be nice to his partner or play lovingly with his children, but this is not for their benefit; it is for his. His periods of being affectionate and fun give his targets false hope that things are not that bad, reducing their ability to recognize just how abusive he really is and increasing their entrapment. To the outside world, a coercive control perpetrator may seem like a violent, dangerous, or hostile man; or, alternatively, he may just as easily be seen as a normal "great guy"—likeable, generous, intelligent, even a pillar of his community. Appearances can be very deceptive.

For children living under the coercive control perpetrated by their father (or father-figure), childhood is a bleak and distorted version of how it should be. He may dislike it when their mother gives them love and attention, and frequently demand that she stop it and focus on him instead. He may be furious when the children make noise, cause mess, or engage in carefree play at home, and make it clear that these normal childhood activities will not be tolerated. Children's healthy attempts to develop their independence by asserting their will against their parents are crushed in relation to their father—he won't allow critiques or disobedience.

Children's lives are also harmed when he harms their mother. When he isolates their mother from her family and friends and makes it difficult for her to go out in the community, the children are also isolated—they may not be able to go to their friend's houses or do after-school activities if their mother is unable to take them, and opportunities to build friendships and socialize are lost. Their father may have plenty of money for himself, but leave their mother chronically poor, meaning she cannot buy the children the things they need, like nutritious food, causing negative impacts on their health. The children know that their feelings matter very little in their family. Although their mother may care deeply about them and may do her very best to look after them, there are limits to what their father will allow her to do, and, overall, it is clear to the children that family life revolves around pleasing their father.

The above summary of childhood under coercive control is drawn from the qualitative research interviews that I carried out in England with 15 mothers and 15 of their children who had lived with and eventually broken free from coercive control. Young Roxie, with whose story we began, is one of these children. Aged 11 when I interviewed her, and having lived apart from her father for four years, Roxie could well remember what life had been like during his campaign of coercive control, and what it had taken for her and her mother to begin to recover from his abuse. These interviews form the heart of this book, giving rich insights into what life was like for children and mothers both during and after coercive control.

Such insights are rare. This book is the first academic book to examine children's experiences of coercive control. The approach it takes represents a deep shift in the children and domestic violence field. We make the shift happen by asking a bold new question. The old question, that has dominated children and domestic violence research for the last several decades, is: "How are children affected by exposure to incidents of parental violence?" The new question, which this book asks, is:

How are children affected by the perpetrator's campaign of coercive control (a campaign that may, or may not, include violence)?

Additionally, the book also asks:

What does the road to recovery look like for children and mothers who have experienced coercive control?

The mothers and children interviewed for this research explained what daily life had been like under coercive control. They reflected on what activities they had to do, or could not do, because of how perpetrators/ fathers would react. From those interviews, a detailed picture emerged of how perpetrators'/fathers' coercive control had constrained children's and mothers' actions and limited their freedoms. However, the picture was not just one of constraints. Children and mothers also bravely resisted perpetrators'/fathers' abuse when and where they could, and had eventually escaped, at least to an extent. Escape was not easy, and usually required much more than separating from perpetrators. As part of their escape, survivors often had to manage family court battles over child custody and contact; ongoing threats, stalking, abuse, and violence by perpetrators/ fathers; and multiple house moves. Because many perpetrators/fathers

PREFACE   xi

attempted to maintain their coercive control post-separation, the road taken by children and mothers toward freedom was often long and dangerous.

By the time they took part in the study, most of the interviewed children and mothers had largely escaped from coercive control. They had built new lives for themselves, usually as single-mother households. (A small number of mothers were in relationships with new partners.) Most children's and mothers' descriptions suggested that, overall, the new lives they had built were much more positive than their life under the perpetrator's/father's coercive control, and were helpful to their recovery and growth.

This book's study of coercive control is also a study of the mother–child relationships between adult victims/survivors and child victims/survivors. Some unique features are present here: In this study, unlike previous studies, children and mothers from the same families were asked to recall how close or strained their relationships with each other had been at different points along their journeys. You, the reader, will be able to see "what happened next" and understand the long-term trajectories that mothers and children experienced, some of which were ultimately very positive and hopeful.

The book is organized as follows. Chapter 1 introduces coercive control in more depth, exploring its tactics, dynamics, and impacts. Chapter 2 introduces the cutting edge and innovative approaches that this book helps pioneer to illuminate children's experiences. Chapter 3 explains the "hows, whats, whens, and whys" of the interviews themselves, such as how mothers and children were contacted, how interviews were designed, and what ethical approaches were followed. Readers who are not interested in these details can skip this chapter! Chapters 4–9 draw on the interviews with children and mothers to explore how their lives were affected by coercive control, and we will close this preface by outlining these chapters in a little more depth.

The purpose of chapter 4 is to show how children were both profoundly harmed by, and also resisted, perpetrators'/fathers' coercive control. This chapter suggests that children and mothers in these circumstances should be understood as co-victims and co-survivors who are both being harmed by the same thing: perpetrators' drive and determination to control others. Implications of this way of thinking for child protection and family courts are set out in this chapter.

Chapter 5 examines how coercive control affects mother–child relationships. Here we will see how the differing circumstances of the different families, and the precise nature of perpetrators' coercive control in each family, impacts on mother–child relationships. This chapter organizes the impacts on mother–child relationships into a "Five Factor Framework," and explains how this framework can be used to understand how some mother–child relationships stayed close and supportive whereas others became much more strained and distant.

Chapter 6 picks up the story of children's and mothers' lives at the point when they had separated from perpetrators. It explores the two main difficulties that mothers and children faced post-separation: contact between children and perpetrators/fathers that allowed perpetrators to stay in their lives and continue their coercive control, and post-separation violence, stalking, and harassment from perpetrators/fathers, which could leave mothers and children in as much danger as ever. This chapter also outlines what circumstances and types of support were required by children and mothers for them to begin to heal from coercive control and start to build new lives.

Chapter 7 highlights the ways in which many of the interviewed mothers and children had helped one another to recover. This was something they had done in the months and years after separating from perpetrators/fathers, through simple but meaningful forms of positive interaction with each other. Woven into the fabric of their everyday lives, their techniques for helping each other included particular methods of giving reassurance, building each other's confidence, and showing care and affection for one another.

Chapter 8 gives a detailed survey of the longer-term outcomes for mother-child relationships after coercive control. These relationships in the period after separating from perpetrators/fathers are described through four patterns, named as follows: (1) positive supportiveness, positive recoveries; (2) high-stakes support, limited recoveries; (3) struggling relationships, struggling recoveries, and; (4) broken relationships, blocked recoveries. Each mother–child relationship in the study was characterized as experiencing one of these four patterns. Some were characterized as experiencing pattern 1, some pattern 2, and so forth. The chapter will reveal what distinctive feature characterized mothers and children experiencing pattern 1—the most positive pattern—and what this means for those who seek to support survivors of coercive control.

As the book starts to come to a close, chapter 9 provides rare insights into what mothers and children themselves wanted from their post-coercive control mother–child relationships: their views, feelings, and outlooks. Interestingly, one particular type of mother–child relationship—that these survivor families had either achieved or wished to achieve—was almost universally aspired-to by mothers and children. The chapter will sketch out what particular, ideal type of mother–child relationship this was.

Finally, chapter 10, the conclusion to the book, provides ten game-changing recommendations for future research, policy, and practice. These ten recommendations—five for research and five for policy and practice—suggest the necessity for bold action in a number of key areas, including how we address perpetrators and how we understand and support children and mothers.

ACKNOWLEDGMENTS

This book began its life as a project funded by the UK Economic and Social Research Council (grant number ES/I011935/1), and I am grateful for their support. I also give my heartfelt thanks and gratitude to the women and children who participated in the study.

Finally I thank my husband and fellow academic, Dr. Joseph Maslen, a tremendously skilled writer and editor who did so much to assist me in making this book happen, day to day, dawn until dusk. Ours is a close working relationship as well as a life companionship; while we publish under separate names, our writing comes out of a collaborative process. As outsiders to each other's specialisms, we help each other in communicating our ideas, and the way the book unfolds reflects this.

1

Understanding coercive control

THE COERCIVE CONTROL MODEL OF DOMESTIC VIOLENCE

If a situation of coercive control were a political system, it would be a dictatorship. The coercive control perpetrator is the dictator. Dictators, able to behave with deceptive politeness on the international stage, are defined by their cruel, ruthless, and paranoid tyranny over their own people. Domestic opposition is usually banned. Contact with people from other countries is heavily restricted. Citizens are likely to be under constant surveillance. Compliance is instilled through terror and threat of punishment. In other words, life with a coercive control perpetrator is like living under one of the most oppressive governments on Earth. And there are millions of these mini dictatorships happening right now on ordinary streets. Quite probably (if you live on one), on your street too.

The understanding that much domestic violence is about one partner seeking to coercively control, dominate, and assert power over another has long been recognized by certain researchers, advocates, and organizations (e.g., Dobash and Dobash, 1979; Dobash et al., 1992; Dutton and Goodman, 2005; Herman, 1992; Pence and Paymar, 1986, 1993; Stark and Flitcraft, 1995). In 2007, Evan Stark's book-length work on this subject, *Coercive Control: The Entrapment of Women in Personal Life*, further increased awareness of how coercive control is at the heart of the most dangerous and harmful cases of domestic violence. In that book, Stark

Coercive Control in Children's and Mothers' Lives. Emma Katz, Oxford University Press. © Oxford University Press 2022.
DOI: 10.1093/oso/9780190922214.003.0001

argued that our criminal justice and social responses to domestic violence were failing victims and were in urgent need of transformation because they wrongly conceptualized domestic violence as discreet incidents or episodes of violence. This incidents-of-violence-based understanding of domestic violence disregards the fact that coercive control perpetrators use many other abusive tactics besides violence—including emotional/psychological abuse, monitoring and microregulation, isolation, and economic abuse—and they use those tactics continuously. Victims/survivors of coercive control are therefore being constantly abused, even if there has not been an incident of violence for months, or ever.

Conceptualizing domestic violence as physical violence therefore leads us to underestimate the risks and harms of coercive control. It also underestimates the true extent of the damage that perpetrators are inflicting, leading to dangerously ineffectual responses. A perpetrator may have brought about a situation where his partner is living like a prisoner in her own home, her every action controlled and monitored, deprived of her liberty, only allowed out under strict conditions, a shell of her former self, her psychological integrity in ruins, and her economic well-being drastically reduced (Moulding et al., 2021); but, because the perpetrator has not beaten her recently or inflicted any major physical injuries on her, the risk of him causing harm to her is perceived as low and she is offered very little help (Stark, 2007). It is still overwhelmingly true across the world that, as Stark (2007) observed, there is no mechanism for criminal justice systems to recognize the enormous harm that has been caused by such perpetrators. This legal vacuum leaves them free to continue their abuse.

As the work of Stark and others has highlighted, there needs to be a fundamental change—a revolution—in the ways that societies understand and respond to coercive control. The model of domestic violence as incidents of violence needs to be set aside in cases of coercive control. In its place, the coercive control model should be adopted. This model emphasizes that multiple tactics of abuse are used by perpetrators, and that they use these tactics continuously. The model highlights how perpetrators' tactics have cumulative effects on victims/survivors, entrapping them, depriving them of liberty, and causing "death by a thousand cuts."

Understanding coercive control

TACTICS OF COERCIVE CONTROL

Numerous studies have helped to illuminate how coercive control operates as a severe and multidimensional form of domestic violence (e.g., Bancroft et al., 2012; Barnes and Aune, 2021; Chantler and McCarry, 2020; Crossman et al., 2016; Douglas, 2018; Douglas and Fell, 2020; Dragiewicz et al., 2021a; Dragiewicz et al., 2021b; Dutton and Goodman, 2005; Elizabeth, 2017; Feresin et al., 2019; Halliwell et al., 2021; Hardesty et al., 2013; Haselschwerdt et al., 2019a; Havard and Lefevre, 2020; Hayes, 2017; Hester et al., 2017; Heward-Belle, 2017; Heward-Belle et al., 2018; Hill, 2020; Humphreys et al., 2009; Lehmann et al., 2012; Lux and Gill, 2021; Mandel et al., 2021; Matheson et al., 2015; Matolcsi, 2020; McDonald et al., 2019; Miller et al., 2010; Monckton Smith, 2020a, 2020b; Monk and Bowen, 2021; Moulding et al., 2021; Pitman, 2017; SafeLives, 2019; Saltmarsh et al., 2021; Sanders, 2015; Sharp, 2008; Sharp, 2014; Sharp-Jeffs et al., 2018; Solace/Women's Aid, 2021; Stansfield and Williams, 2021; Stark, 2007, 2009, 2012; Tarzia, 2021; Tarzia et al., 2019; Thiara and Hauge, 2014; Thiara and Roy, 2020; Thomas et al., 2014; Varcoe and Irwin, 2004; Williamson, 2010; Woodlock et al., 2020). Taken together, these studies have provided us with extensive information about the tactics and behaviors of coercive control perpetrators. These include:

- **Emotional and psychological abuse**, including screaming, belittling, mocking, insulting, humiliating, interrogating, and being contemptuous; using a combination of affection, good times, emotional coldness, and emotional cruelty as part of a system of reward and punishment to habituate the victim/ survivor to behave and feel as the perpetrator wishes; sometimes apologizing and making promises to change in order to create false hope in the victim/survivor; denying, minimizing, and blaming other people for their own abusive behavior; undermining the victim's/survivor's confidence, self-esteem, and sense of self-efficacy by continually commenting on their "faults"; "gaslighting" the victim/survivor by encouraging them think that they are mentally ill or encouraging them to doubt their own memory and perceptions of reality; forcing the victim/survivor to watch, hear, or be aware of a loved one being psychologically, physically or sexually abused; preventing the victim/survivor from showing their loved ones affection or giving them attention; using abuse to make the victim/survivor highly dependent on them and then threatening to permanently separate from/ be unfaithful to them; making threats to remove children or pets from the victim/survivor if they defy the coercive control; threatening to reveal private/personal information about the victim/survivor to others; encouraging the victim/survivor to believe that people in their life laugh at them, hate them, or do not care about them; manipulating the feelings of empathy, guilt, connection, and responsibility that the victim/survivor has for them, and their wish to try to help/heal them, in order to coerce the victim/survivor into acting against their own best interests; threatening/attempting or actually committing suicide, or saying that they will die or become seriously ill due to stress or upset if the victim/survivor does not comply with them; and creating states of terror, constant worry and hypervigilance, shame and self-blame, emotional exhaustion, emotional desperation, and mental ill health in victims/survivors through sustained abusive actions.

- **Control of time, space, and movement**, including the "micromanagement" of the victim's/survivor's daily life, routines, choices, appearance, and behavior. This may involve coercing the victim/survivor into spending more time with the perpetrator than they wish to; coercing them into life-altering actions such as marriage or relocating to a new area; making lists of activities that the victim/survivor must follow, especially around housework; restricting the victim's/survivor's ability to make basic decisions for themselves; unreasonably imposing time limits on activities and setting curfews; coercing the victim/survivor into adopting particular styles of clothing, hair, and makeup; controlling what the victim/survivor can eat; preventing the victim/survivor from engaging in the play/leisure activities that they enjoy; depriving the victim/survivor of resources required for normal daily life, such as access to transportation; and dictating and microregulating how the victim/survivor can behave as a parent.

- **Monitoring and stalking**, including through digital technology. This may involve watching and following the victim/survivor; depriving the victim/survivor of privacy; checking the victim's/survivor's phone and letters to monitor their contacts and communications; monitoring the victim's/survivor's online activities; phoning, messaging, and video calling the victim/survivor frequently and intrusively; and placing digital monitoring devices on the victim's/survivor's person/possessions/car/home. Perpetrators may ask others (including their children) to assist them in their monitoring and stalking, or use others for this purpose without their knowledge.
- **Sexual abuse**, including rape and sexual coerciveness (coercing the victim survivor into sexual acts that they do not wish to take part in or find degrading, frightening, or painful); child sexual abuse; paranoia about infidelity/sexual activity; image-based abuse or threatening to reveal to others details of the victim's/survivor's sexual health, sexual past, or sexual preferences; making the victim/survivor feel sexually degraded and dehumanized; and reproductive coercion (birth control sabotage or coercing the victim/survivor into having or not having a child). Sexual abuse can also include coercing the victim/survivor into prostitution/unwanted sexual activity with third parties.
- **Economic abuse**, including interfering with the victim's/survivor's employment, business, or schooling; unfairly appropriating some or all of the victim's/survivor's income, assets, or savings; preventing the victim/survivor from possessing money, assets, or savings or controlling the amounts that they can access; coercing the victim/survivor into excessive amounts of expenditure on gifts/days out/holidays; refusing to contribute

fairly to bills, household expenses, or child maintenance; creating debt for which victims/survivors are liable; falsely or unreasonably claiming that the victim/survivor owes them money/assets; negatively affecting the victim's/survivor's credit score; and involving the victim/survivor in costly legal proceedings vexatiously (i.e., out of a sense of spite, and to continue their control).

- **Isolation from sources of support**, including family, friends, and professionals. Perpetrators may explicitly ban victims/survivors from accessing support, create practical barriers to victims/survivors accessing support (for example, by attending all of their appointments with them), or use manipulation or intimidation to discourage the victim/survivor from having contact with or confiding in family and friends or accessing professional support. Isolation from family can include isolating the adult victim/survivor and their children from each other, and isolating the children from each other to weaken their sibling relationships.
- **Faith-based and spiritual abuse**, including deriding the victim's/survivor's beliefs, preventing the victim/survivor from practicing their religion, coercing the victim/survivor into religious practices with which they are uncomfortable, and using religion to justify abuse.
- **Manipulating and grooming others** online and in-person in order to gain allies and further marginalize and disempower the victim/survivor. This includes perpetrators creating false narratives to present themselves in a positive light (for example, reasonable, logical, highly talented/a genius, respectable, highly moral, generous, fun, cool, funny, caring, concerned, devoted, a complex but mostly good person, deserving of sympathy, hard-done-by, suffering unfairly, a victim of injustice), and perpetrators creating false narratives about the victim/survivor that present them in a negative light and create doubt about their character, sanity, motivations, and credibility (for example, that they are abusive, violent, a drunk/drug user, mentally unbalanced,

emotionally unstable, sexually promiscuous, lacking in religious observance, emotionally cold, hysterical, self-centered/ narcissistic, a bad mother, a "woman scorned," a "vindictive ex," a "gold digger," an "attention/fame seeker," an out-of-control teen, a coached child, a liar/exaggerator/fantasist).

- **Exploiting systems, institutions, and services** to manipulate, threaten, discredit or harm the victim/survivor. These include the criminal justice system, regulations around immigration, family courts, civil courts, schools, banking systems, health/mental health services, social services, religious institutions, housing services, charities, and NGOs.
- **Coercing criminal activity**, including coercing the victim/ survivor into committing crimes, and threatening to disclose the victim's/survivor's criminal actions to the police unless they remain constantly obedient.
- **Intimidation and threats to commit acts of physical abuse, violence, and homicide** against the victim/survivor, their loved ones (including pets) and their property, including driving a car or other vehicle dangerously to instill fear in the victim/survivor; making threats to beat up, set fire to, throw acid at, or kill people or hire others to do so; displaying/holding/making direct threats with guns and other weapons to intimidate the victim/survivor and demonstrate willingness to kill the victim/survivor in future; and threatening to burn down the family home.
- **Physical abuse, violence, and homicide** against the victim/ survivor, their loved ones (including pets), and their property. This includes destruction of property; sabotaging the victim's/ survivor's car; violence such as pushing, hair pulling, shaking, slapping, kicking, hurling heavy objects, hitting, biting, burning, or scalding; strangulation or other methods of cutting off air; throwing/pushing the victim/survivor into walls, across rooms, down staircases, or out of moving cars; causing sexual injuries such as vaginal abrasions, and hurting with a weapon such as a knife; violence that causes injuries that leave the victim/survivor

with a permanently altered appearance, health conditions, or disabilities, and the perpetrator actually killing the victim, or driving the victim to attempt suicide or to actually kill themselves. Other behaviors that cause physical harm and distress, such as deprivation of necessities such as food, water, a comfortable temperature and shelter; restraining/tying up; forcing the victim/survivor to kneel in the corner of a room or sit on the floor for extended periods of time; withholding medicine, medical care, or access to therapy; coercing the victim/survivor into taking unnecessary medications, having unnecessary/harmful medical/psychological treatments, or having unnecessary "medical" tests such as "virginity testing"; administering drugs and harming the victim/survivor with toxic substances such as poisons, bleach, or acid; regularly disrupting sleep, denying victims/survivors the physical rest they need and causing exhaustion; preventing the victim/survivor from carrying out basic bodily functions such as urinating and menstruating in a dignified way; preventing the maintenance of basic hygiene and personal grooming or demanding excessive standards of hygiene and personal grooming; withholding mobility aids or other equipment needed to assist with a disability; and coercing/forcing the victim/survivor into behaviors that are painful or harmful to their body such as over- or under-eating, excessive exercise, excessive alcohol consumption/substance misuse, or unwanted body modifications.

This list, extensive as it is, is unlikely to be fully comprehensive, and other tactics may occur that are not mentioned here.

The tactics just outlined can be used by perpetrators pre- or post-separation, and most can be targeted at children and young people as well as at adults. For instance, the child of a perpetrator may experience the perpetrator rigidly and malevolently controlling their daily activities, excessively controlling and limiting their contact with friends, hurting their beloved pets, depriving them of access to amounts of money and resources that are normal for their age, exhibiting paranoia about their sexual activity, and sabotaging their educational efforts (e.g., Callaghan et al., 2018; Fellin et al., 2018; Haselschwerdt et al., 2019a; Katz, 2016, 2019; Katz et al., 2020; Øverlien, 2013).

Many of these perpetrator behaviors overlap and could be placed in two or more of the categories in the previous list. For example, sexual coercion is both sexually abusive and psychologically abusive; tactics for isolating victims/survivors from sources of support can involve a great deal of psychological manipulation; and violence can cause economic consequences, for example when the victim/survivor is too injured or ill to work or engage with their education.

All of the abusive tactics we have just examined (including physical and sexual violence) are understood in this book to be part of perpetrators' use of coercive control. This is because perpetrators use these tactics to gain and maintain control over their victim/s, or to flaunt and enjoy the control and dominance they have established over their victim/s (Day and Bowen, 2015; Dutton and Goodman, 2005; Fontes, 2015; Harne, 2011). As Monckton Smith (2020b, p. 1280) states, where there is coercive control, the perpetrator's need for control is the ultimate "driver" behind any of the tactics they use. Monckton Smith (2020a) aptly suggests that we should describe the activities of perpetrators as (and here is a military twist to our political metaphor of coercive control as a dictatorship) "campaigns of coercive control." Perpetrators are willing to execute any tactical maneuver, or use any weapon in the coercive control armory, in order to "win" the campaign. For coercive control perpetrators, winning this campaign means gaining control of their target/s and maintaining that control for as long as they desire.

COERCIVE CONTROL AND SITUATIONAL COUPLE VIOLENCE

Coercive control–based domestic violence of the kind described in the previous section is different from "situational couple violence" (Fontes, 2015; Hardesty et al., 2015; Johnson, 2008). Situational couple violence is violence that occurs during couple conflicts, when verbal aggression escalates into acts of physical violence, but where the perpetrator is *not* aiming to control their partner's life or restrict their liberty (Fontes, 2015; Johnson, 2008). Consequently, situational couple violence, particularly in its less severe forms (less harmful types of violence that occur infrequently and are *not* part of a pattern of wider abusive behaviors), tends to have far fewer negative impacts than coercive control-based domestic violence (Haselschwerdt et al., 2019a; Myhill, 2015; Nevala, 2017). This is reflected in the lower levels of harm usually attributed to situational couple violence (as opposed to coercive control-based domestic violence) by persons reporting it. Especially if it was non-severe violence, situational couple violence may be reported as being at the level of unpleasant or annoying, or even as having no negative impact at all (Barter et al., 2009). Victims of situational couple violence are substantially less likely than victims of coercive control to "seek medical help at hospitals, protection at shelters for abused women, and legal justice in courts" (Øverlien, 2013, p. 278).

A victim of situational couple violence will *not* attempt to avoid a recurrence of the violence by any means necessary, such as by greatly reducing their social life, adopting a new style of dress that makes them feel unhappy, or no longer disagreeing with their partner. Those sorts of responses are the hallmarks of victims of coercive control, not of victims of situational couple violence. If a victim *is* being affected in such ways, this strongly indicates that coercive control is occurring, and that the violence is *not* situational couple violence.

To clarify, then, this book refers to "coercive control–based domestic violence" as distinct from "situational couple violence." The book's sole focus is coercive control, where perpetrators' actions are motivated by their desire to gain and maintain control over their victim's life. However, as Johnson (2008) cautions, it should also be noted that situational couple violence can be very fear-inducing and harmful in those cases where it is perpetrated in a severe way, for example where the perpetrator causes major pain or substantial injury and/or is violent very regularly. Thus, although it is not the focus of this book, we should not underestimate the potential negative impacts of severe situational couple violence on adults or children who are subjected to it, or the dangerousness of those who perpetrate it in severe ways (see Heward-Belle, 2016; Meier, 2017).

At present there is a lack of data that distinguishes between the national prevalence rates of situational couple violence and coercive control. Although studies are emerging into the prevalence of coercive control in particular subsamples of national populations (see later in this chapter), population-level data about "domestic violence" tends not to distinguish between the two phenomena (Myhill, 2015). Within such data, the phrase "domestic violence" is unhelpfully used to classify completely different situations: A man who was once non-injuriously struck by his girlfriend in a relationship that was usually non-violent, non-abusive, and happy (situational couple violence) is categorized in the same way as a woman who was systematically terrorized, regularly beaten, and made to fear for her life by her husband (coercive control). The headline population-level information about domestic violence prevalence that we are familiar with, such as the UK figure "1 in 4 women and 1 in 6 men experience domestic violence," therefore does not inform us of the scale of coercive control within the population.

Population-level data about children's exposure to "domestic violence" suggests that the number of children exposed to it runs into the millions in both the United States and the United Kingdom. In the United States, Finkelhor et al.'s (2009) large-scale study found that "6.2% of children reported they had witnessed one of their parents assaulting the other in the past year, and an average of 16.3% had witnessed parental assault in their lifetime. Among the oldest group of children, 34.6% had witnessed parental assault in their lifetime" (Øverlien, 2013, p. 277). In the United Kingdom, similar research by the NSPCC (National Society for the Prevention of Cruelty to Children) found that "12% of under 11s, 17.5% of 11–17s, and 23.7% of 18–24s had been exposed to domestic violence between adults in their homes during childhood" (Radford et al., 2011b, p. 47).

Yet, again, there is the same definitional problem around which of these cases is coercive control, and which is situational couple violence— meaning that we do not know the total numbers of children per population who experience the one, as opposed to the other (Stark and Hester, 2019). Gathering such data is particularly difficult because, as will be discussed more fully later in this chapter, coercive control perpetrators may abuse their victims *without* using physical violence (Crossman et al., 2016; Halliwell et al., 2021; Nevala, 2017; Stark and Hester, 2019). Consequently, children living with coercive control may not be detected by population-level research questions that focus on children's exposure to violence. In general, further research is required to establish the numbers of children, women, and men experiencing coercive control in general populations.

THE IMPORTANCE OF CONTEXT IN COERCIVE CONTROL

In order to further distinguish coercive control from situational couple violence, two additional factors are important to consider. These are factors of context, which include: (1) the presence of a "credible threat," and (2) the extent and depth of the control. We will consider each of these factors in turn, as well as their impact when they combine to create a state of chronic fear in the victim/survivor.

The presence of a "credible threat"

The presence of a "credible threat" is a defining characteristic coercive control, as Dutton and Goodman (2005) explain. When a coercive control perpetrator sets out his demands and expectations, it will be clear to the victim/survivor (either implicitly, by his past words or actions, or explicitly by him having stated what he will do) that, if they disobey, he will punish them with a negative reaction that they fear, dread, or find profoundly upsetting. This negative reaction will be one that the victim/survivor knows that the perpetrator is capable of carrying out: He will have established at an early stage of his coercive control that he is willing and capable of carrying out his threats, and that any consequences that might ensue for him (such as a night in jail) will not deter him.

The perpetrator's negative reaction is not necessarily a dramatic act of violence; it could be a less dramatic act, for example, withdrawing affection for a period of time after the victim/survivor visits or meets up with a friend. The victim/survivor will be aware of the continual presence of this threat (victims/survivors often report that they "just knew" what would happen if they disobeyed or failed to please the perpetrator); and so they will feel that they have to be extremely and constantly careful with what they say and do ("walking on eggshells"). For example, if a perpetrator withdraws affection not just once but almost every time that their partner socializes with a friend, then, over a number of months, their partner may be coerced into greatly reducing her contact with friends in order to avoid this repeated negative reaction. As a result, she may be left isolated, lacking support, and more dependent on the perpetrator.

The extent and depth of control

Of course, if the woman in this example were financially independent and brimming with confidence, she might leave a partner who made her feel as if she was "walking on eggshells" and stopped her from socializing with friends. However, the perpetrator's other tactics may be ensuring that this is not the case—by the time he starts isolating her from her friends he has probably also started undermining her confidence by suggesting that she has flaws and negative qualities and therefore is fortunate to be with him. He has probably also entangled her finances with his own finances, by way of a joint tenancy or a joint bank account to which her money has been transferred, in order to reduce her financial independence. He may have increased her empathy for him with narratives about his "difficult life," motivating her to stay so she can try to heal him. The perpetrator has therefore made it emotionally, and practically, difficult for his partner to escape the relationship.

Therefore, again, the wider context matters. Understanding the meaning behind an act where one person attempts to influence another—for example: "I expect you to come to the garden center with me on Sundays"; or

"I think you should wear this outfit; that other outfit makes you look bad" (see Hester et al., 2017)—requires more than simply the statements themselves. In fact, these statements may not be abusive at all if the relationship is abuse-free. There needs to be a contextual awareness, therefore, of whether the wider relationship is abusive, and, if so, the breadth and depth of the abuse. What matters here, then, are the *patterns* of abusive behavior.

So, in relation to those statements, the major question is how routinely and insistently the person expects their partner to, for example, come to the garden center, as well as (returning to the "credible threat") what happens if they refuse to do so. Coercive control perpetrators often *routinely* and *insistently* control core aspects of the victim's/survivor's life such as how they dress, who they socialize with, how long they can be out the house for when they go to the shops, what they can buy, or even what feelings they can express; and they convey a credible threat about what will happen if the victim/survivor does not obey. If one instance of these behaviors was occurring in a context of coercive control but was assessed in isolation, it might not be detectable as "abuse"; yet if we consider the patterns of behavior and their cumulative impacts, the abuse becomes evident. Indeed, the cumulative impact of the routines imposed by coercive control perpetrators is extremely significant; it goes to the heart of the victim's/survivor's life, undermining many of their most basic freedoms and human rights (Hill, 2020; Stark, 2007).

The combination of the presence of a "credible threat" and the extent and depth of control

Combined with the cumulative impacts of the perpetrator's patterns of behavior, the presence of the perpetrator's credible threats causes the victim/survivor to exist in a state of chronic fear and anxiety. A hallmark of the victim's behavior in this state is "self-policing": habitually attempting to eliminate actions perceived as bringing about negative reactions by the perpetrator, even at times where the perpetrator is not present to witness those actions (Monckton Smith, 2020a; Stark, 2007). Fear of conflicting with the perpetrator's wishes will therefore usually keep the victim/survivor in a state of long-term and continual dread and compliance.

The fear may be especially acute when a perpetrator behaves unpredictably by "changing the rules": reacting negatively to situations about which they were previously calm (Monckton Smith, 2020a); behaving in a "bizarre way" (Øverlien, 2013); and vehemently reinforcing trivial demands (Hill, 2020). In these moments, the victim/survivor senses that nothing is really safe, predictable or "out of bounds." Living in a state of high anxiety and possibly even terror (and possibly believing the perpetrator's claims that his behavior is all her fault), the victim/survivor redoubles her efforts to self-police and comply in the hope that this will minimize the risks and keep their partner calm.

DYNAMICS AND IMPACTS OF COERCIVE CONTROL

For a perpetrator to succeed in their campaign of coercive control, their behavior must not be constantly, obviously hostile and controlling, at least not at first. Perpetrators have to intersperse and interweave their more obviously hostile and abusive behaviors with periods of seemingly "nice," "caring," and "indulgent/generous/gift-giving" behaviors (Enander, 2011; Fontes, 2015). Such behaviors sit within the category of "emotional and psychological abuse" outlined at the beginning in the chapter. These "positive"-seeming behaviors from perpetrators can have numerous detrimental impacts on victims/survivors: They can keep victims/survivors emotionally invested in their relationship with the perpetrator, provide false hope that "things are better now" or "it's not that bad," and undermine their ability to recognize that the perpetrator is an abusive person (Katz et al., 2020). Perpetrators' displays of seemingly positive behavior can become less frequent over time as perpetrators gain increasing control of their targets. Once perpetrators have become confident that they have their target/s entrapped and that escape is unlikely, they have less need to give the appearance of being "nice" to maintain their control. However, perpetrators may dust off their "nice" behaviors and use them again as needed if they perceive a threat to their control and calculate that a period of "niceness" is the best way to neutralize it, for example if a social worker comes to visit, or if their target is showing signs of breaking free.

A core motivation for controlling an intimate partner and/or family member/s is that the perpetrator wants those persons to willingly devote themselves to meeting his needs, and to abandon their own needs, wishes, independence, and freedom (Bancroft, 2002; Bancroft et al., 2012; Harne, 2011; Hill, 2020; Monckton Smith, 2020a; Pitman, 2017; Richards, 2019). As Bancroft (2002, pp. 64–65, cited in Hill, 2020, p. 24) explains, "when an abusive man feels the powerful stirring inside that other people call love, he is probably feeling the desire to have you devote your life to keeping him happy with no outside interference." Of course, the vast majority of human beings do not wish to submit totally to meeting another person's emotional, physical, financial, practical, and/or sexual needs, day-in-day-out, as though they have no rights and no existence of their own. It is highly destructive to a person's mental and emotional health to exist in a state where their own needs and wishes have been sidelined and their basic freedoms have been taken away (Herman, 1992; Moulding et al., 2021). It is therefore no easy task for perpetrators to achieve their goal of turning a fellow human being into a slave-like figure who exists to serve them.

The *difficulty* of securing such total obedience (especially in societies where people have been raised to believe that they are free individuals) is the reason why perpetrators need to deploy an extensive array of abusive tactics to achieve it. Each tactic brings the perpetrator closer to securing the total obedience they crave. For instance, in the case of a perpetrator using coercive control against an intimate partner, the perpetrator may use verbal and emotional abuse to start to convince their partner that they are too "stupid" and "useless" to manage on their own. The perpetrator may equate obedience with commitment to the relationship, so that if a partner questions the perpetrator's rules they are accused of lacking commitment. As we have noted, the perpetrator may also use phases of positive-seeming behavior to give their partner false hope the relationship "isn't really that bad," or to create the impression that they are acting out of love, care, or protectiveness. Meanwhile, the perpetrator may use economic abuse to strip their partner of the resources that they would need to escape and live independently; may increasingly isolate their partner to stop them from accessing help and support (often using "jealousy" as an excuse for this); and may use periodic threats to harm or kill their partner and/or their partner's loved ones, or use actual physical violence, to scare their partner into compliance. The combined effect of the perpetrator using all of these tactics is that it produces conditions of *entrapment* and *unfreedom* in the perpetrator's target/s (Stark, 2007).

A high sense of entitlement and self-centeredness has been discovered in research and interventions with male perpetrators of coercive control (Bancroft, 2002; Bancroft et al., 2012; Coy et al., 2012; Harne, 2011; Heward-Belle, 2016; Hill, 2020; Kelly and Westmarland, 2015; Monckton Smith, 2020a). Some male perpetrators identify strongly with hegemonic masculinity and believe that men, husbands, and fathers are superior to women, wives, and children (Bancroft et al., 2012; Heward-Belle, 2016; Loveland and Raghavan, 2017). Indeed, more broadly beyond the family unit, these men tend to believe in the patriarchal notion that, as members of the male sex, they are *entitled* to possess power and have an all-encompassing *right* to power across the many different domains of their lives (Hill, 2020). This belief-system contributes to their view that women and children in their family should be under their control and should please and serve them continuously (Bancroft, 2002; Kelly and Westmarland, 2015; Mohaupt et al., 2020). Heward-Belle's (2016) research, involving interviews with Australian men on domestic violence perpetrator programs, reported that "[some perpetrators] described feeling entitled, due to their gender, to use domestic violence." These interviews "were rich in descriptions of how they felt aware, in control, and were active agents who instrumentally deployed violence" (Heward-Belle, 2016, p. 329). The perpetrators in these programs, Heward-Belle (2016, p. 330) noted, "described viewing their needs as supreme, feeling entitled to dictate over others, and to quash resistance with violence and abuse. They described making unilateral decisions for family members, being motivated by wanting to be right, and desiring to be the centre of attention."

Accordingly, research has shown male perpetrators to be rigid and dominant in their parenting, with little interest in their child's perspectives and emotions. Mohaupt et al. (2020) found that several domestic violence–perpetrating fathers in their study viewed their children as property to be owned and controlled (see also Bancroft et al., 2012). Similarly, Haselschwerdt et al. (2019a, p. 1532) reported that some perpetrators/fathers had a "desire to control their daughter's behavior and decisions as they similarly sought control over their wives' [behavior and decisions]." Several children in Callaghan et al's (2018) study described how perpetrators/fathers had exerted high levels of control over both them and over their mothers. As children in Lamb et al's (2018) study stated, "one of our father's favourite mottos was [that] children should be seen and not heard . . . and his wife shouldn't be seen OR heard" (p. 167). Thus, these kinds of male perpetrators are likely to cause considerable direct harm to their children as well as to their girlfriend or wife, as they extend their coercive control over their whole family, and demand to have control over the children in the family as well as to have control over their female partner.

Taken together, perpetrators' coercive control tactics can have devastating impacts, as persons subjected to coercive control may become entrapped in a distorted, totalitarian version of reality (Morris, 2009; Williamson, 2010). As McLeod (2018, p. 6) notes, victims/survivors report "not being allowed or having to ask permission to do everyday things," because the perpetrators' tactics have created the dictatorship to which we referred at the beginning of the chapter: "a world where the victim is constantly monitored or criticized and has every move and action checked." Adult and child victims/survivors also describe routinely attempting to keep the situation calm and safe by complying with the perpetrator's expectations and demands and by convincing the perpetrator of their devotion and loyalty (Cavanagh, 2003; Herman, 1992; Monckton Smith, 2020a). Furthermore, within perpetrators' distorted realities, perpetrators can insist that events and feelings are only true and real if the perpetrator says they are (Morris, 2009). Thus, adult and child victims'/survivors' lived experiences are denied and perpetrators' perceptions are imposed over them, often causing great confusion and psychological difficulties in adult and child victims/survivors (Herman, 1992).

Living inside perpetrators' distorted realities severely restricts victims'/survivors' "space for action"—that is, their freedom to think, say, and do normal things and to meet their own basic needs without worry or fear. For instance, a person who is *not* experiencing coercive control and has high levels of space for action might agree that: "I am free to live the kind of life that I want to," "I can take up employment, education and/or learning opportunities that interest me" and "I am able to visit and meet up with my friends/family whenever I like" (Kelly et al., 2014, p. 138). Such ordinary, everyday freedoms are not possible for a person experiencing coercive control (Moulding et al., 2021; Stark, 2007). Kelly et al.'s (2014) longitudinal research with female domestic violence survivors found that these women's space for action had generally been very restricted while they were in intimate relationships with perpetrators. Once they had ended these relationships, separating from perpetrators, there had been a rebound in their basic freedoms. As one woman explained: "[now I'm out of the relationship] I'm my own person; I can do what I want. I can answer my phone when I want, I can go where I want, I can eat what I want. I can wear what I want—I don't have to get dressed if I don't want to. I can watch a programme if I want. I can have a bath whenever I want. . . . I can do whatever I want to do" (Kelly et al., 2014, p. 124). It is precisely these kinds of *vital* everyday freedoms that perpetrators of coercive control take away from their victim/s.

It is important to recognize, however, that victims/survivors *do* resist perpetrators' attempts to impose coercive control on them (Cavanagh, 2003; Dutton and Goodman, 2005; Hill, 2020; Kelly and Westmarland, 2015). Resistance may take overt forms such as arguing and protesting when the perpetrator treats them unjustly, not following the perpetrators' rules, or shouting at the perpetrator. Victims/survivors may physically fight back or use violence in self-defense (Johnson, 2008), with such actions sometimes leading to an upside-down interpretation where the actual victim/survivor is seen as the perpetrator (and criminalized as such), or is seen as being "just as bad" as the perpetrator (Hill, 2020).

(Indeed, perpetrators may deliberately intimidate and manipulate victims/survivors into acts of self-defensive violence for that purpose, so that they can construct this upside-down interpretation either immediately or at a later date.) Victims'/survivors' resistance can also take place in hidden ways, such as the victim/survivor refusing to think about matters in a way the perpetrator has demanded, or considering ways of escaping while giving an outward appearance of compliance.

Stark (2007) suggests that "arguments" in contexts of coercive control (arguments that run along the lines of "you said this" or "you did that") are not actually about a particular issue. Rather, such arguments are about perpetrators attempting to impose coercive control and victims/survivors resisting this imposition (Cavanagh, 2003; Kelly and Westmarland, 2015). When a perpetrator becomes enraged during a conflict, they are not angry or upset about a particular issue (i.e., their abusive behavior is not "situational," even if it appears to be so). Instead, the perpetrator is enraged that the victim/survivor has responded in a way that they perceive as a sign of resistance to their control (Cavanagh, 2003). For instance, the victim might have complained about the perpetrator's behavior, visited a friend who the perpetrator did not want them to visit, or been dressed or moved in a way the perpetrator did not like. Indeed, the victim may not have done anything at all. The perpetrator may be seeking an excuse to further their control and may invent an issue to "argue" about. Whatever the cause or pretext, the perpetrator will subject the victim/survivor to very negative behaviors (such as verbal and emotional abuse, intimidation, damage to property, or physical violence) in order to try to make the victim/survivor too dispirited, intimated or frightened to resist them in future. So, in cases of coercive control, what may on the surface appear to be an argument or a fight about a particular issue is actually about the perpetrator attempting to *permanently crush all resistance* to their control. Thus, perpetrators' behavior in "arguments" is integral to their harmful campaigns to gain and maintain total control over their target/s. Such arguments are a great deal more serious than they may seem on the surface.

Perpetrators can be skilled in making their patterns of coercive control appear to be isolated, trivial, or ambiguous incidents. When talking about their behavior, coercive control perpetrators have a tendency to greatly minimize their actions by presenting themselves as, for example, only doing what most other men/parents would do in the circumstances, or as having been provoked by a bad wife, irritating child, or troublesome teen. In offering accounts such as these, perpetrators cloak the extent of their abusiveness toward partners and children, and mislead listeners by suggesting that there were good reasons behind the acts of abuse that they committed (Cavanagh et al., 2001; Harne, 2011; Smith and Humphreys, 2019; Williamson, 2010). When setting out the "good reasons" for their behaviors to others, perpetrators may make use of commonly held prejudices and stereotypes about women and children, such as the "nagging wife who constantly henpecks her husband," the "career woman who selfishly puts her career before her family," the "mentally ill woman who can't live a normal life and can't be trusted to make her own decisions," the "hormonal teen who is going through a difficult phase," or "the daughter whose sexuality requires control and oversight to prevent promiscuity." Persons eager to believe the best of coercive control perpetrators may be deceived into accepting perpetrators' warped versions of events. Such persons may include the perpetrators' parents, friends, employers, professionals involved with the family, family courts, and adult and child victims/survivors themselves (Meier, 2017; Monk and Bowen, 2021; Moulding et al., 2015; Naughton et al., 2015; Towns and Adams, 2016).

Narratives that circulate in the media and in courts can also downplay the severity of the acts that the perpetrator has committed, and can portray their behavior as less severe or more justifiable than it was (Monckton Smith, 2012). Indeed, Meier (2017) particularly cautions that family courts in the United States are exploiting Johnson's (2008) typology of domestic violence to assert that men/fathers with histories of coercive control have actually only perpetrated the "lesser offense" of situational couple violence: violence that could be deemed as irrelevant to child contact. In this situation, perpetrators'/fathers' extensive use of coercive control can be lost from the family court's view, and their actions reimagined and recoded as being "really not that bad/serious," with potentially devastating consequences for the safety and well-being of children (Meier,

2017). Meier also cautions that situational couple violence should *not* be perceived as irrelevant to child contact, especially when it has been perpetrated in a severe way. A person who uses violence during conflicts may be an unsafe parent; see also Heward-Belle's (2016) study of domestic violence and fathering.

PERPETRATORS AND VIOLENCE

The extent to which coercive control perpetrators use physical violence, or appear to outsiders as a "violent person," varies considerably (Stark, 2007). While some perpetrators use violence frequently, others use little or none (see e.g., Crossman et al., 2016; Halliwell et al., 2021; Nevala, 2017). As Stark and Hester (2019, p. 91) discuss: "in perhaps as many as a third of all [coercive control] cases, fear, constraints on autonomy, belittlement, and other facets of abuse [create] 'entrapment' without any notable incidents of violence." Similarly, Nevala's (2017) EU wide data (from the European Union's FRA Violence Against Women Survey) found an almost 50/50 divide among women who reported experiencing high levels of control from their current partner. Data showed that 55% were being subjected to violence by their partner, while 45% were not.

One reason why some perpetrators use little or no violence is that they may judge the frequent use of violence to be unwise. For them to maintain coercive control, it is important that their target/s remain as unsupported, isolated, and confused as possible. Extensive physical violence may "give the game away" by making it far easier for victims/survivors, communities, and professionals to realize that the perpetrator is an abuser (Naughton et al., 2019). Such a realization may motivate the victim to seek support, and increase the likelihood of professionals taking the situation seriously. Day and Bowen (2015, p. 67) suggest that some perpetrators possess a high degree of expertise or "competency" in using coercive control and escaping detection: "As 'competency' develops, the use of coercive control tactics become more successful without the need for physical violence." In these circumstances, perpetrators who are highly abusive and harmful are also non-violent. In some cases, it is only when a perpetrator feels that they have failed to achieve control using non-violent coercive control tactics that they will resort to using physical violence to gain control (Loveland and Raghavan, 2017). Perpetrators may also use their extensive competency to maintain a positive public persona, carefully cultivating a public image of themselves as "sociable, charming, likeable, charismatic, talented and sensitive" (Day and Bowen, 2015, p. 66). This further isolates their target/s, who will struggle to gain support and to be believed if they come forward to ask for help (Monk, 2017).

Understood from this perspective, perpetrators who use little or no violence may often be more dangerous and destructive than violent perpetrators (Crossman et al., 2016). This is because they may potentially be more likely to succeed in their goals—namely stripping other human beings of their freedom and self-determination (Stark, 2007), taking away their opportunities to meet their own needs (Kelly and Westmarland, 2015), and coercing them into living horrifically diminished lives that are based around serving the perpetrator.

It is important to state here that what perpetrators of coercive control therefore do, even without physical violence, is subject fellow human beings to sustained attacks. To rephrase the point in a different way, an absence of physical violence does not mean that there have been no "attacks." A victim/survivor of coercive control will have been subjected to horrific and injurious attacks on their emotions, psychological health, their personhood—on their very self (Herman, 1992; Matheson et al., 2015). The concept of "attack" also applies to the perpetrator's negative impacts on the victim's/survivor's financial position and ability to live independently and take up employment (Moulding et al., 2021). These psychological and financial blows represent subtle but devastating types of attack—ones that take place not intensively over minutes or hours, but extensively over months and years. In other words, the perpetrator will have chosen not just to cause injury at one time-point, but to carry on causing injury on a continual basis over the long term. Of course, the results of these psychological and financial attacks are not apparent in the same manner as physical violence—but if they could be, the results would be hideous: bodies grievously hurt, covered from head to foot with wounds, and perhaps in comas or intensive care.

Furthermore, non-violent perpetrators are also dangerous because of what may happen if and when they lose their invisible stranglehold on the victim/survivor. There are a disturbing number of cases where such perpetrators have transitioned directly from little or no physical violence to the ultimate expression of interpersonal violence: to actually kill their target/s (see e.g., Monckton Smith, 2020a; Wate, 2018). This paradox— a non-violent perpetrator instantly becoming the most violent after perceiving that they have lost control—is easy to explain: Such killings are the ultimate way of regaining control (Monckton Smith, 2020a, 2020b). The message is: "I control you so completely that I will take your life, or the life of your loved ones, away from you." The potential for murder to occur should not be underestimated in situations where an extremely controlling perpetrator has previously been non-violent but now believes they are losing control.

COERCIVE CONTROL AS A GENDERED FORM OF ABUSE

Data indicate that coercive control–based domestic violence is mainly perpetrated by males. This is different from situational couple violence (see earlier), where rates of female and male perpetration are more similar (Myhill, 2015). For coercive control, there is much evidence to suggest that females constitute only a small percentage of perpetrators (see also Hester, 2012). For example, in the United States, Johnson et al. (2014) found that "22% of women experienced coercive controlling violence from ex-husbands, while only 5.4% of men experienced coercive controlling violence from ex-wives." Similarly, Myhill (2015) reported that, out of a sample of women and men who stated on the Crime Survey for England and Wales that they had been a victim of domestic violence, 30% of the women and 6% of the men were deemed to have experienced coercive control-based domestic violence. (The remaining men and women in this sample were categorized as having experienced situational couple violence.) Myhill's findings therefore indicated that the vast majority (94%) of men who reported to the Survey that they had been victims of domestic violence had been victims of situational couple violence, rather than coercive control–based domestic violence. Within Myhill's study, respondents to the Survey were classified as victims of coercive control if they reported that their partner had done *both* of the following: " 'Repeatedly belittled you to the extent that you felt worthless' and 'frightened you, by threatening to hurt you or someone close to you' " (Myhill, 2015, p. 362). Hester et al.'s (2017) UK study of heterosexual men accessing the services of GPs (General Practitioners, i.e., medical doctors based in local surgeries) found that only 2.3% of these men had experienced coercive control as victims only. Finally, Barlow et al.'s (2020) research into the policing of coercive control in the northwest of England found that 95% of victims were female. This is *not* to suggest that male victims/survivors of coercive control are any less important than female ones—of course they are similarly important. It is simply to highlight that there are many more female coercive control victims/survivors than male ones.

The disparity is partly due to cultural and structural gender inequalities in societies that tend to make it considerably easier for men to entrap women in coercively controlling relationships than the reverse (Aghtaie and Gangoli, 2014; Stark, 2007). This is a complex issue that is largely beyond the scope of this book, and so it will only be discussed relatively briefly here. There are a number of factors that come together to create "conducive contexts" (Kelly, 2007) for men to coercively control female partners and simultaneously create "hostile contexts" that make it difficult for women to coercively control male partners (Moulding et al., 2021).

One set of factors is structural. Women undertake the majority of housework, childcare, and care for disabled or elderly family members, and more frequently work part-time, have less secure jobs, and receive lower pay compared to men. These are near-ubiquitous structural inequalities in societies that make it more difficult for the average woman, compared to the average man, to leave an abusive partner and live independently (Kuskoff and Parsell, 2020). UK data released by YouGov in 2021 found that "in many couples women rely on their partner to get by financially—even if they work full-time themselves—while among men [this dependence is] much rarer. . . . Women with a partner are entirely (6%) or somewhat (29%) dependent on their other half." For men, the figures were much lower, with 3% entirely and 11% somewhat dependent on their partner (Nolsoe, 2021).

Furthermore, as part of their socialization into feminine gender roles (the ways that females are taught to express femininity in socially acceptable ways), adolescent girls and women are typically encouraged to be sexually attracted to "bad boys," to be nurturing and accommodating and to prioritize the needs of others ahead of their own, to "keep the peace" within families, and to prize being in a romantic couple and avoid singleness and spinsterhood (see e.g., Aghtaie et al., 2018; Budgeon, 2016; Cairns and Johnston, 2015; Castro Sandúa and Mara, 2014; Davies, 2019; Lombard, 2015; Taylor, 2012; Valls et al., 2008). Such socialization provides a platform and a "way in" for male perpetrators who wish to keep women in coercively controlling relationships (Women's Aid et al., 2021).

The platform provided by gender roles is further facilitated by the sets of beliefs that girls and women have already internalized about love. Influenced in part by the cultural media that societies as a whole consume (such as songs, television, movies, and social media), girls and women often grow up believing that real love is difficult, tumultuous yet vitally important, and that they are the ones primarily responsible for making a relationship/family "work" by being patient, understanding, accommodating, and forgiving (Hill, 2020; Women's Aid et al., 2021). Additionally, conservative discourses of femininity and masculinity, which may derive from religion or tradition, supply narratives of male leadership and female submission. These narratives "support and even reinforce the acceptance of [male-against-female] abuse" (Wendt, 2008, p. 152, cited in Barnes and Aune, 2021, p. 14). Thus, when male coercive control perpetrators make demands (for example that their girlfriends/wives need to be more committed to them, to stop "making them jealous" by speaking to others, to share the passwords for their phones/online accounts, and to generally do more to please them every day), these perpetrators are able to disguise their abuse as behavior that is already considered socially normal in everyday heterosexual families/relationships.

In addition to present-day factors, we also have the legacy of historical male/female dynamics to contend with. Historically there have been explicit social and cultural expectations and religious and legal frameworks supporting males to have more power than females in families and intimate relationships (Arnull and Stewart, 2021; Harne, 2011; Monckton Smith, 2020a, 2020b), and these expectations still have considerable influence today (see e.g., Aghtaie et al., 2018; Aghtaie and Gangoli, 2014; Heilman et al., 2017; Lombard, 2015, 2016; Monckton Smith, 2020a, 2020b; Namy et al., 2017). For instance, Heilman et al. (2017) conducted a large-scale study that examined whether young men (under 30 years old) in the United States, Mexico, and the United Kingdom felt that their society told them that: "a man should always have the final say about decisions in his relationship or marriage." The authors found that 55% of the young men in the United States agreed that their society told them so, along with 46% of the young men in Mexico, and 44% of the young men in the United Kingdom. Very similar numbers reported feeling that their society told them that "if a guy has a girlfriend or wife, he deserves to know where she is all the time" (Heilman et al., 2017, p. 25). Such messages may encourage men to be confident in rejecting any attempts their girlfriend/wife might make to establish a campaign of coercive control against them. As Aghtaie et al. (2018, p. 304) found, "young men tended to be much quicker [than young women] to reject controlling or coercive behavior as 'ridiculous' or 'not normal' when it was aimed at them."

In general, then, societal messages tend to normalize boyfriends/husbands having a degree of ownership and possession over girlfriends/wives (Aghtaie et al., 2018; Lombard, 2015, 2016). As Monckton Smith (2020a, p. 132) phrases it, "women do not generally get taught that they have ownership of men—quite the opposite: they are more often taught that they are owned." This in turn makes it more likely that coercively controlling behavior from boyfriends/husbands will be excused or romanticized (for example viewed as a sign of deep love, protectiveness and care, or "natural" male jealousy and possessiveness) and will be viewed as normal masculine behavior by perpetrators, victims, and their friends, family, colleagues, and communities (Aghtaie et al., 2018; Monckton Smith, 2020b). Furthermore, some male perpetrators have been shown to endorse notions of masculinity that emphasize being the head of the family and being the authority on all matters. This sense of entitlement has been shown to be central to some perpetrators' exercise of coercive control over women and children (Bancroft et al., 2012; Downes et al., 2019; Heward-Belle, 2016; Mohaupt et al., 2020; Monckton Smith, 2020a; Women's Aid et al., 2021).

Hence, based on the messages they receive and endorse from their societies about how men and women should behave, male coercive control perpetrators may feel a sense of "cultural authorization" for their behavior (Monckton Smith, 2020b, p. 1281). As Dragiewicz et al. (2021a, p. 3) explain, male perpetrators "leverage patriarchal cultural norms and structural inequalities to manipulate, isolate, coerce and control women in the context of abusive intimate relationships." It is not that most societies directly endorse male coercive control and encourage men to perpetrate it—usually they do not. Rather, it is that "normal" social and cultural expectations of how men should behave are significantly closer to the behavior of coercive control perpetrators than "normal" expectations of how women should behave (Bishop and Bettinson, 2018). Women who are perceived as being assertive and wishing to be in charge (especially in charge of men) are likely to be met, at least sometimes, with unease, disapproval, rejection, and perhaps even violent/abusive backlash. Thus, any woman attempting to impose coercive control on a male intimate partner would find herself very much swimming *against* the tide of dominant norms and social expectations about how men and women are supposed to behave. By contrast, males attempting to impose coercive control on female intimate partners find themselves, to some extent, swimming *with* this tide. It is therefore unsurprising that, worldwide, we observe many more males than females perpetrating coercive control against their partners.

THE INVISIBILITY AND UNACCOUNTABILITY
OF MALE PERPETRATORS

Gender is also a significant factor in male perpetrators' current "invisibility" and lack of accountability for the abuse that they inflict—both in general and in relation to children. In relation to children, gender plays a significant role in our perceptions of male perpetrators and female victims/survivors in their roles as parents. Domestically violent fathers tend to be largely "invisible" in research, policy, and practice on children and domestic violence (Arnull and Stewart, 2021; Brown et al., 2009; De Simone and Heward-Belle, 2020; Edleson, 1998; Heward-Belle et al., 2019; Westmarland and Kelly, 2013). Meanwhile, a disproportionate focus tends to be placed on the child's mother/the victimized parent (Callaghan, 2015; De Simone and Heward-Belle, 2020; Edleson, 1998; Fellin et al., 2018; Humphreys and Absler, 2011; Humphreys et al., 2020; Lapierre, 2008). The focus on the female victim/survivor/mother is influenced by gender norms that place most responsibility for children's upbringings on mothers rather than fathers. Ultimately, the female victim/survivor/mother tends to be viewed as more accountable for the harms caused to children by domestic violence than the male perpetrator/father himself (Arnull and Stewart, 2021).

Challenging the status quo around perpetrators' lack of accountability is relatively common in studies of *adult* domestic violence, but there are relatively few existing studies in the children and domestic violence field that do so. Within the children and domestic violence field, it is women/mothers, not men/fathers, who are generally presented as being responsible for the welfare and well-being of children who have experienced domestic violence (Arnull and Stewart, 2021; Holt, 2017; Heward-Belle et al., 2018; Humphreys and Absler, 2011; Lapierre, 2008, 2010a).

This lopsided approach was noted by Callaghan and colleagues in their corpus analysis of the relevant peer-reviewed literature on children and domestic violence published between January 2002 and January 2015 (Callaghan, 2015). Identifying what discourses and knowledges were dominant in this literature during the 2002–2015 period, they found that the term "mothers" was the fifth most frequently occurring term in the data set, "women" was the 24th, and "maternal" was the 38th. By contrast, "fathers" was the 147th most frequently occurring term. The terms "men," "stepfather," and "paternal" were so little used that they did not appear in Callaghan's results at all. Thus, a body of literature that is primarily concerned with how children are harmed by domestic violence—harm that is usually perpetrated by men/fathers/stepfathers—scarcely refers to these men/fathers/stepfathers at all.

Constructing mothers as "the problem"

The linguistic tendencies identified by Callaghan (2015) reflect the field's frequent investigation of how mothers' parenting may moderate and mediate the impacts of domestic violence on children (see, e.g., Bair-Merritt et al., 2015; Fong et al., 2019; Holmes et al., 2017; Huth-Bocks and Hughes, 2008; Johnson and Lieberman, 2007; Lamela et al., 2018; Letourneau et al., 2007; Levendosky et al., 2006; Rosser-Limiñana et al., 2020; Samuelson et al., 2012; Sturge-Apple et al., 2010). The assumption within much of this literature is that exposure to domestic violence *potentially* damages children, but that the level of damage that children actually sustain depends largely on how well the mother/victim/survivor can maintain "good" parenting and "good" mental health in spite of the abuse the perpetrator/father is inflicting on her (Callaghan, 2015; Lapierre, 2008). A mother/victim/survivor who cannot maintain good parenting and good mental health while the children's father or father-figure abuses her is perceived to be worsening the children's ability to come through the father's/father-figure's domestic violence largely undamaged. Conversely, if the mother can maintain good parenting and good mental health, it is supposed that the children will have a good chance of continuing to function well despite their exposure to their father or father-figure's domestic violence.

Here, grossly unequal expectations are implicitly placed on mothers and fathers/fathers-figures. To maintain their children's well-being, mothers are expected to suffer abuse from the children's father/father-figure while continuing to function as though nothing is happening, at least in terms of their parenting and mental health (an expectation that, in terms of unfairness, is on a par with expecting somebody who has been stabbed not to bleed). Meanwhile, fathers/father-figures can continue to expose their children to domestic violence, as this is not viewed as a core issue for children's well-being. (It is the mothers' coping that is viewed as the core issue.)

Hence, in this dominant approach, it is the children's victimized parent/mother who is positioned as having the potential to harm children in domestic violence contexts through her compromised parenting and mental health. The child's perpetrating parent/father—the cause of the domestic violence—is not positioned in this manner. Indeed, the perpetrator/father is unlikely to be discussed at all. This can be observed in Fong et al.'s (2019) systematic review of 31 previous studies that identify risk and protective factors affecting children exposed to intimate partner violence. The authors conclude by specifically associating mothers, but not perpetrators/fathers, with "risk factors," thus: "interventions provided to families exposed to IPV need to target *both maternal and child risk factors* in order to successfully reduce child externalizing problems" (Fong et al., 2019, p. 149, my italics). Ignoring perpetrators in this way may produce misleading research results. As Edleson (2006, p. 4) explains, "over reliance on data collected from and about battered mothers may lead to partial or inaccurate conclusions. For example, it may be that the perpetrator's behavior is the key to predicting the emotional health of a child. By not collecting data about the perpetrators, we may incorrectly conclude it is the mothers' problems and not the perpetrators' violent behavior that is creating negative outcomes for the children."

Furthermore, in terms of outcomes for female victims/survivors themselves, the overfocus on mothers is exceedingly problematic because, in reality, once the spotlight of concern and intervention is turned on the mother, her parenting and her protection of the children is placed under scrutiny. As Callaghan (2015, p. 17) states, "the male violence that produced the negative consequences for both their female partner and her children is rendered largely insignificant, as the target of concern and intervention becomes the abused woman." This overfocus on mothers can create additional distress, trauma, and injustice for mothers/abuse victims, sometimes resulting in abused mothers losing contact with their children due to concerns about the mothers' fitness to parent (De Simone and Heward-Belle, 2020; Johnson and Sullivan, 2008; Maher et al., 2021). Meanwhile the parenting (non)fitness and (non)protectiveness of perpetrators/fathers may be left unaddressed, enabling them to continue to harm their children (e.g., see Harne, 2011).

However, within research, it is not beyond the realms of possibility to make the leap toward a form of writing that is more perpetrator-focused. For example, Fong et al.'s (2019) conclusion of their systematic review, quoted earlier, could have been: "Interventions provided to families exposed to IPV need to target *paternal risk factors* and to tackle the root cause of child externalizing problems, namely the paternal parent's decision to perpetrate IPV." This alternative conclusion conveys that, in domestic violence contexts, it is perpetrators/fathers who are usually the main obstacle to the positive functioning of children in their families—they are the ones who are causing the domestic violence, and they are responsible for the negative impacts that have occurred because of their abuse (Bancroft et al., 2012; Harne, 2011). Unfortunately, such perpetrator-focused sentences would be unlikely to appear in systematic reviews of research on children and domestic violence. This is because, as will be discussed in what follows, there is currently a paucity of studies (especially quantitative studies) into how children are affected by perpetrators' paternal behaviors. However, for exceptions see, e.g., Bancroft et al. (2012), Harne (2011), Haselschwerdt et al. (2020), Heward-Belle (2016), Mohaupt et al. (2020), Smith and Humphreys (2019), and Thompson-Walsh et al. (2021).

There is much scope for future perpetrator/father-focused studies. For example, research could examine whether children's behavioral problems are associated with the extent to which perpetrators/fathers employ tactics to split the family and undermine children's relationships with their mother and siblings (Bancroft et al., 2012). Such research could also explore whether there is an association between reduced positive functioning in children and perpetrators/fathers preventing mothers and children from spending time with each other on a day-to-day basis, or if there are associations between children's psychological well-being and the extent to which perpetrators/fathers perceive their children as owned objects (Bancroft et al., 2012; Burnette et al., 2017; Heward-Belle, 2016). Such questions have been largely bypassed to-date, but remain ready to be asked by future researchers. Investigating these questions would help to rebalance the field and could influence a shift in policy and practice toward paying greater attention to the parenting behavior and (non)protectiveness of perpetrators/fathers.

Victim-blaming

Sadly, the field's current lopsided focus on mothers/victims/survivors aligns with wider societal practices of victim-blaming (Berns, 2004; Niemi and Young, 2016). Within victim-blaming, attention is focused on how the victim has behaved and responded to what they have suffered. If the victim's behavior/response is perceived to have been incorrect, then they are viewed as having been at fault, eclipsing the perpetrator's accountability. Such blame is unjust; it is similar to blaming somebody for unknowingly eating poisoned food, and then considering them to be at fault for how their body reacted to the poison, while ignoring the accountability of the person who poisoned the food. Victim-blaming ignores perpetrators' active decisions to create harmful situations and enact hurtful, damaging, and/or criminal behaviors (Randell, 2010).

Families who have experienced domestic violence are far from immune to such victim-blaming. For example, Moulding et al.'s (2015) study of adults with childhood experience of domestic violence found that some participants appeared to blame their victimized mother more than their perpetrating father. They criticized their mother's character, believing her to have been insufficiently strong and independent. That their father's character was problematic was not something that these participants seemed to consider (though some children who have experienced father-perpetrated domestic violence do hold their fathers accountable, see e.g., Lamb et al., 2018).

The tendency to ignore the perpetrator's responsibility and blame the victim is further exacerbated in contexts of male-perpetrated domestic violence by the issue of gender norms (Heward-Belle, 2017; McDonald-Harker, 2016). As parents, women tend to have greater expectations placed on them than men. Mothers, not fathers, tend to be viewed as primarily responsible for children's well-being, mental health, and development (Arnull and Stewart, 2021; Callaghan, 2015; Lapierre, 2010a; Maher et al., 2021). This can be observed in Cater and Forssell's (2014) interviews with Swedish 8- to 12-year-olds whose fathers had perpetrated domestic violence. The study's findings indicated that these children had very low expectations about what it meant to be a "good enough" father. To be judged by these children as "good enough," a father needed only to refrain from being violent and to function as a possible reinforcement to the mother's parenting in the rare instances where the mother was unable to do something. In these children's opinions, being "good enough" as a father did not mean providing regular care or participating regularly in the child's life. Children not only held these low expectations about their own fathers—they held the same views about "good enough" fathering in general. This was in sharp contrast to their expectations about their mothers. They expected their mothers to meet all of their needs, effectively acting as their sole parent. Consequently, it would be immeasurably more difficult for such children to perceive the mother/victim/survivor as a successful parent. There was, unjustly, far more scope for them to be angry and disappointed about their mothers' parenting than about the parenting of perpetrators/fathers.

Splitting the identities of "father" and "perpetrator"

The disconnect between condemning a man as a "perpetrator" and viewing him as a "good enough father" is another problematic tendency in responses to domestic violence, especially in family courts (Hester,

2011). A criminal court may have convicted a man of violence toward his partner; and social workers may have viewed him as dangerous to his children while conducting child protection interventions—yet, in family courts, where he is represented primarily as a "father," there is a tendency to view his domestic violence perpetration as unconnected to his fathering (see Hester, 2011).

This split between the identities of "father" and "perpetrator" occurs despite the ample research evidence that male perpetrators of domestic violence present a very high risk of behaving abusively and neglectfully toward their children (see e.g., Beeble et al., 2007; Buchanan, 2018; Burnette et al., 2017; Cater and Forssell, 2014; Clements et al., 2021; Edleson, 1999b; Guille, 2004; Harne, 2011; Haselschwerdt et al., 2020; Heward-Belle, 2016; Mohaupt et al., 2020; Mullender et al., 2002; Salisbury et al., 2009; Stewart and Scott, 2014). Additionally, in policy discourses, the concept of domestically violent *fathers* tends to be absent (Stanley, 2011). Harne (2011, p. 63) has noted how policy leaves a gap around the idea of violent fathers: "Although there is growing recognition in child protection and safeguarding policies that children need to be protected from violent *men* [italics in original] . . . such offenders are rarely referred to as violent fathers or father figures in policy statements."

Using mutualizing language

There is a further problematic tendency in academic, practitioner, and policy discourses—using mutualizing and gender-neutral language such as "parental conflict," "violent arguments," and "high conflict divorce" to refer to cases of male-against-female domestic violence. This language spreads between these different discourses, especially from academic research (which practitioners and policymakers may consult) into policy and practice (De Simone and Heward-Belle, 2020).

Taking scholarly research first, mutualizing language is endemic across many relevant areas of study. For example, in the literature on the co-occurrence of intimate partner violence and child abuse, Bidarra et al.

(2016, p. 17) refer in a mutualizing way to "interpersonal conflicts" and "familial dysfunctioning" as they state that: "Regular interpersonal conflicts or familial dysfunctioning . . . appear to increase the risk of both IPV and CSA. . . . In families where there was IPV, there was [within the family as a whole] a greater tolerance for and trivialization of violence." Mutualizing language of the type found in this quote ("interpersonal conflicts," "familial dysfunctioning," "in families") does not pass critical inspection when applied to a coercive control situation. A family in which there is a perpetrator of coercive control is not "dysfunctional"; it *contains an abuser*. If there is "trivialization of violence" within the family in a coercive control situation, the *trivialization is being imposed or encouraged by the abuser*.

Beyond academic research, where practitioners and policymakers are engaged more directly in handling occurrences of male-against-female domestic violence, the use of mutualizing language has resulted in extraordinary injustice in the misrepresentation of actual cases. Obvious instances of this problem have been highlighted by Humphreys, whose analysis of UK social work case files found numerous examples of domestic violence being minimized through the use of mutualizing language. For example, what was described by a child protection professional in a case file as "an argument between the parents" was actually, "on closer reading," a knife attack by the father against the mother in which he stabbed her while she was holding their baby (Humphreys, 1999, p. 80; see also Humphreys and Absler, 2011; De Simone and Heward-Belle, 2020; Knezevic et al., 2021). In the same vein, mutualizing language is also commonly found in descriptions of coercive control situations that focus on "toxic," "turbulent," or "abusive" relationships (De Simone and Heward-Belle, 2020), rather than on the perpetrator and his beliefs, attitudes, personality, and patterns of behavior (Bancroft et al., 2012; Monckton Smith, 2020a, 2020b). Language that frames the "relationship" as the problem deflects attention from the abuser as the cause of the problem.

The reason why such mutualizing language is inappropriate for coercive control situations is that it apportions half of the blame to the victim, when responsibility for coercive control sits firmly with the perpetrator. The reason why "conflict" may occur regularly in the context of coercive control–based interpersonal violence is *not* because the family members are quarrelsome: Rather, as we have noted earlier, the perpetrator is causing the problem when he attempts to impose his coercive control; the conflict is happening primarily because other family members are, with good reason, attempting to resist his attempts to do so (Dutton and Goodman, 2005). Conversely, if coercive control–based violence and abuse are occurring and family members are appearing not to resist, this is unlikely to be because the victim/s are "tolerant" of violence or abuse: rather, it may be because they are not able to resist at that given moment in time due to the dangers posed by the perpetrator or the tactics of manipulation that he is using against them (Stark, 2007). What differentiates these coercive control situations from situational couple violence (where both parties may, in some circumstances, be mutually creating the problem and mutually using violence to express their frustration at each other or "win" an argument) is the highly unequal power-dynamic generated by the coercive control perpetrator over their target that precludes the possibility of mutuality between them (Hill, 2020).

COERCIVE CONTROL IN OTHER CONTEXTS

Before we move on to the next chapter, it is important to note that although coercive control is most often perpetrated by boyfriends/husbands/fathers/father-figures against their adult female partners and children (Barlow et al., 2020; Callaghan et al., 2018; Hester et al., 2017; Johnson et al., 2014; Katz, 2016; Katz et al., 2020; Myhill, 2015; Stark, 2007), coercive control does occur in other contexts too. For instance, it occurs in childfree or childless couples, in LGBT + couples, in situations where the woman/mother perpetrates coercive control against the man/father (though these cases are, as we have noted in this chapter, rare), and where male or female perpetrators target higher levels of coercive control at their child than they do at their partner/ex-partner. Coercive control can also occur when a grown-up child perpetrates it against a parent, when a carer perpetrates it against somebody dependent on their care, and when multiple perpetrators work together. For example, a husband, father-in-law, and mother-in-law may join forces to perpetrate coercive control against the wife/daughter-in-law of the family. These examples are not exhaustive. Also, not all perpetrators are of working age. A 14-year-old may perpetrate coercive control against his girlfriend; an 84-year-old may do the same against his wife (Addae and Tang, 2021; Aghtaie et al., 2018; Chantler and McCarry, 2020; Fontes, 2015; Hill, 2020; Monckton Smith, 2020a; Raghavan et al., 2019; Solace Women's Aid, 2021; Williamson, 2014).

Nor is coercive control solely confined to intimate/caring relationships or families. The same set of coercive and controlling techniques are used in a variety of other scenarios; for example they are the favored tools of kidnappers, hostage-takers, pimps/sex traffickers, and cult leaders (Hill, 2020; Pomerantz et al., 2021; Stark, 2007). As Herman (1992, p. 76, cited in Hill, 2020, p. 33) states, "the desire for total control over another person is the common denominator of all forms of tyranny." All victims/survivors of coercive control should be able to access the supports that they need, and all perpetrators of coercive control should be held accountable for their abuse.

However, within the study reported in this book, all of the perpetrators were the children's fathers/father-figures and had been the women's boyfriends/husbands. Furthermore, all of these perpetrators had acted as part of the wider social problem of men's gender-based violence and abuse against women and children. It is beyond the scope of this (already quite substantial) book to discuss alternative coercive control contexts in more detail.

2

Coercive control and the agentic child

INTRODUCTION

Picture a child experiencing domestic violence. What do you see?

It might seem unnecessary to do this—you might think that you already "know" what these children are enduring—but actually it *is* necessary to start by re-examining the preconceived idea that flashes into your head. The intention behind this chapter is to put forward a fresh conception of who children "are" and what capacities they have. Whatever we think we may know, our default understandings may be obstacles to the development of a fuller picture of children's experience of domestic violence.

Perhaps most people's instinctive image of children's experience of domestic violence is the type of image that is represented and reinforced by the media: the child crying or hiding in a dark, shadowy room. The teddy bears and dolls clasped for comfort in such images are symbolic of lost childhood innocence—the child's experience of domestic violence is viewed in terms of spoiled innocence and damaged childhood (Kitzinger, 2015; O'Dell, 2008). Alternatively, your image may be less passive, but may still be quite particular—you may picture a child rushing to intervene in a physical confrontation where the mother is being attacked by the father. Yet that too is only a partial image, as this book will explore.

Coercive Control in Children's and Mothers' Lives. Emma Katz, Oxford University Press. © Oxford University Press 2022.
DOI: 10.1093/oso/9780190922214.003.0002

The problem with these images is that our "frame" is distorted in two ways. One distortion (1) is societies' misconceptions of domestic violence as being about a relationship where one adult hits the other. The other distortion (2) is the stereotypical narratives around children and childhood that often present children as passive and damaged victims of adversity. Due to these distorted frames of (1) domestic violence and (2) children, our vision of *children's* experiences of domestic violence tends to be impaired: We tend to view the child's experience in the narrow terms of how they are damaged by their exposure to violence.

In response, this chapter tackles both distortions and creates a new frame that is built out of better solutions in both areas. This involves: (1) broadening beyond the incident to detect the coercive control—not in all cases of domestic violence, but in those cases where coercive control is being experienced; and (2) setting out how there has been, and needs to continue to be, a reconceptualization of children that puts at its heart "agency": that is, a person's capacity to act independently and to influence the world around them.

For those less familiar with the term "agency," it is a sociological term that refers to the ability that humans have to use their free will, to make decisions, and to be active in shaping the course of their own lives. It is a key term in this book. This book is situated within an innovative literature that has explored children's agency in circumstances of domestic violence: and it also does something that no other text has done, which is to focus in depth on children's *relational* agency in circumstances of coercive control, especially the agency they have in their relationship with the victim/survivor parent. Children's relational agency, especially within their mother–child relationships, is a core theme of this book.

TOWARD INCLUDING CHILDREN IN THE COERCIVE CONTROL REVOLUTION

In 2015, the UK Government took the step of criminalizing coercive control in England and Wales. The Serious Crime Act 2015 s. 76 made coercive and controlling behavior in a family or intimate relationship an offense resulting in up to five years in prison, a fine, or both (Bishop and Bettinson, 2018; Stark, 2018). This measure represented significant progress in responses to *adult* victims/survivors and perpetrators. However, *children* who experience parental coercive control were left behind by the Act, which stated that the offense of coercive control only applied if the victim was aged 16 and over. In effect, the Act failed to recognize that children under 16 years old could be victims of coercive control.

This failure within the Serious Crime Act 2015 s. 76 is aligned with a broader lag in thinking in the international children and domestic violence field. It has now been many years since Stark's groundbreaking (2007) book *Coercive Control*, which illuminated the multifaceted and life-encompassing nature of the abuse experienced by many *adult* victims/survivors of domestic violence. Stark called for a revolution in how we understand and respond to coercive control–based domestic violence, urging us to search deeper than the incidents of violence to recognize the full range of coercive and controlling tactics that some domestic violence perpetrators systematically use against their victims. Yet, since 2007, while the field of domestic violence research has been influenced by Stark, the more specific field of research into *children and domestic violence* has generally not been part of this revolution. Rather, it has remained entrenched in the more limited understanding, critiqued by Stark, of domestic violence as incidents of violence.

Thus, the majority of research in the children and domestic violence field has continued to view the "problem" in very narrow terms as children's exposure to incidents of parental violence (Haselschwerdt et al., 2019b). Phrases such as "the domestic/intimate partner violence," "the violence," and "the violent incident" have tended to be used interchangeably in this research (see, e.g., Chanmugam, 2015; De Puy et al., 2019; Fong et al., 2019; Holden, 2003; Holmes, 2013; Holmes et al., 2018; Jaffe et al., 2012; Münger and Markström, 2018; Staf and Almqvist, 2015). This language has reflected the general consensus in the field that, when it comes to children, the physical violence *is* the domestic violence/intimate partner violence. As a result, the issue of how children are affected by the full range of perpetrators' coercive control tactics has remained largely unexplored.

There have been some exceptions to this consensus, and this section will examine those in detail. Some of the first studies to engage with children's experience of coercive control–based domestic violence were by Bancroft and Silverman (2002), Morris (2009), Harne (2011), and Øverlien (2013). Morris (2009) discussed how perpetrators' web-like regimes of control can entrap children as well as mothers. Bancroft and Silverman (2002) recognized that coercive control was central to the fathering practices of many male domestic violence perpetrators, as these perpetrators "tend to be controlling and coercive in their direct interactions with children, often replicating much of the interactional style that they use with the mother" (Bancroft and Silverman, 2002, p. 6). Perpetrators' use of the same interactional style was likewise recognized by Harne (2011). Even when perpetrators directed their abuse toward children via child-specific (school- or play-related) objects, the nature of their abuse was the same as it was with mothers:

> Children and young people [describe] a catalogue of fathers' cruel and emotionally abusive behaviour towards them, such as destroying school work, school reports and toys, harming pets, not allowing children out of the house, not allowing them to speak to their mothers and not allowing friends to phone or come to the house. Some fathers are shown to deliberately emotionally abuse children and young people, insulting them and humiliating them in a similar way to their mothers. (Harne, 2011, p. 28)

Øverlien's (2013) qualitative research also provided important insights into how perpetrators' domineering interactional style transferred onto their interactions with children. She found that fathers/stepfathers were using psychological abuse toward children—continually constraining and monitoring them in a web-like regime:

> [These children] had to endure a form of control that seemed to have no other purpose than making sure children knew who was in charge [i.e., the father/stepfather]. [Fathers/stepfathers] dictated

what the child could wear, or if . . . [they could] socialise with friends and participate in activities. Their behavior, appearance, and schoolwork all had to be flawless and lots of things were "forbidden." One child described how: "If I set a glass on the table, it has to be put right there and not there, I am not allowed to do this and this, I have to do everything without a single mistake." (Øverlien, 2013, p. 280)

Such insights into perpetrators' constraining and monitoring behaviors—of "dictat[ing] what the child could wear"; of deciding if they could "socialise with friends and participate in activities"; and of specifying "things [that] were forbidden" and "ha[d] to be put right there and not there"—suggest the inadequacy of the children and domestic violence field's usual focus on violence. To confine our investigations to how children such as these have been exposed to violence would be to miss out on understanding the range of other forms of harm that these fathers/stepfathers are inflicting on their children as part of their domestic violence perpetration. Without this understanding, interventions to help and support such children are unlikely to meet their needs. The concept of coercive control is clearly needed in the children and domestic violence field in order to accurately identify the experiences and support needs of such children.

Further research has begun to examine the distinction between children experiencing situational couple violence and children experiencing coercive control (see chapter 1). Haselschwerdt (2014, p. 218) called on researchers of children and domestic violence to make this distinction, arguing that reworking our concept of domestic violence in this way would enable research to "specifically examine the experiences of youth exposed to coercive control as opposed to [youth exposed to] conflict that escalates to violence." This distinction between child survivors of situational couple violence and of coercive control was explored by Jouriles and McDonald (2015), who investigated how these two categories of children were affected by experiences of parental violence. They concluded that parental violence motivated by coercive control was linked with greater child adjustment problems. This understanding was then further deepened by Haselschwerdt et al. (2019a), who reported that their sample of young adults who had experienced coercive control during childhood had been exposed to many of the controlling behaviors that their fathers/ father-figures had directed at mothers, including:

> Verbal and emotional abuse, financial abuse, surveillance, and monitoring [of mothers'] behaviour and whereabouts [as well as] control over the mothers' clothing and appearance and exceedingly high expectations for [her] domestic work (e.g. cooking, cleaning, children's appearance). (Haselschwerdt et al., 2019a, pp. 1525–1526)

With a few exceptions, these children also reported exposure to severe and frequent violence perpetrated by their father/father-figure against their mother.

Katz's (2016) qualitative study was the first to focus specifically on perpetrators' *non-violent* tactics of coercive control and how they are experienced by children. This study found that children were particularly affected by perpetrators' control of time, movement, and activities within the home; isolation from sources of support; and economic abuse. Importantly, children were part of the picture not just as witnesses. They were not only "exposed to" fathers/father-figures using those tactics against their mothers; those tactics were also *directly harming and constraining* children's own lives. In contrast to Haselschwerdt et al.'s (2019a) and Øverlien's (2013) findings, Katz's research documented contexts where perpetrators were using little or no violence. About half of the 15 children in Katz's study were being harmed by coercive control in contexts of little or no violence against their mothers. This finding suggested that there might be a subsection of children who are under-represented in research on domestic violence. Such children's answers to survey questions about exposure to violence might be "sometimes" or "never." Yet coercive control dominates their lives. This is in line with Nevala's (2017) finding, discussed in chapter 1, that 45% of women in European Union countries who reported high levels of control from a partner had not been subjected to any violence from this partner.

Further research that has increased our understandings of children's experience of coercive control has also come from Callaghan, Alexander, Fellin, and Sixsmith's study with more than a hundred children in Greece, Italy, Spain, and the United Kingdom. Research papers published from this study (Alexander et al., 2016; Callaghan and Alexander, 2015; Callaghan et al., 2016a, 2016b, 2017a, 2017b, 2018; Fellin et al., 2018, 2019) have: (1) suggested the similarity of child and adult victims' experiences under coercive control, and (2) challenged the typical view of children as passive and "damaged" witnesses to domestic violence by exploring children's agency in their experiences of coercive control.

The similarity of child and adult victims' experience was noted by Callaghan et al. (2018) in their analysis of children's and mothers' descriptions of coercive control. Both mothers and children described having to be continually vigilant and constantly adapting their speech, appearance, and everyday activities to try to appease perpetrators. Callaghan et al. (2018, p. 1564) noted that both children and mothers had to ceaselessly "manage what they said and what they did, as a way of preventing themselves from being too visible, too loud, and too noticeable to the abuser."

Agency was also an important theme in this research. It highlighted that children could develop strategies of resistance in their everyday lives: that they had strengths that could be demonstrated in resourceful responses to the obstacles that the perpetrator was putting in their paths. For example, the researchers found that, when perpetrators prevented children from engaging in normal play behaviors at home, children were determined and adept at finding other places to play such as friends' homes and outside spaces (Fellin et al., 2018). Fellin et al. (2019)—who developed a strengths-based intervention for children, "MPOWER," as part of their research—noted from their data that children found many means of expressing "agency, resilience and resistance":

[Children] maintained a sense of agency, resilience and resistance in a range of ways: through caring relationships; through their use of space and their material environment; through their expression and management of complex emotion; and through their management of what and how they disclose their experiences. (Fellin et al., 2019, p. 172)

Agentic strategies on the part of children were therefore, as the authors put it, taking place "in the material spaces and relational exchanges that characterized [children's] worlds" (Fellin et al., 2019, p. 172).

Overall, then, what is being put forward here is a reframing of children and domestic violence. In place of a passive concept of children being "exposed to" or "witnessing" physical violence, it is possible to build a strengths-based understanding of children's agentic responses to coercive control. The study reported in this book furthers this understanding, providing an exploration of children's vulnerabilities and their agentic capacities when experiencing coercive control.

CHILDREN AND DOMESTIC VIOLENCE: TOWARD THE RECOGNITION OF CHILDREN'S AGENCY

When children and domestic violence research first emerged in the 1980s and 1990s, children tended to be viewed as passive bystanders and silent witnesses who were harmfully exposed to upsetting scenes of violence against their mother (Mullender et al., 2002). In much the same vein as that 1980s/90s portrayal, the majority of the field's research up to the present day has focused on investigating how children are damaged by "exposure" to domestic violence. The focus has been on how such children often develop behavioral, mental health, cognitive, social, physical, and physiological problems (see, e.g., Artz et al., 2014; Carlson et al., 2019; Holt et al., 2008; Kitzmann et al., 2003; Øverlien, 2010). Mullender et al. (2002, p. 13) raised the concern almost 20 years ago that most research in the field was on a "quest [to find] psychopathology in children who have witnessed violence against their mothers." There were some exceptions here; for example, Peled (1993), Holtzworth-Munroe et al. (1997), and Edleson (1999a) each explored the coping strategies of children who "witness" parental domestic violence. However, overall, Mullender et al.'s criticisms have continued to apply to scholarship in the field as the years have passed. Data about the impacts of domestic violence on children has continued frequently to be gathered from their mothers or other adults (Øverlien, 2010). Children, meanwhile, have continued to be defined in terms of psychopathology and, as Mullender et al. (2002, p. 3) had warned against, children have continued to be "marginalized as a source of information about their own lives" (see also Edleson, 1999a). Insofar as children are included in data collection, the approach has tended to be limited and deficit-focused, with children asked to complete questionnaires designed to measure their behavioral and emotional problems.

The field's focus on harms has too often marginalized the recognition of these children's *agency*, *strengths*, and *adaptive coping strategies*. This is not to deny the vital importance of research into how domestic violence harms children. However, research on children's resistance and resilience is also important. As Callaghan et al. (2018, p. 1556) have explained, "children who experience domestic violence are not *just* damaged by the experience but also have a complex range of coping strategies." The result of omitting children's agency from our research is that we may limit the ability of interventions and services to understand children's strengths and coping strategies and build on them.

Against this backdrop of damage-focused studies, there is a small but growing strand of research that does explore children's agency, voices, lived experiences, strengths, and adaptive coping strategies. Mullender et al.'s (2002) book *Children's Perspectives on Domestic Violence* was the first contribution to the field to foreground the concept of agency in relation to children and domestic violence. Based on qualitative interviews with 24 mothers and 54 children in the United Kingdom, the authors found that when children are not listened to and are not taken seriously as persons who are experiencing domestic violence, they can feel "doubly disadvantaged" (Mullender et al., 2002, p. 121). For the most part, the children in Mullender et al.'s study did not want adults to hide from them the difficult truths about the experience. They wanted adults to keep them informed and to include them in decision-making, for example about whether to separate from the perpetrator and what interventions to put in place.

This strand of agency-focused research, following in the footsteps of Mullender et al., has grown over the past fifteen years (see, e.g., Åkerlund and Sandberg, 2016; Alexander et al., 2016; Anderson et al., 2017; Arai et al., 2021; Beetham et al., 2019; Buckley et al., 2007; Callaghan et al., 2016a, 2016b, 2017a, 2017b, 2018; Chanmugam, 2014, 2015; Eriksson et al., 2005; Eriksson and Näsman, 2008; Fairchild and McFerran, 2018; Fellin et al., 2018, 2019; Johansen and Sundet, 2021; Källström and Thunberg, 2019; Katz, 2015a, 2015b, 2016; Lamb et al., 2018; Lapierre et al., 2018; Morris et al., 2015; Naughton et al., 2019; Øverlien, 2010, 2013; Øverlien and Hydén, 2009; Swanston et al., 2014). Such research has explored how children, while experiencing a great deal of fear as a result of fathers' threats and violence, also respond in a number of agentic ways. These include finding safe spaces, attempting to tune out frightening sounds, calling for help, supporting and protecting siblings, intervening to try to protect their mother, and many other coping strategies (Alexander et al., 2016; Arai et al., 2021; Callaghan et al., 2016b; Chanmugam, 2015; Mullender et al., 2002; Øverlien and Hydén, 2009).

More broadly, researchers have examined how children may actively use a range of resources in their daily lives to help them to cope, resist, and achieve some happiness. These resources include supportive friends and family, play, sport, journaling, music, and other forms of creative expression (Fairchild and McFerran, 2018; Fellin et al., 2018, 2019). Children also have the agentic capacity to carefully manage processes of disclosure, attempting to thoroughly assess the risks involved in informing or not informing various people about their experiences (Callaghan et al., 2017b). While some children express confusion about domestic violence, and have difficulty recognizing when their father is using psychological abuse (as opposed to more easily recognized physical violence—Naughton et al., 2019), others are aware that gaining power and control are central motivations behind the range of abusive and violent behaviors that their father has used (Callaghan et al., 2018; Mullender et al., 2002). Post-separation, some children have been able to decide that their fathers would need to show major attitudinal and behavioral changes before they would consider having future contact with them (Lamb et al., 2018).

CHILDREN'S AGENCY WITHIN PARENT–CHILD RELATIONSHIPS

We have now demonstrated how children have agency as individuals; yet children's agency also goes beyond their actions as individuals. Children influence and affect the people with whom they interact, and so their agency extends to the relationships they have with the people in their lives. This premise is central to the research reported in this book— and children's relational agency, especially within their mother–child relationships, is one of this book's core themes. The book shows how, in specific ways, the children within the study used this agency to help and support their mothers. As we will explore in later chapters, such agency did not necessarily involve dramatic individual acts such as phoning the police in a crisis. Rather, it occurred through commonplace, relational acts of support such as treating their mother to a small gift or watching a movie with her.

At present, there are a few other studies that explore relational agency and how some children use it to co-produce strong and supportive relationships that help themselves and others to survive abuse (see, e.g., Callaghan et al., 2016b; Mullender et al., 2002). (Of course, it should be acknowledged that children, like adults, can use their relational agency in negative and destructive ways as well as positive ones.) For the most part, though, research in the children and domestic violence field has not yet explored children's relational agency. The trend of viewing children as passive in relational terms, critiqued by Katz (2015a), has since continued. Within children and domestic violence research, children are often implicitly conceptualized as passive bystanders whose successful "adjustment" depends on the quality of their mothers' parenting (see, e.g., Bair-Merritt et al., 2015; Cully et al., 2021; Fong et al., 2019; Holmes et al., 2017; Huth-Bocks and Hughes, 2008; Johnson and Lieberman,

2007; Lamela et al., 2018; Letourneau et al., 2007; Levendosky et al., 2006; Samuelson et al., 2012; Sturge-Apple et al., 2010). Even studies that foreground children's agency tend to focus on their agency in responding to violence *as individuals*. For instance, they explore how children take individual action to keep themselves safe, call the police, or intervene in a violent incident (see, e.g., Callaghan and Alexander, 2015; Chanmugam, 2015; Øverlien and Hydén, 2009).

The lack of focus on children's relational agency in earlier research can largely be attributed to the dominance within the children and domestic violence field of an outdated model of parent–child relationships. This is the "unilateral" model of parent–child relations shown in Figure 2.1:

As explained by Kuczynski et al. (1999, p. 25), the unilateral model was based on a non-recognition of children's agency in parent–child relationships:

> [Within this model] parents were considered to be active agents capable of meaning construction and intentional action. Children were considered to be either passive recipients or victims of parental practices whose capacities for meaning construction and intentional action was usually ignored.

Within this model, "influence [is] assumed to flow in one direction, from parent to child" (Kuczynski et al., 1999, p. 25). Children's abilities to purposefully initiate actions within parent–child relationships and to influence their parents are not accounted for.

Figure 2.1 The Unilateral Model of Parent–Child Relationships

The unilateral model exists as an unexamined assumption within the children and domestic violence field. According to Kuczynski et al. (2003), the model first emerged as a theory within early developmental psychology. Although there was a formal turn away from this model in the late 1960s, there has been a tendency over the subsequent decades for it to continue, subtly, to underpin research in several child- and family-related fields (Kuczynski et al., 1999). The children and domestic violence field is no exception here, as many studies in the field can be viewed as being implicitly grounded in the unilateral model. For instance, Letourneau et al. (2007, p. 655) stated that they conducted "an analysis of the relationships between parents and children exposed to domestic violence." Yet, in practice, their study only analyzed one half of this relationship: the parenting practices of mothers. Such an approach fails to account for children's contributions to mother–child relationships. Rather, in accordance with the unilateral model, it suggests that mothers' parenting *is* the mother–child relationship.

A "bilateral" model of parent–child relationships was proposed by Kuczynski and colleagues to overcome this parental input/child outcome way of thinking (Kuczynski et al., 2003). As shown in Figure 2.2, this model depicts parent–child relationships as being produced by the ongoing, dynamic interaction between these directions of influence:

The bilateral model views causality in parent–child relationships as "bidirectional": Parents influence children, and children also influence parents (catching up with the lived realities with which parents may be familiar!). The model also assumes that parents and children have equal

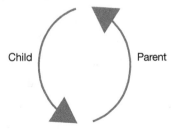

Figure 2.2 The Bilateral Model of Parent–Child Relationships

amounts of agency, although not usually equal amounts of power to exercise it.

It is important to explain the key premise within the bilateral model that children and parents have equal agency. There is a distinction here between agency as an inherent human quality and the power and resources to express agency effectively. Children's inherent agency is, from birth, equal to the inherent agency of their parents. As Kuczynski and De Mol (2015, p. 9) explain, all humans have "inherent capacities to make sense of the environment, initiate change, and resist domination by others." However, children and parents are unequal in power and resources, and consequently children are less able to express their agency effectively. However, as children mature and their power and resources grow, they are able to use increasingly sophisticated strategies to exercise agency and influence their parents and the world around them.

The bilateral model has had far greater influence outside of the children and domestic violence field than it has had within it, underpinning much research on family and parent–child relationships (see, e.g., Arditti, 1999; Burke et al., 2017; Harach and Kuczynski, 2005; James, 2013; Kuczynski et al., 2016, 2018; Marshall and Lambert, 2006; Morrow, 2003; Oliphant and Kuczynski, 2011; Van den Bulck et al., 2016; Walton et al., 2017). Beginning more than 20 years ago, this research highlighted the active and influential roles of children. For instance, drawing on a general community sample in England, Morrow's (2003) research explored how children themselves defined "family" in bilateral ways, finding that: "nearly half of the older children included elements of mutual support in their definitions of what families are for, using phrases such as 'caring for each other', 'sharing' and 'looking after each other.'" As one 13-year-old girl described: "families are for helping you through bad times, cheering you up when you feel down, caring for one another" (Morrow, 2003, p. 120). Arditti's (1999) US study with college students from divorced single-mother households also noted that these students held bilateral understandings of good mother–child relationships. The students positively discussed having relationships with their mothers that involved shared disclosures and friendship. In such studies of family and parent–child relationships, children have emphasized the importance of mutual support within families, viewing themselves as both givers and receivers of care.

Morrow's and Arditti's studies related to older children—yet there is evidence that middle childhood can also be a time of mutuality and reciprocity in parent–child relationships. Oliphant and Kuczynski's (2011) study with a community sample of Canadian parents who had children aged 4–8 found that closeness and companionship were maintained mutually by children and parents in several ways. Instances of care and supportiveness were found in a range of everyday activities and behaviors:

> Having fun together, sharing similar interests, treating each other with mutual respect, communicating with each other on an equal level, displaying affection, and making time to spend with each other. [Parents also described] maintaining a balance with behaviors that preserved their responsibilities as authorities e.g. teaching and guidance. (Oliphant and Kuczynski, 2011, p. 1107)

These findings highlight the active agency of children in parent–child relationships. Influencing and supporting parents, and giving care and attention to parents, *are part of children's roles*.

It is necessary here to stress the difference between the healthy, age-appropriate care and support that children may give in contexts of mutuality, and the much-less healthy situations where children are providing care and support with limited reciprocation from parents. In the more extreme of the latter cases, children are forced to act in ways that go far beyond what is suitable to their age, maturity, and capabilities, as parent(s) are no longer parenting and are expecting the child to take over the parent(s) role. The appropriate term for these extreme cases is "parentification":

> It is generally believed that parentification in the family entails a functional and/or emotional role-reversal in which the child sacrifices his or her own needs for attention, comfort, and guidance in order to accommodate and care for a logistical or emotional need of the parent. . . . In parentification, the parent(s) relinquishes executive

functions by delegation of instrumental roles to a parental child or by total abandonment of the family psychologically and/or physically. (Hooper, 2007, p. 217)

Here we can note that the terms "parentification" and "role-reversal" do *not* correctly apply to healthy situations where a child is giving age-appropriate and reciprocated support to a parent. They only apply to the very particular situations where a child's care and support are not "acknowledged, supervised, and reciprocated" by the parent(s), and the parent(s) do not meet the child's needs for attention, comfort, and guidance (Jurkovic et al., 2001, p. 246). It must also be acknowledged that family relationships are complex, dynamic, and evolving, and do not always fall into neat categories. There may be parent–child relationships that fall short of parentification but where children's care-giving behaviors become very problematic at times.

The field of children and domestic violence research has much to learn from studies in other fields that have used the bilateral model to explore parent–child relationships. Such studies have illustrated that, in families where there is no coercive control and parent–child relationships are healthy, there is reciprocity of care and supportiveness between parents and children. The norm is *not* for children to exist in a state of passive dependency and inaction, but for parent–child relationships to be characterized by mutual agency and mutual influence. A key contribution made by this book is to explore what happens to this reciprocity of care and supportiveness in circumstances of coercive control (see chapters 5–9).

CONCLUSION

This chapter has explored how the problematization of children and domestic violence needs to be reframed in certain ways and how, to bring this reframing about, understandings of both "children" and "domestic violence" need to be reconceptualized. In relation to the reconceptualization of domestic violence, this reframing involves moving away from the language of children "witnessing" the father's/father-figure's abuse against their mother. Children living with coercive control perpetrators cannot be abstracted in this way from the situation: Tactics used by perpetrators/fathers against mothers also directly harm and constrain children's own lives. In relation to the conceptualization of children, this chapter has emphasized children's agency. It has shown how we need to move beyond the language of "exposure" and "damage" that implicitly frames children as bystanders who are shaped passively by the situation and lack an active will of their own. We need a more complex and nuanced view: Children are victims and they are harmed, but they are also copers and survivors.

The issues around how perpetrators of coercive control cause harm to children are picked up again in chapter 4, with an in-depth discussion based on the research findings reported in this book. Meanwhile, the next chapter, chapter 3, explains how that research was designed and conducted. Readers who are not interested in the "whats, whens and whys" of the study are welcome to skip straight to chapter 4 to learn more about the "big picture" of children's experiences and how we might better understand them.

3

Interviewing children and mothers about coercive control

INTRODUCTION

The research reported in this book involved semi-structured qualitative interviews with 15 mothers and 15 children who had experienced coercive control-based domestic violence. Mothers and children from the same families were included. This was an advantage as it allowed for a fuller and more complex understanding of mothers' and children's experiences, and enabled coercive control to be explored from the perspectives of both mothers and children.

The study was unique in its focus. First, it was concerned not with investigating mothers' and children's experiences of "incidents" of physical violence, but with their everyday lives: lives that were conceptualized as contexts where mothers and children experienced coercive control from perpetrators/fathers but could also develop agentic strategies of resistance. Second, the intention was to reach beyond the period when mothers had been entrapped in relationships with perpetrators. The interviews explored what had happened during those relationships, but also ventured into what had happened in the months and years since these relationships had ended. Finally, focusing on children's strengths as well as vulnerabilities and following the bilateral model of mother–child

Coercive Control in Children's and Mothers' Lives. Emma Katz, Oxford University Press. © Oxford University Press 2022.
DOI: 10.1093/oso/9780190922214.003.0003

relationships (see chapter 2), the intention was to understand not only how mother–child relationships had been harmed by coercive control, but also the mutual supportiveness and "ordinariness" in these relationships.

ETHICAL THEORY

Ethical approval for this research was granted by the University of Nottingham's Ethics Committee. Discussions of the ethical approaches taken during the study are included throughout this chapter, but some important information can be introduced here. The ethical framework developed for the research was one that drew on two bodies of ethics literature: (1) feminist scholarship on ways of researching ethically (see, e.g., Campbell et al., 2010; Maynard, 1994; Miller et al., 2012; Skinner et al., 2005), and (2) child-centered literature which suggests strategies for researching ethically with children, including children who have been abused (see, e.g., Alderson and Morrow, 2011; Bushin, 2007; Christensen and James, 2008; Coyne, 2010; Eriksson and Näsman, 2012; Gorin et al., 2008; Kellett, 2010; Kirk, 2007; Lewis, 2009; Mason and Hood, 2011; Morris et al., 2012).

Feminist ethic of care framework

A feminist ethic of care framework was viewed as particularly suitable for research with survivors of coercive control. This framework encourages researchers to ground their ethical decision-making in the circumstances of participants, rather than rigidly applying a set of rules (Edwards and Mauthner, 2012). Furthermore, a feminist ethic of care framework views research relationships as being at their most ethical when they are based on trust, care, empathy, and respect (Campbell et al., 2010).

Child-centered research methods

The child-centered research methods literature was also highly appropriate for this study (see, e.g., Alderson, 2005; Alderson and Morrow, 2011; Christensen and James, 2008; Christensen and Prout, 2002; Gillett-Swan and Sargeant 2018; Kellett, 2010; Kirk, 2007). This literature recognizes children as agentic, competent experts on their own lives (Mason and Hood, 2011). It also stresses the need for researchers to actively reduce power hierarchies between themselves and child participants (Mason and Hood, 2011). Otherwise, as Kirk (2007, p. 1252) notes, "the unequal power relations that exist between children and adults [in wider society] are duplicated in the research process." Researchers drawing on this literature are encouraged to ensure, as far as possible, that potential child participants are in a position to make decisions on their participation based on what they feel is best for themselves.

INCLUSION CRITERIA

The following three inclusion criteria were used in this research:

1. Participants needed to be mothers or children with experiences of domestic violence. It was not specified that participants had to have experienced coercive control–based domestic violence, although, in the event, all those who took part had experienced coercive control.
2. Children needed to be a minimum of 10 years old. The decision to make 10 years old the age-limit for this study was based on a balance between, on one hand, a realization that interviews about coercive control would require a significant degree of maturity and verbal ability from participants, and, on the other hand, the wish to include younger children in the study as much as possible. (There was no upper age-limit set at the

start of this research. However, in order to take part, children needed to be living with their mothers and not yet in their own independent home.)

The decision on the minimum age of participation was made following reflection and consultation, both with previous studies in the field and with a domestic violence survivors' group who advised on the research design at the planning stage. Among the previous studies, age-limits were variable. While McGee (2000) and Baker (2005) interviewed children as young as 5, Mullender et al. (2002), Eriksson (2012), and Swanston et al. (2014) included children from the age of 8 and Øverlien and Hydén (2009) interviewed children from 12 years old. The survivors' group, mostly mothers themselves, were encouraging about the viability of the project. They thought that 10 would be appropriate as a lower age-limit because 10-year-olds would have sufficient maturity to understand the research and decide whether or not to participate. Setting 10 as the age-limit also allowed the study to include the views of children in both primary and secondary school (children in England typically start secondary school at the age of 11).

3. To take part, mothers needed to be separated from perpetrators/ fathers and to be fairly safe in their current daily lives. The study avoided interviewing people who were still experiencing high levels of violence and threats from perpetrators post-separation. The decision not to recruit people in those circumstances was taken because of the need to maintain the participants' and my own safety, and because of the study's interest in exploring families' recoveries. It was acknowledged that, as each family's situation had its own precise characteristics, there was no straightforward threshold of safety that could be applied as a criterion for participation. I therefore made case-by-case judgments about whether mothers and children were sufficiently safe to take part in the study.

FIELDWORK LOCATION AND RECRUITMENT PROCESS

Location

The fieldwork was conducted over 13 months in the central region of England known as the Midlands, and the majority of the participants were from various locations in the East Midlands area. Most participants lived in, or near, market towns or city suburbs. An advantage of participants living in varied locations, and having experienced a range of statutory and voluntary service providers, was that the data were not unduly influenced by the level and quality of service provision in any one local area.

Sampling methods

Participants were accessed through a combination of purposive sampling and snowball sampling (Esterberg, 2002). The aim of the purposive sampling, by which 12 out of 15 of the families were accessed, was to recruit families who had received support from specialist domestic violence services, such as Women's Aid. Snowball sampling, which accounts for the other three families, occurred when mothers who had already participated put me in contact with another mother who they believed would be interested in participating. The families recruited through snowball sampling had also received professional support for their experiences of domestic violence.

Ethical rationale

Recruiting via support services, and recruiting families who had received professional support, was ethically important. This approach minimized the chances that a participant's interview would be the first time that they had talked about such an emotionally challenging topic. It also meant that participants would have ongoing relationships (or, at least, familiarity) with professional organizations, and could call on these sources of support if the interviews raised any issues (Mullender et al., 2002, p. 27).

Gaining access to participants

Recruiting sufficient numbers of participants was challenging. Initially, I contacted organizations by telephone and e-mail and asked if they would help me to contact their current or former service-users who were mothers of dependent children. Twelve organizations were contacted, and six ultimately agreed to help. Those organizations who agreed to help then proceeded to inform mothers about the research. When a mother expressed an initial interest, a worker requested their permission before sharing the mother's telephone number with me. This then allowed me to contact the mother directly to give her more details about the project. However, having a mother's telephone number was no guarantee of her participation, as some mothers never answered my calls. Others did answer, and ultimately took part in the study. Some organizations invited me to attend events they were hosting for service-users, enabling me to approach mothers in person and ask if they were interested in participating. This strategy had mixed results, but it did result in some interviews being arranged.

INTERVIEWING CHILDREN

Gaining access to child participants

Children were recruited via their mothers, and mothers gave consent for children to take part. This approach was taken because, as Mullender et al. (2002, p. 30) stated regarding their own study with children who had experienced domestic violence: "[It] was vital not to usurp the right of women to decide what would be safe or harmful for their children [as these women] had only recently become free of the power and control of the abusers and were newly established as the heads of their households." It was also important to avoid this "usurpation" more generally, given the power relations between myself as a professional researcher, operating with the cultural capital and institutional weight of a University behind her, and women in the community. It was therefore up to mothers to decide if they wished to tell their children about the research, and to ask them whether they were interested in participating. If the children then expressed interest in participating, I proceeded to contact the children.

Children's informed consent

No interview with a child proceeded unless the child gave their own informed consent. Gaining the informed consent of children can be difficult, as children who are approached via parents to take part in research can face a double power-hierarchy: Two adults, one of them the researcher and the other their parent, may both wish them to participate. To minimize the chances that children would participate against their inclinations, I followed the child-centered research approach of giving potential child participants detailed yet easy to understand information about the research, emphasizing their right to say no, and endeavoring to put them at ease so that they would feel comfortable expressing their wishes.

Children's ongoing consent

Consent was viewed in the way recommended by Lewis (2009, p. 406), as "an ongoing process that begins from the very first point of contact and [continues] throughout all further arrangements." This understanding of consent places the onus on the researcher to consider, from the first meeting until the last agreed contact, whether participants wish to be involved in the study.

A minority of children (although, contrary to my initial expectations, not the youngest) were nervous and uncommunicative at the beginning of their interviews. This variation in children's responses to being interviewed is in line with the experiences of other researchers. For example, Mullender et al. (2002, p. 41) noted, "There was a wide range in how forthcoming the children and young people were [...]. Some found it difficult to speak, while others talked without stopping." My approach, when children seemed nervous before an interview, was to continue to give them information about the research in a friendly way. If they gave consent to take part, I carefully monitored how the children were feeling once the interview began, and rechecked their ongoing consent explicitly by asking them during the interview if they wished to continue.

Rechecking children's ongoing consent enabled some children to modify the terms of their participation during their interview by saying that they did not wish to speak about the period when they had experienced coercive control. In these instances, the child and I agreed to focus on the child's life since they had separated from the perpetrator/father and their current relationship with their mother. This refocusing of interviews based on children's preferences produced a more equal power-relationship between child participants and myself.

Children's non-verbal cues and ongoing consent

Many researchers have noted the need to read non-verbal cues that may indicate that a participant's consent is becoming less enthusiastic. Eriksson and Näsman (2012, p. 4) suggest, "We have to take responsibility to end the interview if we get indications that the informant does not wish to continue, even if this is not expressed verbally." The concept of reading such non-verbal cues in this way was in place for all of the interviews in the study—those with adults as well as children—however, in practice no adult reacted to being interviewed with the negative non-verbal cues that were occasionally evident in the child participants.

When these situations occurred (i.e., when a child participant's non-verbal cues suggested that they were feeling some stress), I attempted to react in a sensitive way. I asked the participant if they wanted to take a break, to skip over a question, or to end the interview. In one instance, I decided to terminate an interview early, as the child was looking down at the floor, giving short and barely audible answers, and had not "warmed up" after the interview's first few minutes. Not wishing to end abruptly, I thanked the child for their time and said to the child that the interview had been very helpful.

COMPOSITION OF THE SAMPLE

The same number of mothers and children were interviewed in the study—15 children and 15 mothers—but this symmetry was a coincidence; I did not interview one mother and one child per family. There were 11 families where a mother and one or two of her children were interviewed, and four families where it was only possible to interview the mother. Collectively, the 15 women who were interviewed were mothers to 47 children, 15 of whom were interviewed and 32 of whom were not. There were two main reasons why these 32 children were not interviewed; many fell outside the study's age-limit/living circumstances criteria, and some did not wish to take part.

Of the 15 interviewed mothers, there were four who were interviewed without an interview taking place with any of their children. Three of these mothers had children who were within the study's age-limit but who did not wish to be interviewed. According to these mothers, their children were (1) in an early phase of recovery and did not currently wish to discuss their experiences (Jack); (2) had been through an extensive period of talking and recovery and now wished to "put the past behind them" (Zara); or (3) had a highly conflictual relationship with their mother and was not interested in participating (Tanya). The fourth mother did not have a child who was sufficiently old to participate (her oldest child—Carly—was 7) but she still wished to take part herself. During the data analysis, care was

Interviewing children and mothers

taken to avoid assuming that these mothers' data represented children's experiences within their families. It cannot be known whether the non-participating children would have agreed with their mothers' accounts.

Table 3.1 provides detailed information about the sample. All names are pseudonyms:

Table 3.1 THE SAMPLE

Type of interview	Mother's name	Child/ren's name/s	Children's age and sex	Time since mother and perpetrator separated
Mother and one child interviewed	Ellie	Shannon	10, female	4 years
	Isobel	Bob	12, male	3 years
	Eloise	John	20, male	4 years
	Kimberley	Elle	14, female	4 years
	Marie	Leah	11, female	3 months
	Alison	Jane	11, female	7 years
	Bella	Roxie	11, female	4 years
Mother and two children interviewed	Ruby	Thomas & Katie	10, male & 12, female	1 year
	Akeela	Brock & Vince	12, male & 13, male	8 years
	Violet	Angel & Joe	12, female & 14, male	9 years
	Lauren	Zoe & Grace	12, female & 14, female	9 years
Mother-only interviews	Charlie	Tanya (not interviewed)	14, female	6 years
	Lucy	Zara (not interviewed)	11, female	7 years
	Ria	Carly (not interviewed)	7, female	4 years
	Sybil	Jack (not interviewed)	11, male	8 months

DEMOGRAPHIC AND OTHER FACTORS

Age and sex

Six boys and 9 girls were interviewed. Mothers' ages ranged from 26 to 50, with the majority being in their 30s or 40s. Two mothers (Marie and Ria) had given birth to their first children with the perpetrator while they were still in their teenage years. The 15 interviewed children were all (apart from one 20-year-old) aged 10–14. This age range encompasses both "children" and "young people," so when this book uses the term "children" to refer to these participants, the term is being used in a relational sense (i.e., that we remain our parents' children at any age).

Ethnicity

Of the 15 mothers, 13 were White British, 1 was Black British, and 1 was British South Asian. Among the children, 10 were White British, 2 were Black British, and 3 were British South Asian. This was broadly in line with the demographics of the East Midlands region of England, where 13 of the 15 families lived (two families were from the neighboring West Midlands). The population of the East Midlands is 85.4% "White British," 6.5% "Asian," and 1.8% "Black," with the remainder being associated with other ethnic categories (HM Government, 2018).

Experience with refuge services

Only a minority of families in the study (4 out of 15) had accessed refuge services. This meant that the sample was not overly skewed toward participants who had used this provision.

Perpetrators' relationships to children

In 12 out of 15 families, the perpetrator was the children's biological father. In the other 3 families, the perpetrator was either the children's step-father or their mother's boyfriend.

Time since separating from the perpetrator

At the time of interview, mothers had been separated from perpetrators/ fathers for an average of 5 years. Nine mothers had been separated for 4–7 years, while a further 3 mothers had separated 8–9 years ago. Three mothers had separated more recently, one year or less before the interview.

Children's contact with perpetrators

A minority of the interviewed children (3 out of 15) were still having contact with the perpetrator at the time when they took part in the study. In the interviews with these children, an attempt was made to avoid imposing a linguistic framework that might be distressing (such as the term "domestic violence") when discussing the father's actions. Instead, space was given for these children to describe their father's actions in their own ways.

INTERVIEW LOGISTICS

Venue

All but one of the interviews were conducted in participants' homes. (The one interview not conducted in a home was held, at the participant's request, at the offices of a local domestic violence organization.) The home environment provided several benefits as a location for the interviews:

- suitability as a setting for discussion of highly personal topics
- power for participants, being a space which was theirs, and in which I was a guest
- opportunities for me to build rapport with participants, by thanking them for their hospitality, commenting positively on their homes and engaging with their pets
- practicality for interviewing both mothers and children on the same visit, as mothers and children could be interviewed one after the other and could keep busy with their usual daily routines while the other interview(s) took place

Who to interview first

Mothers and children were usually interviewed on the same day. Sometimes the mother was interviewed first, sometimes the child, depending on what was convenient for the family. I learned during the process that it was helpful to interview the mother first, because mothers' accounts were usually richer in detail and helped me to build an understanding of the sequence of events that had been experienced by the family.

Length of interviews

Mothers' interviews were usually about twice the length of children's, as mothers tended to give fuller answers. The average duration of mothers' interviews was 1 hour 35 minutes: the longest being 2 hours 30 minutes, and the shortest, 50 minutes. The children's interviews lasted on average 40 minutes, varying between 15 minutes and 1 hour 10 minutes. Some children's interviews were relatively short because they had been very young during the period when their mother and the perpetrator/father had been in a relationship, and therefore remembered little about what their life had been like at that time. In this situation, several of the interview questions were inapplicable. These interviews normally lasted between 20 and 30 minutes, focusing on the child's recovery process and their life in the present.

Remuneration

All participants were given a £10 gift voucher from a retailer of their choice to thank them for their participation.

ETHICS AT THE INTERVIEW STAGE

Confidentiality and joint/separate interviews

It is standard within the field to offer complete confidentiality except if anything is said that makes the researcher concerned about a child's safety (Mullender et al., 2002; Baker, 2005). This was the approach taken in this research. In accordance with the recommendation of Baker (2005), information about this policy was included on the study's consent forms and participant information sheets.

At the outset of the research, it was decided that the aim would be to hold mothers' and children's interviews separately. As well as helping to better maintain confidentiality between the mothers' and children's interviews, it was felt that holding separate interviews would better enable participants to talk openly about negative aspects of their mother–child relationships.

In the event, mothers and children were interviewed separately in all but four of the families, and these interviews were confidential, as mothers chose for the interview to take place in an enclosed room that no other person was using. However, in four of the 15 families, mothers and/or children requested that they be interviewed jointly. The overall impact of holding these interviews jointly was difficult to determine. On the one hand, some participants suggested that joint interviews made them feel more comfortable and aided their memories. However, joint interviews may have also prevented some mothers and children from discussing their more negative feelings regarding their mother–child relationships.

Anonymity and data security

Data security and the protection of participants' identities was vital, given that breaches of security could endanger participants. Participants self-selected a pseudonym. Participants were also protected by the removal of identifying information from the data (Wiles et al., 2008). First, references to real names of people or places were omitted from field notes and interview transcripts. Second, when quotations from the interviews were used in academic publications based on the study (including in this book), they were screened and, where necessary, modified to make potentially identifying information less specific. Finally, the paper and electronic documents relating to the interviews were stored securely: consent forms in a locked cabinet, and computer files containing interview recordings and transcriptions on an encrypted USB device.

Information sheets and consent forms

Participant information sheets and consent forms were written in a manner that was easy to understand (Kirk, 2007; Mason and Hood, 2011). The consent form stated the purpose of the study and the voluntary nature of participation. It stressed the fact that participants could withdraw whenever they wanted, and did not have to talk about matters that they preferred not to discuss. The form explained what would happen to the study's results, how participants' identities would be protected, and arrangements for confidentiality. Children and mothers were separately given consent forms to read and sign.

Reducing power imbalances with participants

I was aware of the need to reduce power-hierarchies between myself and participants as much as possible. A useful aid to this process was that, as a non-driver, I usually traveled to interview participants on trains and buses, and, in then reaching the participant's home by foot, often took wrong turns. This unfortunate tendency happily allowed me to follow the recommendations of Eriksson and Näsman (2012) and light-heartedly tell participants about my poor sense of direction. This approach to opening conversations with participants may have helped to put participants at ease, by foregrounding that I was an ordinary person with flaws. This was potentially useful given the power imbalance between participants and myself as a professional researcher, operating with the cultural capital and institutional weight of a University behind me (as mentioned earlier).

Rapport with participants

I adopted a friendly and positive interviewing approach with participants—in line with the feminist ethic of care framework discussed earlier, and its valuing of research relationships based on empathy and respect (Campbell et al., 2010). I attempted to use good interpersonal skills throughout, with positive body language, tone of voice, and filler sounds such as supportive "hmm" noises at appropriate times.

INTERVIEW STRUCTURING AND DESIGN

Order of questions

The first question, asked to both mothers and children, focused on the present: "Could you tell me a bit about you and your mum/children, and the things that are good or not so good about your lives at the moment?" The questions in the middle part of the interview covered the experiences of coercive control, the leaving process, and experiences of services, in that order. The latter part of the interview returned to participants' current lives, asking questions such as: "Out of all the people in your mum's/child's life, who do you think has helped them the most?"

Sequencing questions to minimize distress

The questions were sequenced so that the interviews could begin and end on a positive note. Starting the interview with a question about the present generally provided an easy and non-threatening opening (Kirk, 2007). Once the participants had become more comfortable, the questions in the middle part of the interview took them into the difficult subject matter of their past experiences. The questions in the latter part of the interview allowed participants to reflect positively on their recoveries and the improvements that had occurred in their lives, minimizing the chances that the interview would leave them feeling distressed (Radford et al., 2017).

A strengths-based approach

The interviews included questions about the strengths and positive aspects of participants' current lives as well as the abuse that they had previously experienced. This represents good practice because a solely negative focus in interviews can be harmful to participants and communities. Alderson (2005, pp. 28–29) has pointed to the link between a methodological focus on deficiency and interpretations that reinforce social injustice:

> If the research questions and methods concentrate on children's needs and failings, so will the reports emphasize problems and deficits. This can increase shame, stigma, prejudice and disadvantage for whole groups of children. Yet these children may, in some respects, be strong, resilient, knowledgeable and resourceful. Fair, ethical research therefore involves asking children about positive as

well as adverse aspects of their lives, in order to avoid biased reports that may compound their problems.

Accordingly, this study deliberately paid attention to the "strong, resilient, knowledgeable and resourceful" aspects of the participants' lives and experiences, not only their adversities. Because it dismisses neither the positive nor the negative, this attention to strengths as well as harms can be viewed as ethically helpful, as well as useful in delivering more nuanced findings.

Asking similar questions to enable comparisons between mothers' and children's experiences

In the interviews, similar questions were asked to the mother and children within each family, in order to draw out comparisons between mothers' and children's answers about: (1) themselves, (2) each other, and (3) their relationship with each other. For example, both mothers and children were asked: "Thinking back to the time just after the separation, could you tell me about your memories of how you and your mum/children were during that time, and how things were between you?"

Mothers were usually engaged and talkative during their interviews. Children's interviews were more varied in this respect. Some talked enthusiastically, appearing to enjoy the interview experience, while others were more nervous. In retrospect, other methods besides one-to-one semi-structured interviews could have been more helpful with the nervous children. For example, it might be that these children would have felt more comfortable drawing or using photographs or diaries to convey their experiences (Baker, 2005).

DATA ANALYSIS

A thematic analysis was conducted using the approach developed by Ritchie and Spencer (2002). Initially, this approach involved me producing a thematic framework that could be used to code and sort the data. This framework was drawn from the study's interview questions, then refined gradually as it was applied to a selection of interview transcripts. At this stage, the thematic framework consisted of 15 themes and over 100 subthemes. For example, one theme was "mother–child supportiveness after separating from perpetrators." The subthemes within this theme included "understandings of supportiveness," "feelings about support," and "ways of supporting." These themes and subthemes were used as a means of coding the transcripts.

The next stage of the analysis involved charting the data by working out "the range of attitudes and experiences" for each theme and subtheme (Ritchie and Spencer, 2002, p. 317). I created a table for each theme with the participants' names listed in rows and the subthemes in columns. These tables were then filled out with summaries of each participant's experiences of the various subthemes, referenced with a page and line reference from their interview transcript (Barnard et al., 2012). This meant that every participant's response to a subtheme was present on the same table and could be compared.

Once charting was complete, the final stage of "mapping and interpretation" began. This involved "defining concepts, mapping the range and nature of phenomena, creating typologies, finding associations [and] providing explanations" (Ritchie and Spencer, 2002, p. 321). Throughout the analysis, I endeavored to respect the thoughts and feelings expressed by participants and to maximize the authenticity of the research.

LIMITATIONS

Cultural situatedness

Culturally, the study does not claim any global applicability in its representation of the topic. It was situated in a particular part of the world and a particular type of society. Taking place in the United Kingdom, it was situated in a Western country that has one of the world's larger economies and a primarily non-religious population (Curtice et al., 2019). It is not known to what extent the findings may apply in countries beyond the United Kingdom.

Size of the sample

Thirty children and mothers took part in this research, which is a relatively small sample, though comparable with many other qualitative studies in this field. The study makes no claims to representativeness, as these 30 people were also by no means representative of coercive control survivors as a whole. Caution is required in considering to what extent the findings might apply to wider populations of survivors.

Demographics of the sample

The participants had specific demographics. Broadly in line with the demographics of the East Midlands of England, the regional location of most of the interviews (see earlier), the participants were mostly White (13/15 mothers and 10/15 children were White), and most lived in, or near, market towns or city suburbs, rather than in rural locations. Again, caution is therefore required in considering to what extent the findings might apply to survivors from a diverse range of ethnicities, and to survivors living in rural areas.

Recruitment via support services

Participants were recruited via support services, meaning that all of the participants had received formal supports for their experiences of domestic abuse (although the extent of those supports varied considerably). Therefore the study lacked the voices of more vulnerable and marginalized survivors who had not accessed such services.

Specific focus on the most frequent context/type of coercive control

The study also focused on a certain type of situation, where the mother and children were the victims/survivors and the perpetrator was the children's father/father-figure. As discussed in chapter 1, coercive control can be perpetrated in a number of different contexts, including by women/mothers against men/fathers and children. Such cases of coercive control are significantly rarer (see, e.g., Barlow et al., 2020; Hester et al., 2017; Johnson et al., 2014; Myhill, 2015), but do nonetheless occur, and warrant further research in their own right.

Personal and present-day perspectives

All of the accounts given in the interviews represented the participant's views and understandings at the time when the interview took place. Although participants' discussions of their current lives were contemporaneous, their recollections of how life had been at the height of the coercive control were retrospective.

As mentioned earlier, in 4 out of the 15 families it was not possible to interview the children, and so mothers were the only ones interviewed. When children's views were absent, we cannot assume that the children would have agreed with the mothers' accounts.

Conversely, in the few cases where joint interviews were held, the accounts may have been shaped by perceptions of what *the other person* wanted to hear. This may have constrained participants' discussions of negative aspects of their mother–child relationships.

CONCLUSION

In keeping with ethical framework developed for the research, and the feminist and child-centered scholarship on which it draws, the study was conducted in a way that prioritized the well-being of participants throughout. Clear information was given to participants about the study and what taking part would involve. Decisions about what questions to ask, to whom, how and where were all carefully considered.

The results of this research are unfolded in the remaining chapters. The research yielded a rich picture of how these children and mothers had been harmed by father/father-figure perpetrated coercive control, and how they were endeavoring to recover.

4

Coercive control

Harms to children

INTRODUCTION

In this chapter we begin to explore the results of the research reported in this book by examining the harms caused to children by perpetrators'/ fathers' coercive control. This chapter also explores how children actively resist coercive control, and how, in cases of coercive control, treating "domestic violence" and "child abuse and neglect" as two different categories is misleading.

The chapter makes a series of important arguments. The first part of the chapter argues that perpetrators'/fathers' drive to gain control was the underpinning factor behind harms that they caused to both mothers and children—especially punishing and constraining mothers and children for supposedly "being bad" or "doing wrong," and for attempting to gain independence and interpersonal connection with each other or anyone beyond the perpetrator/father himself. A key point here is that coercive control by perpetrators/fathers dominates entire *homes*, creating overarching conditions of entrapment and constraint that affect children as well as mothers. The second argument is that resistance was woven into the everyday lives of child victims/survivors. So, what might for example appear to an outsider to be an unexceptional bag of shopping, or an easily forgotten argument or tantrum, may in fact be part of ongoing efforts of

Coercive Control in Children's and Mothers' Lives. Emma Katz, Oxford University Press. © Oxford University Press 2022.
DOI: 10.1093/oso/9780190922214.003.0004

resistance in which children make resourceful use of their limited space for action. The third argument, made in the latter part of the chapter, is that it is unhelpful to treat as two separate phenomena children's experiences of coercive control and their experiences of abusive and neglectful behavior by the perpetrator parent. Perpetrators'/fathers' abuse and neglect of their children seemed from the data to be *part of* their coercive control. The chapter instead suggests the usefulness of having a single concept of coercive control as a multi-stranded form of abuse that harms both children and adults.

Explaining how this multi-stranded form of abuse works and what forms it takes, the chapter highlights two factors that often result in the children and the victim/survivor parent having no escape from the perpetrator: namely, perpetrators' persistence, dangerousness, and resistance to change, and the "pro-contact culture" of family courts. The chapter also discusses how, in cases of coercive control, the conventional framing of the victim/survivor parent as having "failed to protect" her children is inappropriate and unsuitable.

CONCEPTUALIZING HARM

As described in the previous chapters, this study is based on qualitative interviews with 15 children and 15 mothers who had separated from male perpetrators of coercive control. Most of the children were aged 10–14 at the time of interview, and in most cases it was the child's biological father who had been the perpetrator. The accounts of these children and mothers showed that the children had *experienced* coercive control alongside their mothers, and had been *co-victims* and *co-survivors* of their father's/father-figure's coercive control (see also Callaghan et al., 2018). These children were harmed not only because they were witnesses to the coercive control that their father was directing at their mother (i.e., they were not only being indirectly harmed via seeing, hearing, or knowing about the ill treatment of another); rather, fathers'/father-figures' coercive control was also *harming children's own lives.*

Monckton Smith (2020a, p. 169) describes how coercively controlling behavior "is a campaign, and like most campaigns it has a purpose and a plan. The [perpetrator's] plan [to control their target/s] is often rigid and takes priority over anything and everything." This concept is useful in relation to understanding the relationship between the perpetrator and their children: For the perpetrator, the plan to control the target/s is so important that it takes priority over their children's safety, well-being, and health. In the present study, perpetrators/fathers seemed to fall into two categories: (1) those whose "plan" was to control their partner, and (2) those whose "plan" involved controlling both their partner and their children. In families harmed by the first type of perpetrator/father, the direct harm caused to children by the father was as a byproduct of the father's obsession with controlling the mother. For example, when perpetrators/fathers prevented mothers from visiting family and friends, children's social worlds were limited too, and children experienced social isolation in their own lives. These perpetrators/fathers seemed to have been unconcerned about what was happening to the children as a result of their actions. Yet their specific intention was to (to take this particular example) socially isolate the mother rather than socially isolating the children.

However, in families harmed by the second type of perpetrator/father, the direct harm to children seemed to have occurred because perpetrators/fathers had deliberately targeted coercive control at children as well as partners, *intentionally* extending their coercive control over the whole family (Fellin et al., 2018; Morris, 2009; Øverlien, 2013). For example, these fathers expected their children to be as obedient and submissive as they expected their girlfriend/wife to be, and punished the children for non-compliance in the same ways that they punished their girlfriend/wife. For the second type of perpetrator, targeting their children as well as their partner was perhaps occurring because these men viewed themselves as the superior, masculine, head of the household (Downes et al., 2019), *entitled* to coercively control the lives of their children as well as their girlfriend/wife (Bancroft et al., 2012; Heward-Belle, 2016). As this chapter will go on to show, irrespective of their fathers'/father-figures' intentions, all the children in the study were harmed by coercive control. It is therefore appropriate to view the children as *co-victims and co-survivors* of perpetrators'/fathers' campaigns of coercive control.

DIRECT HARMS CAUSED TO CHILDREN BY COERCIVE CONTROL

Isolation and control of time, movement, and activities

Here we will begin to explore in more detail the children's experiences of these harms, beginning with perpetrators/fathers controlling mothers' movements outside the home. This form of control severely restricted children's social lives by preventing them from engaging with wider family, peers, and extracurricular activities. Extracts from the interviews highlight the isolation that was imposed on children as well as mothers by these perpetrators'/fathers' controlling tactics:

> [Because of the perpetrator's/father's control] I just didn't go out, so then the children didn't go out. It was just school and home. So they missed out on days out, family trips, socializing with people. And they've missed out on knowing what healthy relationships are about in other families, because children don't make as many friendships if you can't mix with other mums. (Marie, mother)

> Kids' parties were another problem because he'd be accusing me of trying to "get off" [have sexual relations] with one of the dads, so parties were out the question. We couldn't do any after-school clubs because I had to be back by a certain time. Me and the kids weren't allowed to go round to see his [perpetrator's] mum. (Isobel, mother)

These mothers' descriptions illustrate how some perpetrators'/fathers' controlling tactics could severely limit children's opportunities to create resilience-building relationships with non-abusive people outside of their immediate family. Children gain social skills, confidence, and resilience from positive experiences with grandparents, friends, or in after-school clubs; but, because of perpetrators'/fathers' control, Marie's and Isobel's children were living in the same isolated, lonely worlds as their mothers, unable to benefit from those developmental opportunities. This deprived state was especially experienced by younger children, who were more reliant on mothers to facilitate their access to friend's houses, playgrounds, and days out.

Children could also be used instrumentally by perpetrators/fathers as a means of controlling the mother. One mother, Isobel, experienced her children being used by the perpetrator as informants on her everyday activities. When she went out shopping, the perpetrator made her take one of her non-infant children with her, in order to be able to interrogate the child about the outing when they returned home:

> If I wanted to go shopping then I had to take a speaking child with me, he would ask them where we'd been and what we'd been doing. (Isobel, mother)

In this subtle but insidious tactic of control, the perpetrator/father was making the child a contributor to the regime of constant surveillance that he was using to narrow the mother's space for action.

Undermining children's education

Children's education could also be directly undermined by perpetrators/ fathers. Isobel explained how her husband had told their children that they "shouldn't bother" to do their homework. Isobel suggested that this perpetrator/father was attempting to present himself to his children as fun and heroic, while casting her as "the baddy," thereby increasing his power and influence over the children and isolating and disempowering her within the family (see also Monk and Bowen, 2021). On the same theme of schoolwork, a jointly interviewed mother and son, Eloise and 20-year-old

John, described the perpetrator/father making John miss an important educational deadline:

> JOHN: I had to get my coursework in. I must have left my folder at home. He said he was going to come in the car and bring it to the school at lunchtime. Lunchtime came and went and nothing happened.
>
> ELOISE: I asked him to bring the folder in and leave it on reception for John and he said: "no I'm not, he can come out to the car" and I said: "no he can't, they won't let him out, you can't get out unless you've got a doctor's appointment or whatever." I said: "look, you've got to bring it into the reception," but he said he wouldn't do it . . . he used to do things like this to cause problems.

This perpetrator's/father's motivation for making his son miss the deadline was unclear. Possibly he may have enjoyed this opportunity to exercise control and domination over his son and wife, or he may have been punishing them for some perceived transgression against his control. Either way, these examples illustrate how perpetrators/fathers can be willing to sabotage their children's education in order to further their own campaigns of coercive control.

Imprisonment and neglect

Some children and mothers described how perpetrators/fathers deprived them of basic resources such as food and heating and subjected them to periods of imprisonment within the home:

> ELOISE: He'd tell us we couldn't touch the food in the fridge, that we weren't allowed to eat, he'd lock us in the house a lot of the time so we couldn't get out, he'd unplug the phone

JOHN: He'd take out the power because in the hall we've got an old electrical box where you can take things out and that's it—you've got no power

ELOISE: He used to take an element out of the central heating so we'd have no heating. He'd lock us in the house and go out. He'd take the modem so John couldn't do his homework and I couldn't do my banking on the computer. So we were prisoners in a way.

He'd lock us in the house. (Roxie, age 11)

There was no food in the house . . . He would buy expensive food [for himself] and I was living on water when I was breastfeeding. (Ria, mother)

These behaviors from perpetrators/fathers, particularly the deprivation of food, risked severely damaging children's health, and, if taken far enough, could have been fatal. Perpetrators'/fathers' decisions to, at their whim, subject children and mothers to the experience of being imprisoned can be understood as a form of psychological abuse toward them both. These perpetrators'/fathers' actions may have made these children feel powerless and conveyed to them that they were "bad" or "worthless." Such examples again highlight that children were experiencing fathers'/father-figures' coercive control alongside their mother; that both the mother and the child(ren) were direct victims of his crimes.

Thinking more broadly, such actions are part of a wider "traditional" belief-system that places the man at the "head" of the household. Such a belief-system may seem relatively harmless in its milder forms, but it carries—as the actions of these perpetrators/fathers show—a potential for severe brutality. Heward-Belle (2016) identified this type of belief-system in some Australian perpetrators (see chapter 1) who felt that the man is naturally the head of the family, with the right to control and punish "his" women and children as he feels is appropriate (see also Downes et al., 2019).

Child sexual abuse

The extreme end of perpetrators'/fathers' sense of entitlement and possession was experienced by one family in the study: Lucy and her daughter Zara. The perpetrator/father in this family had sexually abused Zara when she was under 5 years old; abuse that Lucy had only discovered post-separation when Zara began to make disclosures. According to Bancroft et al. (2012), incest in these circumstances is usually, though not always, perpetrated against daughters, and is strongly linked to perpetrators'/fathers' sense of entitlement, self-centeredness, and belief that they own the child. Bancroft et al. (2012) suggest that these perpetrators are not sexually attracted to children per se. Rather, they are aroused by situations of sexual dominance and power imbalances. Sexually abusing children who are dependent on your parental care is clearly one such situation. These perpetrators are likely to also be simultaneously sexually abusing their adult girlfriend/wife, whom they can also dominate and have power over during sexual activities because of their coercive control.

Preventing mother–child interactions

The interviews also illustrated how perpetrators/fathers operating with the "head of household" belief-system may seek to prevent the flourishing of interactions between mothers and children. Mothers and children in the study described perpetrators/fathers who seemed to show jealousy toward the relationships that children had with their mothers:

> Lots of times when Mum was giving me attention he'd tell her to go over to him, so she'd have to leave me to play by myself. (Shannon, age 10)

> There was no fun, no playtime allowed. Like when [my daughter] Leah used to want me to sit and brush her hair—that wasn't allowed

because he'd be jealous. He'd say: "You've spent enough attention on her, what about *my* attention?" (Marie, mother)

I think he was jealous of me and my mum's relationship. I know he was jealous of me because if I was ever with my mum he would come into the room because he was jealous . . . and say I'd be cuddling up to my mum and then he would come and then I'd walk off because I didn't want to cuddle up near him. (Katie, age 12)

Preventing mothers and children from spending time together contributed to maintaining perpetrators'/fathers' dominance in families. Children described feeling sad, annoyed, and angry at being unable to spend time with their mothers. The limited maternal attention and restricted opportunities for fun and affection that resulted from perpetrators'/fathers' behaviors may have contributed to the withdrawn or aggressive behaviors that most of the children in this study had developed while living with coercive control.

Stalking

Although in most cases mothers and children did not describe perpetrators/fathers physically stalking them while mothers were still in relationships with perpetrators, this did occur in one case. John described how, when he was a young teenager, his father had followed him on his paper round, behaved in a very threatening manner, and "almost ran me over":

He used to chase [Mum and me] in the car. . . . He chased me on my paper round. I used to do a paper round and he almost ran me over . . . and [after that] I had to go out with a hammer on my paper round [for self-protection] just in case. (John, age 20)

Such behavior by this perpetrator/father might have been intended to constrain his adolescent son's increasing independence and freedom of

Coercive control: Harms to children

movement outside the home. It may also have been intended to remind John that, although he was coming closer to adulthood, he was still under his father's power.

Constraining and distorting children's behavior

Many children were harmed by living with narrowed space for action within their homes—that is, they had very limited freedom to say and do normal, age-appropriate things (Kelly et al., 2014). One child matter-of-factly described having to constrain his behavior and voice in the family home:

> I would be sort of quiet, I didn't shout-out or run around. (Bob, age 12)

Some perpetrators/fathers appeared to demand that their children periodically "disappear" by making no noise and keeping silent about their needs. At these times, young children had to constrain their own normal, healthy behavior in order to comply with their father's/father-figure's demands. One mother, Lauren, described how the perpetrator's/father's behavior meant that her daughters sometimes had to live as though they did not exist:

> When he came home from work he'd want to spend time with them and they were always *his* girls. . . . He used to say to Zoe: "You're my little angel." . . . But at the same time they couldn't shout, they couldn't make noise, they couldn't be children around him unless it was on his terms. It was alright if he wanted to play with them, but at other times it was like he wanted them to disappear. (Lauren, mother)

This perpetrator's/father's regime of constraint may have contributed to developmental delays for the children. Lauren reported that her daughter Zoe "didn't really speak" while living with her father. Delayed speech in these circumstances would usually be attributed to the trauma that Zoe suffered from being exposed to physical violence against her mother. However, it was also possibly linked with Zoe being a direct victim of her father's coercive control, particularly the narrow space for action that her father was imposing on her. It may be that living under a coercive control regime where her father often demanded that she make no noise led to Zoe constraining her own voice as a strategy of adaptation/survival.

Another aspect of perpetrators'/fathers' coercive control that was illustrated in the interviews was that if perpetrators/fathers were "in the mood" to engage with their children, they expected children to switch effortlessly from a state of disappearance and non-existence to a state of gratitude and affection:

> If *he* wanted to do something like go out for the day or something we were supposed to be like little puppies, like you know if he wanted to make a fuss of us we were supposed to be like "ooh, ooh, thank you master" you know, and if he let us down then we were supposed to say: "oh yeah okay then fine." (Isobel, mother)

Isobel's use of "us" and "we" once again highlights how perpetrators/fathers could direct coercive control at both partners and children, in this case by requiring them to be pleased at any attention he chose to give them. Furthermore, Isobel and her children were apparently not supposed to show normal emotional responses when this perpetrator/father "let them down"; an unhealthy constraint of their real feelings. This perpetrator/father therefore appeared to have enjoyed a state of non-accountability within his family (see also Morris, 2009). He was able to act as he wished without experiencing consequences—at least until his wife and children ultimately escaped him after approximately 15 years of his coercive control.

Punishing children for resistance to coercive control

The work of Stark (2007) suggests that if women and children resist coercive control by showing displeasure or protesting, perpetrators/fathers will suppress and punish this resistance, often by using verbal and emotional abuse, intimidation, damage to property, and/or physical violence. To someone unaware of how perpetrators punish resistance, such situations might appear to be a mutual "argument" or "fight" in which the woman or child is equally culpable. It may even seem that the woman is being ungrateful, cold, or "not making an effort," and/or that the child is being disobedient or "out of control." Such misunderstandings mask the real motivation behind perpetrators' behavior—to gain and maintain control.

A number of the interviews in the study illustrated how, for perpetrators/fathers, pursuing their objective of gaining and maintaining control involves finding ways of, and creating opportunities for, punishing children. One child, Roxie, described a situation where she and a sibling had been set up to fail by the perpetrator/father; given an age-inappropriate task to do and then brutally punished for not completing the task perfectly:

> [My dad] asked me and my half-brother to like sort his paperwork out for his work and we did it and we got it mixed up a bit and so he, like, hit us to the point where we had to go to school the next day with make-up on, because he like bruised us and stuff. (Roxie, age 11)

John similarly described being set up for punishment by the perpetrator/father when he was forced to participate in a sport and then abused for not winning:

> JOHN: He'd force me to swim, wouldn't he?
> ELOISE: Yeah forcing him to swim when he didn't want to . . . and the abuse he used to give to him when he didn't win [swimming competitions] was awful.

The potential results of such punishment in reducing a child's space for action in the most everyday ways, and to the smallest of levels, were apparent in the words of another mother, Sybil:

> [My son] wouldn't do things like make his own sandwich, he'd be too scared of doing it wrong. (Sybil, mother)

Because they were being punished routinely by a perpetrator/father for supposedly being bad or doing wrong, it is not surprising that children in these situations may have become scared of making mistakes in even the most everyday parts of their lives.

Another interview illustrated how perpetrators/fathers may punish children who show signs of resisting their campaign of coercive control; a subject about which there has been very little previous consideration. An instance of a perpetrator/father punishing a child for showing signs of resistance can be shown in the account of Bella, who described how her ex-partner had reacted to his young daughter's independence. Bella's daughter Roxie (whose experience of being punished we have just noted) had been a child who did not unquestioningly obey the perpetrator/father. Roxie had been punished by the perpetrator/father for being "opinionated":

> My kids, they've always been opinionated . . . that's one of the things he didn't like about [our daughter] Roxie, like, when he got violent with her he'd say: "you're just like your mum," because I'd argue back at him and Roxie's also very opinionated . . . so he'd kind of knock it out of her, and then she was more quiet, more reserved in what she did, more cautious. (Bella, mother)

According to Bella, this perpetrator/father claimed that Roxie (who was aged 4–7 at the time) was "just like her mum" because both mother and daughter did not bend to his will. As we have noted, this man's belief that he was entitled to an obedient child (as well as to an obedient partner) had led to him using violence against them both. As this father narrowed his daughter's space for action, she became quiet, reserved, and cautious, possibly because she was fearful of further punishment. Roxie therefore seemed to have experienced classic coercive control: The perpetrator made the victim/survivor fearful of negative consequences, and this coerced the victim/survivor (in this case his child) into compliance (Stark, 2007).

Distorting family dynamics with hyper-entitlement

This chapter is demonstrating how the children in this study were being profoundly negatively affected by perpetrators'/fathers' excessive sense of entitlement. We have encountered perpetrators/fathers demanding that families be oriented around continually meeting their needs without question or complaint, and punishing children and mothers for any resistance; a highly distorted family dynamic. We have noted how perpetrators/fathers created unreasonable and constricting rules for children and mothers to follow, and punished them when they made mistakes or did not live up to the perpetrator's/father's expectations. Many of the children in this study, as well as their mothers, had been forced to follow these rules, even at very young ages. For example:

> The kids were only tiny and you'd know, as soon as he came through the door, we'd be playing, me and the children, and you'd know as soon as he was coming home because the atmosphere would change, because all of a sudden, there were certain things we couldn't do because it might upset Daddy. (Lauren, mother)

Perpetrators'/fathers' negative moods could dominate homes to such an extent that children and mothers were prevented from laughing and having fun:

> [If we were] laughing, we would have just been told to "shut up." It was just a completely miserable experience. It was just angry and miserable and grumpy all the time. So there was just no fun in the house, no laughter. (Marie, mother)

In all of these scenarios, children's own needs were disregarded by perpetrators/fathers (see also Mohaupt et al., 2020). As described earlier, participants' accounts suggested that if a perpetrator/father wanted his children to stop laughing, be quiet and "disappear," he expected them to do so. If he wanted to monopolize their mother's time and continually deprive them of her attention, he expected mothers and children to comply. If he wanted to undermine children's education, deprive them of food and heating, and/or imprison them and their mothers in the home to exert his power and control, then he did so.

Mothers' and children's descriptions suggested that children's well-being and welfare had not been considered by perpetrators/fathers. Instead, perpetrators'/fathers' overwhelming priority appeared to be maintaining their control and dominance over their family. The children in this study had therefore lived under the same conditions of entrapment and constraint as their mothers. Like their mothers, many children were experiencing isolation from wider family and peers. Like their mothers, children were living with narrowed space for action—their ability to say and do normal day-to-day things and to display normal emotions was limited by what perpetrators/fathers would allow. However, also like their mothers, children did not tend to be passive victims. Instead, as we will now explore, they often used their own agency to survive and resist perpetrators'/fathers' coercive control.

CHILDREN'S RESISTANCE TO COERCIVE CONTROL

Several previous studies have highlighted children's resistance to domestic violence (see, e.g., Callaghan et al., 2018; Fellin et al., 2018; Houghton, 2015; Mullender et al., 2002; Øverlien and Hydén, 2009). However, with some exceptions (particularly Callaghan et al., 2018, and Fellin et al., 2018), this work has mainly focused on children's resistance to "incidents" of physical violence, rather than their resistance to fathers'/father-figures' full range of ongoing, everyday coercive control tactics. The accounts of the children and mothers in this study suggest that they took opportunities to resist many different tactics of coercive control, not just physical violence. They did this whenever they could within the constraints that perpetrators/fathers placed on them, and in accordance with whatever space for action they had.

Because coercive control involves perpetrators trying to fundamentally change the nature of their target/s' everyday lives (so that the target/s' everyday lives become devoted to pleasing the perpetrator), much of children's and mothers' resistance to coercive control took place at the level of their everyday activities, as mothers and children battled to maintain everyday lives that were tolerable and included some experiences of autonomy and self-fulfillment. This section will focus on how children and mothers engaged in such resistance through the everyday interactions they had with each other (i.e., how everyday mother–child relationships provided opportunities for resistance), something that has received very little previous attention.

Resisting economic abuse and lack of freedom

Children's and mothers' resistance to coercive control could take place in very subtle ways. By resisting perpetrators'/fathers' rules when possible, children and mothers strengthened their sense of agency and independence. For example, in cases where children and mothers were able to leave their homes together to experience periods of freedom and autonomy, they did so:

> [Me and my son] did things together. When we went to the cinema or we went shopping we could just "let our hair down" and do what we wanted to do. We were going to the cinema two or three times a week to get out of the house. (Eloise, mother)

Here, Eloise describes the self-determination of being able to "do what we wanted to do" that she and her son enjoyed when away from the perpetrator/father. It is this self-determination that perpetrators of coercive control seek to destroy as part of their agenda to turn partners and/or family members into beings who exist solely to serve them.

Eloise and her son John also co-created opportunities to resist economic abuse by working together to hide their "forbidden" purchases:

JOHN:	When we would come back with shopping bags, some-times we had to hide them . . .
ELOISE:	. . . . We used to throw them over the hedge . . .
JOHN:	. . . Into the garden so he wouldn't see them . . .
ELOISE:	. . . Clothing or anything I'd bought John, because he would go mad [that I'd spent money on John].

Here, what an outsider would perceive as an ordinary set of shopping bags was instead, in the understanding of this mother and child, a symbol of defiance.

Resistance via spending positive time together and giving support

Many children and mothers also seized opportunities to resist restrictions within the home. Times when perpetrators/fathers were absent from the home or were sleeping were particularly useful:

> Well some days he [perpetrator/father] would be out, and me and Mum would watch a movie and have some time together, which he wouldn't let us do when he was there. (Katie, age 12)

> He always made her [Ellie's daughter Shannon, then aged 1–6] sleep on her own you see, but she wouldn't go to sleep without me being next to her. So I'd wait for him to go to sleep and then I'd get in next to her or she'd get in next to me. (Ellie, mother)

By spending time together against perpetrators'/fathers' wishes, children and mothers were providing each other with emotional support, reducing one another's isolation, and maintaining the closeness in their mother–child relationships. The descriptions so far illustrate how mothers and children can find opportunities to positively increase each other's well-being even when their actions are being heavily restricted by perpetrators'/fathers' coercive control.

Some children resisted coercive control by providing their mothers with emotional support. Children tended to mention times when they had supported mothers after particular "incidents" (perhaps because these were the most vivid in their memories), while mothers discussed how children had supported them in more general, everyday ways:

> He'd lock us in the house, so my mum . . . she got upset and stuff, so I just, like, gave her hugs and stuff and told her it's going to be okay. (Roxie, age 11)

> When he had a tantrum and went off to the pub and left us and then I'd just comfort [Mum] and hug her and she'd hug me as well. (Shannon, age 10)

> [My son] John's been so emotionally supportive. . . . He would say to me: "Mum don't go to bed tonight in his [perpetrator's/father's] room; come and sleep with me." So I'd get into John's bed and John had a beanbag and he'd lay on the floor and say—"shall I put us a movie on Mum, what do you want to watch?"—to cheer me up. (Eloise, mother)

> [My daughter] Jane really did get me through it. . . . She was really close to me and massively supportive. . . . There were lots of hugs and she'd make me pretend cups of tea with her plastic kitchen set. (Alison, mother)

The emotional supports provided by these children highlight the important roles that children were playing in their mothers' well-being. Children's actions were often commonplace and "age appropriate," such as (in the previous examples) presenting a pretend drink to their mother using a plastic kitchen set or inviting her to watch a movie with them. Yet, children's actions assumed great significance because they took place in contexts where perpetrators/fathers were directing a campaign of verbal, emotional, and psychological abuse at mothers with the aim of making them feel worthless and useless. Children's efforts to support mothers partly countered perpetrators'/fathers' campaigns of abuse by giving mothers a sense that they were valued and liked and that their feelings mattered. However, as we will find in the next chapter, not all children supported their mothers in the ways just discussed, as some mother–child relationships became very strained and distant under the perpetrator's/father's regime of coercive control.

Resisting emotional manipulation

Some children also resisted perpetrators'/fathers' attempts to emotionally manipulate them with apologies and gifts. Ellie described how her daughter Shannon had developed resistance to this manipulation over time, as she gained more experience of her father breaking his promises:

> He would use Shannon to get out of the situation, he would cry his eyes out and he would say: "oh Daddy's really sorry, Daddy's really sorry" and really sob and she would feel really upset then because he was crying and because she's a child, she doesn't like to see anyone upset, she would go and get tissues and she'd wipe his eyes for him and he'd really love her up saying: "oh I love you, Daddy's silly, I'm really, really sorry" and then she'd say: "it's okay Daddy, we forgive you" and he's like: "I promise I'll never do it again, I'll never do it again," and she'd say: "it's okay," so then it's taken out of my hands then and I'd be like [*sighs with exhaustion*]. But then this was happening all the time and Shannon started saying: "he keeps promising that he won't do it again Mummy, but he keeps breaking his promise . . . [As Shannon got to about age 5] he would always bring a present for Shannon so she would be okay with him but then what she would do is . . . anything that he'd brought her she destroyed and

she'd pull its head off or you know tear it to pieces and throw it in the bin. (Ellie, mother)

This account highlights how perpetrators/fathers can directly target children with manipulative behavior as part of their strategy to keep both children and mothers entrapped. The response Shannon had developed at around the age of 5—destroying the gifts that this perpetrator brought her—suggests her ability to see through this manipulation (see also Katz et al., 2020), and that she had (rightly) become furious with his behavior and was no longer willing to tolerate it. If taken out of context, destroying presents might be categorized as emotional dysregulation and problematic behavior (Callaghan et al, 2017a). However, when viewed in the context of coercive control, it can be recognized as an empowering form of resistance for this young child.

Reflections on resistance

The accounts explored in this section highlight that children's and mothers' resistance to coercive control can be subtle and easy to overlook. Many of the acts of resistance that they undertook would be taken for granted by most people, such as when a mother and son "let their hair down" (i.e., relaxed) and "did what they wanted to do" on trips to the cinema, when a mother and daughter cuddled up on the sofa together to watch a movie while the perpetrator was out of the house, or when several children within the study gave their mother a hug when they perceived that she was upset. The significance of undertaking such actions for children and mothers experiencing coercive control was that it gave them opportunities to maintain some of the core attributes that perpetrators were trying to take away from them—a sense of autonomy and freedom, a feeling that they were valued and that somebody wanted to spend time with them (rather than being "worthless" and "useless" as perpetrators implied), and a sense that their feelings actually did matter and were important within a family context.

COERCIVE CONTROL AND CHILD ABUSE

This chapter has demonstrated how perpetrators of coercive control were usually psychologically abusive, sometimes physically abusive and neglectful, and, in one case, sexually abusive toward their children. Perpetrators'/fathers' child abuse and neglect were part of these children's experiences of coercive control. Exploring the implications of this observation, the latter part of the chapter will outline why the usual approach to understanding co-occurring domestic violence and child abuse is unsuitable in cases of coercive control–based domestic violence, and why a different approach is required.

To begin with, the usual conceptual approach to the issues of domestic violence and child abuse and neglect is to separate the two topics apart from each other. In this conceptualization, because the perpetrators in these families harm both the children and the mother, there are two separate harms taking place: (1) children's "exposure" to domestic violence/ IPV against the mother, and (2) child abuse/maltreatment. This conceptual separation is evident in the substantial previous research that has been conducted into situations where children suffer from "exposure" to parental domestic violence and are child abuse victims. In those studies (e.g., Appel and Holden, 1998; Chan, 2011; Edleson, 1999b; Hamby et al., 2010; Jouriles et al., 2008; Osofsky, 2003; Sijtsema et al., 2020), the child abuse and the "exposure" to domestic violence are treated as conceptually distinct phenomena that are taking place in the same family, as signified by the commonly used terms "co-occurrence" and "dual exposure." According to those studies, a child in these circumstances has two different problems—(1) being "exposed" to parental domestic violence, and (2) being a direct victim of child abuse and neglect.

Some researchers (e.g., Finkelhor et al., 2007; Hamby et al., 2010) have used the term "polyvictimization" to describe the various different harms children can experience, such as witnessing partner violence, sexual abuse, physical abuse, psychological abuse, bullying, and witnessing community violence. The particular way in which those researchers have framed the problem is expressed in Finkelhor et al.'s (2007, p. 8) statement that "children who experience one kind of victimization are at greater risk of experiencing other forms of victimization." It is important to note that the concept of "polyvictimization" is being used here in a similar way to the concepts of "co-occurrence" and "dual exposure": Each form of abuse is considered to be discrete from the other abuses being experienced by the child, though they have cumulative impacts.

These approaches are problematic from the point of view of this book. The problems are, first, the foregrounding of a terminology of "exposure" to discuss the child's experience of domestic violence/IPV and child abuse/maltreatment, and, second, the attempt to separately categorize the perpetrator's actions in those respective areas. Against those approaches, this section makes three key propositions:

1. That the vocabulary of "exposure" does not fit well with the experiences of the children in this study.
2. That the same identical actions from perpetrators harmed children and mothers.
3. That a preferred alternative would therefore be to have a single concept to describe what the perpetrator was doing, not two concepts.

Questioning the concept of "exposure"

The first step, then, is to consider how the vocabulary of "exposure" makes little sense for the children in this study. The reason why "exposure" is an unsuitable term here is that the children were *harmed directly* by perpetrators'/fathers' coercive control-based domestic violence. Indeed, there were multiple ways in which children could be harmed directly by coercive control. These included: (1) perpetrators/fathers not deliberately harming the children directly but nevertheless doing so as a byproduct of the ways that they were restricting, undermining, and controlling the mother's everyday life and resources; (2) perpetrators/fathers causing direct harm to children deliberately as part of their coercive control against the mother; and (3) perpetrators/fathers deliberately and purposefully harming the children as well as the mother as part of their campaigns of coercive control.

We will begin here with the perpetrator/father (1) not necessarily deliberately harming the children directly but nevertheless doing so as a byproduct of the ways that they were restricting, undermining and controlling the mothers' everyday life and resources. This could occur in numerous ways. One way in which it could occur was via the mother's lack of freedom to leave the home and move about freely in her community, and the consequent social isolation that she experienced. When the perpetrator/father prevented the mother from leaving the home, the children's freedom to leave the home also deteriorated (especially when the children were too young to be permitted to travel and visit others alone); and when the perpetrator/father increased the mother's social isolation, the children also experienced direct social isolation and social exclusion from their own peer group and wider family.

As we noted earlier in this chapter, this link was observed by two mothers in the study, Marie and Isobel. Marie said that she "didn't go out, so then the children didn't go out," and discussed the direct ways in which the perpetrator/father had limited her children's lives. Events such as "days out, family trips, socializing with people" were all made impossible by this perpetrator's/father's coercive control; and Marie also noted that, as a general rule, "children don't make as many friendships if you can't mix with other mums." Isobel gave examples of this link between her own lack of freedom and the lack of freedom of her children. One example was that her children were unable to access children's parties "because he'd be accusing me of trying to 'get off' with one of the dads." The other example was that her children's access to after-school extracurricular activities were restricted by a curfew ("I had to be back by a certain time") whereby the perpetrator prevented her from being outside at the time in the evening when such activities were due to end and the children would need to be collected.

Similarly, when perpetrators/fathers demanded the mother's time and attention, the children were directly affected by being denied the attention of their mother. This link was pointed out by 10-year-old Shannon, who said that when her mother Ellie was repeatedly told by the perpetrator "to go over to him," the result was that she was deprived of her mother's attention, as "she'd have to leave me to play by myself," something which occurred frequently and caused Shannon distress. Marie mentioned how her daughter Leah "used to want me to sit and brush her hair," but that this "wasn't allowed" due to the perpetrator's demands for Marie's attention.

Economically, when perpetrators/fathers refused to pay their fair share of the household expenses and instead saved or spent the money on their own desires, the children were affected (see also Fogarty et al., 2021). Ria's experience, mentioned in this chapter, was that the perpetrator purchased expensive food for himself while leaving "no food in the house" for anybody else and forcing her to live "on water" while she was breastfeeding. Eloise also described how the perpetrator would "go mad" if Eloise spent money on their son (for example by buying him new clothes), leaving her with no choice but to hide her expenditure as best as she could. In situations such as Ria's and Eloise's, children's ability to have their daily and yearly needs met—including their needs for nutritious food or larger clothes and shoes for their growing bodies—is compromised by perpetrators/fathers, with fundamental effects on the children's lives as they are growing up.

With these instances of "cut-through" to children's lives occurring as a byproduct of harms that perpetrators/fathers were causing to mothers, the language of children simply being *exposed to* domestic violence is insufficient. What perpetrators/fathers were doing to mothers had clear, distinctive impacts on children's own lives. What these children were experiencing—emotional and physical neglect, deprivation, and social exclusion—they were experiencing specifically because of their fathers'/ father-figures' coercive control of their mothers.

Perpetrators harming children as part of coercive control

Let us now move on to the second and third ways in which children could be harmed directly by coercive control, beginning with (2) the perpetrator/father harming the children deliberately as part of his coercive control against the mother. This has been examined in several studies, and perpetrators have been found to harm children in this way both pre- and post-separation (e.g., Beeble et al., 2007; Clements et al., 2021; Dragiewicz et al., 2021b; Heward-Belle, 2017; Humphreys et al., 2006; Monk and Bowen, 2021; Nikupeteri et al., 2021; Rivera et al., 2018; Varcoe and Irwin, 2004; Wuest et al., 2003). Often referred to as "using the children as tools of abuse," this second form of direct harm occurs, like the first, in several ways. One aspect that is highlighted in previous research is where perpetrators use children as a monitoring and surveillance tool. For example, a perpetrator may interrogate the children about where the mother has been over recent periods of time, putting children in a deeply unpleasant and stressful situation. In this chapter we have encountered Isobel's experience of having to take one of her children out with her on shopping trips so that the perpetrator/father could interrogate the child about her actions when they returned home. Children in these scenarios are being placed in an impossible bind by perpetrators/fathers. For example, if a male acquaintance has said hello to their mother at the supermarket, children would have to decide whether or not to be honest and report this event to the perpetrator/father, perhaps knowing that it may cause him to become enraged and harm their mother.

Another tactic covered in this book is perpetrators upsetting and weakening the mother by hurting the children, or by manipulating the affections of the children so that they begin to dislike her. This was another of Isobel's experiences and is explored more in the next chapter, along with the experiences of another mother, Bella. Both will also be briefly discussed here, beginning with Isobel, who (as we noted earlier in this chapter) suffered because of how the perpetrator portrayed himself as "the goody" in his interactions with her children. This meant that for Isobel: "it was quite hard really, getting them to do their homework, because he was saying: 'they don't need to do homework.'" With the perpetrator behaving in this way, the result was that Isobel became "the baddy" in the children's eyes; she was the one who had to persuade them to do their homework and other unappealing tasks such as cleaning their teeth and having a bath.

Bella, meanwhile, described the perpetrator insulting her and treating her "like a second-class citizen" in front of the children, as well as overriding the guidance that she was giving to them. The perpetrator's/father's behavior in this family led the children to treat Bella with disrespect, talking to her "like dirt" and "ignoring everything I said."

In these scenarios, children's feelings and needs were treated by perpetrators/fathers as disposable; the children were collateral damage in the perpetrator's/father's campaign of attack on the mother. In this chapter we have explored these behaviors from perpetrators/fathers at the pre-separation stage; that is, before mothers had separated from perpetrators/fathers. Later chapters will also highlight the ways in which perpetrators/fathers used their children at the post-separation stage as part of their ongoing campaigns of coercive control. A key point here is that a perpetrator/father may behave ruthlessly in these situations, with no concern for the side-effects caused to the children who are caught up in the cruel theater they are creating. This point reminds us of Monckton Smith's (2020a, p. 169) observation, quoted earlier, about perpetrators' tunnel vision: "The [perpetrator's] plan [to control their target/s] is often rigid and takes priority over anything and everything"; including their children.

Finally, there were cases of perpetrator/fathers (3) deliberately and purposefully targeting the children as well as mothers for coercive control. We have encountered in this chapter how John, in particular, experienced a number of instances of this behavior from his father. The perpetrator/father stalked John on his paper round and set up John for punishment by forcing him to participate in sports events and then abusing him for not winning. There were also situations where John and Eloise were co-victims who were targeted directly at the same time by the perpetrator, experiencing the same harms due to his actions. These instances included, for example, John and Eloise being chased by the perpetrator when they left the home, which resulted in John feeling constrained in his independence and freedom of movement in public spaces. This perpetrator/father also locked John and Eloise in the home together with the phone unplugged and the heating and electricity turned off and with orders not to eat or touch the food in the fridge—again, situations where child and mother were simultaneously both being directly targeted. Particular harms were caused to John in these instances. In the example of being locked inside without power, he was deprived of the necessary internet access to complete his homework. Roxie, as we have noted, also experienced the same situation of being locked in the house with her mother Bella. In cases such as these, exerting power, control, and domination over a child's life may have been as important for a perpetrator/father as controlling the mother's life (see Heward-Belle, 2016).

Overall, with each of these strands of abuse, there is a central point to make about *why* the perpetrator was taking these actions. The point is this: That it is likely that such actions were being carried out by perpetrators because of their intense drive and motivation to control their target or targets (Monckton Smith, 2020a). Specifically, in these instances there seemed to be a single patriarchal motivation behind both control of the child and control of the mother (see also Heward-Belle, 2016). Within such a patriarchal outlook, a male perpetrator identifies in an overarching way as the head of the household, and feels that in occupying this position he has a right to control all other members of the family. We encountered this outlook in the experience of Roxie and Bella, who were both punished in the same ways by the perpetrator/father when they tried to resist his domination. This perpetrator/father claimed that his very young daughter was "just like" her mother because she argued back to him in the same way her mother did, and he attempted to "beat this out" of this very young daughter just as he did with her mother.

The parallel between what perpetrators did to mothers and did to children was not only one of motivation; it was also one of impacts. In many of the children's behaviors and emotions, we can observe the behaviors and emotions of the classic (adult woman) coercive control victim/survivor (e.g., Stark, 2007). As was illustrated earlier in this chapter, children who were being severely punished for not constantly obeying and pleasing the perpetrator could in response become quiet and subdued. These children had internalized the knowledge that it was dangerous when the perpetrator was upset and had drastically modified and constrained their behavior to try to avoid upsetting him. The children, like their mothers, also sometimes attempted to resist the injustices of coercive control, to enjoy moments of autonomy, to stand up for themselves, and to try to protect and comfort the other victims/survivors (their mother and any siblings) in the home.

Coercive control as a multi-stranded form of abuse that harms both children and adults

For the children who took part in this study, child abuse and coercive control were deeply intertwined: and so categorizing them as two separate issues would make little sense. Returning, then, to the issue of how coercive control should be understood in relation to child abuse, this section has suggested that they are impossible to untangle from one another. Instead, rather than attempting to separate them, children in these circumstances should be recognized as *child victims/survivors of a campaign of coercive control*, a campaign that included the perpetrator subjecting them to acts of child abuse and neglect, as well as to other aspects of coercive control, such as severely restricted freedom, monitoring and stalking, and all of the other acts that the perpetrator committed. Meanwhile, the adult victim/survivor should also be recognized as a victim/survivor of the same campaign of coercive control. We should be clear, overall, that *coercive control is a phenomenon that includes many strands of abusive behavior that harm both adults and children*. It encompasses abusive acts toward the victimized parent, abusive acts toward children that would be categorized as child abuse and child neglect, and many other harmful behaviors. For a fuller engagement with the many different varieties of abuse used by coercive control perpetrators, see chapter 1.

Coercive control is also a phenomenon that needs to be recognized for its uniqueness. Some of the impacts that it causes to victims/survivors are ones that are particular to coercive control, as distinct from other types of violence and abuse. So, if we are referring to child victims/survivors of coercive control, there are impacts that would be different than those experienced by children who have a father who is, for example, violent but not coercively controlling; emotionally abusive but not coercively controlling; or neglectful but not coercively controlling.

There are some key differences, to begin with, if we compare the coercive control experience with a child who lives with a father who is violent without being coercively controlling (for example, hitting the children during moments of high anger and stress). This is not in any way to minimize the potential harm of such violence: Such a child may anticipate their father's violence, be afraid of it and possibly be traumatized (and in other ways negatively affected) by it in profound ways. However, what marks out such an experience as qualitatively different from an experience of coercive control is that the child's everyday life will not be constrained in the ways that we have documented previously. For example, the mother will (if other circumstances permit) be able to take the child to after-school clubs and other children's birthday parties. Mother and child will not be living under the constant pressure of the father's obsessive monitoring and surveillance. They will also not be subjected by the father to periods of joint imprisonment within the home or purposefully deprived of food and heating. The same distinction applies if we imagine other types of fathers who are harmful but not coercively controlling. To take the example of a father who is emotionally/psychologically abusive but not coercively controlling, such a father might call the child insulting names and cause harm to the child's self-image: yet what would be absent in this behavior is the element of constant control that is experienced by, and impacts on, child victims/survivors of coercive control.

The behavioral patterns of perpetrators of coercive control therefore create what are in some ways different and unique situations than those created by non-coercively controlling yet harmful parents. Coercive control takes a toll on the child's entire existence, permeating multiple layers of ordinary everyday life (Callaghan et al., 2018; Fellin et al., 2018; Haselschwerdt et al., 2019a; Katz, 2016, 2019; Katz et al., 2020; Øverlien, 2013). Life under coercive control is a life of fundamentally and constantly constricted freedom. Therefore a child's space for action—the amount and range of activity that they can undertake and feelings and behaviors that they can express—is continually narrowed and compressed (Callaghan et al., 2018; Fellin et al., 2018; Katz, 2016; Katz et al., 2020; Øverlien, 2013).

Thus, for a practitioner hoping to help a child in these circumstances, it may be particularly useful for them to be able to identify and record in writing that, for instance: "8-year-old Sarah is experiencing physical and psychological abuse from her father as part of his campaign of coercive control." In this one sentence, the practitioner has captured several important facts: "Sarah" is a victim of physical and psychological abuse carried out by her father; "Sarah" is living in a home dominated by coercive control; it is her father who is perpetrating the coercive control; and the root cause of the child abuse against Sarah is the father's coercive control. This sentence would also imply that Sarah's mother is likely to be a co-victim/co-survivor of coercive control and may require appropriate assistance. (For more practical examples of how perpetrators can be suitably identified and their behavior cataloged in reports, see De Simone and Heward-Belle, 2020.) By contrast, alternative, less helpful sentences that do not recognize the link between the coercive control and the child abuse may include: "8-year-old Sarah is experiencing physical and psychological abuse from her father"—this sentence records the child abuse but does not recognize the coercive control. Similarly, the sentence "8-year-old Sarah is being exposed to domestic violence" greatly minimizes what Sarah is experiencing. Another alternative sentence, "8-year-old Sarah has a father who perpetrates coercive control," fails to recognize the child abuse. Each of these three sentences would be less effective for the practitioner in terms of recording their knowledge of what is happening to "Sarah."

Coercive control perpetrators' persistence, dangerousness, and resistance to change

There are other important reasons why we need to recognize the uniqueness of the child abuse and neglect that occurs as part of a campaign of coercive control. One reason is the particularly high level of dangerousness of coercive control perpetrators as a particular "type" of abuser (Monckton

Smith, 2020a). As already mentioned, coercive control perpetrators are usually—due to the intensity and rigidity of their desire to control—highly single-minded in their pursuit of control. A consequence of this single-mindedness is that, if they feel that they are losing control, perpetrators can take extensive, extreme, even lethal actions to maintain or regain their control and punish their target/s for breaking free. These actions are likely to continue post-separation.

As has been highlighted in an extensive body of previous research, co-ercive control perpetrators typically refuse to "take no for an answer"; and so, if the mother has left them, they may continue to monitor, stalk, ma-nipulate, and attack her, causing ongoing harm to both mother and children (e.g., Fleury et al., 2000; Humphreys and Thiara, 2003; Katz et al., 2020; Kelly et al., 2014; Nikupeteri and Laitinen, 2015; Radford and Hester, 2006; Sharp-Jeffs et al., 2018; Thiara and Gill, 2012; Thiara and Humphreys, 2017; Varcoe and Irwin, 2004; Woodlock, 2017). These are post-separation forms of abuse that we may not necessarily observe in fathers who are *not* coercively controlling but are in some other way harmful to their children. For example, a father who was neglectful of his children but not coercively controlling may simply break off contact with his ex-partner and children post-separation and have no further involvement in their lives, rather than, say, putting in the effort required to relentlessly stalk them (Katz et al., 2020; Monckton Smith, 2020a; Nikupeteri and Laitinen, 2015). Furthermore, in terms of the dangerousness of coercive control perpetrators, a history of coercive control has been identified in a high number of the cases where perpetrators/fathers have killed their children and left mothers without their children (filicide), or killed mothers and left children motherless (femicide), or killed both mothers and children. Such acts are often accompanied by the perpetrator/father committing su-icide himself, and appear frequently in our news media (though it is rare for the news media to present the story as a case of coercive control).

The single-mindedness of coercive controllers is such that official sanctions of the type that perpetrators commonly receive are unlikely to act as a deterrent. The perpetrator may be fined, reprimanded, or arrested by the police, or, more rarely, be convicted and receive a custodial prison sentence, yet nevertheless may persist in their attempts to control. Where they cannot continue to control ex partners, they may find a new target such as a new girlfriend and begin a new campaign of coercive control against them (Monckton Smith, 2020a). In some instances, perpetrators who have lost control of their ex-partner may in response focus more of their attention on coercively controlling any children they share with her (Hill, 2020; Monk and Bowen, 2021). The children provide the perpetrator with vulnerable and accessible new primary targets. Furthermore, from the perpetrator's perspective, the targeting of children has the "added bonus" of causing a great deal of psychological distress to their ex-partner: distress which perpetrators may think their ex-partner deserves as punishment for daring to break free (Monckton Smith, 2020a).

A further aspect of the dangerousness of coercive control perpetrators is that they often possess a great deal of skill in charming and manipulating professionals involved with the family (Campbell, 2017; Rivera et al., 2012; Silberg and Dallam, 2019). As Monk (2017, p. 207) puts it: "whether it is by being charming, articulate and well-presented . . . or whether it is by being abusive, intimidating or threatening . . . perpetrators seem to control professionals using tactics that are indistinguishable from those employed to control their victims." As explained in chapter 1, a key means by which perpetrators can manipulate professionals is by spreading narratives among the people in their lives that present them in a positive light, and/ or by spreading narratives that present their target/s in a negative light. These narratives can shape the ways that professionals (including social workers, court professionals and police) come to understand a situation of coercive control. In these circumstances, the perpetrator may come to be viewed as a "great guy," as a "caring father," as "trying their best," or as the victim. Meanwhile, their adult or child target is perceived as the "problem" and as the one "causing trouble" (e.g., Saltmarsh et al., 2021; Silberg and Dallam, 2019). The more that an adult or child victim/survivor protests against this perception, the more negatively they may be viewed. For example, adult victims' attempts to "set the record straight" may be interpreted as evidence of their manipulativeness, their "love of conflict," their uncooperativeness, or their mental instability (Laing, 2017). In the case of children, their attempts to explain the truth may be viewed as evidence of their having been "coached" into spreading falsehoods, or as indicating their inability to distinguish reality from fantasy (Silberg and Dallam, 2019).

A third key feature of coercive control perpetrators that may differentiate them from some other types of abusive or neglectful parents is their general lack of amenability to intervention. Bancroft (2002) found that highly controlling male perpetrators are generally unwilling to change; only a small number do the extremely hard work required to cease their use of coercive control. Bancroft (2002) suggested that those who are more likely to change are characterized by a lower self-centeredness and higher genuine empathy for their partners than is typical in coercive controllers.

Kelly and Westmarland's (2015) evaluation of a high-quality UK perpetrator intervention program showed that while the program was usually successful at eliminating perpetrators' use of physical and sexual violence, it appeared to be less effective at reducing coercive control. Though very positive reductions in coercive control *were* observed in *some* perpetrators (Westmarland and Kelly, 2013), it was found overall that reductions in coercive and controlling behaviors were more limited than the reductions observed in perpetrators' use of physical and sexual violence (Kelly and Westmarland, 2015). For example, when adult victims/survivors were surveyed to assess the extent of the change that had occurred since the perpetrator intervention program, results showed only a 5% decrease (from 36% to 31%) in affirmative responses to the proposition: "domestic violence perpetrator asks the children to report on what I am doing and where I have been." Almost half (48%) of the adult victims/survivors stated that the perpetrator still insisted on "knowing where I am and what I am doing." Furthermore, affirmative responses to the proposition "I feel like I have to be very careful around the domestic violence perpetrator if he is in a bad mood" had only decreased from 96% to 75%, and affirmative responses to "domestic violence perpetrator blames me for his abusive behavior" had only reduced from 84% to 61%.

Perpetrators who have stopped using violence and rape but persist in being highly controlling and emotionally manipulative may continue to cause a great deal of harm to adult and child victims/survivors. For example, they may continue to use children as tools of abuse in their campaigns against children's mothers (e.g., see Beeble et al., 2007; Clements et al., 2021; Dragiewicz et al., 2021b).

UNDERSTANDING THE POSITION OF THE VICTIM/ SURVIVOR PARENT

Recognizing the victim/survivor parent's limited space for action

The situation of a victim/survivor parent (usually, though not always, the mother in the family) is especially difficult. A mother who finds herself in a situation where her children's father/father-figure is behaving harmfully toward the children but is *not* a coercive controller may (depending on circumstances) have choices in how to respond. She may be able to safely separate from the perpetrator and greatly reduce the perpetrator's negative impacts on the children's everyday lives (though again, this depends on circumstances, such as her financial resources).

However, a mother whose children are being harmed as part of the father's/father-figure's campaign of coercive control has very little power or choice in how to respond. First, the perpetrator/father will have comprehensively entrapped the mother via an array of strategies. These strategies may include: economic abuse; psychological abuse; surveillance; isolation; the spreading of false narratives about her, himself, and the relationship; and threats, which often include death threats or threats that he will take the children from her—threats that the victim/survivor knows from past experience are credible and real. The perpetrator/father will, as a result of these strategies, be causing the adult victim/survivor to experience chronic fear and/or chronic psychological distress (Rivera et al., 2018; Stark, 2007; Thomas et al., 2014). Furthermore, the perpetrator/father is likely to have made it clear to the mother that any attempts she makes to interfere with his treatment of the children, to question his behavior toward them, or to attempt to reason with him will be treated as acts of disobedience on her part and will be unsuccessful.

Recognizing the constrained mother's micro-level strategies for protecting her children

The key point to remember here is that the perpetrator's/father's campaign of coercive control will have profoundly limited the scope of what the mother could have done differently. It will have severely constrained her ability to protect the children, leaving her with very little space to take evasive or preventative actions. She has probably achieved all that she can, operating at the micro level, to protect her children via the many small strategies that could be carried out without the perpetrator punishing her or the children for her "disobedience" (Buchanan 2018; Buchanan et al., 2013; Haight et al., 2007; Wendt et al., 2015).

An instance of one of these micro-level strategies was provided by one of the extracts quoted earlier in the chapter, in which the perpetrator insisted that Ellie's very young daughter Shannon had to sleep on her own even though this frightened her. Ellie was forced to go along with this arrangement, but, once the perpetrator was himself asleep, Ellie would quietly go to Shannon's room, or Shannon would sneak into bed next to Ellie, and Shannon was able to feel comforted for a while. This was of course risky— the perpetrator could have awoken at any point and discovered them—but Ellie and Shannon bravely persisted nevertheless. The risk in this instance was perhaps perceived by Ellie to be manageable. However, attempting to permanently break free from the perpetrator entailed greatly elevated levels of risks and numerous major difficulties (e.g., her and Shannon becoming homeless). As we will show later in this book, Ellie and Shannon did eventually break free, but only at great cost.

In general, mothers living under perpetrators'/fathers' campaigns of coercive control may have previously attempted to extricate themselves and their children away from the perpetrator (maybe calling the police multiple times asking for help), yet found such actions ineffective because each time, within a day or two, the perpetrator was released without charge and would return to the home to continue his coercive control (Stark, 2007). Mothers may also have found that, each time they attempted to leave, economic circumstances or the perpetrator's manipulation or threats coerced her and the children into going back again. Furthermore, even when the mother takes the (often very difficult and dangerous) step of permanently separating from the perpetrator/father, doing so may not provide safety because as we have noted, perpetrators/fathers often continue their coercive control post-separation. Post-separation coercive control will be explored in more detail in chapter 6.

The victim-blaming discourse of "failure to protect"

When a child has been abused or neglected by a domestically violent father/father-figure or has been "exposed" to the perpetrator's/father's domestic violence, a common response is to place the mother/victim/survivor under scrutiny and blame the harm that the perpetrator/father has caused to the child on the mother's/victim's/survivor's supposed "failure to protect." Mothers accused of "failure to protect" may even lose custody of their children (e.g., De Simone and Heward-Bell, 2020; Douglas and Walsh, 2010; Ewen, 2007; Humphreys and Absler, 2011; Johnson and Sullivan, 2008; Kelton et al., 2020; Maher et al., 2021; Meyer, 2011; Stanziani and Cox, 2021).

However, this mother-blaming response is based on the ideas that: (1) domestic violence is nothing more than incidents of physical violence; (2) the victim has the power to control if, when, and where the perpetrator uses violence against her so as to avoid the child being exposed to it (an idea grounded in the assumption that victims are partly or wholly causing the perpetrator's violence against them, for example by being unreasonable or provoking the perpetrator); and (3) the victim has a great deal of freedom between each incident, including the freedom to permanently leave the perpetrator without any major risks or difficulties. Furthermore, when a mother has acted harmfully toward the children herself (such as by hitting them or excessively yelling at them) *because of* the negative impacts that the perpetrator's/father's coercive control was having on her (see Damant et al., 2010), then she may mistakenly be viewed as being "just as bad" as, or even worse than, the perpetrator/father.

As we have observed, these ideas are fundamentally at odds with the realities of coercive control–based domestic violence. Yet once we understand coercive control, perceive the adult and child/ren as *co-victims/ survivors*, and recognize that the harms to children were part of the perpetrators' campaign of coercive control, then we can understand the urgent necessity of rethinking the notion of "failure to protect" in contexts of coercive control. At the same time, the findings of this book indicate that when children are being harmed in contexts of coercive control, it would be beneficial for state responses (including the responses of official bodies such as criminal justice systems, social services and family courts) to give stronger emphasis to tackling perpetrators and effectively eliminating their ability to continue their campaign of coercive control.

One important point to add here is that it is likely that, in a minority of cases, mothers who are coercive control victims/survivors will also be problematic parents in their own right, and would have maltreated their children even if their partner had been totally non-abusive himself. These rare cases require different approaches compared to cases where the mother would be an unproblematic parent if she were not being subjected to the father's/father-figure's coercive control.

COERCIVE CONTROL AND FAMILY COURTS

The incident of violence model and the pro-contact culture

Family courts, like child protection systems, tend to draw on problematic incident-based understandings of domestic violence. Often the assumption is that the domestic violence consisted of isolated incidents of violence that took place between the parents, and that therefore the domestic violence is not relevant to the perpetrator's fitness as a parent (Silberg et al., 2013; Silberg and Dallam, 2019; Stark, 2009). A domestically violent father is likely to be viewed as a "good enough dad" (Women's Aid, 2016). There may also be an assumption that the domestic violence occurred because of a "relationship problem," and that therefore once the relationship has ended, the perpetrator will no longer be violent or abusive. Domestic violence is then labeled as "historic" and assumed to be irrelevant to child contact.

In family courts, these views sit alongside a tendency to uphold a "pro-contact culture" (Hunter et al., 2020; Macdonald, 2017). Within this culture, parent–child contact is viewed as being nearly always beneficial for children, and the absence of parental contact is assumed to be extremely detrimental to children, even if the parent is abusive (Hill, 2020; Women's Aid, 2016). As such, it is unusual for a family court to completely deny an abusive parent contact with their child post-separation/post-divorce (Barnett, 2014). In Britain, less than 1% of family court cases result in a parent being denied contact (Macdonald, 2017).

Yet we have demonstrated in this chapter how incorrect these understandings and assumptions are when one parent is a coercive control perpetrator. At a minimum, a perpetrator of coercive control will have been willing to subject their child to all of the negative consequences that they chose to bring about when they decided, month after month, year after year, to coercively control the child's other parent. Often the perpetrator will have terrorized their children and inflicted acts of child abuse and neglect on them as part of their coercive control (Callaghan et al., 2018; Fellin et al., 2018; Haselschwerdt et al., 2019a; Katz, 2016, 2019; Katz et al., 2020; Øverlien, 2013). Furthermore, as implied earlier in the chapter, dissolution of the relationship is unlikely to have brought the perpetrators' coercive control to an end. Where there has been a campaign of coercive control, the cause is not "relationship problems," but the perpetrator's deep-rooted drive to control (Monckton Smith, 2020a); a drive which is rarely fully eliminated, even via a high-quality perpetrator intervention program (Bancroft, 2002; Kelly and Westmarland, 2015).

Perpetrators'/fathers' manipulation of family court systems

A substantial body of research from multiple countries has highlighted how, at present, perpetrators who are inclined to do so are able to use family court systems to ensure that, post-separation, they can continue their campaign of coercive control—a campaign that includes child abuse and neglect and other harms caused to children (Bancroft et al., 2012; Beeble et al., 2007; Clements et al., 2021; Coy et al., 2015; Dragiewicz et al., 2021a; Dragiewicz et al., 2021b; Elizabeth et al., 2012; Eriksson et al., 2005; Feresin et al., 2019; Galántai et al., 2019; Harne, 2011; Harrison, 2008; Holt, 2017; Humphreys et al., 2019; Hunter et al., 2020; Jouriles et al., 2018; Katz et al., 2020; Laing, 2017; Macdonald, 2016; Mackay, 2018; Monk and Bowen, 2021; Radford, 2013; Radford and Hester, 2006; Stark, 2009; Thiara and Gill, 2012; Varcoe and Irwin, 2004; Watson and Ancis, 2013; Wuest et al., 2003). Not all separating parents have their child contact arrangements decided in the family courts; most parents come to informal agreements without recourse to courts. However, informal agreements are likely to be problematic in domestic abuse cases, and such cases may be referred to family courts. The majority of the cases heard in family courts feature domestic abuse. (The number of family court cases featuring domestic abuse in the United Kingdom was estimated at 62% by CAFCASS and Women's Aid in 2017.)

For perpetrators/fathers, it is a significant victory when family courts order contact between them and their children: Their ex-partner and children may have no escape from them until the children reach the age of legal adulthood (which may be as far away as 18 years if the child is a baby). Under these circumstances, the perpetrator and his coercive control will remain firmly in their lives, causing on-going harm.

Mothers are routinely dismissed when they attempt to challenge the inclinations of family courts that post-separation contact must take place between children and perpetrators, and that they must co-parent with their abusers. They may be described as "high conflict," "pathological," "hostile," "unfriendly," or "alienating" mothers (Barnett, 2014;

Harrison, 2008; Hester, 2011; Silberg and Dallam, 2019). If mothers and children inform family courts about the perpetrator's/father's domestic violence and acts of child abuse and neglect, and state that they believe that this contact would be unsafe, then mothers are at high risk of being disbelieved and, in some cases, labeled as engaging in "parental alienation" (Meier, 2009; Meier, 2020; Silberg and Dallam, 2019). Furthermore, children who voice their fears about contact may be told by family courts that their mother has "coached" them into making false accusations or has manipulated them into fearing their father when, in the court's view, they have no good reason for fearing him (Silberg and Dallam, 2019).

The successful use of "parental alienation" accusations by perpetrators/fathers

When courts disbelieve mothers and children that the perpetrator/father has a history of abuse and still poses a grave threat to their well-being, this represents a very serious turn of events. Findings on this are presented in Meier's research into family court outcomes: a federally funded, comprehensive study of the situation across the United States (see Meier, 2020; Meier et al., 2019). This research found that, for fathers, claiming to be a victim of "parental alienation" was a very successful strategy. Of the cases where mothers claimed fathers were abusive but fathers counterclaimed the mother was engaging in "parental alienation," mothers' abuse claims were disbelieved 77% of the time. There was also a 50/50 chance that the court would take the children away from their mother and put them in the custody of the father: That outcome occurred in 50% of those cases. Almost three-quarters of mothers lost custody to the father when courts were actually persuaded by the father's claims of "parental alienation": Among those cases, the rate was 73%. In discussing these statistics, we should remember Monk's (2017) observation mentioned earlier in the chapter that perpetrators often have the ability to "control professionals using tactics that are indistinguishable from those employed to control their victims," and part of that ability lies in persuasiveness: a mask of "being charming, articulate and well-presented" (see also Campbell, 2017 and Rivera et al., 2012).

Fathers' ability to achieve a positive outcome for themselves using the strategy of accusing mothers of "parental alienation" was often effective even in cases where courts believed that the father had been domestically violent. If the court believed that the father had been domestically violent, but he meanwhile managed to convince them that the mother was engaging in "parental alienation," the court was still quite likely to be amenable to giving him custody: The rate in those cases was 43%.

It is important to make a couple of points here. First, it has been shown that these negative family court outcomes are not only a US phenomenon. Negative outcomes in cases where fathers claim parental alienation have been found in other countries, including (but not limited to) the United Kingdom, Australia, New Zealand, Canada, Spain, Italy, and others (see, e.g., Barnett, 2020; Birchall and Choudhry, 2021; Casas Vila, 2020; Elizabeth, 2020; Feresin, 2020; Hill, 2020; Hunter et al., 2020; Laing, 2017; Lapierre et al., 2020; Mercer and Drew, 2021; Rathus, 2020; Sheehy and Boyd, 2020; Zaccour, 2020). Second, courts' responses were gender-biased in favor of men/fathers. As Meier et al. (2019) noted, when mothers claimed fathers were abusive but fathers counterclaimed that the mother was engaging in "parental alienation," the father gained custody of the children 50% of the time. By contrast, in cases where fathers claimed that mothers were abusive and mothers counterclaimed that the father was engaging in "parental alienation," outcomes were almost 70/30 in the father's favor: The rate of mothers gaining custody in those circumstances was only 29%.

Mothers' struggle to be believed by family courts

Even when mothers are not accused by fathers of parental alienation, mothers still struggle to be believed by family courts when they report that the father has a history of abuse. Meier et al.'s (2019) US study showed poor outcomes for mothers in cases where the mother reported to the family court that the father had been abusive, and where, simultaneously, there was also no suggestion from the father that the mother had been engaging in parental alienation. In 59% of those cases, mothers were disbelieved. Furthermore, breaking down the data by type of abuse, Meier et al. (2019) found that of the mothers who reported to the family court that the father had been sexually abusing the child, 85% were disbelieved (see also Webb et al., 2021).

This is despite research suggesting that false accusations from mothers in these circumstances are rare. For example, Trocmé and Bala's (2005) analysis of a nationwide Canadian child abuse and neglect study found that false accusations occurred at a rate of 12% in custody disputes (88% of the accusations were true). In cases of false allegations, it was non-custodial parents (usually fathers) who were most likely to make false accusations of child abuse or neglect: Non-custodial parents were responsible for 43% of the false accusations. Custodial parents (usually mothers) were only responsible for 14% of the false accusations, and children were responsible for only 2% of the false allegations. (The remainder of the false accusations were made by others, such as family members, neighbors, or others in the community.)

Yet, returning to Meier et al.'s findings, in the cases of mothers reporting to courts that the father was abusive, the figures for mothers then losing custody to the father are remarkable. Of the mothers who reported to the family court that the father had been abusive, and were doing so where there was meanwhile no suggestion from the father that the mother had been engaging in parental alienation, 26% of mothers lost custody to the father. Of the mothers who reported that fathers had both sexually and physically abused the children, 50% lost custody to the father. Even narrowing this down to those mothers who *were believed* by the family court when they reported that the father had physically abused the children, 20% still lost custody to the father. Summarizing these findings, Meier et al. (2019, p. 26) concluded that "courts are excessively skeptical of child physical and sexual abuse reports, are likely

The aftermath of family court judgments for mothers and children

Once family courts have reached these outcomes, mothers and children are put in an extremely difficult and also extremely ironic situation. They may be jailed or subjected to other punitive responses for not complying, or for continuing to report that the perpetrator is still abusing the child (Dallam and Silberg, 2016; Dispatches, 2021; Hunter et al., 2020; Mercer, 2019; Silberg and Dallam, 2019). Children may therefore be left with no choice but to carry on partly or wholly living with the perpetrator/father and be subjected to his ongoing coercive control, despite the substantial harms associated with this outcome (e.g., Hill, 2020; Silberg and Dallam, 2019). Data suggest that, in the United States, more than 58,000 children a year are placed in the custody of an abuser (Silberg and Dallam, 2019). A minority of these cases are life-ending: The father goes on to kill the child (Hill, 2020; Silberg and Dallam, 2019; Women's Aid, 2016).

The irony of such a situation is that here the mother has been punished for *attempting to protect* the children from the domestic violence perpetrator, having possibly already been punished in the child protection system for "failing to protect" their children from him. Under the child protection system, mothers are punished for "exposing" their children to a perpetrator by not moving them away from him or excluding him from the family home. Yet when a mother complies with the demands of the child protection system and separates herself and the children from the perpetrator, within a few months she may find herself in the family court being punished for trying to keep the children safe from the domestic violence perpetrator by limiting his access to the children (see Hester, 2011; Saunders and Oglesby, 2016).

Reforming family court responses to coercive control

This book is by no means unique in raising these issues about the family courts, but the book's findings around the far-reaching negative impacts that perpetrators of coercive control can have on children's lives strengthen existing calls for change. In particular, this chapter has highlighted the negative impacts on children of perpetrators' tactics of isolation, economic abuse, curtailed freedom to leave the home, surveillance, and microregulation of everyday life; negative impacts which have received little previous attention. For the children in this study, those impacts occurred whether or not the perpetrator had ever used violence as part of his coercive control, highlighting that family courts should be alert to the harms caused by coercive control perpetrators even when they have not been physically violent.

Hence, a fully reformed and well-functioning family court system would be one that is routinely able to identify when a parent has been engaged in a campaign of coercive control for the past several months or years, and would be able to take substantially greater account of five key points: (1) perpetrators of coercive control cause harm to their children; (2) the perpetrator is unlikely to have abandoned their campaign of coercive control following separation from their partner; (3) on the contrary, the campaign is still likely to be "live" and ongoing; (4) perpetrators' requests for contact may well be part of the campaign of coercive control; and (5), if the request for contact is part of the campaign of coercive control, then granting contact would be unsafe and detrimental to the child (see Bancroft et al., 2012; Beeble et al., 2007; Clements et al., 2021; Coy et al., 2015; Dragiewicz et al., 2021a; Dragiewicz et al., 2021b; Elizabeth et al., 2012; Eriksson et al., 2005; Feresin et al., 2019; Galántai et al., 2019; Harne, 2011; Harrison, 2008; Hill, 2020; Holt, 2017; Humphreys et al., 2019; Hunter et al., 2020; Jouriles et al., 2018; Katz et al., 2020; Laing, 2017; Macdonald, 2016; Mackay, 2018; Monckton Smith, 2020a; Monk and Bowen, 2021; Radford, 2013; Radford and Hester, 2006; Stark, 2009; Thiara and Gill, 2012; Varcoe and Irwin, 2004; Watson and Ancis, 2013;

Wuest et al., 2003). To frame point (5) more positively, denying the contact would help to bring an end to the perpetrator's campaign of coercive control, and would give children and mothers the opportunity to begin to heal from the severe abuse that they have experienced (Holt, 2017; Katz, 2015b).

CONCLUSION

The central message of this chapter has been that coercive control is a multi-stranded form of abuse that harms children in ways that transcend the notion of a conceptual separation between "coercive control" and "child abuse and neglect." The chapter emphasized coercive control perpetrators' persistence, dangerousness, and resistance to change, the problematic tendency to position the victim/survivor parent as someone who is to blame for "failure to protect," and the urgent need for family courts to move away from the "pro-contact culture" that often means that the victim/survivor parent and child have no escape from the perpetrator.

The first part of the chapter discussed precisely how and why perpetrators of coercive control caused direct harms to children. The perpetrator's/father's tactics include, as we noted, an array of harms: social isolation and the restriction of movement, monitoring and surveillance, deprivation of basic resources such as food and heating, imprisonment in the home, brutal and unjust forms of punishment, and imposition of inappropriate rules and expectations of what could be said or done in the home. Children were vulnerable to every one of these tactics. In all of these scenarios, children's own needs were disregarded by perpetrators/fathers.

The chapter also explored how children and mothers found ways to actively resist coercive control. What was highlighted especially here was under-the-radar resistance: the secret, guerrilla campaign of resistance that takes place between children and mothers on an everyday basis in order to "get around" the wrath of the domestic dictator (see chapter 1).

Examples have included simple acts: watching a movie, secret shopping, sleeping next to each other, hugs, and make-believe tea-making. These might be underestimated as "little" things, but they were important. They deprived the perpetrator/father of complete victory by sustaining the feelings of self-worth and autonomy that the perpetrator was attempting to drain away from mothers and children.

Finally, illustrating the considerable similarities between children's and mothers' experiences of coercive control, the chapter showed how children and mothers were caught in the same twisted "world" that the perpetrator/father had created. Due to the perpetrator's/father's actions, both children and mothers suffered from social isolation, and in some cases, as we have illustrated, physical imprisonment. To avoid angering perpetrators/fathers, both children and mothers had to habitually constrain and modify their behavior. Children and mothers were not free to play, laugh, or spend time with each other as they wished to. Some perpetrators/fathers appeared to view their children in the same way as they viewed their female partners, expecting constant obedience and feeling justified in punishing perceived disobedience. Perpetrators/fathers could also use the same emotionally manipulative tactics against both children and mothers, such as crying, apologizing for abuse, and gift-giving. Children and mothers were co-victims and co-survivors of perpetrators'/fathers' tactics.

Overall, we encounter complex issues with numerous implications when we begin to focus on how coercive control affects child and adult victims/survivors, and when we begin to examine the full extent of the harms that perpetrators cause. Addressing these harms effectively involves rethinking many existing models and approaches, both for researchers and official bodies. This book is part of the beginnings of this rethinking. Other work has also examined some of the issues that this book is raising, and this book adds to that direction of travel. Momentum is gathering for further research and revised policy and practices responses that better name, recognize, and respond to the harms that children experience in contexts where one of their parents/parental-figures is engaged in a campaign of coercive control.

This chapter, then, has provided a "big picture" illumination of how coercive control directly harms children, how they actively resist it, and how the conceptual separation of "domestic violence" and "child abuse and neglect" is misleading. The next chapter moves on to the more specialized question of how coercive control affects mother–child relationships.

5

Mother–child relationships under coercive control

INTRODUCTION

The previous chapter suggested how children may be harmed by, and resist, coercive control-based domestic violence. This chapter has a more particular focus: It considers how the relationships between mothers and children were affected by perpetrators'/fathers' coercive control. The focus of the chapter is on exploring what happened to mother–child relationships, but, in doing so, we will also necessarily learn much about the relationships between the children and their coercive-control-perpetrating fathers. The father–child relationships were, as one might expect, influential in what happened to the mother–child relationships: Specifically, they influenced how some mother–child relationships were more harmed than others by the coercive control.

Mother–child-relationships can be a key obstacle to the perpetrator/ father gaining total control. This is a fact that is noted in the existing literature on domestic violence, for instance by Herman (1992, p. 79)—"As long as the victim maintains connections [with persons other than the perpetrator], the perpetrator's power is limited"—and by Bancroft et al. (2012, p. 99), who similarly conclude that the perpetrator/father's "access to power and control is threatened if solidarity [within the family] exists." Bancroft et al. (2012) observe that: "In cases where mothers and children

Coercive Control in Children's and Mothers' Lives. Emma Katz, Oxford University Press. © Oxford University Press 2022.
DOI: 10.1093/oso/9780190922214.003.0005

succeed in remaining unified, [perpetrators] lose much of [their] ability to control and manipulate family members."

Attacking and undermining mother–child relationships is therefore integral to the success of father-perpetrated coercive control (as is undermining closeness between siblings, though that is not a focus of this book). However, previous research has shown that while many mother–child relationships are harmed, some profoundly so, by coercive control, others appear to remain close and supportive (Bancroft et al., 2012; Chanmugam, 2014; Humphreys et al., 2006; Lapierre et al., 2018; Monk and Bowen, 2021; Mullender et al., 2002; Wendt et al., 2015). The task of this chapter—which makes no claim to universal application beyond the 15 families who took part in the study—is to explore why, in the families of the interviewed mothers and children, there was this difference in outcome. This task involves assessing what circumstances were occurring in the families that were making mother–child relationships more or less close and supportive or, alternatively, distant and strained.

Three categories of mother–child relationship are identified: "Very close," a type of mother–child relationship where the main experience was of feeling emotionally interconnected; "Very distant and strained," where the main experience was of feeling emotionally disconnected and separate from each other; and "Mixed." The main experience in the "Mixed" category was that the perpetrator's/father's behaviors had undermined the mother–child relationship, but that the mother and child(ren) had still maintained some closeness with each other.

There are numerous factors, many of which fell outside the scope of this study, that may have impacted on closeness and distance between mothers and children. However, in this study, five factors were identified as being particularly important in determining the category of the mother–child relationship in each of the 15 families. These are:

1. The perpetrator's/father's behavior toward the child(ren): whether it was mostly hostile/mostly disinterested, or varied over time between hostility, disinterestedness, and superficially "nice" behaviors

2. The perpetrator's/father's use of domestic violence: whether he abused the mother in front the children or secretly, and the degree of severity in the coercive control he perpetrated
3. The perpetrator's/father's undermining of the mother–child relationship: the extent to which he was determined to do so
4. The mother's ability to emotionally connect to the child(ren): to what extent her ability to do so was affected by the perpetrator's/father's abuse
5. The child(ren)'s views of their mother and the perpetrator/father: the extent to which they wished to talk to, spend time with, and be close to, their mother or the perpetrator/father

These factors were identified in the "Five Factor Framework" summarized in Katz (2019). What this chapter does, going beyond Katz (2019), is provide an in-depth, comprehensive breakdown of how the five factors applied in all 15 families in the study.

As this chapter will demonstrate, variance in the five factors meant that the mother–child relationships in the interviewed families differed widely. In some families, the development of mother–child supportiveness was obstructed by the perpetrator/father to such an extent that little-to-no supportiveness was occurring. As perpetrators'/fathers' coercive control increasingly undermined these mother–child relationships, a culture of noncommunication or a "conspiracy of silence" developed between these abused mothers and children (Humphreys et al., 2006). In other families, however, mother–child support was still occurring, and could have a positive impact on children's and mothers' well-being.

As this chapter will explore, closeness and supportiveness could coexist with strains, confusions, and negative feelings. Mothers who felt close and supportive toward their children could also feel exceedingly guilty about their children's experiences of coercive control. Children could behave in challenging ways toward their mother, yet also support their mother when they perceived that she was upset. Overall, the findings presented in this

CATEGORIES OF MOTHER–CHILD RELATIONSHIP

From the interviews with mothers and children, it was clear that some had been able to maintain much closer mother–child relationships than others in the face of coercive control. In four families, mothers and children described their mother–child relationships as being very close. In a further four families, mothers and children described their relationships as being very distant and strained. In the remaining seven families, relationships were described by mothers and children as quite close but also quite strained and distant. Mothers' and children's statements usually matched each other, e.g., in families where a child described their mother–child relationship as very close, their mother also described it as very close. Table 5.1 categorizes these three types of mother–child relationship:

Table 5.2 shows how each mother–child relationship within the study was categorized:

It is important to note here that mother–child relationships are complex, multifaceted, and fluid. Mothers and children can hold many different and contradictory feelings for each other simultaneously, and relationships can shift over time. Some of this nuance is inevitably lost by placing relationships into categories. The categories used in this study should therefore not be taken to represent the full complexity of participants' mother–child relationships. Rather, they should be understood as describing the feelings and beliefs about their mother–child relationships that participants chose to express at the time when they were interviewed.

Table 5.1 CATEGORIES OF MOTHER–CHILD RELATIONSHIP

Category	Definition	Example from the data
Very close and supportive	Participants' main experience of their mother–child relationship was of feeling emotionally connected to each other.	"This was our closeness. . . . We opened up to one another, we told each other things. . . . We did things together"
Mixed	Participants' main experience of their mother–child relationship was that the perpetrator's/father's behaviors had undermined their mother–child relationship, but they had still maintained some emotional connection to each other.	"We were always close, it's never been a case of, you know, not being [close, but . . .] our relationship probably broke down a little bit"
Very distant and strained	Participants' main experience of their mother–child relationship was of feeling emotionally disconnected and separate from each other.	"My kids started to shut down. . . . [My kids] just shut down and left me to it and I had to deal with it [the coercive control] myself"

Table 5.2 SAMPLE BY CATEGORY OF MOTHER–CHILD RELATIONSHIP

Very close and supportive	Mixed	Very distant and strained
Ellie–Shannon	Lucy–*Zara*[1]	Kimberley–Elle
Eloise–John	Akeela–Vince–Brock	Charlie–*Tanya*[1]
Ruby–Katie–Thomas	Violet–Joe–Angel	Marie–Leah
Alison–Jane	Lauren–Grace–Zoe	Ria–*Carly*[1]
	Isobel–Bob	
	Sybil–*Jack*[1]	
	Bella–Roxie	

[1] The names of the four children who were not interviewed, but were discussed by their mothers, appear in italics (see chapter 2). We cannot know if these children would have shared their mothers' views about how close, supportive, distant, and strained their mother–child relationships were.

THE FIVE FACTOR FRAMEWORK

The Five Factor Framework consists of the five factors that repeatedly arose during participants' discussions of closeness and distance in their mother–child relationships. Mothers' and children's accounts suggested that each of these factors had either increased mother–child closeness or increased mother–child distance and strain, depending on how it was experienced within a family. The Five Factor Framework depicted in Figure 5.1 represents these processes.

Table 5.3 lists the five factors and provides a definition of each factor:

Taken separately, each of these factors has been the subject of previous research. For example, Fogarty et al. (2021), Humphreys et al. (2006) and Morris (2009) examined perpetrators' strategies for undermining mother–child relationships. Burnette et al. (2017), Heward-Belle (2016) and Mohaupt et al. (2020) explored perpetrators' attitudes toward their children. However, this chapter takes the five factors together. Going beyond previous research, it shows the impacts that each of the five factors, *experienced together*, had on closeness, supportiveness, distance, and strain within mother–child relationships.

Factor 1: Perpetrator's/father's behavior toward the children

How perpetrators/fathers behaved toward children played a significant role in what happened to mother–child relationships. In the accounts of the mothers and children interviewed, approximately half of the perpetrators/fathers were described as nearly always being hostile or disinterested toward their children. The other half were described as inconsistently alternating between indulgent, hostile, and disinterested behaviors toward their children. The children of perpetrators/fathers who were nearly always hostile or disinterested discussed how they disliked this treatment. These children had usually developed negative views of the perpetrator/father and strongly negative feelings toward him (views and feelings that

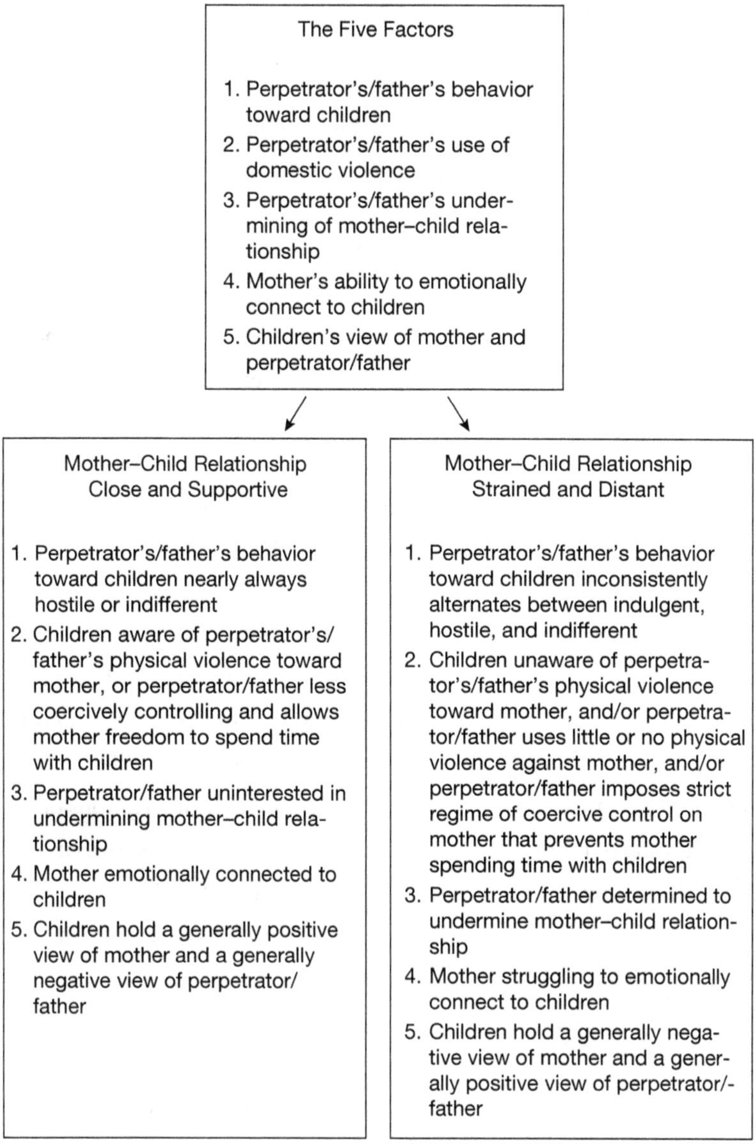

The Five Factors

1. Perpetrator's/father's behavior toward children
2. Perpetrator's/father's use of domestic violence
3. Perpetrator's/father's undermining of mother–child relationship
4. Mother's ability to emotionally connect to children
5. Children's view of mother and perpetrator/father

Mother–Child Relationship Close and Supportive

1. Perpetrator's/father's behavior toward children nearly always hostile or indifferent
2. Children aware of perpetrator's/father's physical violence toward mother, or perpetrator/father less coercively controlling and allows mother freedom to spend time with children
3. Perpetrator/father uninterested in undermining mother–child relationship
4. Mother emotionally connected to children
5. Children hold a generally positive view of mother and a generally negative view of perpetrator/father

Mother–Child Relationship Strained and Distant

1. Perpetrator's/father's behavior toward children inconsistently alternates between indulgent, hostile, and indifferent
2. Children unaware of perpetrator's/father's physical violence toward mother, and/or perpetrator/father uses little or no physical violence against mother, and/or perpetrator/father imposes strict regime of coercive control on mother that prevents mother spending time with children
3. Perpetrator/father determined to undermine mother–child relationship
4. Mother struggling to emotionally connect to children
5. Children hold a generally negative view of mother and a generally positive view of perpetrator/-father

Figure 5.1 The Five Factor Framework

Table 5.3 THE FIVE FACTOR FRAMEWORK

Factor	Definition
1. Perpetrator's/father's behavior toward children	Participants' qualitative descriptions of perpetrator's/father's attitudes toward, and treatment of, the children
2. Perpetrator's/father's use of domestic violence	Participants' qualitative descriptions of domestic violence perpetrated by perpetrator/father, e.g., physical violence, threats, isolation, emotional and psychological abuse, economic abuse, sexual abuse, control and microregulation of activities. Participants' qualitative descriptions of the extent of children's awareness of any physical violence perpetrated by perpetrator/father. Participants' qualitative descriptions of how frequently and how severely the perpetrator/father perpetrated domestic violence.
3. Perpetrator's/father's undermining of mother–child relationship	Participants' qualitative descriptions of perpetrator's/father's attitudes toward mother–child relationship and tactics used by perpetrator/father to undermine it
4. Mother's ability to emotionally connect to children	Participants' qualitative descriptions of how perpetrator's/father's behaviors affected mother's ability to feel emotionally close with the children, and extent to which mother felt emotionally close or emotionally distant and separate from the children
5. Children's views of mother and perpetrator/father	Participants' qualitative descriptions of how the children perceived the mother and the perpetrator/father

were logical and reasonable in the circumstances), and tended to feel very positive about their mother:

> He was continually belittling [our son] John. Saying how stupid and thick he was. How fat and lazy he was. (Eloise, mother)

> I love Mum with all my heart and soul, and I did back then. I just hated that man and worried what he'd do to her. . . . I just wanted to be there for Mum to look after her. (John, age 20, Eloise's son)

This dislike of the perpetrator/father on the part of children contributed to the development of closer relationships between children and mothers. These children often chose to (metaphorically speaking) stand beside their more nurturing parent:

> He used to hit us a lot. . . . I didn't like him and I didn't talk to him that much. I wanted to stay with my mum, because my mum is much nicer. (Vince, age 13)

By contrast, other perpetrators/fathers behaved in more subtle and manipulative ways toward their children, mixing hostility and disinterestedness with periods of indulgence and attention as part of their overall pattern of abuse. This tactic can be likened to the manipulative behavior that perpetrators use against their partners by sometimes appearing to be "nice," "caring," and "indulgent/generous/gift-giving." This "Jekyll and Hyde" behavior (Enander, 2011) confuses the victim/survivor, giving them false hope, and keeping them emotionally locked into the abusive relationship. Some of the children in the study had experienced "Jekyll and Hyde" perpetrators/fathers. These perpetrators/fathers had engaged with the children on some occasions while at other times seemingly wanting them to disappear, or had indulged them with money and "junk food" while also physically and emotionally abusing them:

> When he came home from work he'd want to spend time with them and they were always *his* girls. He used to say to Zoe: "You're

my little angel." But at the same time they couldn't shout, they couldn't make noise, they couldn't be children around him unless it was on his terms. It was alright if he wanted to play with them, but at other times it was like he wanted them to disappear. (Lauren, mother)

His way of being nice to the kids was Christmas and he'd go out and he'd spend a couple of grand [i.e., around £2,000]. He'd throw money at them. . . . [But] he didn't bother with the kids at all, unless it was to discipline them his way, which was with his fists all the time. (Bella, mother)

Mothers discussed how children were very confused by the perpetrator's/father's unpredictable behavior, and explained how this confusion impacted on their mother–child relationships. In the family of Bob and his mother Isobel, Bob had always wanted "to please" the perpetrator/father:

ISOBEL: When he wanted to, he could be Superdad. He'd promise them the world, say we'd go out somewhere, then he'd ring me up from the pub [to cancel the plans]. . . . Bob was always trying to please his dad . . .

EMMA: What different kinds of feelings do you think the children had toward you back then?

ISOBEL: Confusion I think. He was a "Jekyll and Hyde" character. I don't think they understood why he could be nice one minute and not the next. I suppose they loved me and that, but it was just a confusing time for them.

Isobel here recognized (even using the exact phrase) the "Jekyll and Hyde" character of the perpetrator/father: the character of someone who could be "nice one minute," or even a "Superdad when he wanted to," but then disappointed them in a way that the children could not understand. These perpetrators'/fathers' inconsistent behaviors, periodic indulgences, and broken promises created an overall climate of confusion and unpredictability in households. As Isobel's account suggests, this unpredictable behavior from perpetrators/fathers undermined mother–child closeness, and could leave children desperate for their father's approval.

Across the study, children with inconsistent and manipulative fathers usually had different views of their parents compared to children with more continuously hostile or nearly always disinterested fathers. For instance, Isobel's son Bob explained in his interview that he had loved his father as much as his mother, and simply wished for his father's negative behavior to cease. Bob's feelings contrasted with those of John, who, as we have just observed, described hating his continuously-hostile father and loving his mother, a mother who John described as a kind and nurturing parent. Children with fathers who were almost always hostile or disinterested toward them were usually more able to perceive their fathers in an accurate, largely negative way, and, rationally, preferred their mother accordingly. There were no suggestions in children's or mothers' interviews that mothers' behaviors were responsible for how children had felt about perpetrators/fathers; rather, it seemed that it was the perpetrators'/fathers' own treatment of the children—the ways that fathers behaved toward children on a day-to-day basis—that was influencing how the children felt about perpetrators/fathers.

Notably, none of these perpetrators/fathers appeared to have parented in a satisfactory way, and this finding is in keeping with other studies into the parenting of domestically violent fathers (e.g., Bancroft et al., 2012; Harne, 2011; Haselschwerdt et al., 2020; Heward-Belle, 2016; Humphreys et al., 2019; Katz et al., 2020; Mohaupt et al., 2020; Overlien, 2013; Smith and Humphreys, 2019; Thompson-Walsh et al., 2021). The children in this study seemed to have experienced one of two "bad options": they either had (1) a father who was nearly always hostile or disinterested in them, or (2) a "Jekyll and Hyde" father who combined hostility and disinterestedness with periods of unhealthy and self-serving indulgence and attention. Children with the latter kind of father were especially disadvantaged by the confusion, instability, and longing that their father's highly changeable behavior caused in them.

It is likely that both groups of children would have benefited from professional supports to help them to make sense of, and to heal from, the negative parenting practices of perpetrators/fathers. Such supports may have been particularly beneficial if they had emphasized that (1) the children were not to blame for their father's treatment of them, and that (2) the children deserved to be parented in warm, empathetic, nurturing, consistent, boundaried ways. (Supports should provide examples of what such parenting involves, so that the children can be equipped with practical information about how they should be treated by parents.)

Factor 2: Perpetrator's/father's use of domestic violence

Many mothers' and children's accounts suggested that the levels of distance and closeness in mother–child relationships were affected by the ways that perpetrators/fathers used domestic violence; particularly the extent to which they were controlling and the frequency and severity of their physical violence. Coercive control tends to escalate over time, and higher levels of control made it harder for mothers and children to stay close to each other. There were two families in the study where levels of coercive control were escalating but still relatively low at the time when mothers separated from perpetrators/fathers, a situation described by Johnson (2008) as "incipient intimate terrorism." (The relevance of this concept will be flagged up at appropriate moments during the chapter.) The lower levels of coercive control experienced by these mothers (Ruby and Alison) and their children allowed them to spend more positive time together, and for mothers to maintain more autonomy over their parenting:

> I spent a lot of time in their bedroom playing with them and teaching them things; coloring, reading, baking. I also took them out a lot and kept them busy. I had a very consistent night-time routine with them, and I tried to keep life as normal as possible for them. [My daughter] Jane and I were very close. (Alison, mother)

Alison's experiences suggest how beneficial it may be for mother–child closeness and well-being when perpetrators/fathers choose not to prevent mothers from investing time and energy into their children. Alison was able to exercise freedom over her own activities in ways that were forbidden to many of the other mothers in the study (see also Buchanan, 2018).

By contrast, some perpetrators/fathers, as part of their coercive control, forced mothers into grueling schedules that made it impossible for them to engage with their children:

> I was constantly working in the house and I did long shifts at work. . . . I wasn't allowed to be on my own. He would always take me to work, pick me back up. . . . I had to have a spotless house. . . . It was a nightmare. (Charlie, mother)

Mothers and children living under these restrictive regimes described how they had experienced more distant and strained mother–child relationships, and felt isolated and disconnected from each other. Some of these mothers and children described situations where the mother had felt debilitating guilt for not being able to spend time with their children, and where children were left feeling unsure about whether or not their mother loved them.

A further issue impacting on mother–child closeness was whether children were aware of their father's physical violence toward their mother. Approximately half of the mothers in the study (Ellie, Eloise, Kimberley, Charlie, Lucy, Ria, Akeela, and Bella) described how their partners had subjected them to every form of abuse associated with coercive control, including frequent and severe physical violence, threats, psychological and often sexual and economic abuse, and having their lives controlled and monitored:

> We had broken furniture because he threw it at me. . . . He would say I was cold and that I didn't understand him. . . . He would buy expensive food [for himself] and I was living on water while I was breastfeeding. (Ria, mother)

> There was no peace for me in that house; it was echoing with him shouting, screaming, yelling for little petty things. [. . . In bed] he'd treat me like meat. No love or tender care. (Akeela, mother)

> Once I got home a few minutes late. He started banging my head against the wall, calling me all these names, saying: "where have you been you bitch?" and Shannon was just shaking like mad and crying. (Ellie, mother)

The children in the study who were living with more frequent and severe physical violence against their mothers generally had more of an understanding about what was occurring. This finding was in line with Thiara and Gill's (2012, p. 43) observation, based on their interviews with 45 mothers and 19 children, that, "Where children were directly abused or witnessed repeated abuse, they held 'antidad' views." The children of the interviewed mothers experiencing a higher level of physical violence were more likely to recognize the perpetrator's/father's abuse of their mother as wrong and to have a closer relationship with their mother (again, a reasonable and logical response from children).

By contrast, children in families with less or no physical violence were often less aware of the full scale of the perpetrator's/father's abuse of the mother. There were five such families in the study. For the mothers in these families, physical violence was either less frequent (Isobel, Marie, and Lauren) or absent completely (Sybil and Violet). For Isobel, Marie, Lauren, Sybil, and Violet, the coercive control principally took the form of unrelenting and continual monitoring, psychological abuse—often alongside sexual and economic abuse—and threats about what might happen if the perpetrator's/father's authority was disobeyed:

> Keeping you down, chipping away at you; he used to say "if you leave me no one else is going to want you, you're ugly." He'd say "I'm going to ring your parents now and tell them that you're the worst daughter on this planet and they'll never speak to you again." (Lauren, mother)

> If I went out, he said it was because I wanted to look at other men or phone my lover. I couldn't go anywhere without having to explain myself. At times I had 5 minutes to get home from work and if I was any later than that then there were consequences. (Isobel, mother)

Children in these families tended to feel more confused about what was occurring, and about their parents (see also Naughton et al., 2019). As one mother, Isobel, described, "[the children] always loved him [the perpetrator/father] because they didn't know quite what was happening."

However, it was not *always* the case that children in families with a high level of physical violence sided with the mother and, similarly, it was not always the case that children in families with a lower level of physical violence were more confused. With any given one of the five factors, if another (or more than one) of the other five factors was pointing in a different direction, then the impact of the given factor could be muted. So it was with factor 2. For example, in families where mothers were struggling to emotionally connect with their children (factor 4, later), children did not necessarily feel close to their mother, even if they were aware that she was being subjected to severe physical violence from the perpetrator/father.

Factor 3: Perpetrator's/father's undermining of mother–child relationship

The accounts of the interviewed mothers and children suggested that some perpetrators/fathers had been much more interested than others in undermining mother–child relationships. Unsurprisingly, those mother–child relationships that were more undermined by perpetrators/fathers were often the ones that were more strained. Perpetrators'/fathers' tactics for undermining mother–child relationships have been identified in previous studies (see, e.g., Bancroft et al., 2012; Buchanan, 2018; Heward-Belle, 2017; Humphreys et al., 2006; Lapierre, 2010a; Monk and Bowen, 2021; Morris, 2009; Radford and Hester, 2006). For the mothers and children in this study, these harmful undermining tactics included:

- Openly disrespecting mothers in front of children, encouraging children to form negative views of their mothers, and encouraging children to have little respect for their mothers.

- Reducing mothers' confidence in their parenting, thereby targeting and undermining an important element of mothers' identities.
- Preventing mothers and children from spending time together and showing each other affection. Perpetrators/fathers often controlled and monitored space and time within the household, and demanded that they receive the majority of the mother's attention. This prevented mothers and children from participating in activities together and generating positivity in their relationship. It could also confuse children, giving them a sense that their mother did not love them because she was not spending time with them, and could make mothers feel guilty and disconnected from their children.
- Overriding mothers' attempts to maintain discipline and keep children in a stable routine. Some perpetrators/fathers adopted a permissive parenting style to make the mother appear to the children as the stricter parent. This could set children against their mother's attempts to guide or "parent" them. It could also make mothers feel that they would not be able to "handle" the children on their own if they separated from the perpetrator/father, thus further entrapping them.

Many mothers noted how children exposed to these tactics had lost respect for them, and had begun to resent and reject their parenting:

> It got to the point where the kids were talking to me like dirt, and ignoring everything I said, because that's all they saw from their dad. It was so stressful. . . . Anything I said to the kids he would override on purpose. I was nothing in that house. (Bella, mother)

> It was quite hard really, getting them to do their homework, because he was saying: "they don't need to do homework." So it was like fighting a battle with him all the time. He was sort of "the goody" and I was "the baddy." I was like: "you've got to clean your teeth and have a bath and do your homework." (Isobel, mother)

Mothers discussed how these harmful undermining tactics by perpetrators/ fathers had distorted children's beliefs around what constitutes normal, positive parenting behavior. The mothers described situations where they believed their children had come to perceive negative behavior (such as bullying, verbal abuse, and degrading and humiliating other people) as positive and desirable. It was in this context that Bella had experienced violence from her male step-child (child-to-parent violence).

However, perpetrators'/fathers' attacks on mother–child relationships were not always successful. The extent to which perpetrators were able to undermine mother–child relationships depended on the orientation of the other four factors. In families where factors 1, 2, 4, and 5 were mostly oriented toward mother–child closeness, some children and mothers described how children had been able to resist perpetrators'/fathers' undermining tactics. This was exemplified by one of the mothers, Ruby:

> Even if [the perpetrator] had said bad things about me, they wouldn't have believed him. Kids know the truth. Things have to be in a bad, bad way for them to believe lies like that. (Ruby, mother)

Ruby and her children lived in a situation where the perpetrator (not the children's father) was usually hostile toward the children (factor 1), where Ruby was strongly emotionally connected to the children (factor 4), and where the children recognized the perpetrator's behaviors as wrong and unjust (factor 5). These circumstances help to explain why Ruby expressed confidence that the perpetrator would not have been able to undermine her mother–child relationships.

Similarly, in another family, Brock (age 12) described being able to reject the perpetrator's/father's attempts to undermine his relationship with his mother. Brock's account suggested that the perpetrator/father was usually hostile toward him (factor 1), physically violent to his mother in front of him (factor 2), and that Brock disliked the perpetrator/father (factor 5). Brock discussed how his father had tried to manipulate him and his brother into moving out of their mother's house and living with him instead. However, Brock and his brother had perceived that this was unwise and had chosen to remain with their mother, being aware from previous experience that once they were living with him he would "hit us, shout at us, not let us do anything and lock us in our room." Brock showed perceptiveness about the reasons why their father had tried to convince the children to live with him, stating that he was doing it just "so Mum would feel upset," rather than because he genuinely wished to care for his children.

Factor 4: Mothers' ability to emotionally connect to children

Mothers who had been harmed by perpetrators/fathers in ways that left them less able to emotionally connect to their children tended to have more strained mother–child relationships. As reported in other studies (see, e.g., Lapierre, 2010b; Radford and Hester, 2006), several mothers experienced numbness, disassociation, and disconnection from their children. These mothers described feeling emotionally shut down, "robotic," or as if they were on "auto-pilot":

> I was on auto-pilot as a mum. I was looking after them, but with no energy to enjoy the relationship—you're just completely gone. It's like you're outside your own body, just looking at someone else's life, just doing what you can to get by. It's like being on autopilot: You're just functioning because you have to. (Lucy, mother)

> I didn't feel close to [my son] Jack back then. I felt like I was his protector, but not like I could enjoy him. . . . It's hard to play [with your child] when you're feeling sad and anxious all the time. . . . I was so ground down by it all. (Sybil, mother)

Although most of these mothers did not discuss these experiences in terms of named mental health conditions, it is likely that as a result of perpetrators'/fathers' coercive control they were experiencing conditions such as depression, anxiety, and complex-PTSD (Dutton and Goodman, 2005; Fogarty et al., 2021; Herman, 1992; Humphreys and Thiara, 2003; Khan, 2020; Moulding et al., 2021). Some mothers also mentioned physical ill-health as a barrier to closeness with their children, describing themselves as "drained," "exhausted," and physically "weak" while the perpetrator's/father's abuse was ongoing.

One theme that emerged in some of the interviews was mothers feeling emotionally disconnected from children (see also Fogarty et al., 2021). This emotional disconnection could occur when perpetrators/fathers were violent toward children and would not allow mothers to protect them. Mothers in this situation retreated emotionally from the devastating experience of having children who they were powerless to shield from harm. This was the situation for Marie, whose experiences will be explored in depth toward the end of this chapter:

> The way I got through it was putting a wall up and blocking the kids out emotionally, because he could be quite physical with my son sometimes. He'd leave handprints on him if he'd smacked him. . . . When I did say something, he [the perpetrator/father] would soon make it clear he was going to carry on anyway, so there wasn't anything I could have done. (Marie, mother)

Another context in which this emotional disconnection occurred for mothers was when the perpetrator/father had targeted their pregnancy for particular abuse, for example by hitting their abdomen, or telling them that their pregnant body was disgusting. Two of the mothers in the study, Marie and Ria, discussed how they had felt unable to connect with their children when they were babies because of such behavior from perpetrators/fathers (see also Buchanan, 2018).

However, there were several instances within the study of mothers who had maintained a strong emotional connection between themselves and their children. In one family, the accounts of the mother and daughter suggested that they had maintained their emotional connection despite the mother struggling with poor mental health and substance misuse due to the perpetrator's/father's abuse (see De Simone and Heward-Belle, 2020). This mother, Ellie, made great efforts to continue spending positive time interacting with her daughter when possible:

> [My daughter] Shannon and I used to play, usually upstairs. The upstairs was sort of our area and the downstairs was his area. . . . I made this wonderful fairy-tale world for her upstairs in her bedroom, and just all upstairs really, and we spent most of the time together up there. (Ellie, mother)

It was notable within the study that the mothers and children who had been able to spend fairly regular time together on enjoyable activities (such as playing, cooking, watching television, going out to the park, movies, and shopping) were usually the ones who reported greater closeness during the years that they had lived with perpetrators/fathers. Conversely, the mothers and children who were prevented from spending enjoyable time together were also the ones who described their mother–child relationships as being more distant. Whether or not enjoyable mother–child time could take place was influenced by the five factors discussed in this chapter. For example, mothers' and children's accounts suggested that mothers who were feeling emotionally disconnected from their children (factor 4) were generally unable to fully engage in "fun" activities with them. The sharing of enjoyable mother–child activities was also prevented when perpetrators/fathers chose to heavily control and curtail mothers' time and movements (factor 2). Finally, as outlined in the next section, factor 5 also affected the extent to which children themselves wished to spend time with their mothers.

Factor 5: Children's views of mother and perpetrator/father

Children's relative preference for their mother or the perpetrator/father— the question of which of these two people they most wanted to talk to, spend time with and be close to—was a major factor influencing how close and distant mother–child relationships became. The views of children in this regard were strongly related to the other four factors discussed previously. Children who were closer to their mothers usually held more positive views of their mothers. Mothers' and children's accounts suggested that these were the children who were experiencing most or all of the following:

1. A father who nearly always behaved in a hostile or disinterested way toward them.
2. Awareness of their father's physical violence toward their mother (making it easier for the children to realize that he was an abuser), or a father who was less coercively controlling and allowed their mother more freedom to spend time with them (enabling mother–child closeness to develop).
3. A father who was less interested in undermining their relationship with their mother.
4. A mother who was able to be more emotionally connected to them.

Conversely, children whose mother–child relationships were more strained and distant tended to hold more confused, ambivalent, or negative views of their mothers. Mothers' and children's accounts suggested that these were the children who were experiencing most or all of the following circumstances:

1. A father who inconsistently alternated between indulgent, hostile, and disinterested behaviors toward them.
2. A father who hid his physical violence from them so they were not aware of it, and/or perpetrated little or no physical violence (making it harder for them to realize that he was an abuser), and/or who imposed a strict regime of coercive control on their mother that prevented her from spending time with them (so mothers and children had insufficient opportunities to maintain closeness).
3. A father who was determined to undermine their mother–child relationship.
4. A mother who was less able to emotionally connect with them because of how the father was harming her mentally and physically with his coercive control.

Mother–child relationships were not maintained by mothers alone. Rather, they were jointly maintained by mothers and children. Children's view of their mother (influenced by the four factors outlined earlier), played a significant role in how close or distant mother–child relationships became.

Impacts of the five factors on mother–child relationships

In each family, there was a link between how many of the factors were oriented toward closeness or distance, and the levels of closeness and distance in mother–child relationships. Among those who had very close relationships (four families), mothers' and children' accounts suggested that all of the five factors were usually oriented toward closeness. The only exception to this general rule was that perpetrators/fathers in these families could make some attempts to undermine mother–child relationships (factor 3). However, the contributions to mother–child closeness made by the other four factors meant that they were largely immune to those attempts. The levels of closeness in these families were exemplified in statements such as Alison's:

> [My daughter] really did get me through it. . . . She was really close to me and massively supportive. (Alison, mother)

It was not the case within these families that mothers and children never argued, became angry with each other, or felt the feelings of misplaced blame and guilt that are common in victims/survivors (Moulding et al., 2015; Mullender et al., 2002). They did. Rather, mothers and children suggested that closeness ran alongside, and in some ways counterbalanced, those more negative elements of their relationship. Mother–child closeness was beneficial partly because it gave children and mothers a sense that they were not alone—that they had somebody with them who loved them. Furthermore, mothers and children described closer mother–child relationships as sources of much-needed positive and enjoyable interactions in the context of an otherwise very negative home life.

Mixed mother–child relationships were experienced by seven families. The mothers and children with these relationships—that is, relationships that were both quite close and quite strained and distant—were in situations where two or three factors leaned toward closeness while the other two or three created conditions that produced more strain and distance. For example, in a family with mixed mother–child relationships, the mother may have been able to emotionally connect with the children and spend positive time with them (factor 4), but the perpetrator's/father's behavior toward the children was inconsistently indulgent (factor 1), the perpetrator/father was determined to undermine the mother–child relationship (factor 3), and the children's views of their parents were confused (factor 5). These factors produced a difficult combination of closeness and strain. In these circumstances, mother–child relationships were a mixture of close and distant, but did not break down completely:

> We were always close, it's never been a case of, you know, not being [close, but . . .] our relationship probably broke down a little bit. (Lucy, mother)

> Our relationship was okay . . . we rowed [argued] a lot (Roxie, age 11)

Finally, in the very distant and strained relationships (experienced by four families), mothers' and children's accounts suggested that all or nearly all of the factors were oriented toward distance and strain. These mother–child relationships contained very little closeness, and mothers and children felt disconnected and isolated from each other:

> I cut myself off emotionally from the kids, and just put a kind of wall up and like just cared for them on autopilot I suppose. (Marie, mother)

In families with very distant mother–child relationships, some mothers suggested that their children leaned more toward the perpetrator/father and came to favor him (for example by siding with him, developing a strong dislike of their mother, and/or continuing to live with the perpetrator/father after their parents separated).

It was also possible for a mother who had two or more children to have closer/more strained relationships with some of her children than others. This variance was particularly the case if the perpetrator/father behaved differently toward one child compared to their siblings, for instance by lavishing time and money on his favorite child while ignoring and criticizing the others. In such families, mothers' accounts suggested that the perpetrator's/father's favored child had a more strained relationship with their mother than the other children in the family.

Professionals working with families where there is, or was, coercive control-based domestic violence may find the Five Factor Framework useful in helping them to understand what has occurred in the families they are engaging with. If a relationship between a child and their victim/survivor parent appears to be strained, professionals could use the Framework as a basis for sensitively asking questions about the dynamics in the family. Asking questions around each of the five factors could help to provide a detailed picture of how the perpetrator's behavior has affected the children and the victim/survivor parent. Once issues of concern have been identified (such as that the perpetrator/father has not allowed the mother and children to spend sufficient positive time together, or that the perpetrator's/father's denigration of the mother has caused the children to lose respect for her) then plans could be developed and interventions used to tackle these harms. The Five Factor Framework could therefore sit alongside broader interventions for helping children and victim/survivor parents to become free, safe and, ultimately, recovered, from perpetrators'/fathers' coercive control.

This chapter will now go on to explore mothers' and children's experiences of their mother–child relationships in more depth, first turning to the closest and most supportive relationships, then to the mixed relationships, then finally to the relationships that were most distant and strained.

VERY CLOSE AND SUPPORTIVE RELATIONSHIPS

The four families where mother–child relationships were very close and supportive were:

- Ellie and her daughter Shannon, age 10 (Shannon's age while Ellie and the perpetrator were together was 1–6)
- Eloise and her son John, age 20 (John's age while Eloise and the perpetrator/father were together was 0–16)
- Ruby and her children Katie, age 12, and Thomas, age 10 (Katie and Thomas's ages while Ruby and the perpetrator were together were 8–11 and 6–9)
- Alison and her daughter Jane, age 11 (Jane's age while Alison and the perpetrator/father were together was 0–3)

Ellie and Shannon and Eloise and John experienced closeness in the context of severe coercive control. Ruby, Katie, and Thomas, and Alison and Jane's experiences were quite different; they seemed to have experienced Johnson's (2008) "incipient intimate terrorism"—that is, abusive behavior from the perpetrator/father that had not yet escalated into full coercive control. Given these different contexts, we will explore the mother–child relationships in the two sets of families in turn.

Closeness and supportiveness in cases of severe coercive control

For Ellie and Shannon and Eloise and John, the five factors all favored mother–child closeness. The children in these families frequently experienced perpetrators/fathers physically assaulting their mothers, and Shannon experienced the perpetrator (who was not her biological father) rape her mother in front of her (factor 2). Perpetrators/fathers were usually hostile toward the children, and John's father also directly physically abused him (factor 1). In these families, then, mothers and children were experiencing much of the coercive control together. They described an intense closeness, and a feeling of connection in their suffering:

> We felt like we were a unit, and then there was him. (John, age 20)

> To a large extent, we're like one person, and I think that's because we've been together more or less constantly through all the domestic violence; we've been to rock bottom together. (Ellie, mother)

These children's and mothers' accounts of co-experiencing coercive control reflected this togetherness in their use of "we" and "our" in their descriptions:

> Me and Mum kind of lived in fear, definitely when it was night. Because he'd get angry and start being nasty like a few times a week or something, and most of the time his behavior was just unacceptable. And it just wasn't nice and we just didn't like it. (Shannon, age 10)

> ELOISE: It was like a yo-yo situation: we'd forgive him then he'd do it again. We used to have to barricade ourselves in John's bedroom, many a time.
> JOHN: We used to push my furniture against the door . . .
> ELOISE: . . . But he'd still push in.

Here, closeness was linked with jointly living in fear, jointly perceiving the perpetrator's/father's behavior as wrong, and working together to protect themselves against the perpetrator's/father's abuse. John in particular noted the strong feelings of love and hatred that he had developed, through living in these circumstances, for his mother ("Mum") and father ("that man") respectively (factor 5):

> I love Mum with all my heart and soul, and I did back then. I just hated that man and I worried what he'd do to her. (John, age 20)

Both mothers, Ellie and Eloise, reported providing high levels of support to their children within the confines of the situations that they faced, despite experiencing poor mental health because of the perpetrator's/father's coercive control (see De Simone and Heward-Belle, 2020). Eloise was depressed and crying every day. Ellie, coerced by the perpetrator, was taking illegal drugs. Nonetheless, both made great efforts to try to prevent their children from witnessing violence and from being hurt. Furthermore, they were generally warm and loving toward their children. Both persisted in spending time with their children whenever possible.

In relation to factor 4, then, these mothers appeared to have retained the ability to emotionally connect with their children, even though the coercive control was having a very negative impact on them. They enjoyed each other's company and created a sphere for entertainment and play in the manner described in chapter 4:

> He wanted all of me, all the time when he was home. [. . . But when he was at work] Shannon and I used to play, usually upstairs. The upstairs was sort of our area and the downstairs was his area. . . . I made this wonderful fairy-tale world for her upstairs in her bedroom, and just all upstairs really, and we spent most of the time together up there. (Ellie, mother)

ELOISE: We did things together. When we went to the pictures or we went shopping we could just "let our hair down" and do what we wanted to do.

JOHN: When we would come back with shopping bags, sometimes we had to hide them.

ELOISE: We used to throw them over the hedge.

JOHN: Into the garden so he wouldn't see them.

ELOISE: Clothing or anything I'd brought John, because he [the perpetrator/father] would go mad [that I'd spent money on John].

These times of "letting their hair down" appeared to have played a pivotal role in these mother–child relationships, helping mothers and children to maintain closeness and positivity with each other. Eloise and John's description of going shopping may be understood as an example of mutual resistance, as they worked together to hide their purchases from the perpetrator/father. Shannon also described how she and Ellie mutually supported each other when the perpetrator/father had been abusive and then left the house. At these times, Shannon and Ellie provided each other with reassurance and comfort by hugging each other and saying "it's going to be okay."

In addition, Eloise provided John with more general emotional support. She talked to him about what life should be like, dealt with his misdemeanors in a sensitive way, and encouraged him to talk to her when he was experiencing problems. Eloise suggested that these supports were successful, with her and John "open[ing] up to each other" and "[telling] each other things" in a way that promoted closeness in their relationship. John reflected on this pivotal "bond":

Mum's helped me a lot because, if you have a bond with your mum, that can help strengthen you, get you through it. Loads of people out there going through this don't have a bond with either parent, with anybody, so it's just themselves, but if you've got somebody, at least one person, that can be tremendous. (John, age 20)

Communicating in these ways may have reduced Eloise and John's isolation by helping them to feel as though they had somebody with whom they could speak and confide their feelings.

Child-to-mother support was also occurring in these families. Shannon had lived with the coercive control only until the age of 6, but described how even at this young age she had supported her mother by being "nice" to her:

I'd just be very good to her, like I'd be polite and be, like, nice to her and happy and just very smiley to her. . . . I never said any bad stuff to her or anything because I love her, and if I threw a bit of a tantrum, after seeing Dad doing that to her, I'd remember how much I loved her and I'd start being very nice to her again. (Shannon, age 10)

Here, Shannon suggests that she supported her mother by changing her own behavior; becoming more "nice" and "polite" and avoiding saying "bad stuff." This support strategy on the part of a young child—attempting to regulate her own behavior—is one that could easily remain unrecognized by adults, but was experienced by Shannon as important.

John's forms of support were more overt. Having lived with his mother and father up to the age of 16 (ten years longer than Shannon), John had frequently intervened physically to protect his mother from his father. John also provided direct emotional support. As Eloise described, he was "like a counselor" and acted as a general companion:

He's been so supportive. In an emotional way he was supportive to me. . . . He would say to me: "Mum don't go to bed tonight in his room; come and sleep with me." So I'd get into his bed and John had like a bean-bag and he'd lay on the floor and he'd say: "shall I put us a movie on Mum, what do you want to watch?"—to cheer me up. He was like a counselor; he had to grow up so quickly because of his father's bad behavior and attitude. (Eloise, mother)

John also recalled his wish to support Eloise (factor 5):

I just wanted to be there for her to look after her. (John, age 20)

John's actions in supporting Eloise were aimed at helping her to maintain a happier mood. In taking the initiative and suggesting that she watch films with him, John was doing what he could to counter his mother's depression, and creating opportunities for them to spend time together. Eloise's quote about John being "like a counsellor" also suggests that he tried to help her to cope with her more negative feelings, although neither of them gave details about this form of support in their joint interview.

It is also notable that both John and Shannon were only-children. This may have produced more intense emotional connections between these children and mothers, as no siblings were present to divide their attentions from each other. However, there was not always closeness in this context. As will be shown later in this chapter, Ria and her only child, Carly, had a more strained and distant relationship.

Although these mother–child relationships were close and supportive, they also contained anger and guilt. Ellie reported that Shannon had felt "angry" toward her while they had lived with the perpetrator/father:

> She was really angry at me but she couldn't express it. She would just look at me with this really angry look, sort of furrowed brow, and just be quiet really. [Sometimes] she would say: "you don't love me; you only love him," and I would just think: "oh God." It used to kill me. (Ellie, mother)

Shannon's own comments (discussed earlier) suggest that she was actually attempting to support her mother by not expressing her feelings. However, Ellie's interview suggests that these feelings sometimes burst out, and that, for Ellie, Shannon's feelings were still painfully evident. Ellie described how she had suffered from feelings of guilt about what Shannon was experiencing, and felt unable to host Shannon's school friends in the family home:

> I couldn't invite her friends from school, because I didn't know what he might do. But I used to play with her, and one time, when she was about 5, she'd made all these paper cut-outs of like little people and she said: "these are my friends," and I just felt terrible. I felt so guilty. (Ellie, mother)

Ellie's feelings of guilt were an obstacle to her openly communicating with Shannon about the coercive control that they were experiencing, although, as we have noted, they were still supporting in each other in a number of ways, including by hugs and reassurance:

We didn't actually talk to each other about what he did or what he would say. We'd just be: "Oh he's just being naughty, just shouting, that sort of thing," and just push it under the carpet, never actually [talk about it]. I felt too guilty, too embarrassed, and didn't want to accept the way that it was, let alone sort of think that I was letting Shannon down so much actually. (Ellie, mother)

As Ellie's comments suggest, pushing the perpetrator/father's behavior "under the carpet" was part of her emotional survival strategy at that time.

Closeness and supportiveness in cases of less severe coercive control

Ruby and her two children, Katie and Thomas, and Alison and her daughter, Jane, appeared to have experienced "incipient intimate terrorism" (Johnson, 2008) from the perpetrator/father. The perpetrators in these families were certainly abusive. Ruby's partner subjected her to sexual coerciveness, hair pulling, pushing, and shoving, and could behave in a mean and domineering way with the children. Alison's partner harmed her with violence and economic abuse, the latter of which also left her daughter impoverished. However, neither mother appeared to have experienced severe emotional/psychological abuse such as being belittled into feeling worthless. Nor had they experienced isolation from the outside world, or intense micromanagement of their everyday lives. It seemed that neither Ruby nor Alison had been highly afraid of their partners until near the ends of their relationships, when perpetrators'/fathers' actions began to escalate and became increasingly severe (which, in Alison's case, meant that she and her children ultimately had to flee to a refuge). Ruby and Alison were also not regularly prevented from spending time with their children (factor 2). Analysis of their interviews suggested that these mothers had more confidence than other mothers in the study because they were not being severely emotionally/psychologically abused by perpetrators/fathers (factor 4). Finally, because the perpetrators/fathers in these families were either hostile or disinterested toward the children (factor 1), Katie, Thomas, and Jane appeared to have found it easier to remain close with their mothers.

Because Ruby had not been afraid of her partner until near the end of their relationship, she had been able to maintain a high degree of control over her parenting. Ruby's autonomy as a parent had given her children Katie and Thomas (age 8–11, and 6–9 while their mother and the perpetrator/father were together) a sense that they could consult her whenever they had problems:

If I ever needed anything I'd just go to my mum. (Katie, age 12)

Katie also described how her mother had ignored the perpetrator when he stated that she should punish her children more severely (something that Ruby was in a position to ignore because the perpetrator had not made her feel high levels of fear toward him). Ruby had made it clear to her partner that if he ever hit her children (he was not the children's biological father) it would be the end of their relationship. This marking-out of acceptable conduct was effective, and the children were not hit. Ruby also explained how, when arguments broke out between her and the perpetrator, she was able to relocate the children out of the way, often telling them to go upstairs. Ruby was therefore protecting her children from harm in multiple ways (see also Wendt et al., 2015). (It is worth noting here that the perpetrator in this case had disguised his abuse in such a way that Ruby had thought he was a good person at heart, who sometimes behaved badly. It was only when the perpetrator's abusive behaviors began to escalate that Ruby was able to understand what was really occurring, at which point she began to plan for her and the children to escape).

Alison also described how she had worked extremely hard to keep her young children (Jane and a younger sibling) away from the perpetrator's/father's illegal drug use and violence toward her. In her efforts to shield them, Alison provided the warm and consistent parenting that shaped their early years. Her ability to create a life "as normal as possible" for them appeared to have largely protected them from the harmful effects of the perpetrator's/father's behavior:

> I tried to keep the kids away from their dad's addiction [to illegal drugs] as much as possible. . . . I spent a lot of time in their bedroom playing with them and teaching them things, coloring, reading, baking. I also took them out a lot and kept them busy. I had a very consistent night-time routine with them, and I tried to keep life as normal as possible for them. Jane and I were very close. (Alison, mother)

Similarly, Ruby and Katie were able to spend time with each other when the perpetrator was absent from the house. Ruby and Katie both described these times together as a form of mutual support:

> Well, some days, [the perpetrator] would be out, and me and Mum would watch a movie and have some time together. I used to help cook tea with my mum because I enjoy cooking so we'd, like, help each other. (Katie, age 12)

> The children and I, we've always had a laugh together, so on those days when we were alone we would snuggle up on the sofa and watch films together, and we always emotionally supported each other then. (Ruby, mother)

Ruby also attempted to support her children to deal with the emotional impacts of the perpetrator's behavior. As Thomas described, she acted to lessen the impact of his verbal abuse:

> Mum helped me a lot because, when [the perpetrator] told me off, she said: "it's alright, it doesn't matter." (Thomas, age 10)

As Thomas says here, Ruby's emotional reassurance was important in minimizing the harm caused by the perpetrator's verbally abusive behavior.

The closeness between Ruby and her children also helped to protect their relationship from being undermined by the perpetrator (factor 3). Ruby commented that any attempts by the perpetrator to turn her children against her would have been unsuccessful:

> It wouldn't have washed with my kids at all, because they would have told me straight away anyway, and they would have told him where to go. (Ruby, mother)

Katie and Thomas's close relationships with their mother therefore had the beneficial effect of helping them to reject the perpetrator's potential attempts to undermine those relationships.

As with Ellie and Shannon's relationship discussed earlier, Ruby and her children's relationships also contained some strains. One of the strategies used by Katie and Thomas to support their mother was to withhold their true feelings: Katie described how she and Thomas had disliked the perpetrator as soon as they had met him, but had not told Ruby because they did not want to upset her or ruin her new relationship. Again, this highlights how mothers and children could be very close and supportive, yet remain silent about the issues relating to perpetrators'/fathers' abusive behaviors.

Ruby had been aware of Katie's and Thomas' negative feelings toward the perpetrator. She believed that her children's wish to have the perpetrator out of their lives had caused some tensions in their mother–child relationships at the time. However, Ruby also thought that these negative feelings had been outweighed by positives in their relationships. She felt that this was because she had been able to continue parenting Katie and Thomas in a warm and loving way, and to maintain a positive emotional connection with them (factor 4). Ruby and her children had continued to communicate about general matters in life and to spend time with each other:

> I just think they probably thought I was letting them down in some way or not protecting them. But I was still their same old mummy,

and they were still close to me, and we still did the same things we always did and we still talked, so I think in many ways that made up for them at some points feeling: "I want to go Mummy [i.e., separate from the perpetrator]; why aren't we going?" . . . But I think mostly they would have felt the same things toward me that they'd always felt [i.e., love and closeness]. (Ruby, mother)

Ruby's suggestion that her relationships with her children had remained fundamentally close was supported by Katie's comment that:

I didn't get along with [the perpetrator], but me and my mum were always fine. (Katie, age 12)

Similarly, Alison affirmed how supportive Jane had been toward her:

There were lots of hugs and she'd make me pretend cups of tea. . . . She really did get me through it . . . me and Jane are very close. She was just, like, three and a half just before we left, and I knew that she'd seen things and she picked up on things that were happening in the house and she'd see me upset. Even then, she was very caring and very supportive to me, in a way and I do think that if I didn't have the children, I don't know how I would have actually got out of the relationship really, so I think [the children] were a massive support to me. (Alison, mother)

Jane's specific acts of support (hugs, pretend cups of tea) were simple and were similar to what young children in "normal" families might do (Oliphant and Kuczynski, 2011). In the particular context of the "things that were happening," Alison had experienced these acts as profoundly helpful. Jane's "very caring" behavior was perhaps "a massive support" because it reaffirmed to Alison that she was loved and recognized as important by her children.

Reflections on the very close and supportive relationships

The accounts of the mothers and children who had very close and supportive relationships suggest that these relationships generally increased their well-being and helped them to survive. Mother–child supportiveness took several forms, including protecting each other from abuse and comforting and reassuring each other. On an everyday level, mothers and children supported each other by spending time together when they were apart from perpetrators/fathers. Some children also engaged in more negative forms of support. These involved not sharing their feelings with their mothers because they believed it would upset them. In one case, the child supported the mother to the point of acting in a similar way to a counselor, and in other cases in more age-appropriate ways. Within all of these families, support and closeness ran alongside negative feelings such as anger and guilt in a complex mixture—perhaps with the exception of Alison and Jane, who did not report experiencing any negative feelings.

Within these families, the coercive control was either so severe for mothers and children that it brought them together, or significantly less severe, meaning that mothers and children were largely free to relate to each other as they wished. It was notable that all of the perpetrators/fathers in these families appeared to have behaved in hostile or disinterested ways toward the children. This consistent hostility or disinterestedness may have made it easier for the children to dislike perpetrators/fathers and stay closer to their mothers.

MIXED RELATIONSHIPS

The "mixed" mother–child relationships contained some closeness and supportiveness, but they also contained a significant sense of emotional distance and disconnection between mothers and children. The seven mothers and children with mixed relationships were:

Mother–child relationships under coercive control

- Akeela and her sons Vince, age 13, and Brock, age 12 (Vince and Brock's ages while Akeela and the perpetrator/father were together were 0–4 and 0–3)
- Lucy and her daughter Zara, age 11 (not interviewed) (Zara's age while Lucy and the perpetrator/father were together was 0–4)
- Violet and her children Joe, age 14, and Angel, age 12 (Joe and Angel's ages while Violet and the perpetrator/father were together were 0–5 and 0–3)
- Lauren and her daughters Grace, age 14, and Zoe, age 12 (Grace and Zoe's ages while Lauren and the perpetrator/father were together were 0–5 and 0–3)
- Isobel and her son Bob, age 12 (Bob's age while Isobel and the perpetrator/father were together was 0–9)
- Sybil and her son Jack, age 11 (not interviewed) (Jack's age while Sybil and the perpetrator/father were together was 0–10)
- Bella and her daughter Roxie, age 11 (Roxie's age while Bella and the perpetrator/father were together was 0–7)

First, the factors contributing to closeness and supportiveness in these relationships will be analyzed, and this will be followed by an exploration of the factors that contributed to strains and distance.

Closeness and supportiveness in mixed mother–child relationships

In some families, a main factor that appeared to have contributed to closeness between mothers and children was perpetrators'/fathers' hostile or disinterested relationships with their children (factor 1):

He used to hit us a lot. . . . I didn't like him and I didn't talk to him that much. I wanted to stay with my mum, because my mum is much nicer. (Vince, age 13)

In accounts such as these, perpetrators'/fathers' consistently negative treatment of the children appeared to have made it easier for those children to dislike the perpetrator/father and build a stronger relationship with their "much nicer" mother (factor 5).

In other families, the main factor that seemed to have contributed to closeness between mothers and children was the mother's ability to maintain a close emotional connection with her children (factor 4) and to spend positive time with them. For example, Lauren was able to persist in playing with her children, Grace and Zoe, while the perpetrator/father was absent from the home:

> EMMA: Why do you think you and the girls were close?
>
> LAUREN: Well, before I left him, I was only working three days a week so, while he was at work, we always spent a lot of time together as mother and daughters. When he came home from work, then [he insisted that] they were his children, not mine, so I just had to sort of step back . . . but we've always spent time together, so we would, you know, cuddle up on the sofa, reading stories, things like that.

According to Lauren, the perpetrator/father in this family had an inconsistent relationship with Grace and Zoe, sometimes appearing "fun" and playful and at other times ignoring them (factor 1). Thus, factor 1 was oriented toward mother–child distance, while factor 4 was oriented toward mother–child closeness. This combination of factors appeared to have resulted in Grace identifying positive elements in both of her parents (factor 5):

> At the time, I kind of saw my dad as the fun parent and my mum as the stable parent who always looked after us. (Grace, age 14)

Thus, although the perpetrator/father had managed to position himself as "fun" in his child's eyes, he had *not* managed (as some perpetrators/fathers do, see Bancroft et al., 2012; Monk and Bowen, 2021) to create a situation where the child had developed a negative view of their mother. Grace's mother's consistent care and the positive time that she spent with Grace appeared to have a protective effect on their mother–child relationship, enabling them to maintain some mother–child closeness despite the coercive control that they were experiencing.

Some children with mixed mother–child relationships mentioned that they had emotionally supported their mother when they perceived that she was upset, suggesting that they were attuned to her feelings and wanted to have a positive impact on her well-being:

> If I saw Mum was upset, I'd give her a cuddle or something like that, try and make her feel happy. Stuff like that really. (Bob, age 12)

> I was worried about Mum quite a lot, and I did things to try to help her. . . . When we were locked in the house, and Mum was upset, I would hug her and tell her it was going to be okay. (Roxie, age 11)

Interestingly, Roxie's mother Bella described her children as having a very disrespectful attitude toward her. Yet, Roxie's account suggested that she was still worried about her mother's welfare and wanted to support her during the distress of the perpetrator/father locking them in the house. Roxie was perhaps closer to her mother than her mother thought: the only occasion in the study where there was this difference in perception of closeness between a mother and child.

Mothers with mixed mother–child relationships made many attempts to protect and support their children with the means that were at their disposal, though perpetrators/fathers often severely restricted what they could accomplish. Sybil wanted to protect her son Jack from the perpetrator's/father's abusive parenting, but had limited ability to do so because of the perpetrator's/father's power in the home:

> Jack would beg me to do things like give him a bath because his dad used to do it so roughly, getting shampoo in his eyes and things. Sometimes, if he was in a good mood, he'd let me, but other times he would just refuse. (Sybil, mother)

Similarly, Violet described how she had argued against the way that the perpetrator/father treated their children (he often slapped them), but the perpetrator/father had reacted to her protests by "getting in her face" and intimidating her. Lauren discussed the difficult balance she had constantly strived to maintain between meeting her children's needs and not angering the perpetrator/father, as he disliked Lauren meeting anyone's needs but his own.

Lauren's description of the perpetrator provides particular nuance to the concept of domestic dictatorship with which we began chapter 1. The most obvious way in which a perpetrator/father could assert his position as a dictator, and position the mother as being under his power, was by asserting how "above" her he was. (We have just observed this type of dynamic in the experiences of Sybil and Violet, and will observe it in the experiences of Bella, Isobel, and Marie later in this chapter.) However, he could also do so by positioning himself as a needy child below her who could "throw tantrums" if overlooked or ignored. This tactic was experienced by Lauren (and by Marie, against whom the perpetrator/father pursued both techniques). In Lauren's family environment, the perpetrator/father could assert control by acting in childlike way toward her as a little emperor in the home:

> He was jealous, I think, of the children, you know, because when I had the girls the world didn't revolve around him anymore. . . . He was like a child. It was like having a third child in the house and he'd throw tantrums if we did something wrong . . . there were certain things you couldn't do. . . . You're trying to keep him happy and trying to love the children. So, it was just a case of just trying to keep him happy, but then trying to keep the girls happy as well. (Lauren, mother)

For mothers such as Lauren, experiencing the perpetrator/father playing this role, space for action was highly compressed (Kelly et al., 2014, see also chapters 1 and 3). Room for any parenting of the children was continually limited by the perpetrator's/father's demands on their time and energy. This tactic by perpetrators/fathers harmed children, and it also represented a powerful defense of their privilege within the family. If perpetrators/fathers perceived that mothers were challenging their privilege in the family context, they could respond with "tantrums," intimidation, and refusals to moderate their behavior.

Strains and distance in mixed mother–child relationships

As we have just observed, in some ways, mothers and children with "mixed" mother–child relationships could feel close to each other and try to support one another. However, there were also significant elements of strain and distance in these mother–child relationships.

In some families, a major contributor to strain and distance appeared to be the perpetrator's/father's treatment of the children (factor 1). Some perpetrators/fathers undermined mother–child relationships by being overly indulgent at times. Isobel's partner told their children that they did not have to do any homework or clean their teeth. Bella's partner allowed their children to consume excessive "junk food" and "fizzy drinks," leading to them becoming overweight. Isobel and Bella discussed feeling particularly undermined by this strategy, as it set their children against their attempts to guide or "parent" them:

> It was quite hard really, getting them to do their homework, because he was saying: "they don't need to do homework." So it was like fighting a battle with him all the time. He was sort of "the goody" and I was "the baddy," you know. I was like: "you've got to clean your teeth and have a bath and do your homework." (Isobel, mother)

> If I gave a rule to the children, he'd purposely come in and override it. I felt like I was constantly just talking, but the kids didn't listen to anything I said, so it was just horrendous really. (Bella, mother)

These perpetrators/fathers made mothers appear to children as stricter, less likable parents (factor 5). Mothers became the rule-makers and "baddies," perpetrators/fathers posing as the "fun" rule-breakers. Their acts of overriding mothers were corrosive, not just to the children's futures—dismantling the helpful regimes in areas such as dental hygiene, cleanliness, and schoolwork that mothers were attempting to construct—but also to mother–child relationships.

In some families, mothers attempted to protect children by hiding perpetrators'/fathers' abusive behavior from the children as best as they could. (Of course this was not possible in every family, as some perpetrators/fathers were determined to behave abusively in front of their children.) In families where mothers were able to hide much of the perpetrator's/father's abuse, this concealment could create emotional distance between mothers and children. Isobel described how, when her children were concerned about her well-being, she would gently rebuff their inquiries and not share with them any "detail about it":

> If I was crying and they'd say: "what's up Mum?" I'd say: "oh I'm just a bit upset today," I wouldn't go into detail with them about it. (Isobel, mother)

Mothers in this position were attempting to conceal many of their emotions and experiences from their children. The potential result was that mothers were made to feel alone and isolated within the family, becoming emotionally detached from their children, who may have had a sense that they were not being allowed into their mother's emotional world.

Several mothers discussed how perpetrators/fathers had actively attempted to undermine their mother–child relationships (factor 3) by reducing mothers' esteem within households. For Lauren, the perpetrator's/father's resentment at her status as a beloved parent led to him keeping her apart from her children while trying to convince her that they hated her:

> He would manipulate my relationship with those children, he did not like the fact that they loved me, he hated that, he hated the fact that those children loved me, so he would say things such as, "oh,

they don't love you, they hate you, you're a bad mother" and all this sort of thing . . . he would always try and keep me away from them, try and take my time away from them. (Lauren, mother)

Some perpetrators/fathers attempted to reduce the status of mothers as parents by verbally demeaning them in front of the children. This tactic could be deployed through profanities and the cultural currency of misogynistic insults about women's bodies and sexuality (Nikupeteri et al., 2021). Bella had been derided by the perpetrator/father in this way as a "f'ing fat whatever" and Isobel as "a slag or something":

His attitude toward me with the children was demeaning. Anything I said, he would override it. He'd say to the kids, "your mum's an f'ing fat whatever," there was no respect there whatsoever, he'd just totally belittle me to the kids, and treated me like a second-class citizen. (Bella, mother)

He'd call me a slag or something, and [my son] Bob would say: "my mum's not one of them," and [the perpetrator/father] would say: "well you don't know about your mum." (Isobel, mother)

The consequences of perpetrators'/fathers' open disrespect for the children's mother—how it encouraged children to form negative opinions of their mothers, and even disgust toward them—could be severe. Bella described how her children had been led by the perpetrator/father to show no respect for her, ignoring everything that she said and speaking to her "like dirt."

Another barrier to mother–child closeness and supportiveness in these families was the impacts of perpetrators'/fathers' coercive control on mothers' abilities to emotionally connect with their children (factor 4). Akeela emphasized that coercive control had caused deteriorations in her mental and physical health. By the time she separated from the perpetrator/father, she had felt "emotionally drained and physically gone." Similarly, Lucy, speaking of being "just completely gone," described how the coercive control had taken the enjoyment out of her mothering:

I was on auto-pilot as a mum. I was looking after them, but with no energy to enjoy the relationship—you're just completely gone. It's like you're outside your own body, just looking at someone else's life, just doing what you can to get by. It is like being on autopilot: You're just functioning because you have to. (Lucy, mother)

Similar to Lucy speaking of having "no energy," Sybil described how she had been "ground down" by the perpetrator's/father's coercive control over a period of years:

I didn't have enough energy for him [son]. . . . It's hard to play when you're feeling sad and anxious all the time. . . . I was so ground-down by it all. I felt like a sad little woman locked away in a house. (Sybil, mother)

Feeling too "sad and anxious all the time" to be able to play with her son, Sybil's self-esteem had suffered. Sybil described being aware of how she felt, and aware that she should play with her son, but not having "enough energy" to take positive action.

Another mother, Isobel, shared Lucy's feeling of losing her alertness to the situation. Similar to Lucy, who as we noted, described "being on autopilot," Isobel explained how she had been kept so busy dealing with the demands of her family that everyday life became "robotic":

I was working full-time at the time, so I'd get up early in the morning. I'd make sure all their uniforms were set out. . . . I'd do the lunches, I'd make sure the school bags were packed, everything was ready for school. . . . I'd go to work. [Later] I'd go and get the kids from school, come back, do their tea, homework, bath, telly. It was just robotic. I didn't have time to think about anything really; that was it. (Isobel, mother)

Isobel was coping in a way that helped her to avoid Sybil's feelings of sadness and anxiety. Yet she was trapped in a daily cycle of routines. Under the pressure of the perpetrator's/father's coercive control, her life was reduced to a demanding list of jobs that had to be performed correctly and on time. In her consciousness, as she described it, there was no "time": no time to "think" or to reflect on "anything" other than the immediate rigors of the next task to be performed. The result described here by Isobel, as with other mothers in similar situations in the study, was numbness toward her mother–child relationships. Overall, there was a sense in many families that perpetrators/fathers had harmed mothers so much that their emotional connection to their children was significantly reduced.

Reflections on the mixed mother–child relationships

The "mixed" category of relationship usually involved two or three out of the five factors being oriented toward closeness and supportiveness and two or three factors being oriented toward strains and distance. In some families, mothers and children still felt quite close to each other and were trying to support each other. Yet their relationships also contained some significant strains, and some mothers and children appeared to have felt partly, though not totally, emotionally disconnected from each other.

Behaviors and experiences in these families were very complex and multilayered. For example, a child might usually be disrespectful to their mother (behavior encouraged by the perpetrator/father), but then attempt to support and comfort her when they perceived that the perpetrator/father had particularly upset her. A child might be manipulated by the perpetrator's/father's inconsistent parenting into perceiving him in a positive way, and not understand how manipulative and abusive his behavior was, yet still also value their mother because of the love and care she gave them.

The fact that these mixed mother–child relationships did not break down completely and still retained some closeness may have become significant after these mothers and children separated from perpetrators/fathers. As chapters 6–9 will show, many of these mother–child relationships were able to improve significantly once they were no longer being harmed by the perpetrator's/father's coercive control.

VERY STRAINED AND DISTANT RELATIONSHIPS

The four families where mother–child relationships were very strained and distant were:

- Kimberley and her daughter Elle, age 14 (Elle's age while Kimberley and the perpetrator were together was 7–10)
- Charlie and her daughter Tanya, age 14 (not interviewed) (Tanya's age while Charlie and the perpetrator/father were together was 0–8)
- Marie and her daughter Leah, age 11 (Leah's age while Marie and the perpetrator/father were together was 0–10)
- Ria and her daughter Carly, age 7 (not interviewed) (Carly's age while Ria and the perpetrator/father were together was 0–3)

Notably, none of these mothers and children reported spending positive time together, or having any form of positive relationship with each other, while mothers were still with perpetrators/fathers. A main issue undermining Kimberley and Elle's relationship was that the perpetrator had manipulated Kimberley into accepting his negative treatment of the children. Kimberley and Elle's family were one of the three families in the study (the others being Ruby, Katie, and Thomas, and Ellie and Shannon) where the perpetrator was not the children's biological father. The relationship between Kimberley and the perpetrator occurred when Elle was aged 7–10. Kimberley also had other children in their teens, and a baby with the perpetrator.

This perpetrator was coercively controlling toward both Kimberley and her children. Kimberley reflected in her interview that, at the time, she had regarded this situation as a price worth paying to have a "family unit" that contained a father/father-figure (a feeling perhaps made stronger for

Kimberley as a Black woman of African-Caribbean heritage, who may have experienced pressure to avoid the racist social stigma that is often directed at Black single mothers):

> I was spending more time with him than with my children. Now I think I should have really put my children first, but because I wanted this family unit, and he kind of knew that, he just took over so he was controlling the whole family. . . . He put fear into my children regarding, like, what time they had to come home at night and dressing a certain way—"do as you're told" . . . I was thinking: "well is this normal or not normal?" [. . . Now I see that] I was more on my ex's side than on my children's side, and I should've told him to stop it, it's wrong. [. . . But back then] I just wanted this family unit to work. (Kimberley, mother)

In hindsight, Kimberley realized that her responses had increased the distance between her and her children. Furthermore, the perpetrator's coercive control was having a physical effect, leaving her drained of energy and unwell. This impact meant that, ultimately, she and her children largely stopped spending time together, reducing their emotional connection with each other (factor 4).

The situation was compounded by the fact that Kimberley's children were largely unaware that she was being abused by the perpetrator (factor 2). This lack of awareness had resulted from Kimberley's attempts to protect her children from knowing about the perpetrator's abusive behavior toward her:

> I couldn't tell my kids what was going off [happening], because my kids never saw. . . . There were a lot of things that my kids didn't see or hear because I think it's not right for a child to see or hear any arguing or violence in the house. (Kimberley, mother)

Although this concealment protected the children in some ways, and can be considered an act of support by Kimberley, it further undermined

Kimberley's mother–child relationships. The children's lack of awareness made it difficult for them to understand their mother's behavior. Rather than connecting with her or trying to support her, they disconnected from her:

> My kids started to shut down. We never used to communicate [about what was going on], because my kids never saw. . . . I think [my kids] just shut down and left me to it, and I just had to deal with it myself and end it myself. (Kimberley, mother)

In her interview, Kimberley's daughter Elle found it difficult to talk about how she had felt during this time. However, she did say that she had been "sad," and often stayed in her bedroom. There was therefore a sense that Kimberley and Elle were affected by the coercive control separately, sitting in different rooms and not communicating together about what was upsetting them.

Ria experienced similar difficulties to Kimberley in emotionally connecting with her daughter. The coercive control that Ria experienced escalated during her pregnancy, and this seemed to have contributed to Ria's sense of detachment in this mother-child relationship (factor 4):

> It was a very stressful pregnancy. It [the coercive control] got worse when I was pregnant. I felt ugly and alone. . . . I've struggled with giving Carly affection; I've struggled showing her love; I've struggled just cuddling her. (Ria, mother)

These struggles may have been exacerbated by the perpetrator/father preventing Ria from caring for Carly as a baby (factor 3). Ria recalled an incident, dating from when Carly was a newborn, in which the perpetrator/father kept Carly in the room while he and his friends took illegal drugs. Eventually Carly needed breastfeeding and began to cry, but the perpetrator/father would not allow Ria to take Carly out of the room. This incident led to Ria separating from the perpetrator/father, but he manipulated her into offering him another chance and was "in and out of

Carly's life" until she was 3 years old. Ria explained that she had given the perpetrator/father more chances partly because she was finding it so difficult to show love toward Carly:

> Every child wants consistency—they want love, and I felt I couldn't give her that love, and maybe her dad could give her more. That's where I was wrong. (Ria, mother)

This decision to allow the perpetrator/father to return may therefore be understood as an attempt by Ria to support Carly by providing her with a source of love. However, Ria indicated, the perpetrator/father proved to be incapable of providing his daughter with love. Overall, Ria's accounts suggested that she had felt extremely disconnected from Carly during the period when she was in a relationship with the perpetrator/father.

The situation experienced by Charlie was unusual in the study because two factors in her family were oriented in a way that usually contributed to closeness, yet she and her children (Tanya and a younger sibling) had very strained and distant mother–child relationships. The perpetrator/father had a consistently hostile relationship with the children (factor 1) and the children were aware of the perpetrator's/father's frequent physical violence toward their mother (factor 2). Charlie described how she and the children all experienced the coercive control:

> We were always walking on eggshells, tiptoeing around. (Charlie, mother)

The key reason why this shared experience did not contribute to closeness and supportiveness between Charlie and her children appeared to be factor 4—the perpetrator/father successfully blocked Charlie's ability to emotionally connect with the children, and factor 2—the children did not understand that what their father was doing was wrong, despite their having extensive awareness of his abuse.

Turning to factor 4 first, Charlie explained the severe coercive control exercised over her life by the perpetrator/father. He reduced her space for action to an absolute minimum, compressing her time and personal independence so tightly that she was almost sleepwalking through her life. There was no space in her mind for reflection on her mother–child relationships:

> Basically, I didn't have time to think about how it was affecting me and the kids, because I was constantly working in the house. I did long shifts at work, had to come home, bathe the kids and stuff, because he didn't do it. I wasn't allowed to be on my own. He would always take me to work, pick me back up. . . . I had to have a spotless house. . . . It was a nightmare. (Charlie, mother)

As we have illustrated, mothers such as Lauren who worked less frequently than perpetrators/fathers often made use of their time alone with the children to build and maintain closeness and positivity in the mother–child relationship. By contrast, Charlie was disadvantaged by the severity of the coercive control imposed by the perpetrator/father (factor 2), leaving her with no window of time or energy to build close mother–child relationships.

Furthermore, Charlie believed that her children had little understanding that the perpetrator's/father's abuse was wrong. In her interview she stated her view that this lack of understanding was natural for young children:

> Children don't know what's right or what's wrong, depending on how old they are. If they see their dad hit, they probably think: "that's what he should be doing." (Charlie, mother)

As we have demonstrated earlier, this was not generally the case in the interviews undertaken for the study. Many of the children who had experienced frequent physical violence against their mother did have a clear sense that it was wrong. The reason for Charlie's children's lack of understanding may have been partly connected to the way that their mother presented the situation to them. Part of Charlie's own coping strategy was to tell her children that she was "alright." Indeed, Charlie may have needed to convince herself that she was "alright" in order to cope with the perpetrator's/father's ongoing abuse:

> They knew that I was sad and hurt because of the injuries I used to have, and they were concerned about me, but I always used to say I was okay and: "I'm alright, I'm tough," and just left it at that. . . . I tried to just be strong and get on with things. (Charlie, mother)

Although Charlie was attempting to reassure her children by saying that she was resilient, this reassurance may also have had the effect of discouraging her children from supporting her. Charlie was also perhaps inadvertently encouraging them to think that it is permissible to be violent and cause injuries, providing that the victim is "tough" enough to take it. However, it is important to remember that the person primarily responsible for giving these children the message that violence is acceptable was the perpetrator/father himself.

The final mother whose very strained and distant relationships with her children we will consider here is Marie. Marie, in her interview, gave an extraordinary amount of depth and insight into what was a particularly devastating campaign of coercive control by a perpetrator/father. First, she experienced relatively little physical violence (factor 2), making it difficult for her children to understand what was happening. As Marie explained, the abuse was mostly economic, sexual, and emotional:

> He wasn't that physically violent throughout the relationship. It kicked off more when I tried to leave. It was control, anger. I walked on eggshells around him. Financially—I'm on benefits now and I've got more money now than I've ever had—he kept us short of money and he was sexually abusive [toward me] as well. So, in terms of physical violence, the kids didn't see much because there wasn't that much really. (Marie, mother)

So this was an instance of a perpetrator/father who was very controlling in ways that did not include "that much" physical violence, making the abuse less visible than it might otherwise have been to the children.

In addition to using these hidden forms of abuse—economic, sexual, emotional—that left no physical trace visible to the children or to outsiders, the perpetrator/father was systematically undermining Marie's mother–child relationships (factor 3) (see also Monk and Bowen, 2021). One strategy he used was to insult Marie in front of her children and encourage them to laugh at her. As with the choice of hidden forms of abuse, the concealment of verbal aggression in humor seemed to be part of the perpetrator's/father's strategy to pursue coercive control in a covert way that would be less easily identified and resisted:

EMMA: Did he ever say bad things about you in front of the kids?

MARIE: Yeah, definitely. He'd put a joke at the end of it, so it would seem like: "oh it's okay, he's just joking," but to the children—no, because he's constantly putting Mum down. So I think that affected them, because their level of respect for me was not very much at all. I was nothing in the relationship, so they didn't see me as worth anything I don't think.

One strategy that the perpetrator/father in Marie's family decided that he would generally *not* employ was being the "goody." (As described in chapter 4, he told Marie and the children to "shut up" if they were laughing, and was "angry and miserable and grumpy all the time.") However, he *did* choose to assume the role of the "goody" in the particular moments when Marie attempted to discipline the children:

If I tried to discipline them when I was with him, he would just override it straight away, so they didn't see that they had to listen to me. (Marie, mother)

Here the perpetrator/father was targeting the children's sense of whether they should pay attention to their mother when she was providing (helpful) discipline in their lives. More generally, similar to the situations described by Lauren, Bella, and Isobel earlier in this chapter, the target of the perpetrator's/father's attack was the bond of esteem between children and mother that underpinned the mother's status as a respected member of the household.

This perpetrator/father meanwhile gave markedly more "positive" attention to one particular child than he did to the other children. The perpetrator/father had several children with Marie (he had used reproductive coercion to pressure her into multiple childbirths), one of whom was interviewed for this study (their daughter Leah). With all but one of the children, the perpetrator/father was usually hostile or disinterested (factor 1). However, Marie mentioned that one of their children, Louise, was the perpetrator's/father's favored child and received special attention from him (factor 1). For instance, Louise played for a local sports team, and he would take her to matches and support her from the sidelines. It was not clear from Marie's interview how her mother–child relationship with Louise was affected by the perpetrator's/father's close and preferential relationship with Louise while the coercive control was still occurring. However, as we will discover in chapter 8, after Marie had separated from the perpetrator/father, Marie's relationship with Louise was more damaged than her relationships with any of her other children.

Marie also suggested that the perpetrator/father prevented her and the children from spending time together because he believed that he was entitled to Marie's attention at the expense of the children. Similarly to Lauren, Marie described the perpetrator as having a dictatorial attitude, asserting his own privilege in a kind of childish little-emperor petulance:

He wouldn't allow me and the kids to build a relationship. He wanted me to just do the basic caring for the children—clean them, put them to bed—but there was no fun, no playtime allowed. Like when Leah used to want me to sit and brush her hair—that wasn't allowed because he'd be jealous. He'd say things like: "You've spent enough attention on her, what about my attention?" (Marie, mother)

Leah confirmed in her own interview that she had barely been able to spend any time with her mother:

> The only time we were together was when we were clearing up and that. We didn't talk or anything. We didn't, like, talk to our mum, sit on the settee [sofa], watch a film or anything, and we didn't go to the shops together, except in the summer holidays. . . . It was like Mum wasn't there. . . . It felt like she wasn't there, because I didn't spend time with her or anything. (Leah, age 11)

Leah's comment that it felt as if her mother "wasn't there" suggests that she too felt emotionally disconnected from her mother (factor 4). This situation was the opposite of "being there"—being around as a warm and supportive presence—discussed in chapter 7. The mother was physically there, but did not appear to be "there" in a real, interpersonal sense as a fellow family member with whom she could share fun or mutual support.

Finally, Marie stated that the perpetrator/father had made it impossible for her to protect her children from his harmful treatment of them, making it too painful to be emotionally connected to them (factor 4). She explained how the only way she could cope with the pain of not being able to stop the perpetrator/father from hurting her son was by "blocking the kids out emotionally":

> I cut myself off emotionally from the kids and just put a kind of wall up, and like just cared for them on autopilot I suppose. . . . It was a protection thing for me—the way I got through it was putting a wall up and blocking the kids out emotionally, because he could be quite physical with my son sometimes. He'd leave handprints on him if he'd smacked him; things like that. (Marie, mother)

Marie "put a kind of wall up" between herself and the whole situation—"It was a protection thing for me." Indeed, not only had the perpetrator/father placed Marie in a position where she had no control over her children's upbringings and could not protect them, he would also force her into submission on the "odd occasion" when she tried to resist him:

> I was too frightened most of the time to say anything [about his treatment of the children]. I think I just cut myself off. On the odd occasion when I did say something, I soon shut up because he'd make it clear he was gonna carry on anyway and he wasn't gonna listen to me. (Marie, mother)

Marie believed that her children may have been worried about her at times—but, similar to Charlie, she "put on a brave face" in a way that discouraged them from expressing their concerns:

> EMMA: Do you think the kids were ever worried about you?
>
> MARIE: Sometimes if I was, like, upset and crying because of whatever he'd done, then yeah, they would be concerned then. I think I put such a brave face on it, and sort of hid it so well, that probably not, no. I don't know, like I say, we didn't communicate that much about feelings or anything, so I suppose if they had been concerned they maybe didn't voice it?

Overall, the array of coercive control tactics that the perpetrator/father deployed against Marie, and the mastery with which he deployed them, had a devastating effect on her relationships with her children. She and the children were almost entirely disconnected from each other for much of their childhoods.

Reflections on the very distant and strained mother–child relationships

In this section, we have observed the particularly damaging effects that coercive control can have on mother–child relationships. In the four families with the most distant relationships, circumstances were such that children were unable to understand that perpetrators/fathers were using coercive control against mothers, or that this was wrong. Perpetrators'/fathers' actions prevented these mothers from emotionally connecting with their children. These actions also often directly undermined mother–child relationships.

Supportiveness in these families was consequently limited. Mothers attempted to support their children by attempting to protect them from knowledge of the perpetrator's/father's abusive behavior. They often "put on a brave face" and minimized the distress they were feeling (an act that was simultaneously an act of support, part of their own coping strategies, and an obstacle to the development of understanding or supportiveness between these mothers and children). Within this climate of emotional distance, there was nothing in these mothers and children's interviews to suggest that the children had given their mothers any support during the years that they had lived under the perpetrator's/father's coercive control.

Overall, the mother–child relationships discussed in this section were the ones most damaged by the coercive control. As we will explore in chapter 8, this high level of damage to mother–child closeness was long-lasting in these four families. It was in these four families that mother–child relationships appeared to have recovered the least after separation from the perpetrator/father.

CONCLUSION

We have observed in this chapter how mother–child relationships were influenced by the "five factors" identified and discussed previously. As we have demonstrated, each factor's orientation toward closeness and supportiveness, or, conversely, toward distance and strain, influenced the level of harm caused to the mother–child relationship. For example, if the perpetrator's/father's behavior toward children was predictably hostile or disinterested (factor 1), children were more likely to prefer to be with their mother (factor 5) and the mother–child relationship was more likely to remain close. Mother–child relationships were also more likely to be close and supportive if the children were aware of the perpetrator's/father's physical violence toward their mother and if the mother was allowed more freedom to spend time with them (factor 2), if the perpetrator/father was less interested in undermining the mother–child relationship (factor 3), and if the mother had been able to maintain an emotional connection with the children (as opposed to experiencing numbness and dissociation as a consequence of the perpetrator's/father's abuse) (factor 4). The fewer breaks there were in this orientation toward closeness and supportiveness—in other words, the fewer factors there were that pointed in the other direction—the likelier it was that the mother–child relationship had remained strong.

Reflecting on such an in-depth chapter, there are many aspects to consider, and perhaps the most notable is the importance of the extent to which the perpetrator's/father's tactics were or were not hard to "read" and understand. Perpetrators'/fathers' consistent hostility or disinterestedness toward children (factor 1) tended to be easier to read for children, and sometimes led to increased mother–child closeness. Furthermore, the children who perceived clear and unambiguous abuse of the mother by the perpetrator/father (factor 2) were often the least "taken in" by him. These children were more aware of the full scale of the perpetrator's/father's abuse of the mother, and felt more passionately that the coercive control that their mother was experiencing was wrong (see also Naughton et al., 2019). Conversely, when perpetrators'/fathers' abuse was more subtle and harder to "read" (for example less violent, or disguised by humor), then children tended to be more confused and had more distant and strained relationships with their mothers.

As mentioned in the introduction to this chapter, the intention in this analysis is not to claim that only five factors exist. There are numerous other factors which fell outside the scope of this study that may have impacted on closeness and distance between mothers and children. Some of these include, for instance, whether the family was in circumstances of poverty or affluence, the educational qualifications of the parents, the existence of any pre-existing parental mental ill-health, and whether mothers had previous experiences of abuse in childhood or from other partners. As data were not gathered in relation to these topics, it cannot be known if they were also impacting on the mother–child relationships analyzed in this study.

Chapters 4 and 5 have demonstrated how coercive control perpetrators harmed the children in the study, and how the relationships between mothers and children were affected. The next chapter, following on from these discussions of mother–child relationships, will focus on the obstacles that were blocking mothers' and children's paths to recovery post-separation, and what was required for their recoveries to begin.

6

Ready to recover?

Challenges faced when breaking
free of coercive control

INTRODUCTION

With chapters 4 and 5 having demonstrated how perpetrators'/fathers' coercive control harmed the children and mothers in this study, we now re-
sume the narrative at a later point in time, when the mothers had separated
from perpetrators/fathers. It is beyond the scope of this book to focus on
mothers' experiences of deciding to leave perpetrators/fathers; the topic is
a complex one in its own right (see Anderson and Saunders, 2003). Here
we will just note that the "last straw" that led mothers to try to break free
was often (though not always) centred on the danger that perpetrators/
fathers posed to children (see also Rhodes et al., 2010):

> That final incident [perpetrator verbally abusing son] was so bad and
> so over-the-line that I knew that was the time to leave him. . . . There
> was no question those children needed to know that that wasn't ac-
> ceptable and we were going. (Ruby, mother)

Coercive Control in Children's and Mothers' Lives. Emma Katz, Oxford University Press. © Oxford University Press 2022.
DOI: 10.1093/oso/9780190922214.003.0006

He punched the glass and he showered the girls with glass and I knew then that I couldn't carry on . . . that was when I realized: "I've got to get them away." (Lauren, mother)

As Shannon got older and became more and more aware of what was going on, it was far more difficult for me to stay with him. I couldn't, when I could see it was increasingly damaging her, I couldn't stay. (Ellie, mother)

Separation brought with it the possibility of recovery. However, recovering from coercive control is far from easy. Firstly, adult and child survivors need to be able to shift their focus from emotional and physical survival to making sense of, and recovering from, their experiences (Ford-Gilboe et al., 2005; Wuest et al., 2003). To make this transition, they need to be living lives that are largely peaceful, safe, and stable. However, as we will explore in this chapter, establishing such lives can be difficult. Perpetrators of coercive control frequently have no intention of respecting their partner or family member's decision to end their relationship, and continue to terrorize and distress them post-separation (Bancroft et al., 2012; Beeble et al., 2007; Clements et al., 2021; Coy et al., 2015; Dragiewicz et al., 2021a; Dragiewicz et al., 2021b; Elizabeth, 2017; Eriksson et al., 2005; Galántai et al., 2019; Harne, 2011; Harrison, 2008; Hayes, 2017; Heward-Belle et al., 2018; Hill, 2020; Holt, 2017; Katz et al., 2020; Kelly et al., 2014; Mackay, 2018; Nikupeteri et al., 2021; Nikupeteri and Laitinen, 2015; Radford, 2013; Radford and Hester, 2006; Sharp-Jeffs et al., 2018; Stark, 2009; Thiara and Gill, 2012; Thiara and Humphreys, 2017; Wuest et al., 2003). The mothers and children in this study experienced two major and often overlapping barriers that initially obstructed them from starting to recover: (1) ongoing violence, stalking, and harassment from perpetrators/fathers; and (2) perpetrators/fathers using contact visits with children to continue harming and manipulating children and undermining mother–child relationships.

However, for most of the mothers and children in this study, these barriers did not remain in place permanently. In the majority of cases (though not all), they had lessened within a year or two of separation (though the harms perpetrators/fathers caused in that year or two were often severe and should not be underestimated, and in some cases the post-separation abuse continued for much longer). Mothers' and children's accounts suggested that there were various reasons why barriers to recovery reduced: including that mothers and children had been forced to relocate to a new area and perpetrators/fathers no longer knew where they were; that perpetrators/fathers had lost interest in them (often because they were focusing on new victims); that legal measures such as non-molestation orders had been largely successful in keeping perpetrators/fathers away, or that children had decided not to see perpetrators/fathers anymore and their decisions had been accepted.

As we will discover in this chapter, once mothers and children felt sufficiently safe and secure, they were able to begin to make significant strides with their recoveries. Aspects of these recoveries for children included gaining a healthy understanding of their experiences of coercive control (particularly by no longer blaming themselves or their mother), learning to handle feelings and emotions in positive ways, and being in a position to start to overcome any emotional or behavioral difficulties. Also important to recovery were mothers and children finding constructive ways to talk about their experiences of coercive control, and mothers feeling less guilty and more confident as parents. All of these elements of recovery strengthened mother–child relationships, enabling those relationships to become powerful sources of resilience and growth in children's and mothers' lives (Cameranesi et al., 2020; Yule et al., 2019).

The question of how mother–child *relationships* recover in the aftermath of domestic violence, explored in this chapter, is vital yet underresearched. Although some previous studies have addressed this topic, they have mostly focused on investigating the efficacy of particular interventions that help to heal mother–child relationships (see, e.g., Humphreys et al., 2011; Kong and Hooper, 2018; McManus et al., 2013; Smith et al., 2015). Widening the focus beyond such interventions to explore mother–child relationship–recovery more generally, this chapter represents a novel shift. We turn now to the issues identified by children and mothers themselves as most important to their recoveries.

OBSTACLES TO RECOVERY

Ideally, mothers' and children's recoveries would begin on the day that they separate from perpetrators/fathers. Yet this is unlikely to be the case. For recoveries to get underway and to start having transformative impacts, mothers and children need to be experiencing little ongoing abuse, to feel safe and secure, and to have largely regained control over their lives (Ford-Gilboe et al., 2005; Knezevic et al., 2021; Wuest et al., 2003). Achieving such circumstances can be exceedingly difficult, with mothers and children frequently facing many obstacles and barriers (Heward-Belle et al., 2018). As highlighted by research from multiple countries, these obstacles and barriers include perpetrators'/fathers' post-separation violence, stalking, and harassment (Fleury et al., 2000; Humphreys and Thiara, 2003; Katz et al., 2020; Kelly et al., 2014; Knezevic et al., 2021; Nikupeteri et al., 2021; Nikupeteri and Laitinen, 2015; Radford and Hester, 2006; Sharp-Jeffs et al., 2018; Thiara and Gill, 2012; Thiara and Humphreys, 2017; Woodlock, 2017), and ongoing contact between children and perpetrators/fathers (Bancroft et al., 2012; Beeble et al., 2007; Campbell, 2017; Coy et al., 2015; Dragiewicz et al., 2021a; Dragiewicz et al., 2021b; Elizabeth et al., 2012; Eriksson et al., 2005; Feresin et al., 2019; Galántai et al., 2019; Harne, 2011; Harrison, 2008; Hayes, 2017; Hill, 2020; Holt, 2017; Humphreys et al., 2019; Hunter et al., 2020; Jouriles et al., 2018; Katz et al., 2020; Laing, 2017; Lux and Gill, 2021; Macdonald, 2016; Mackay, 2018; Monk and Bowen, 2021; Radford, 2013; Radford and Hester, 2006; Stark, 2009; Thiara and Gill, 2012; Varcoe and Irwin, 2004; Watson and Ancis, 2013; Wuest et al., 2003).

Most of the mothers and children in this study experienced these problems in the first 1–2 years after separating from perpetrators/fathers, and in some cases for much longer, blocking their ability to start recovering.

Post-separation violence, stalking, and harassment

For several mothers and children in the study, ongoing violence, stalking, and harassment were major problems, and consequently many mothers and children had not had a safe place to live. Mothers' ex-partners were rarely sent to prison for perpetrating domestic violence. During the time when this study took place, only one of the 15 perpetrators was in prison. (He had received a much longer sentence than is typical for domestic violence perpetrators. This was because, during a violent incident, he had attacked police officers with a weapon.) So, despite the fact that most perpetrators/fathers had already committed multiple and repeated criminal offences, they remained at liberty, often doing "normal" jobs, free to continue their violence, stalking, and harassment of ex-partners and children.

One mother, Kimberley, described the post-separation abuse that she and her children had experienced, and the effects that it had on all of them:

> My ex has had no real consequences for his actions. . . . He used to come round and bang on the door, and be abusive on the telephone. . . . He threatened to kill me a couple of times. . . . [The kids and I] were all looking over our shoulders. . . . I used to feel paranoid and they used to feel paranoid. . . . My daughter used to check the doors all the time; even when we went on holiday she used to get paranoid and check the doors. (Kimberley, mother)

For Kimberley, one consequence of living with this constant threat from the perpetrator was that she struggled both physically and emotionally (Dutton and Goodman, 2005):

EMMA: What was it like trying to be a mother while all that stuff with your ex was going on?

KIMBERLEY: It was hard because I felt weak and I was very emotional, and I was working as well, so I found it hard communicating with my kids and having that family relationship.

Kimberley's feelings (a normal reaction to being under severe threat) were having a domino effect on her relationships with her children. Because of the communication problems that these feelings were causing, it was difficult for her to build the "family relationship" with them that she wanted to develop.

Another issue discussed by several families was how post-separation violence, stalking, and harassment prevented mothers and children from going out and having the carefree time together that children, especially, often described as important for strengthening their mother–child relationships. In each of these families, perpetrators'/fathers' post-separation coercive control had continued to deprive mothers and children of their freedom and liberty (Stark, 2007). Mothers and children described how their movements had been restrictively shaped around efforts to avoid perpetrators/fathers. For example, Isobel and her children had faced continuing threats to their safety from post-separation stalking:

> ISOBEL: The first time I pressed charges, he got a few months for battery and he got let out after just a few weeks. He started to stalk us. . . . We used to stay out of the house and away from him for as long as possible . . . then when we'd come in we'd lock the gate, pull the curtains across, lock all the doors, put the alarm on, and then go upstairs out of the way. We'd just live upstairs and then try and get out when we could.
>
> EMMA: So when did that actually end?
>
> ISOBEL: When he attacked me again and he got remanded in custody.

With this constant threat causing them to "lock the gate, pull the curtains across, lock all the doors, put the alarm on, and then go upstairs out of the way," Isobel and her children were suffering a highly constrained space for action (Kelly et al., 2014; Sharp-Jeffs et al., 2018) just at the time when they wished to begin moving forward. Under these circumstances, it was impossible for Isobel to begin to help her children to recover. Rather, the family continued to face levels of adversity, fear, and stress comparable to those experienced pre-separation.

Other families discussed the constant dangers, violence, and adversities that they faced. One mother who described such situations was Ellie, whose ex-partner subjected her and Shannon to a brutal attack post-separation:

I woke up at 3 in the morning and he's above me with a knife to my throat, so then he superglued all of the windows . . . and locked us in for two days. For nearly 24 hours Shannon was locked in her bedroom while he just repeatedly beat me and raped me. (Ellie, mother)

This harrowing attack came to an end when a concerned neighbor called the police. The perpetrator was taken into custody. However, even this did not result in long-term safety for Ellie and Shannon (then 6 or 7 years old):

When we were staying at a refuge, he'd served so long [remanded in custody] and his trial hadn't come up, so he was given bail, and we had to carry round rape alarms with us in case he attacked us. Shannon had to carry one to school in case he turned up. [. . . By the time] we moved here [current home] I wasn't very well [mental ill-health] and I didn't like going outside. (Ellie, mother)

Meanwhile, Ellie and Shannon had been inappropriately rehoused and left penniless by their local council on several occasions in the years after they separated from the perpetrator. As a result of the perpetrator's violence and this inadequate response from their local council, their safety and well-being had been undermined:

The pressure is on to leave and to be "safe" but what place are you leaving to? I've lived in some awful places for short periods of time. . . . We got moved into a place—concrete floors, there's no carpets, no bed, no furniture, no cooker, no fridge, no freezer, no washing machine, nothing, nothing. It was the 17th of December, freezing cold. . . . I stood there, I remember so clearly, crying and thinking "What have I done? What have I done? Where have I brought Shannon to?" (Ellie, mother)

The problem of a local authority's hopelessly limited interpretation of "safety" was evident to Ellie here. On another occasion, she and Shannon had been placed somewhere free from the perpetrator/father, but not even free from the more general threat of violence, let alone—given that they had no money and little comfort—giving them any freedom to live independently for a sustained period of time:

> Because [the services involved with the family decided] we "had to be safe" we were put into this bed and breakfast. [We had] no money, absolutely nothing. My daughter's asking me "where are my toys Mummy?" There's literally a mattress on the floor and then drug addicts trying to kick our door in at four in the morning and I've got my 6 year-old daughter in the room with me, so what do I do? (Ellie, mother)

Several other mothers in the study also discussed how they had been relocated by local councils into dangerous, inappropriate temporary accommodation. Mothers in this situation were experiencing a triple problem—still under attack from the perpetrator post-separation, with inadequate financial resources, and living in housing that was unsuitable for their needs. Ellie continued to care for her daughter during this frightening period, but, as with Kimberley and many other mothers in the study, she described how the strain of this post-separation experience further undermined her mental health, leaving her unable to begin recovering.

In another family, a child described his own experiences of his father's terrifying post-separation behavior:

> He used to bring some other men and try to break into the house, and me and my brothers feared for our lives because he used to smack on the doors, and I used to hide. (Vince, age 13)

This ongoing violence continued to traumatize Vince, his brothers, and their mother, Akeela.

Another child, Roxie, was also affected by her father's frightening behavior, including death threats written in places that were visible to Roxie and her siblings:

My dad's injunction ran out, he kept turning up at the house. . . . Then he wrote something on the back door, he wrote "dead bitch," and my mum tried to get it removed before we could see it, but I saw it before it got removed. (Roxie, age 11)

Perpetrators'/fathers' choices to expose children to the attacks and death threats that they were making against the children's mothers may have been particularly harmful. Children's experience of intense fear and worry about their mother's safety has been linked with "poor adjustment." This includes, in child survivors of domestic violence, "problems in virtually all spheres of functioning including social, psychological, emotional, behavioral, intellectual, and physiological domains" (Cameranesi et al., 2020, p. 117).

Roxie's mother, Bella, experienced negative and unhelpful responses from the police over this incident and over other instances of post-separation coercive control:

Within a few months of leaving him he'd start ringing up, threatening me, at one point he had someone carve death threats onto my back door. I was given a print-out of things he had said online, of him threatening to kill me. An officer came out to me and it happened to be his brother's friend and he was like: "I think everything you say is lies" and he basically called me a liar in his uniform. So I ended up having to speak to a different officer and in the end, even with that print-out, even with all threats, everything, he got a slap on the wrist, no arrest, no warning, nothing. (Bella, mother)

As Bella's account illustrates, threats by a perpetrator/father might not necessarily be taken seriously by officials: particularly in a more enclosed community where a perpetrator/father could have, or be cultivating, a powerful network of people who carry authority locally. Bella was describing the same type of situation that Kimberley discussed, where (in Kimberley's words) the perpetrator had "no real consequences for his actions." This unaccountability (see chapter 1) not only creates injustice; it is also likely to embolden perpetrators, as "weak justice responses lead perpetrators to believe they are immune to consequences. . . . When this belief is reinforced for offenders time and again, they feel free to abuse with impunity" (Hill, 2020, p. 288).

Overall, in each of these families, as well as in several others, it seemed that perpetrators/fathers had enjoyed a great deal more freedom than victims/survivors post-separation. Perpetrators/fathers had been at liberty to continue their crimes, while mothers' and children's freedoms to feel safe at home or to move about in their communities remained as distant as ever. These experiences highlight the need to intervene much more vigorously with perpetrators of coercive control, with a level of intense resolution that surpasses the resolution of perpetrators themselves to carry on abusing. As we will discover later in this chapter, in numerous families in the study, it was only when perpetrators'/fathers' threatening and violent behavior had, finally, reduced to lower levels that mothers and children could start the challenging work of recovery.

Children's contact with perpetrators/fathers

Another significant obstacle to recovery was children having post-separation contact with perpetrators/fathers. Most of the children in the study had experienced some post-separation contact with perpetrators/fathers. However, contact was usually no longer occurring at the time of interview. Sometimes this was because perpetrators/fathers appeared to have lost interest in maintaining contact, often because they had found new partners to control and were fathers/father-figures to new children and were parenting them in abusive ways (Monckton Smith, 2020a). Alternatively, it was because children had changed their minds about wanting contact and had been able to stop. Only three of the interviewed children—Leah, Angel, and Zoe—were still having contact with their father during the time when they participated in this study. These low rates of contact may not be typical of the experiences of domestic violence survivors, but may instead be a reflection of the fact that one of the study's inclusion criteria for participants was that they needed to be fairly safe from post-separation abuse. As child-contact is one of domestically violent fathers' main avenues for post-separation abuse, it is unsurprising that families who were sufficiently safe to participate were also ones where child contact had, for the most part, ceased by the time they were interviewed.

Mothers' and children's narratives suggested that, in the initial post-separation years, perpetrators/fathers had used contact visits to continue their pre-separation behaviors of abusive fathering and/or active undermining of mother–child relationships. For example, as reported by Kimberley, one perpetrator/father had used contact visits with their young son to tell him that he was not being cared for adequately by his mother:

[He said:] "Look at your clothes, your mum dresses you like a tramp, your mum doesn't even clean you properly." (Kimberley, mother)

Marie (mother of Leah and other children who did not take part in the study) described how the perpetrator/father was continuing to harm and emotionally manipulate their children during contact visits:

He's still really putting them through it emotionally. He told them that if we moved here [to our new house] they'd get shot and stabbed because that's what happens in our area, things like that, so he's really still hurting them emotionally. . . . When they come back [from contact visits], they're awful. Their behavior's really bad, and normally I'm getting verbally attacked by my son who's having a go at me. (Marie, mother)

Marie's children were having court-ordered contact with the perpetrator/ father on a twice-weekly basis, and she explained the debilitating impact of this frequency of contact:

> Contact is awful. I hate it. A few hours before it I get really stressed and panicky, and don't want to have to go to where I know he is. . . . When they come home, I have to spend the next two hours unpicking all the rubbish he's just put in their heads (exhausted sigh) and try to carry on to a normal level again. (Marie, mother)

So, for Marie, each visit was preceded by hours of feeling "stressed and panicky," and afterward she had to expend intense effort undoing the harm that it had caused. There was little respite from this destructive cycle and its cumulative effects, not only on what was "in the heads" of her children but also in what was happening to her own mental health. In this case, family court–ordered contact was undermining the resilience and recovery of the children and their mother (Cameranesi et al., 2020; Holt, 2017; Yule et al., 2019).

Other mothers gave similar statements about the difficulties caused by contact and its aftermath. Violet and Lauren, mothers of Angel and Zoe respectively, discussed how their children were left distressed or angry by contact in ways that affected their mother–child relationships:

> He'd say he was coming to see the kids and then not turn up, so I used to get the backlash from them. (Violet, mother)

> It's really hard for Zoe because she loves him because he's her dad. . . . Zoe's always kept her feelings about him bottled up, and then every now and then she'd have a meltdown and I'm the one who gets it in the neck. (Lauren, mother)

What statements such as these suggest is that mother–child relationships can continue to be strained and conflictual because of the emotional distress caused by contact, just at the time when recovery processes should be beginning.

Harm was also caused when perpetrators/fathers had moved in and out of the family's lives post-separation. This was described by two mothers whose children were no longer having contact with their father:

> Working up to the court-case was bad, and then that was over and I thought "right this is it now." And then he got out of prison, and then it was the injunction so that dragged us back a bit more. And then we were fine, and then he applied for contact and we were dragged back down again, and then that's come out okay [he was denied contact]. So we were always just alright, but these things keep dragging us down and then we'd bounce back up again. (Isobel, mother)

> The first couple of years were hard—the children had to adjust—and then when he came back into their lives everything blew up again. . . . We'd have good days, and then he'd come in and everything would blow up and I'd have to rebuild everything regarding the kids' behavior. . . . It wasn't until things died down with him that I was able to sort the kids out. Now he's not in their lives, they're on a more even level. (Bella, mother)

The statements of Isobel and Bella illustrate how the presence of the perpetrator/father in mothers' and children's lives was experienced as a "drag" or a "blowing up"—an impediment to smooth forward/upward movement. Each new intrusion set back the progress that the family had been making.

Another obstacle for mother–child relationships, also identified in previous research (see, e.g., Beeble et al., 2007; Clements et al., 2021; Feresin et al., 2019; Humphreys et al., 2006; Monk and Bowen, 2021; Radford and Hester, 2006) as well as in the "tramp" comment from Kimberley quoted earlier, was that contact gave perpetrators/fathers the opportunity to make negative comments to children about their mothers. As we are about to explore, Kimberley was not the only mother in the study who had the experience of perpetrators encouraging children to form negative views of their mothers. In the post-separation period, Isobel's ex-husband had told their son Bob that everything would be alright, and he would become the perfect father, if only Isobel would give their marriage another chance:

> He was saying he was going to take Bob for fun days out, that we were going to go on holidays, [and saying]: "everything's going to be fine now Bob, it's just your mum stopping us from being a family." (Isobel, mother)

In this upside-down, blame-shifting narrative (see also chapter 1 for discussion of perpetrators' attempts to construct upside down versions of events), Isobel was being portrayed as the obstacle to the family's togetherness. Meanwhile, it was the perpetrator/father himself who was attempting to destabilize the family, physically hurting Isobel and then (while she attempted to carry on as normal and protect the children from upset) exploiting her suffering to turn her children against her:

> [After we had separated] he promised the kids we were going to go out somewhere on my birthday and then he came and attacked me the night before and, um, threatened me with a knife and hit me so I couldn't walk properly. Then he turned up on my birthday as if nothing had happened and we had to go out walking around everywhere. I was in pain but I wasn't saying anything, but he was saying to the children "look: it's your mum who's the miserable one."

These examples indicate how perpetrators/fathers could strategically use the tactic of making negative remarks to children about their mother (see chapter 5). Blaming and demeaning the victim/survivor parent while elevating himself in the children's eyes, this perpetrator/father was driving a wedge between mother and children, creating strains in mother–child relationships (Monk and Bowen, 2021).

Perpetrators/fathers presenting themselves to their children as victims (see Katz et al., 2020), and blaming mothers for the family's problems, could confuse and distress children, preventing mother–child relationships from beginning to heal. Another mother, Ria, also described this upside-down situation—the perpetrator/father presenting her as a villain and himself as her victim:

> He would tell [daughter] Carly: "Mummy doesn't love me anymore and she kicked me out," and things like that, so he filled her head with all these lies. He's always playing the victim kind of thing and that's what's been drilled into her. (Ria, mother)

This perpetrator's/father's use of contact visits to influence Carly with a mother-blaming narrative was one of the main reasons why Ria and Carly's mother–child relationship was still strained at the time of interview, four years after Ria had separated from the perpetrator/father.

The power of perpetrators'/fathers' narratives, shifting blame onto children and mothers, could be devastating. One of Lauren's daughters, Grace (age 14), described how her father's behavior during their court-ordered contact visits had harmed her and her sister emotionally to the point where her sister had been too distressed to attend school. This perpetrator/father had used contact visits to communicate his blame-shifting narratives to his daughters:

> He'd say "oh your mum makes me cry, your mum makes me do this stuff; I can't see you because of your mum," he'd just paint such a bad picture of her . . . he blamed her and us for everything. . . . He said he was on antidepressants because I wasn't seeing him often enough. . . . I felt very small and bad. . . . [After our weekend visit with our father, my sister Zoe] would be off school most Mondays because she felt so ill, she was on the sofa being held by Mum and crying. . . . He would call [my sister Zoe] and say "you're the only one who really loves me" . . . I was just so drained and I felt like crying all the time. (Grace, age 14)

Via this blame-shifting onto "her and us" [Lauren and the children], the perpetrator/father was burdening Zoe and Grace with a feeling of responsibility for his coercive control and the post-separation distress he claimed to be feeling: hence, as Grace says, "I felt very small and bad." Moreover, by claiming he had to take antidepressant medication because Grace was not seeing him sufficiently often, as well as by saying "your mum makes me cry" and "you're the only one who really loves me," he was emphasizing to Grace and Zoe that he depended on their visits for his emotional well-being (a disturbing example of parentification). By doing so, he was instilling in Grace and Zoe a sense that they were obligated to look after his emotional needs with frequent visits—even though his behavior during these visits was agonizing to them, making them feel "ill," "drained," and extremely upset. This father's manipulation may have instilled the belief in his children that their own mental and physical health, well-being, and feelings did not matter; that what matters is that they meet another person's needs, whatever the cost to themselves. Receiving such messages could harm children in the short term and also in the longer term, including increasing their vulnerability to being abused as women in adult relationships.

The findings discussed thus far contribute to the body of research on post-separation violence, stalking, and harassment and children's contact with perpetrators/fathers (Bancroft et al., 2012; Beeble et al., 2007; Clements et al., 2021; Campbell, 2017; Coy et al., 2015; Dragiewicz et al., 2021a; Dragiewicz et al., 2021b; Elizabeth, 2017; Eriksson et al., 2005; Feresin et al., 2019; Galántai et al., 2019; Harne, 2011; Harrison, 2008; Hayes, 2017; Hill, 2020; Holt, 2017; Humphreys et al., 2019; Hunter et al., 2020; Jouriles et al., 2018; Kelly et al., 2014; Knezevic et al., 2021; Macdonald, 2016; Mackay, 2018; Monk and Bowen, 2021; Nikupeteri et al., 2021; Nikupeteri and Laitinen, 2015; Radford, 2013; Radford and Hester, 2006; Stark, 2009; Thiara and Gill, 2012; Thiara and Humphreys, 2017; Varcoe and Irwin, 2004; Woodlock, 2017; Wuest et al., 2003). In particular, these findings highlight how mother–child relationships are impacted negatively by perpetrators'/fathers' post-separation abusive behaviors.

As we have observed so far in this chapter, in these cases of coercive control-based domestic violence, *leaving did not stop the abuse.*

Perpetrators/fathers continued with their campaigns of coercive control post-separation. As Hill (2020, p. 244) explains, women can "choose to leave an abusive relationship. But the choice to end the abuse is not in their hands. If the perpetrator is hellbent on maintaining control, they don't need the victim in physical proximity: they can control them through the system. The courts, child support, social security, a rental tribunal—these can all become another weapon in their armory. For women with children, however, no system is as punishing—or as dangerous—as the family law system."

Therefore, rather than asking the classic victim-blaming question of "why doesn't she just leave?," it would be more appropriate to ask "what is the state (including, for example, national/local governments, welfare agencies, police, and legal systems) doing to make it *possible* for adult and child victims to become free of perpetrators' abuse?" In particular, the key questions are around what the state is doing to ensure that adult and child victims can:

1. Separate safely from the perpetrator/father.
2. Live a life that is truly free from the perpetrator's/father's post-separation abuse, including being free from the abuse that happens through child-perpetrator contact arrangements.
3. Have a safe and suitable place to live and have sufficient money to live on.
4. Access the support they need to recover from the psychological, physical, sexual, social, and/or economic harm that the perpetrator has subjected them to, and to build new lives.

Furthermore, it would be useful to ask: "Are the state's actions in each of these areas usually timely, sufficient, and suitable for the situation?" For many of the mothers and children in this study, the state's actions had *not* been timely, sufficient, or appropriate to protect them from months or years of perpetrators'/fathers' post-separation abuse.

As we will explore in the remainder of this chapter, once post-separation abuse did finally reduce (on average, 1–2 years after the

mothers and children had separated from perpetrators/fathers), significant improvements usually began to occur in children's and mothers' lives.
Yet it is important to note that this eventual reduction in post-separation
abuse may not be typical among the general population of survivors. It
may instead to some extent be a feature of types of families who took part
in this study: that is, families who had sought help from domestic violence
services post-separation, and were not experiencing high levels of post-
separation abuse at the time of their participation.

BEGINNING TO RECOVER

The mothers and children who participated in the study discussed several key issues that were important to the recovery of their mother–child
relationships:

- Having a safe home and sufficient money to live on
- Children breaking free from perpetrators'/fathers' distorted
  version of reality
- Addressing negative feelings and increasing mother–child
  communication
- Mothers feeling more confident as parents

One of the important sources of formal support identified by participants—
alongside refuge workers, Women's Aid outreach workers, and some
counselors, social workers, and parenting programs—were specialist
abuse-recovery programs for children and mothers with experiences of
domestic violence, which followed what is known as "the Ontario model."
Approximately half of the participants in this study had used these
programs, based on a child-centered, psychoeducational model first developed in the city of London in Ontario, Canada. Use of these programs
is much less than 50% in the general population of survivors; the relatively
high use of the programs by participants in this study reflects the fact that

organizations providing these programs were among those that assisted with the study's participant recruitment. In the Ontario model, children work with a group of peers and adult facilitators over approximately 12 weeks to discuss their experiences of domestic violence, find healthy ways of expressing feelings, overcome feelings of self-blame, and develop safety plans. As part of such programs, a concurrent group is also held for the children's mothers, to help mothers to support their children's engagement in the sessions.

In the United Kingdom, Ontario-based programs (i.e., programs that follow the Ontario model to a large extent) run under various names, including CEDAR (Children Experiencing Domestic Abuse Recovery) (Sharp et al., 2011), the Community Group Programme (Nolas et al., 2012), and DART (Domestic Abuse: Recovering Together) (McManus et al., 2013; Smith, 2016; Smith et al., 2015; Smith et al., 2020). Henceforth, all of these programs will be referred to collectively as "Ontario-based programs," rather than using their various names. This will help to avoid confusion in this and subsequent chapters, as participants' experiences of these programs are discussed.

Having a safe home and sufficient money to live on

For participants, having a home that was safe to live in was a prerequisite for recovery. However, "safety" in the context of the home did not simply involve the absence of the perpetrator/father. It required a domestic space that was suitable for mothers' and children's needs, and for them to have sufficient money to live on once there (Kelly et al., 2014; Moulding et al., 2021).

For these participants, the turning point in recovery had only arrived when safety was truly achieved. One mother, Ellie, had been through a number of particularly harmful experiences before finally achieving this safety. Ellie's and her daughter's recoveries had only been able to start three years post-separation, when they were finally given a safe and suitable permanent home. This moment was the beginning of recovery: Once in a suitable home they had gradually been able to start engaging in basic activities such as "venturing out", making friends, and visiting friends' homes:

> She was 6 when we left and she's 10 now. . . . We stayed with my sister, we stayed in a maisonette, a hotel, a safe house, we stayed in lots of different places. We moved to the women's refuge, and then a year ago we moved in here [current home]. So since she's been 6, her life's been up and down, up and down. She's had no normality except for this last twelve months [when we got our current home]. Well, even then she wouldn't go outside to play. And it's only probably in these last 5–6 months that she's started to venture out and do more things. And I've sort of made a couple of really good friends that we can go and visit; she's become friends with their kids. So it's really only in about the last six months that we've started to gain some sort of normality. (Ellie, mother)

Another mother, Kimberley, also identified the time when safety was achieved as a turning point in her and her daughter's recoveries:

> [Post-separation] he used to come round and bang on the door, and be abusive on the telephone. I had to stop him from coming round to the house [non-molestation order]. . . . Since he hasn't been around, it's been better. I sat down with my daughter and said: "something's happened that was wrong, what he did was wrong." She still doesn't say much, but our communication is better than it was before. (Kimberley, mother)

For Kimberley, safety had been achieved when she had been able to "stop him from coming round to the house." Only then had she been able to "[sit] down with my daughter" to explain the situation in a calm way and start the journey towards better mother–child communication.

Meanwhile, children in the study who had been suitably rehoused spoke with great positivity about their new homes, and the features and atmosphere that made these new domestic spaces feel safe and secure:

I knew it was safer because we had all builders coming in and stuff and we have, like, a fire-proof letterbox and stuff, so it's cool. (Bob, 12)

This may not be a mansion, but I like it. I love it here. It's nice and cosy. It's just better and the best. (Shannon, 10)

In different ways, these children expressed the emotional benefits of living somewhere where they felt safe.

The roles played by housing in children's and mothers' recoveries is an underresearched area, but has recently been considered by Bomsta and Sullivan (2018). In their US study, they found that housing stability can have multiple benefits for children and mothers with experiences of domestic violence. Among their participants who were in stable housing, children felt happier and more comfortable, showed improved behavior, and performed better academically. Bomsta and Sullivan's findings also suggested that positive emotional reciprocity developed between children and mothers who achieved housing stability. Children were less stressed because their mothers were less stressed, and the reverse was also true. Living in a safe neighborhood has also been linked to increasing resilience in child domestic violence survivors (see Cameranesi et al., 2020). These findings, alongside the findings presented in this chapter, suggest the importance to policymakers of taking a holistic approach to children's and mothers' housing needs. Child and adult survivors of coercive control/domestic violence do not just need to be safe "on paper." To be able to recover and thrive in their new lives, they need to be living in conditions that meet their practical and psychological needs.

Returning now to the present study, by the time of their interviews (an average of five years post-separation) most participants were fairly safe. Ongoing abuse from perpetrators/fathers had often been particularly intense for the first 1–2 years after separation, and then reduced. This is not to say that the mothers and children felt totally safe. They were still worried about certain possibilities. For example, they were concerned about encountering the perpetrator/father while out walking or driving locally, or were afraid that he would track them down in their new homes.

For most survivors, waiting for complete safety, in the home or outside it, is not an option. Sadly, the legal frameworks and systems that currently exist in Western countries for dealing with domestic violence and coercive control are unlikely to make mothers and children 100% safe from perpetrators (see, e.g., Hester, 2006; Kelly et al., 2014; Knezevic et al., 2021; Sharp-Jeffs et al., 2018; Stark and Hester, 2019). So, when discussing the conditions needed for recovery, the question (unjustly but pragmatically) becomes: "How safe is safe enough for recovery to happen?"

It is not possible to provide a precise answer to this question that applies to all of the families in this study: They had different experiences. Yet the overall findings suggested that, to make significant progress with their recoveries, these mothers and children needed to feel sufficiently safe to redirect their energy away from emotional and physical survival. Their lives needed to feel significantly less frightening, upsetting, and unpredictable, and significantly more peaceful, positive, and secure, and the more this was the case, the better.

Children breaking free from perpetrators'/fathers' distorted versions of reality

It is well known that perpetrators of coercive control manipulate and confuse their partners using various tactics of denial, minimization, justification, and "gaslighting" (Cavanagh et al., 2001; Harne, 2011; Towns and Adams, 2016; Williamson, 2010). Perpetrators' aim in doing so is to surround their partner with a distorted version of reality where (1) they did not "really do anything that bad"; and (2) they were not really responsible for their own behavior. Perpetrators act to trap their partners within this harmful version of reality, causing a partner, for example, to believe that "it was my fault really, I'm just so useless," or "he only acts this way because he loves me so much." As Cavanagh et al. (2001, p. 695) explain, domestically violent men "seek to impose their own definitions upon their partner and thereby neutralize or eradicate her experience of abuse and control." However, until now much less attention has been paid to how *children* are affected by this behavior.

The descriptions of several participants in the study suggested that children had indeed been caught in perpetrators'/fathers' distorted versions of reality. For example, Isobel described how, as part of his coercive control, her ex-husband had told their children that he was blameless for the family separation and that she was to blame (see earlier). One of their children, Bob (then 9 or 10 years old), had reconciled the version of reality that his father was imposing on him with his own lived experience by blocking out his memories of his father's abusiveness to the point where he no longer remembered key events that had occurred just a year or two previously. It was only after Bob had undergone counseling sessions that he was able to overcome these memory-blocks and re-engage with his memories of his fathers' abusive actions. Similarly, Grace described how she had been unable to perceive that people were attempting to help her until a counselor had enabled her to identify her father's manipulative behavior:

> I used to say sometimes, years ago, that I wanted to go and live with my dad. . . . I stopped seeing him a couple of years ago. . . . I'm a lot closer to my mum now. . . . I've spoken to two counselors. One gave me these exercises to help me see what Dad was doing [being emotionally manipulative], and how people around me were trying to help me. That helped my confidence; it helped me to realize that I could talk to people. (Grace, 14)

Counseling helped Bob and Grace to make sense of their fathers' behavior. Realizing that their father was abusive, and understanding that their relationship with him was causing them distress, was an important step in these children's recoveries. Both Bob and Grace had then made the decision not to have any further contact with their father, a decision they discussed positively in their interviews.

As noted earlier in this chapter in our discussion of perpetrators'/fathers' blame-shifting narratives, several participants also explained how children had been drawn by the perpetrator/father into blaming their mother and/or themselves for their father's coercive control. Post-separation, it was therefore important for these children to be supported to escape those blame-shifting narratives and to develop healthier understandings of coercive control. These supports eased tensions in children's mother–child relationships, and promoted children's and mothers' resilience and recoveries:

> I think [the Ontario-based program] did Bob the world of good. . . . It sort of gave him an understanding so we could talk about things, like a common sort of bond. . . . It sort of helped me as well, because I knew that he got why things had happened. . . . We're at a stage now where the children understand what's happened, and it's not their fault or mine. (Isobel, mother)

> Shannon used to say to me: "It's your fault" but now she knows that's it's not my fault, and that's because of the education thing that she's been through [with the Ontario-based program] helping her to understand. (Ellie, mother)

> Carly didn't understand why she couldn't see her dad, and it was really difficult because I didn't want to say anything bad about him to her. . . . Recently my sister explained to her: "Your daddy hurt Mummy, and it upset you." . . . Hearing it from somebody else was quite upsetting for Carly at the time, but it's eventually got there [been beneficial]. I think now is definitely the time to start talking to her about it more. (Ria, mother)

These accounts suggest that, like mothers themselves, children were affected by perpetrators'/fathers' denial of responsibility and tendency to blame those around them for their behavior (see also Moulding et al., 2015). Consequently, children needed support to break free from the distorted versions of reality created by perpetrators/fathers that shifted blame onto themselves and/or their mothers. Receiving this support and rejecting those false realities reduced the underlying feelings of anger that some children had developed toward their mothers, and strengthened children's and mothers' relationships with each other. These findings indicate that, ideally, more professionals should be trained to help child survivors to break free of perpetrators' distorted versions of reality. Skills around how to help children overcome victim-blaming/self-blaming could be incorporated into future training packages on domestic violence/coercive control for professionals who regularly work with children and young people, including counselors/psychologists and teachers.

Dealing with feelings and increasing mother–child communication

As we have noted throughout this chapter, separating from a perpetrator/father is no "magic wand" for problems; and that fact also applies to issues around feelings and communication. Domestic violence often stifles communication between mothers and children (Humphreys et al., 2006, 2011; Lapierre et al., 2018; Mullender et al., 2002), and is associated with emotional and behavioral difficulties in children (Fong et al., 2019; Holt et al., 2008; Hungerford et al., 2012). These issues were being encountered by mothers and children in this study as part of their recovery processes in the months and years after separation. One mother, Ellie, powerfully described how difficult these aspects of recovery are, and how families often need help to accomplish them:

> You need to be able to say what you want to say, but in the right kind of way to each other. If the child is angry they've got to be able to say: "Look Mum; I'm really angry: You've done this, this, and this," and the thing is, the truth really hurts, doesn't it? Getting

to that point is bloody difficult, and you need a lot of help. (Ellie, mother)

Several of the mothers and children discussed receiving help for this difficult and painful task via abuse-recovery programs. Receiving these supports had multiple benefits for many of the mothers and children in this study. Participants spoke about how they had learned to express their feelings (something strongly discouraged by perpetrators, who attempt to silence all feelings except the ones that please them), thereby reducing their arguments and communicating better.

In particular, the supportive environments present within abuse-recovery programs had allowed for the safe expression of feelings that had built up over a number of years. A cathartic sense of release is evident in Ellie's description of her daughter Shannon's engagement with this opportunity:

The way [the Ontario-based program] worked with Shannon, she was able to express all of her feelings and her anger in different ways. . . . They had one day where they could just do whatever they wanted with paints to express how they felt about the [perpetrator] and about life, and she just sort of spattered all these different colors but mainly red on this big wall, and she loved doing that. (Ellie, mother)

Other mothers also spoke of how professional interventions had helped children to address, and let go of, the emotions built up by their experiences of coercive control:

Our communication is better than it was before; [my daughter's] confidence has built up much, much better because she goes to counseling and [the Ontario-based program] and they kind of helped her get her emotions out, what she was bottling up inside. (Kimberley, mother)

Ready to recover? 209

The kids saw a Women's Aid worker; she went into their school and worked with them on ways of dealing with their emotions and the kind of flare-ups they were having. . . . They've really calmed down now. We still argue, but they're like different kids compared to how it was. (Bella, mother)

Collectively, these statements touch on the idea of children being helped to exhale the poisonous, combustible, corrosive feelings that they had previously been "bottling up inside." The children had emerged from this process calmer and more confident.

The transformational process of releasing these feelings was entwined with an improvement in these children's relationships with their mothers. Being supported to understand their experiences of coercive control, many mothers and children began to feel more confident in discussing it together without upsetting each other:

[The Ontario-based program] helped, because, you know, you wanna say things to the kids and the kids wanna say things to you but you don't want to, like, upset them and set it all off again. So it was sort of like a big black ball that's sort of there, but going to the program has helped us come to terms with it. (Isobel, mother)

We were always close—it's never been a case of, you know, not being—but [the Ontario-based program] opened up communication on what happened; it helped her to understand more. I think it sort of consolidated everything that's gone on, and helped us to understand it. (Lucy, mother)

Through communicating constructively with each other, children and mothers were addressing their feelings, opening up and deconstructing the "big black ball" of "everything that's gone on," and moving forward with their recoveries. (A note for readers: In the absence of an Ontario-based program in their local area, mothers and practitioners could use the workbooks *Talking to My Mum: A Picture Workbook for Workers, Mothers and Children Affected by Domestic Abuse* (designed for use with younger children) or *Talking about Domestic Abuse: A Photo Activity Workbook to Develop Communication between Mothers and Young People* (designed for use with older children) by Skamballis et al. (2006a, 2006b). These workbooks, which are available to purchase online, are designed to help children to open up with their mothers about their experiences of domestic violence (Humphreys et al., 2006). These workbooks may not provide all of the benefits of an Ontario-based program, but they could still be a useful aid to recovery.)

It was not only children who needed supports to deal with their feelings. One of the mothers, Ellie, discussed how she had been helped to move beyond feeling extremely guilty that her daughter had lived with the perpetrator's/father's coercive control (see also McCarry et al., 2021):

> My daughter and I are far more open with each other, and I think that's got a lot to do with the fact that we went to [the Ontario-based program] which was absolutely fantastic. . . . I'm able to be more comfortable now. . . . I do still feel guilty and know that I shouldn't, but I do, but nothing in comparison to how it crippled me before. So I'm able to answer painful questions that she puts to me about the past, because I have to, I need to. It's not easy, but I think that if you can get that honesty with each other then it does bring you closer together. (Ellie, mother)

Ellie's words highlight that mothers who are feeling intense guilt over what their children have experienced may have difficulty engaging with children's expressions of anger toward them. The provision of help to reduce such guilt is therefore another important factor in recovery. Without such supports, mothers may understandably avoid the open communication with children that may be necessary to improve the mother–child relationship. With supports, however, mothers are better placed to "hear" their children, and more able to support their children to understand— and move on from—the past.

Mothers feeling more confident as parents

After years of being subjected to abuse, many of the mothers in the study had begun their recoveries with very little confidence in their abilities as parents. This lack of confidence was to be expected given the way that perpetrators of coercive control attack their target's sense of self-worth and sense of their own capabilities, making them feel "stupid," "useless," and dependent on the perpetrator (Matheson et al., 2015; SafeLives, 2019). However, as mothers' recoveries progressed and they started to feel more generally self-confident and relaxed, they tended to gain more confidence in their parenting skills:

> [I think my relationships with the kids has improved because] I've probably just chilled, I've just learnt to just chill out and not worry so much, and everything's just calmed down. (Lucy, mother)

> I've definitely grown as a person; I've come out of my shell. Now I'm more open and more able to have a laugh with the kids. (Bella, mother)

Some mothers also discussed how they had gained new parenting skills that had made them more able to support their children:

> I did the Triple P parenting course: I thought I was a bad mother, but [through the course] I worked out that I wasn't (laughs); it was him saying that I was. But now I've got like a toolkit, so if anything does arise I can put it into place, like talking to the kids and stuff, all that. Like you have to look at them when you're talking, and I've heard somewhere that teenagers just need a hug so I keep trying to get Tom [teenage child] up in a corner and give him a cuddle which doesn't always go to plan! (Isobel, mother)

> A lot of women, they're "on the go" all the time, they don't want to sit down, because then they'll think about all the abuse and stuff, so

they'll keep themselves busy. But now I'm patient, and I will stop in my tracks and I will sit down and I'll make sure that I am listening and hearing what [my daughter's] saying to me and I'll talk back to her, you know, communicate. (Ellie, mother)

By pausing to engage and listen, or by showing affection, these mothers were successfully strengthening their mother–child relationships. The extra confidence that they were showing in their interactions, such as laughing more, or staying calm when problems arose, was helping them to meet their children's emotional needs. Empowering mothers with confidence as parents was therefore another important factor in children's and mother's recoveries from coercive control.

CONCLUSION

We have demonstrated in this chapter that there were many keys to recovery. A vital starting point was mothers and children having a home that felt safe to live in, where they were not "under siege" from post-separation violence and abuse, or being continuously distressed by perpetrators'/fathers' behavior. Once this first building block was in place, mothers and children could redirect their energy away from emotional and physical survival and toward recovery. An important aspect of recovery from coercive control for children was breaking free from the denial, minimization, justification, and "gaslighting" being fed to them by perpetrators/fathers. For recovery, it was also important for children to be able to access supports for any emotional and behavioral issues that they were experiencing as a consequence of living with coercive control, as well as for mothers and children to be able to communicate with each other effectively, and for mothers to feel more confident as parents. As each of these steps towards recovery were achieved over time, children's and mothers' well-being in their everyday lives appeared to increase substantially.

Mothers' and children's recoveries were deeply intertwined. When children made progress with their recoveries—for example by communicating more openly rather than "bottling up" their feelings and learning how to express anger in healthy ways—then the children's progress also helped mothers to move forward. Similarly, when mothers received supports to reduce their feelings of guilt and to feel more confident in talking to their children about the past, these supports benefited not only them but the children too.

As mother–child relationships strengthened, they became an important source of positivity, resilience, and growth in children's and mothers' lives. This strengthening was particularly assisted by Ontario-based programs that worked with both children and mothers. This is in keeping with the findings of Cameranesi et al. (2020) that community services tend to play important roles in the resilience of families. By increasing "family functioning" and "positive family relationships" (Cameranesi et al., 2020, p. 130), Ontario-based programs were helping to create mother–child relationships that became sources of resilience for children. However, mothers and children in some areas had no access to an Ontario-based program, either because one had not been developed in their town/city, or because their local program had closed due to funding cuts. Some mothers in this study reported with anger and sadness that the program in their area, that they had attended and benefited from a year or two previously, had since been closed due to a lack of funding (see also McCarry et al., 2021). The findings of this study indicate that the funding of such programs should be prioritized, as they made highly valuable contributions to some child and adult survivors' resilience and recoveries. They could also substantially reduce various emotional, behavioral, and relationship difficulties that may otherwise cause long-term problems (see also Howarth et al., 2015; Howarth et al., 2016; McManus et al., 2013; Nolas et al., 2012; Sharp et al., 2011; Smith, 2016; Smith et al., 2015; Smith et al., 2020).

In the next chapter, we will explore how mothers and children helped each other to recover using their own agency, emotional intelligence, influence, and skill. We will learn how children and mothers can play important roles in each other's recoveries, and how their support for each other is built into their everyday lives and ordinary interactions.

7

Helping each other to recover

Mothers' and children's strategies

INTRODUCTION

In this chapter we will learn more about the strengths, abilities, and agency of mothers and children who have survived coercive control-based domestic violence, as we explore rare insights into the positive aspects of their post-separation lives. Recovery processes within mother–child relationships are still under-researched, although some progress has been made gradually over the past 20 years (see, e.g., Goldblatt et al., 2014; Humphreys et al., 2011; Kong and Hooper, 2018; Wuest et al., 2004). Understandings of how children develop strategies for assisting their mothers' recoveries – into which this chapter delves in depth – are almost non-existent.

Exploring children's strategies for assisting their mothers' recoveries means revisiting the concept of children's agency discussed in chapter 2. As summarized in that chapter, children's "agency" refers to their capacity to act independently and to influence the world around them. It is well-established that children have agency in responding to domestic violence as individuals, for example taking individual action to keep themselves safe, calling the police, or intervening in a violent incident (see, e.g., Callaghan and Alexander, 2015; Chanmugam, 2015; Øverlien and Hydén,

Coercive Control in Children's and Mothers' Lives. Emma Katz, Oxford University Press. © Oxford University Press 2022.
DOI: 10.1093/oso/9780190922214.003.0007

2009). However, what is less often explored is children's *relational* agency within post-separation mother–child relationships. As we will observe in this chapter, the children in this study exercised this agency not through dramatic acts, but through small acts of support in everyday life such as treating the mother to a gift or watching a movie with her. However, it is important to stress (again revisiting a theme from chapter 2) that this agency did not occur as "parentification." As noted in chapter 2, parentification means "a functional and/or emotional role reversal" where the child supports the parent but the parent does not support the child (Hooper, 2007, p. 217). Rather, the agency explored in this chapter was bilateral (Kuczynski et al., 2003). Support was given in both directions, from child to mother and from mother to child.

This chapter focuses on two different kinds of mother–child supportiveness. The first part of the chapter examines the supports taking place between mothers and children that were directed toward recovery from coercive control:

- Reassurance about the past, present, and future
- Mothers helping children to understand coercive control
- Mood-lifting and helping to overcome emotional and behavioral impacts
- Rebuilding each other's confidence
- Communicating openly with each other
- Showing affection and spending time together
- Children indirectly supporting their mothers' recoveries

The second part of the chapter will explore the more general supports that mothers and children gave to each other, not directly related to coercive-control recovery:

- Supporting each other through upsets or tiredness
- Being attentive to each other's feelings

- Children's practical support for mothers
- "Being there"

These two different kinds of supportiveness, though somewhat distinct, often reinforced each other. For example, a mother's experience of receiving general support from a child, such as the child noticing her tiredness and making a cup of tea, could indirectly assist her recovery. Her well-being, and hence her recovery process, could be enhanced to a certain extent by being treated with kindness and consideration in such a way (the opposite of how perpetrators/fathers had treated mothers). Similarly, children felt comforted and taken care of when mothers expressed that they were "there for" them, and would help them with any problems they were having. For children, the feeling of being supported by their mothers was a "safety net"; it enabled children to become more confident and relaxed when attempting new activities, in contrast to the atmosphere of fear and tension that pervaded family life when perpetrators/fathers had been present.

Many of the children and mothers in the study played key roles in helping one another to recover. However, it is important to note that not all mothers and children were supporting one another to the same extent: Some mother–child relationships were more supportive than others post-separation. So, while several mothers and children were providing each other with most or all of the forms of support listed earlier, some mothers and children were providing each other with only a few, and some children did not appear to be supporting their mothers at all. The mother–child relationships that were the most mutually supportive were the ones where mothers and children were no longer experiencing major obstacles to recovery, and had been able to engage, when necessary, with professional help to strengthen their mother–child relationships. Other mothers and children in the study had not yet reached this point, and were therefore less able or unable to support each other. This issue is discussed in detail in chapter 8.

Helping each other to recover

MOTHER–CHILD SUPPORTS DIRECTED
TOWARD RECOVERY FROM COERCIVE CONTROL

Reassurance about the past, present, and future

Reassurance about the past, present, and future was very important to the mothers and children in the study. It played an important role in recovery, providing a good illustration of the significance of the recovery work that occurred through their mother–child relationships. Future-centered reassurance involved mothers and children reducing each other's fears and worries about what was to come and encouraging each other to think optimistically:

> Whenever I'm upset, [Mum will] give me a cuddle and tell me things are going to be alright. It's helped me get through things. (Grace, age 14)

> The most helpful things [Shannon has] said to me is that she loves me and not to worry about the future. (Ellie, mother)

Reassurance about the past, by contrast, involved dealing with feelings of confusion and self-blame. Central to this reassurance was confirmation that the coercive control was not the mother's or child's fault. When children were asked: "what are the most helpful things that your mum has said to you?," several emphasized their mother telling them that they were not to blame:

> A long time ago, I used to think that my parents' divorce was my fault; my mum told me it wasn't. (Grace, age 14)

> EMMA:　　　　What do you think are the most helpful things your mum has said to you?
> BOB (AGE 12):　That it's not my fault.

Such reassurance about the past appeared to have greatly helped some children, removing a source of confusion and worry. This is in line with the finding of Miller et al. (2014) that the absence of self-blame is a significant predictor of resilience in child survivors of domestic violence.

Reducing self-blame was not only useful for children; it helped mothers too. Some children reported that they had reassured their mother that she should not feel guilty or to blame about what had happened:

> Sometimes she'd say she felt like a bad mum because she moved us away from our dad, and I'd tell her she shouldn't feel guilty. (Grace, age 14)

For children, reassuring mothers about the past was an advanced form of support. It required children to comprehend that their mother was experiencing distressing memories, and understand how to respond in an effective way. This support from children appeared to be beneficial, providing mothers with validation and relief.

Overall, in their reassurances about the past and future, these mothers and children perceived one another as agentic, and were influenced by each other's opinions. This fits with the bilateral model of parent–child relationships proposed by Kuczynski (Kuczynski et al., 1999, 2003; Kuczynski and De Mol, 2015—see chapter 2). One mother, Violet, cried during her interview when she described an occasion when her children had told her that their father's behavior was not her fault. Her emotion suggested that she viewed her children as having their own separate opinions about the coercive control, and valued the reassurance that they gave her.

Reassurances about the present, mainly provided by mothers, often focused on promoting a feeling of safety in the post-separation phase. After leaving perpetrators/fathers, many children in the study experienced fears over their own and their mothers' safety. Several children carried out obsessive checking of doors and windows, and were frightened to sleep alone or let their mother out of their sight (Katz et al., 2020). In cases where mothers and children were living in safety, reassuring children that these behaviors were unnecessary was relatively easy for mothers. However, in the face of ongoing harassment and/or violence from perpetrators/fathers, mothers faced a difficult task. One mother, Ruby, had been raped by her ex-partner after separating from him. (Notably, this perpetrator had not committed any major acts of violence pre-separation, highlighting how abuse can increase post-separation as perpetrators seek to punish and regain control. Post-separation rape has been found to be most common among perpetrators who were controlling but not particularly violent pre-separation, see Stark and Hester, 2019.) Ruby's children became aware of the rape through police visits to their home, though ultimately the police did not arrest the perpetrator after he claimed that the rape was consensual. Ruby described how she had felt that this attack and the subsequent lack of justice had destroyed her children's sense of safety, and how she had therefore attempted to frame it for them in a way that reassured them:

> I told them: "the worst thing has happened; I'm still here, you're still here, and we're going to get through this. It's not killed me, we're still here and it's not going to happen again." (Ruby, mother)

Ruby believed that this strong reassurance had been largely successful in helping her children to cope in the present, and to continue moving forward with their recoveries in the months following the attack (though the children remained horrified by the lack of justice in this case, something that Ruby was powerless to remedy).

Helping children to understand coercive control

Several mothers in the study helped their children to make sense of their experiences of coercive control. Mothers' support often complimented and enhanced the formal supports that children were receiving from specialist domestic violence organizations. For example, Isobel discussed how an Ontario-based program (McManus et al., 2013; Smith et al., 2015; Smith et al., 2020; Smith, 2016—see also chapter 6) had helped her son Bob to understand that the perpetrator/father had been responsible for his own actions. She described how she had reinforced this message to Bob and her other children:

> I think one of the most helpful things I've said is that it's not their fault and it's not my fault either. Their dad chose to do what he did, and it didn't matter what we said or did; it wouldn't have changed him, he'd have carried on doing it. And the best thing for us was to stay away and to keep him away, basically. And that it wasn't us that sent him to prison—it was a judge—and, um, that he'll always be their dad, and it's okay for them to love him. (Isobel, mother)

These messages from Isobel to her children demonstrate her awareness of her children's concerns: their worries about whether they could have changed the perpetrator/father to make him a better person, and whether it was them who had sent him to prison. Bob's statement in his own interview that Isobel had helped him by telling him that the coercive control was "not my fault" (see earlier) suggests the effectiveness of her support.

Another mother, Ellie, described a similar situation. Initially, an Ontario-based program had helped her daughter Shannon to overcome the belief that Ellie was to blame:

> Shannon used to say to me: "It's your fault, why did you have him back?" but now she knows that's it's not my fault, and that's because of the education thing that she's been through [with the Ontario-based program] helping her to understand. (Ellie, mother)

After this breakthrough, Ellie had continued to support Shannon to further understand coercive control by answering Shannon's ongoing questions:

> Now I'm able to answer painful questions that she puts to me, because I have to, I need to. It's not easy, but I think that if you can get that honesty with each other, between mums and their kids, then it does bring them closer together. (Ellie, mother)

This dialogue highlights the ongoing bilateral process taking place between Ellie and Shannon, through which mother and child were becoming closer. Ellie supporting Shannon to understand coercive control was creating a climate of honesty as well as understanding, creating a steady upward spiral of mutual supportiveness in this mother–child relationship.

Another mother, Ria, had asked her sister to help improve her daughter Carly's understanding of the coercive control experienced by the family. In this family, the mother–daughter relationship was too damaged for Carly to listen to her mother. However, Ria was aware that, for their relationship to improve, Carly needed to gain a better understanding of the coercive control, and so had enlisted her sister's help. Ria believed that this approach had been beneficial:

> She used to have it that it was me—I was stopping her dad from seeing her, because he would tell her: "Mummy doesn't love me anymore and she kicked me out," whereas I—I've never said anything bad about him. . . . Recently my sister explained to her: "Your daddy hurt Mummy, and it upset you, and maybe when you reach 16 if you want to see your dad, I'm sure your mum will support you in that." I think that hearing it from somebody else was upsetting for Carly at the time, but it's eventually got there [been beneficial]. . . . Now she's beginning to understand why she can't see him. (Ria, mother)

Ria believed that hearing the truth from a third party had been helpful for Carly. Previously, while Ria had refrained from "saying anything bad about" the perpetrator/father, the perpetrator/father had been telling Carly that Ria was to blame. So Carly (who was only 3 years old when her parents separated) knew that her mother's stance was that she could not see her father, but she did not know why her mother was taking this stance, and was understandably confused and angry. Being eventually told by Ria's sister that "your daddy hurt Mummy and it upset you" had been initially distressing for Carly. However, in the longer term it had helped Carly to make sense of what had taken place in her own past, and to understand why things were as they were in her present.

Some children demonstrated agency in deciding what to know and what *not* to know about the past. One of Lauren's daughters, Zoe, had actively decided that she did not want to be given the full information about the coercive control. Zoe was still having contact once a month with her father when interviewed. Having been very young when her father and mother had separated, she had few memories of what had occurred. Zoe explained that she preferred not to have complete knowledge about her father's behavior. Otherwise, she believed, she would not want to see him again. She was therefore grateful to her mother for not deepening her understanding of the coercive control:

> [What are the most helpful things Mum's said?]: (Pause) I think it's more about what she hasn't said, because if I knew everything Dad had done I wouldn't want to see him anymore. (Zoe, age 12)

In Zoe's view, therefore, her mother's incomplete disclosure was a supportive act.

Zoe and Grace also discussed how they valued Lauren's stance of respecting their agency regarding contact with the perpetrator/father:

> [Mum supports me because] she lets me see him and say, if it was like 11 o'clock at night, I remember Mum letting me ring Dad at that time one night because I was worried, I had like this nightmare that he died or something, so she let me ring him. So even if she doesn't like him and she does say stuff about him sometimes, she's supportive. . . . And even though [my sister] Grace has stopped seeing Dad now, Mum still says to her: "if you want, you can go back and see him." (Zoe, age 12)

Grace similarly confirmed that her mother had respected her personal agency in relation to contact:

> [Positive tone of voice] Mum's always told me it's my choice whether or not I want to see my dad. (Grace, age 14)

Here both Grace and Zoe spoke positively of how Lauren had not been hostile toward their contact with the perpetrator/father, and had told them that they could see him if they wished.

Lauren discussed in her own interview how she had overcome a very difficult situation by being supportive of her children's wishes regarding contact. She did feel strongly that the family courts should not have allowed contact to occur in the first place, as the perpetrator's/father's relationships with Grace and Zoe had been unhealthy and harmful to the children both pre- and post-separation. Yet, had Lauren attempted to have the contact stopped when Grace and Zoe were very young (they were, respectively 5 and 3 years old when she separated from the perpetrator/father), then it was likely that she would have been accused of being an alienating or implacably hostile mother in the family courts, and that contact would have continued despite her concerns (Harrison, 2008; Hunter et al., 2020; Radford and Hester, 2006). Furthermore, Lauren discussed how Grace and Zoe had initially "hated" her for taking them away from a father who they adored, and had wanted to continue to see him. After contact had been court-ordered, Lauren seemed to have felt that the best way of protecting her daughters was to be supportive of contact so that the children would have no further reasons to feel resentful toward her. Maintaining a supportive stance toward the contact was therefore a way for Lauren to avoid a major long-term rift developing in her mother–child relationships. Once such a rift had been averted, Lauren was able to focus on strengthening her relationships with Grace and Zoe into very solid and supportive ones that enhanced the well-being of both children. The interviews with Lauren and with Grace and Zoe (which took place nine years post-separation) suggested that this strategy had been very successful (see later in this chapter and chapters 8 and 9).

Some children had independently determined that their father was a negative presence in their lives—and, though they had *not* come to this conclusion in order to support their mother, some mothers in the study discussed how helpful this awareness by their children had been:

The boys have judged it for themselves in not wanting him in their lives anymore; they know the stress he's given us all. They know why he can't be in their lives, so it's easier for me because I don't need to explain it to them. (Akeela, mother)

[Positive tone of voice] Grace knows that her dad's an idiot, but she learnt it for herself. It wasn't something she learnt from me. (Lauren, mother)

These judgments seemed to be powerful because mothers valued their children's independent perspectives on their father's behavior. By separately coming to similar conclusions about the coercive control they had experienced, children were helping to validate and confirm their mother's own understandings.

Mood-lifting and helping to overcome emotional and behavioral impacts

The children and mothers in the study tended to approach mood-lifting and helping to overcome emotional and behavioral impacts in different ways. Children tended to lift their mother's mood in the short term, whereas mothers tended to give their children longer-term support to overcome the emotional and behavioral impacts of their experiences. Mothers' efforts—helping their children to become calmer and to express their feelings more constructively—contributed to the children's healthy psychological functioning and may have reduced their likelihood of experiencing emotional and behavioral problems in adulthood.

Children used the strategy of mood-lifting when they believed that their mother was worried or upset. Sometimes this strategy involved simply telling their mother not to experience everyday events negatively, such as unkind comments by acquaintances. For example, Brock described how he advised his mother:

"Ignore what people say; don't get upset." (Brock, age 12)

Roxie (aged 11) explained that she sometimes said "I love you" when she felt her mother needed cheering up.

Other children attempted to intervene by doing something positive for, or with, their mother. The sons and daughters in the study tended to have different approaches. The daughters tended to engage with their mother in shared activities, such as applying face masks and talking together:

> I'd buy her creams to make her more relaxed, and face masks for me and my mum to do, and I think that used to help her a bit. (Katie, age 12)

> When I think Mum's worrying about the past now, I'll ask her if she's okay and make her cups of tea and sit with her and talk to her about everyday things, and it's just nice. (Grace, age 14)

The sons' approaches tended to be more direct, giving encouragement in the manner of a sports coach or mentor, or giving a comedic performance. Vince (aged 13) discussed giving his mother Akeela "pep talks" when she had been crying. Similarly, Eloise, mother of 20-year-old John, explained how helpful it was when John made her laugh:

> He's very supportive and he's funny; he makes me laugh, and that's a really good quality—do you know what I mean? He's made me laugh a lot. . . . Any bad news brings me down; it brings it all back to me. . . . So he'll make me laugh; he'll put a smile back on my face. (Eloise, mother)

In taking these steps, which were much valued by their mothers, these children showed that they were attuned to their mothers' emotions, and able to actively engage in attempts to change them.

Many interviews revealed how, over a sustained time-period, mothers had supported their children to deal with the emotional and behavioral impacts of perpetrators'/fathers' coercive control that the children had experienced. Various techniques were used by mothers to help their children to address withdrawn/risk-averse behavior, aggression, and compulsive behavior. For example, 11-year-old Roxie discussed how her mother, Bella, had helped her to feel less angry, while Bella herself reported how she encouraged her children to resolve problems in a calm manner. This support appeared to have been effective. Bella reported that, although Roxie still occasionally had "temper problems," she had become calmer, "like a different child." The ways in which Bella successfully helped Roxie to transform the way she expressed her feelings exemplifies how positive parenting from mothers can increase the resilience and healthy functioning of children who have lived with domestic violence (Cameranesi et al., 2020).

Mothers also gave their children the message that making mistakes is normal and is not a catastrophe to be feared. This was the opposite of the messages that perpetrators'/fathers' coercive control had instilled in children, leaving children reluctant to learn new skills in case they "got it wrong" (see chapter 4). Eloise described situations where she had encouraged her son John to persevere with activities even when mistakes occurred, and how this new freedom and encouragement was building his confidence:

> John was painting the bathroom, he never would have done that before—[the perpetrator] wouldn't have allowed it. And he dropped the paint, he thought I was going to go mad. So I come along and he said "you're probably not going to ask me to paint anymore" and I said "don't worry John, I will," things like that that [the perpetrator] wouldn't have allowed him to do. [John] said to me the other day "Mum, will you teach me how to make pastry?" because he wants to learn. (Eloise, mother)

Now that Eloise had created the conditions in which he could safely learn new skills, John was able to use his agency to identify those he wanted to develop, such as cooking skills. He was also able to actively ask someone—here, his mother—to help him gain proficiency in those areas.

Several children's accounts also suggested their active agency in engaging with their mother's support. This was notable in the account of Lauren and her 14-year-old daughter Grace. Grace discussed how her mother had encouraged her and her sister to disclose problems, to cry when upset, and not to "bottle things up." Grace explained that she had engaged with this advice and also actively modified it, adding the additional step of writing down her feelings and then showing them to her mother or maternal grandmother, enabling them to talk matters through with her. In another family, Ruby's 12-year-old daughter Katie had developed some compulsive "hoarding" behaviors. She had followed her mother's suggestion to try to overcome this behavior, aware that her mother found her hoarding distressing. This supportiveness contained a significant element of mutuality: Ruby helped Katie to overcome her compulsive behavior, and Katie did so partly to protect Ruby from distress. Both mother and child were attuned and responsive to each other's emotional needs.

Rebuilding each other's confidence

It is well known that domestic violence victims/survivors often have greatly reduced confidence (see, e.g., Matheson et al., 2015); yet there has been little attention to how confidence may be rebuilt through mother–child relationships, and especially through children's agency within them. In this study, some mothers and children played vital confidence-building roles. Generally, mothers and children had similar desires and capacities to support each other's confidence, and used similar techniques to do so.

Mothers' primary techniques involved building their children's self-esteem and independence. Some mothers described how they had increased their children's confidence by stressing to them that they loved them, saying "you're my world" or "you're beautiful," and praising their achievements. Other mothers discussed how they had arranged and encouraged their children's involvement in confidence-building hobbies and activities.

Mothers viewed increasing their children's confidence as a means of reducing their children's vulnerability to having abusive relationships of their own as adults. Ellie described how she now gave helpful advice to Shannon about the importance of inner well-being, and of having a wide circle of supportive friends rather than relying on a particular romantic partner:

> I try to encourage Shannon and give her confidence to be how she wants to be, and I sort of tell her that what's important is how she thinks and feels inside, not what's on the outside, that's important, and she believes that as well which is really, really good. . . . And I do stress the fact that she doesn't have to [have romantic relationships]. It's really important that she gets happiness from herself and from her friends, and doesn't depend on one person for it. It's nice to care for other people, but you're just as important as they are. (Ellie, mother)

Similarly, Bob discussed receiving helpful advice from Isobel. Partly this advice was similar to the guidance given to Shannon by Ellie about listening to the inner self. There were also other elements, including that Bob should not put himself under pressure to do things perfectly, and should avoid thinking of himself as "always right":

> The most helpful things she's said are: "It doesn't matter what they say, as long as you think it's right." And also: "You're not always right." That's important because you do have to get things wrong, because if you get everything right, and then you get one thing wrong, it can make you feel really bad about yourself. (Bob, age 12)

This quote is one that deserves particular attention. It can be noted first that, in encouraging Bob to stand by his own conscience regardless of any negative comments by others, Isobel was guiding him toward a more resilient sense of personal conviction. She was also, by telling him that he was "not always right," steering him away from a perspective that is common to perpetrators of domestic violence: that they are the one in the family or relationship who knows best (Downes et al., 2019). It was interesting too that, from Bob's perspective, he interpreted this point that "you're not always right" (which could be a demeaning one in a different context) as a removal of pressure. As Bob noted, it was liberating him from certain feelings of shame ("if you get . . . one thing wrong, it can make you feel really bad about yourself"); and it was also liberating him from aggressive feelings, too, because if a person assumes they must always be right, shame can turn into rage when something happens that upsets this self-perception (Hill, 2020). Taken together, Isobel's advice seemed to point toward Bob developing a kinder, more understanding, and more emotionally secure way of being a young man.

For Lucy, confidence-building had felt particularly important in the case of her daughter, Zara. Unknown to Lucy pre-separation, Zara had been sexually abused by the perpetrator/father (see chapter 4). After separating from the perpetrator/father, and now knowing that he had sexually abused Zara, Lucy had encouraged Zara to attend dance lessons. Her aim was to promote Zara's confidence in her body, and to minimize any long-term harm caused by the sexual abuse:

> Zara does seven dance lessons a week, which may be a bit like "pushy mother," but I think I've done everything to compensate, in a way, because I always wanted her to be confident; I never wanted her to doubt herself. I think one of my worries is, because of it being a sexual thing, when it comes to the time when she becomes sexually aware of boys, or whatever, I don't want her feeling worthless or anything like that. I've always wanted her to have a lot of confidence. (Lucy, mother)

For her son, Stewart, Lucy had this approach:

> I've started him with rugby to try and build his confidence. It must be a thing that's in my head: make sure they're confident. (Lucy, mother)

These quite gender-specific strategies, equipping each child, a son and a daughter, to deal with men, seemed nuanced. Lucy wanted Zara to have the physical confidence to engage successfully in intimate relationships as a young woman. She possibly hoped that Stewart's participation in a masculine and sociability-driven team sport would help him to interact closely with other men, especially physically imposing and self-confident ones, and find a satisfying, safe outlet for aggression.

Many children also helped to rebuild their mothers' confidence, particularly by encouraging and praising their engagement with the outside world, and praising them as mothers. For example, Ellie described how Shannon had voiced appreciation of her personal courage and her "importance" in making a difference for others in her community:

> Shannon always says she thinks I'm brave, which is really good, and she's so proud of me for going to court, and she's so proud of me for doing the stuff that I'm doing now with my volunteer work, and she obviously thinks I'm a very important person. I am [important] in her world; it's just lovely. (Ellie, mother)

For Ellie, Shannon's appreciation was clearly a source of happiness and pride, and increased her sense that she "mattered" to her daughter (Marshall and Lambert, 2006). Shannon's praise was focused on her mother's public side—her work, and her ability to fight for herself in court—possibly reflecting Shannon's desire to encourage and validate Ellie's actions in these areas. Bob similarly described how he and his siblings had helped Isobel by validating her actions. In this instance, the validation was in relation to gift-giving:

> We've helped her and shown how much we like things [gifts] when we get them, show how good things are and stuff like that, it helps her feel she's done something to be proud of. (Bob, age 12)

By expressing happiness in this way, these children were making a conscious effort to give Isobel an important gift in return: a sense of having "done something to be proud of."

Another mother, Eloise, discussed how her son John gave her confidence by encouraging her to "do things" that would be helpful for her. This form of support overlapped with the mood-lifting discussed earlier, especially the "pep talks" mentioned earlier as a support given by Vince to Akeela. Eloise discussed how her confidence had been raised by the pep talks given to her by John, especially at times when she had encountered opportunities to participate in exciting but challenging activities:

> He'll say: "it would be good for you Mum [to do it]," which is important because when you've had so many bad things happen, it does make you feel a "downer" and you do doubt. I doubt myself a lot, and what I'm capable of doing, but John gives me encouragement to do things. (Eloise, mother)

Eloise's account suggests that John's support helped her to move beyond self-doubt, and to take actions that she might otherwise have not felt confident to undertake. Eloise also described the supportiveness between herself and John as mutual:

> We've been supportive of one another. We encourage each other: "you can do it." We try to bump each other's confidence up, you know, which is important. (Eloise, mother)

The "you can do it" described here by Eloise is similar to the way in which mutually supportive sports-players interact with each other when playing for a team. These supports exchanged between Eloise and John, as supportive team-mates in life, may therefore be understood as bilateral—the child encouraging the mother while the mother encourages the child.

Comments from children praising their mother's mothering may have been particularly powerful where mothers had viewed themselves as "bad" mothers during the time when the perpetrator/father was abusing them. These self-perceptions were often partly the result of negative comments that perpetrators/fathers had made about their mothering (see also Heward-Belle, 2017). In the post-separation period, some children were responding to the abuse and helping their mothers to recover by making positive comments:

> [Smiling] Jack's said lots of helpful things—how wonderful
> I am, [and] "you're a great mum." He didn't say them be-
> fore. He says he knows how lucky he is. (Sybil, mother)

EMMA: What are the most helpful things that your children have said to you?

ISOBEL: Um . . . : "You're the best mummy in the world."

As Sybil and Isobel described, when children said that their mothers were "wonderful," "a great mum," or "the best mummy in the world," it was helpful to mothers' self-confidence. Esteem from their children was helping to transform the negative self-image built up by the perpetrator/ father during the coercive control into the positive one of a mother who is highly competent as a parent and beloved by her children.

Communicating openly with each other

Several children reported finding it helpful when they talked with their mothers about everyday events and feelings. Some mothers and children had always been able to communicate in this way. For others, however, communication had been restricted while they had lived with the perpe-trator/father, causing emotional distance between children and mothers (see Mullender et al., 2002). In some of these latter families, professional supports received during their recoveries had led to increased communi-cation, enabling mothers to support their children more extensively:

> I didn't used to talk to Mum that much. I was always at friends'
> [homes], or in my bedroom—that wasn't so good. This woman at the
> refuge helped me and Mum to talk more. Now, when I get upset, we
> sit down and talk about what's happened. (Angel, age 12)

> I talk to my mum more now about what I've been doing. (Joe, age 14)

We talk a lot more than we used to about stuff, like how school is. (Vince, age 13)

These statements include mothers and children communicating about "what's happened" in order to help the children to overcome negative feelings, and also communicating about the present in positive conversations focused on the children's everyday lives. The interviews in the study suggested that both of these types of communication were important for mothers and children in moving forward. Becoming more open and communicative at an everyday level was a significant step in many families' recoveries.

Showing affection and spending time together

Most of the mothers and children in the study discussed how, once living apart from perpetrators/fathers, they took the opportunity to spend more time together and be more affectionate with one another. This increased time and affection was often described as a dramatic difference that brought improvements to their mother–child relationships:

EMMA: Could you tell me a bit more about how life's changed since you moved in here, and any ways that things between you and your mum have changed or improved?

LEAH (AGE 11): Um, spending time together and just doing things together, watching films together and going out.

[My brother Thomas] didn't have much time with my mum, but now he can spend time with her, and he can just come and sit, and he can talk or cuddle or whatever he wants to do, because there's no one stopping him doing that now. (Katie, age 12)

I feel like now I can show him how much I love him, and how fun and interesting he is, and take an interest in him, without worrying that his dad will stop me. We play lots of games together now. I've taught myself to play with him. (Sybil, mother)

As these mothers and children noted, such supports had not been possible when they had been entrapped in perpetrators'/fathers' coercive control. Some perpetrators/fathers had strongly disliked mothers and children being affectionate with one another (see chapters 4 and 5); their tactics for undermining mother–child relationships often included preventing children and mothers from spending time together and showing each other love. It is therefore unsurprising that it was fulfilling and enjoyable for mothers and children to spend time together in the post-separation period.

Overall, mothers' and children's comments suggested that being able to spend time together, share enjoyable experiences, and show affection for each other were vital forms of support. The previous quotes demonstrate how this feeling was increasing mothers' and children's sense of being connected to each other. Sybil and Katie spoke of playing games, sitting together and cuddling, while Leah emphasized the importance of being able to go out and have fun with her mother; an activity which, as Radford et al. (2011a, p. 107) suggest, may be helpful in recovering from harm. Through these behaviors and activities, the families in this study were creating the conditions present within families who have not experienced coercive control, where value is placed on: "having fun together, sharing similar interests [. . .] displaying affection, and making time to spend with each other" (Oliphant and Kuczynski, 2011, p. 1107).

Children indirectly supporting their mothers' recoveries

Children supported their mothers' recoveries not only directly and intentionally, but also in ways that were indirect and unknowing. Several mothers discussed how their children had helped them to persevere, particularly during the early stages of recovery. They also described how their parenting responsibilities had given a vital structure to their day, and how witnessing their children's recoveries had enhanced their own well-being.

In some families, mothers talked of how, if it had not been for their children's presence, they would have committed suicide while they had lived with the perpetrator/father, or soon after leaving him. At the times when they had felt suicidal, mothers were facing major problems with depleted emotional resources. One mother (not named because she did not want her child to know that she had felt suicidal) described the numerous feelings that were pushing her toward suicide:

> There were times after leaving, especially prior to the court case, that I just didn't feel that I could carry on. I just felt that I wouldn't be missed basically, that I'd made massive mistakes, that I was worthless and nobody would miss me, and that [my child] would probably be better off without me. But then it was like—there were two occasions when I nearly did something stupid, and it was only that [the child] happened to be in the same room, in bed, and I thought: "I can't do that to [them]."

In this and other instances, mothers believed that their relationships with their children had made a life-and-death difference during the most difficult parts of their experiences.

In other families, it was the need to care for their children that had pushed mothers to continue with their daily routines. Everyday parenting tasks, such as getting children ready for school, had helped mothers to persevere through their depression and trauma:

> I think it helped me to carry on, like if they've gotta go to school, then you've gotta get up to get them to school. (Isobel, mother)

> You've got kids that *need* you to keep going. So, in many ways, it's the children who make you get up the next day. I had to get up. . . . In many ways they're definitely a life-saver. (Ruby, mother)

For some mothers, supporting their children's recoveries was beneficial to their own recoveries:

> Having the children helps you to recover, because you have to focus on them and sort them out. (Lauren, mother)

> Being there for the kids helped me to get over what I was going through. (Bella, mother)

Having practical and emotional responsibility for children therefore helped to motivate these mothers to continue moving forward with their recoveries.

Several mothers discussed how they had benefited from their children becoming more content and expressing satisfaction with their new lives. For example, Bella described how enthused she had felt when her children expressed happiness at Christmas—making clear to her that they found their new situation to be far superior to life with the perpetrator/father despite its material disadvantages:

> During our first Christmas, they only had small presents compared to what they used to have before; but they said "this is the best Christmas we've ever had." That gave me a big boost. (Bella, mother)

The "big boost" felt by Bella illustrates again how mothers could be influenced by their children's feelings and statements (De Mol and Buysse, 2008). When children expressed such appreciation, mothers could feel reassured about their decision to leave perpetrators/fathers.

Some mothers also said that the overall experience of having a child and being engaged in a mother–child relationship was vitally important to them. They described their children as integral to their lives, and as people to whom they were devoted:

> John being here has been really important to me. . . . I wanted a child, and I'm glad I had John. To have John in my life, to have a child, is very precious. (Eloise, mother)

I just love her; I love her to bits. She's my world, my absolute world. (Ellie, mother)

My children have helped me the most: My whole life revolves around them. (Alison, mother)

These mothers were describing situations in which they had a positive focus for their lives: a focus provided by children who were "really important" and "precious" to them, who they loved, and who helped them to enjoy life.

GENERAL MOTHER–CHILD SUPPORTS NOT DIRECTLY RELATED TO COERCIVE CONTROL

Having outlined the ways in which mothers and children supported each other's recoveries, we will now turn to the general supports that mothers and children gave to each other as part of their everyday lives. As we will observe, the acts of everyday supportiveness and attentiveness described by the participants in this study were similar to those that occur in families that have not experienced coercive control (Marshall and Lambert, 2006; Morrow, 2003; Oliphant and Kuczynski, 2011).

Supporting each other through upsets or tiredness

Supporting each other through upsets or tiredness was a common practice among the families in the study. Alison described how her daughter Jane had given her hugs after bad days. Other children made their mothers cups of tea, drew them pictures, or provided practical help with housework and care of siblings when their mother was ill or tired. These practical supports will shortly be discussed in further detail. Overall, mothers described feeling positive about these actions by their children, as such actions showed that their children were sensitive to their needs and cared about their well-being.

Mothers supported their children emotionally in several ways. Akeela described encouraging her sons to cry when they felt distressed. Alison had comforted her children after one of their school friends had died. Several other mothers described how their children came to them with general worries or concerns. These supports from mothers helped children to constructively manage difficult situations in their lives.

Being attentive to each other's feelings

Attentiveness and consideration of each other's feelings was a support provided by both mothers and children in this study. One mother, Lauren, described how her children generally responded to her in a caring manner:

They [my daughters] both have a really nice supportive attitude. (Lauren, mother)

Examples of mothers' attentiveness to children's feelings included responding well when children shared information in confidence, not saying "that's stupid" or becoming unreasonably angry, and being interested in what had happened during the school day. Bob reported that one of the best qualities about his mother was how emotionally attuned, well informed, and sensitive she was about his everyday life (Cameranesi et al., 2020; Yule, 2019):

She's smart, because she knows how I'm feeling, like what moods I'm in, what school was like, and things like that. (Bob, age 12)

Bob's mother Isobel also commented on how mutually emotionally attuned to each other's feelings she and her children had become:

Now me and the kids pick up if anybody's upset or anything, and ask them if they're okay and stuff, and they'll say: "are you alright Mum?" (Isobel, mother).

Overall, mothers and children described enjoying the climates of emotional attentiveness that had developed in their homes.

Children's practical support for mothers

Many families discussed the practical supports given by children. (Practical supports by mothers were barely mentioned, perhaps because they were taken for granted.) Children's practical supports included doing age-appropriate, routine tasks for, and with, their mother. These could include helping out with cooking and cleaning, and, in the case of older children, providing money toward household expenses.

Several children also made decisions to adjust their expectations of what their mother could accomplish in everyday life in accordance with her financial and health constraints. Akeela believed that her children chose not to ask for gifts or treats in order to help her to manage financially and to spare her from feeling guilty. However, she found their sacrifices distressing:

> I get upset, because sometimes in the summer the ice cream van is outside the school and they want ice cream, but I can't give it them because I haven't got my benefits this week, and sometimes I do get them an ice cream, but sometimes they know—they know when Mum gets her benefits, and they'll say no: "no Mum we don't want an ice cream leave it, leave it," but I know they want an ice cream. For them it's a treat, so it upsets me. (Akeela, mother)

Bob (one of several children) discussed how he understood that Isobel had many parenting responsibilities, and therefore tried not to make excessive demands on her. Another mother, Ruby, explained that her children supported her by accepting that the perpetrator's/father's abuse had undermined her health, so on some days she had to rest in bed for a while rather than playing with them.

"Being there"

The phrase "being there" occurred frequently in mothers' and children's interviews. Overall, "being there" appeared to be a valued support because it provided a sense of emotional security. Mothers and children had helped one another in the past, and felt that they would be supported through problems again in the future.

It was most common for mothers to describe "being there" for their children, although some children also said that they were "there for" their mothers. For mothers, a major aspect of "being there" was being available to talk to their children and help them through their problems:

> I think the most helpful thing I've said to them is that they can always talk whenever they want, about anything they want, and no matter what they say or do, you know there's nothing they can't tell me. I might not like it (laughs), but no matter what happens or what they do in life, I'm always there. (Lucy, mother)

> Jack knows I'm always there for him. He knows he can try things out, and have a go at new things, with his mum there to support him. (Sybil, mother)

When children noted their mothers' commitment to "being there," they described how they valued their mothers saying to them that they would not have to face any future difficulties alone:

> [Mum said] if you're ever upset, just talk to me and I'll be there for you. (Angel, age 12)

> [Mum said] if you've got a problem, just come and talk to me no matter what I'm doing. (Grace, age 14)

Another major way in which children perceived their mothers as "being there" was in being dependable to help in any circumstance:

Helping each other to recover 241

She's always there, and she's kind and she helps. (Jane, age 11)

Mum makes everything better. She's always there for me; she would do everything in her power to help me. (Grace, age 14)

Mum's the parent I can rely on. (Joe, age 14)

Some children discussed "being there" for their mothers in similarly consistent and valued ways. Children suggested that they had already "been there" for their mothers, and that they would continue to "be there" in the future:

[I think the most helpful things I've said to my mum are] that I'll help her with anything. . . . If she ever needs me, she can talk to me, if she wants me to help or anything that's what I'll do. (Katie, age 12)

[I think the most helpful things I've said to my mum are] that I'll always be there for you no matter what, and I'll help you if you need help. (Angel, age 12)

EMMA: Out of all the people or things in your mum's life, which do you think's helped her the most?

ANGEL: Us being there for her, and taking care of her—if she ever needs help, we help her, and if there's anything she wants done, we do it.

JOE: Just us being there for her and caring for her, and her friends being there for her.

Finally, some mothers discussed mutual "being there" within their family:

We all look after each other —that's how they've been brought up— whether it's emotionally or physically. You still love each other, no matter what's going on outside our group of three [mother and two children]. You still love each other and support each other, and that's the reason you keep going. (Ruby, mother)

They're just there, and we just do support each other. [. . . We support each other through] cuddles, cups of tea and chocolate. We'll put a film on and just snuggle up together. We just know we're going to be there for each other, and we do help each other. We know that we love each other. (Lauren, mother)

These mothers described a predictable and enduring sense of themselves and their children "being there" for each other as the norm in their families. Being there for each other "no matter what's going on outside our group of three," and "just know[ing] we're going to be there for each other," was a comforting and secure state-of-affairs in their post-separation lives.

These cultures of "being there" for each other are in line with findings discussed by Williams (2004, p. 17) that, "Day-to-day activities [that are] central to the sustaining of family lives and personal relationships [include] helping, tending, looking out for, thinking about, talking, sharing, and offering a shoulder to cry on." In enacting such everyday practices, the mothers and children in this study were creating new and more positive family lives that were in many ways the opposites of the "regimes of systematic coercion and control" (Morris, 2009, p. 417) that they had previously experienced.

Reflections on children's and mothers' contributions to each other's recoveries

Many of the mothers and children in this study had developed strategies and techniques that were effective for helping each other to recover, setting their mother–child relationships on course for positive longer-term outcomes. These strategies and techniques had not necessarily emerged immediately after the mothers and children had separated from perpetrators/fathers; rather, they had developed during the following months and years. The analysis provided in this chapter on what worked for these families will hopefully provide some useful insights not only for researchers but also for other children and mothers who have recently separated from perpetrators, for professionals, and for anyone else who wishes to support families who are in the midst of the multiple difficulties covered in this book.

The particular types of strategies and techniques that worked for the mothers and children in the study can be concisely summarized in the following terms. First, it was beneficial for recovery when the mothers and children spent positive time together, communicated love and affection to each other as well as hope about the future, and built up one another's confidence, for example by praising each other's achievements and reassuring each other about the past. In terms of reassurance, mothers and children found it helpful to hear from each other that the coercive control had not been their fault; that the perpetrator was responsible for his own actions; and that any consequences he faced were the result of his actions, not theirs. In terms of praise, occasions when the children expressed happiness about their mothers' mothering could be particularly transformational for women who had previously viewed themselves as "bad" mothers. Also, the children benefited from having sufficient information about the past to make sense of what had happened and to understand their current family circumstances. This was especially the case when children had been very young at the time when mothers had separated from perpetrators/fathers. Finally, it was beneficial when the mothers and children reassured each other that it was okay to make mistakes—the opposite of life under coercive control, where mistakes could result in violence and aggression by the perpetrator.

One final general observation is that, over time, it was possible for very difficult situations to be turned around. For example, as we found in this chapter, when Lauren had first separated from her abusive partner, her daughters Grace and Zoe (then 5 and 3 years old) greatly resented her for taking them away from him. Lauren reported that their resentment lasted for around two years, and Grace had even considered going to live with the perpetrator/father. Grace and Zoe had continued to have court-ordered contact with the perpetrator/father over several years, during which time he emotionally/psychologically abused them. Yet, as the children grew up, positive outcomes had occurred through Lauren's strategies for managing the situation, which included respecting the children's wishes regarding being in contact with the perpetrator/father, non-judgmentally supporting both children through the severe distress that they felt after contact visits with him, providing them with consistent, warm, boundaried, and nurturing parenting herself, and arranging for them to have counseling. By the time Grace and Zoe took part in this study at the ages of 14 and 12, their relationships with Lauren had become strong and healthy. Though the harms their father had caused them could not be undone, Grace and Zoe appeared to be managing well psychologically. It also seemed that the perpetrator/father had lost much of his negative influence over the children, with Grace deciding for herself to end her contact with him, and Zoe now able to recognize that his behavior did not represent good parenting. (Zoe complained during her interview that her father was disinterested in her during their monthly contact visits and was instead overly focused on speaking negatively about Lauren and Grace; behavior which Zoe was able to correctly identify as wrong.)

CONCLUSION

Many of the children and mothers in this study were making vital contributions to each other's recoveries. Their recovery-promoting actions were often woven into their everyday lives and ordinary interactions, and involved small but powerful acts of praise, encouragement, attentiveness, care, affection, and communication. Mothers' and children's support for one another often reinforced and built on the professional help that they had received since separating from perpetrators/fathers, further enhancing their well-being. In exploring how children and mothers can help each other to recover, we have recognized the agency, strengths, and abilities of these survivors. Far from being inadequate mothers or emotionally dysregulated children, many participants demonstrated that they had considerable emotional intelligence and skill. Indeed, their narratives help to illuminate *why*, in contexts of domestic violence, children who have mothers that are warm, sensitive, and attentive to their feelings tend to be "resilient"; that is, *why* they tend to demonstrate both an "absence of adjustment problems and high functioning (e.g., high self-esteem, self-efficacy, and constructive problem-solving abilities)" (Cameranesi et al., 2020, p. 117). It may well be that the examples of support from mothers outlined in this chapter are exactly the kinds of everyday maternal supports that bring about these positive outcomes for children.

It is also particularly noteworthy that several children in the study were having a positive influence on their mother's recoveries. As De Mol and Buysse (2008, p. 184) argue, within Western social-cultural discourses "there is plenty of room for the influence of parents on children, but not for the inverse direction." In other words, there is little language available to describe positive child-to-parent influence: It is a phenomenon that does not fit within our "common sense" ways of thinking. Recognizing the active roles that children can play in mothers' recovery is therefore significant: It helps us to disrupt those limited understandings of children. The children in this study may be seen as complex beings who have been harmed, but can also be agentic, skilled, influential, and effective.

8

And they lived happily ever after?

Outcomes for mother–child relationships
after coercive control

INTRODUCTION

Chapters 5, 6, and 7 have shown why some mother–child relationships are more harmed than others by coercive control-based domestic violence, what circumstances are needed for recoveries to begin, and how mothers and children can promote each other's recoveries. This chapter now explores what happens to mother–child relationships in the years after separation from perpetrators/fathers, drawing on the perspectives of the 15 mothers and 15 children who took part in the study.

As noted in chapter 5, perpetrators'/fathers' coercive control affects mother–child relationships to different extents. Whereas some mothers and children are able to sustain close and supportive relationships while living with perpetrators/fathers, other mother–child relationships become more damaged and distant. Therefore, some mothers and children begin their recovery phases with closer mother–child relationships than others. Those with the most strained relationships face the greatest struggles to heal them.

As the mothers and children in the study moved forward with their lives, their mother–child relationships developed into different patterns.

Coercive Control in Children's and Mothers' Lives. Emma Katz, Oxford University Press. © Oxford University Press 2022.
DOI: 10.1093/oso/9780190922214.003.0008

Through its exploration of these patterns, this chapter provides (to the best of the author's knowledge) the first typology of what happens to mother–child relationships after mothers and children separate from perpetrators/fathers. (As in chapter 5, no claim is made to the universal application of this typology beyond the families who took part in the study.)

Previous research highlights the diverse range of outcomes experienced by families recovering from domestic violence. While some young adults show considerable resilience and post-traumatic growth (see, e.g., Anderson and Danis, 2006; Anderson et al., 2011), others can experience long-term negative impacts and may go on to become abusive themselves (see, e.g., Barter et al., 2021). Similarly, some researchers have identified substantial improvements in mother–child relationships post-domestic violence (see, e.g., Goldblatt et al., 2014; Wuest et al., 2004), while other studies illustrate how mother–child relationships can be disrupted and broken in the years following domestic violence (see, e.g., Humphreys et al., 2006; Monk and Bowen, 2021). Elements of all of these outcomes were found among the 15 families who took part in this study. Some families thrived much more than they struggled, whereas others struggled a great deal more and showed fewer signs of thriving. This chapter analyzes these different outcomes, and explores how they were being experienced by mothers and children.

LEVELS, CONTEXTS, AND IMPACTS OF SUPPORTIVENESS

To understand the different paths that mother–child relationships can follow in the aftermath of coercive control, this chapter constructs a "levels, contexts, and impacts" framework to assess supportiveness between the mothers and children in the study. This framework makes it possible to explore the complexities of mother–child supportiveness and the different forms it can take. Taking levels, contexts, and impacts in turn, the criteria for each are as follows:

Levels of supportiveness—From high levels of support
to no support

- The number of strategies of support used by the mother and child
- The number of strategies used by the mother, the number used by the child, and the overall balance of support (i.e., whether the mother is giving most support, the child is giving most support, or they are giving equal amounts of support)
- The presence/absence of mutual support

Contexts of supportiveness—From very positive contexts to
very problematic contexts

- The status of the mother's mental health and how the mother is coping with her mental health (e.g., she feels she is coping well/ she feels she is struggling to cope)
- The extent to which the mother and child have formal (i.e., professional) and/or informal supports (i.e., family and friends) to help them
- The "stakes" of child-to-mother support (i.e., low-stakes, such as a child cheering up their mother but not having any major worries about her, or high-stakes, such as a child supporting a suicidal mother)
- The degree to which there are ongoing problems and conflicts in the mother–child relationship

Impacts of supportiveness—From very positive impacts to very
negative impacts

- The extent to which the mother's and child's support for each other is effective in meeting their emotional needs

- The mother's feelings about the support they give and/or receive from their child
- The child's feelings about the support they give and/or receive from their mother

Applying this framework of "levels, contexts, and impacts" to the data provided by the mothers and children in the study, four different patterns of mother–child relationships were identified, as shown in Table 8.1.

LINKS BETWEEN THE FOUR PATTERNS AND PROFESSIONAL SUPPORT

Which pattern a mother–child relationship followed was strongly related to the extent of the supports (formal and informal) that they had received to help them to recover from their experiences of coercive control. As outlined in this section, only mothers and children experiencing pattern 1 (the most optimal pattern) had experienced sufficient supports to meet their recovery needs.

Pattern 1: Positive supportiveness, positive recoveries

Pattern 1 mothers and children were able to interact and communicate very positively with each other, and give one another effective supports. These mothers and children were the only ones in the study who had been able to access sufficient supports, and this was a key reason why their mother–child relationships were functioning so well by the time they took part in the study (on average 5 years post separation from perpetrators/fathers). In their interviews, pattern 1 mothers and children explained how, over periods of months and years after separating from perpetrators/fathers, multiple supports had largely resolved their problems. Such supports included help from specialist domestic violence services, social workers,

Table 8.1 THE FOUR PATTERNS

Pattern 1: Positive supportiveness, positive recoveries

- Mothers and children are at an advanced stage in their recoveries
- Mother–child relationships are close with few conflicts
- Mothers and children are giving each other mutual supports, and children's support for mothers is low-stakes because mothers are in good mental health, or are coping well with their mental health struggles
- Mothers and children are positive about their mother–child relationships

Pattern 2: High-stakes support, limited recoveries

- Mothers and children are somewhat recovered, but mothers are still struggling significantly with their mental health
- Mother–child relationships are close but also are conflictual
- Mothers and children are mutually supporting each other, but children's support for mothers is "high-stakes" because mothers are experiencing significant mental health distress
- Mothers and children have mixed feelings about their mother–child relationships

Pattern 3: Struggling relationships, struggling recoveries

- Mothers are somewhat recovered, but children still have significant behavioral difficulties and low levels of understanding of coercive control
- Mother–child relationships are strained and conflictual
- Mothers are trying to support children, but children are not supporting mothers
- Mothers and children wish to improve their mother–child relationships

Pattern 4: Broken relationships, blocked recoveries

- Children have sided with perpetrators/ fathers and may be living with them, and mothers are therefore struggling to or are unable to recover, and children are unable to recover
- Mother–child relationships have broken down, and mothers may be out of contact with children
- Mothers may wish to support children but cannot, and children are hostile to mothers and do not wish to support them
- Mothers wish to improve their mother–child relationships

counselors, parenting programs, and Ontario-based mother–child abuse-recovery programs (McManus et al., 2013; Smith et al., 2015; Smith et al., 2020—see chapters 6 and 7), as well as from friends and family. Many different problems arising from perpetrators'/fathers' coercive control—misplaced anger and blame, communication problems, severe mental health distress, alcohol and drug misuse, and behavioral problems—had all been successfully tackled by these mothers and children (see chapters 6 and 7). Pattern 1 mothers and children had reached stages of being largely happy with their mother–child relationships.

Pattern 2: High-stakes support, limited recoveries

Pattern 2 families required additional supports to improve the mother's mental health (Khan, 2020). These mothers and children were endeavoring to support each other. However, mothers were still experiencing high levels of mental health distress as a result of perpetrators'/fathers' coercive control (Dutton and Goodman, 2005; Moulding et al., 2021), and had not received adequate professional supports to help them to rebuild their mental health (Khan, 2020). This mental health distress made it harder for pattern 2 mothers to support their children (McFarlane et al., 2017), and meant that the support that children gave to their mothers was high-stakes and, for the children themselves, potentially more worrisome. These mothers had engaged with various professionals since separating from perpetrators, but the help that they had been given was of insufficient duration, was unsuitable for them, and/or was helpful for other issues but had not been aimed at improving their mental health.

Pattern 3: Struggling relationships, struggling recoveries

Pattern 3 mothers and children were in need of more intensive and longer-term interventions to build strong and supportive mother–child relationships. These mothers and children had also not received adequate professional supports to recover from their experiences of coercive control. However, unlike for pattern 2 families, it was not mental health that was the main issue, but ongoing strains and tensions in their mother–child relationships. The pattern 3 mothers and children were the ones who had experienced very strained and distant mother–child relationships before mothers had separated from perpetrators/fathers (see chapter 5).

Pattern 3 mothers and children therefore entered their recovery phase with particularly damaged mother–child relationships, and had greater support needs in relation to strengthening their mother–child relationships than any others in the study (with the exception of those experiencing pattern 4, see the next section). At the time when they took part, these needs had not been met. Mothers and children were still somewhat disconnected from each other, and the levels of supportiveness between them were low. These mothers and children had tried to resolve these issues. For example, most had attended Ontario-based programs. However, because they had very high support needs, these programs, though slightly helpful, had not been sufficient to bring about major improvements.

Pattern 4: Broken relationships, blocked recoveries

Pattern 4 mother–child relationships were relationships that had been effectively destroyed by perpetrators/fathers. This pattern is put forward more tentatively than the other three patterns, as this type of relationship was only being experienced by one mother in the study (Marie, in the relationship she had with her daughter Louise), though such relationships have been identified in other research (see, e.g., Bancroft et al., 2012; Monk, 2017; Monk and Bowen, 2021; Morris, 2008, 2009). Pattern 4 occurred when the perpetrator's/father's tactics for sabotaging the mother-child relationship (such as encouraging the children to ignore their mother and not allowing mothers and children to spend time together) were so devastating that the child sided with the perpetrator/father and rejected the mother. This situation continued post-separation; the child with the pattern 4 mother–child relationship in this study continued to live full-time with her father after her mother and siblings had separated from him.

The pattern 4 mother and child in this study had received no professional support to help them to build a positive relationship. However, research by Monk and Bowen (2021) and Morris (2008, 2009) suggests the types of professional interventions that may be needed for pattern 4 mothers and children. First, legal interventions are likely to be required to end or greatly reduce the perpetrator's/father's contact with the child. Second, a great deal of sensitive, specialized recovery work by professionals who understand the dynamics of coercive control may be needed in order to undo the harms caused by the perpetrator/father, help the child and mother to heal, and enable the child and mother to develop a positive relationship with each other. Importantly, any such interventions with children in these circumstances should tread carefully to support the child without leaving the child feeling disempowered and unheard.

Which pattern a mother–child relationship followed was open to change. In some families, relationships transitioned between patterns over time. The supports that mothers and children were able to access were central to these shifts. Effective supports could help mother–child relationships to transition, for example, from pattern 2 to pattern 1.

The four post-separation patterns of mother–child relationships have now been introduced. It is now time to examine the characteristics of each pattern in greater depth, starting with pattern 1.

PATTERN 1: POSITIVE SUPPORTIVENESS, POSITIVE RECOVERIES

Eight families were experiencing pattern 1 at the time when they took part in the study. The main features of pattern 1 families were:

- Mothers and children felt positive about the supportive nature of their relationships, and tended to describe these relationships with great happiness
- Mothers and children had developed warm, mutually supportive relationships with one another, and these relationships were

playing significant, positive roles in mothers' and children's recoveries

Also, in pattern 1 families:

- Mothers and children were exchanging moderate-to-high levels of support
- Mothers were providing as much as, or more, support than children
- Because mothers' mental health was currently good or well-managed, children's support was low-stakes, and children were not particularly concerned about mothers' mental health
- Mothers tended to report feeling skilled, confident, and comfortable in their parenting
- There were few ongoing problems or conflicts in the mother–child relationships
- Mothers and children usually had access to helpful support from friends and family
- The supports that mothers and children were exchanging were generally meeting their emotional needs
- Mothers and children had mainly positive feelings about one another and the supports that they were exchanging

The eight families experiencing pattern 1 were:

- Ellie and Shannon
- Isobel and Bob
- Alison and Jane
- Bella and Roxie
- Ruby, Thomas and Katie
- Lauren, Zoe, and Grace
- Lucy and Zara
- Sybil and Jack

Notably, before they had separated from perpetrators/fathers, all of the mothers experiencing pattern 1 had either been experiencing "very close and supportive" or "mixed" mother–child relationships (see chapter 5). Where mother–child relationships had previously been mixed (that is, quite close but also containing some significant distance and strains), their post-separation development into pattern 1 represented a significant improvement. The mothers and children who had achieved this improvement were: Isobel and Bob; Bella and Roxie; Lauren, Zoe, and Grace; Lucy and Zara; and Sybil and Jack. Over time, recovery from coercive control (see chapter 6) had healed some of the harms done to the mixed mother–child relationships, bringing these mothers and children closer together.

Pattern 1 supportiveness

The mothers and children experiencing pattern 1 used many strategies to support each other. Mothers gave their children high levels of ongoing support. They gave this support by showing their children love and affection, being generally attentive and responsive to their children's feelings, comforting them when they felt upset, and giving them a strong sense that they were always "there for" them and would help them with any problems. These mothers were also actively and effectively helping their children to recover by giving them reassurance about the past, present, and future. They particularly gave this reassurance by explaining to their children that the coercive control had not been their fault, and by giving them age-appropriate information about it.

Some mothers experiencing pattern 1 were still rebuilding their mental health, which had often been deeply undermined by perpetrators/fathers, but they felt that they were managing their mental health successfully. These mothers supported their children by minimizing their children's awareness of any low moods or worries that they were experiencing, so as not to concern their children. Pattern 1 mothers helped their children to overcome any emotional or behavioral impacts from the coercive control they had experienced, for example by supporting children to develop constructive ways of dealing with anger. These mothers helped to boost their children's confidence, and encouraged them to become independent and compassionate people.

Finally, these mothers tended to be attuned to their children's emotional needs and were skilled in responding to them. Some mothers discussed how they had been conscious that their children would be unsettled during the periods of transition when they relocated to new homes, and so they carefully framed what was happening in positive terms. One mother explained how she had consistently reassured her children by telling them:

> We'll be able to get through this. It's going to be better than the old house. It's going to be a bumpy ride, but we'll get there. (Ruby, mother)

This sensitive support by mothers helped pattern 1 children to maintain their well-being, and to cope with their difficult experiences.

Children experiencing pattern 1 were also providing their mothers with many forms of support. On an everyday level these included: being generally loving and supportive toward their mother; being helpful when their mother was tired or ill (for example by making her a hot drink, or by drawing her pictures); providing low levels of practical support such as occasionally helping to look after younger siblings; and offering to be "there for" their mother if she was having problems. Importantly, however, these children were rarely their mother's only source of support. Pattern 1 mothers usually had other sources of helpful supports, most often their own mother and/or a network of trusted friends who provided a "supportive and empathetic" presence (Kong, 2021, p. 8) in mothers' lives. These additional sources of support further reduced any pressure pattern 1 children might have felt to support their mother, as they knew that their mother had other supports available. In line with the findings of previous research (see, e.g., Beeble et al., 2009; Coker et al., 2003; Kong, 2021; Mburia-Mwalili et al., 2010), the strength, security, and comfort that mothers and children gained from being embedded in wider networks of support were impacting positively on their overall well-being.

Pattern 1 children also tended to support their mother to recover from her experiences of coercive control. Their techniques for doing so included: reassuring her about the past, present and future, particularly by telling her that the coercive control was not her fault; lifting her out of negative moods by cheering her up or distracting her with an enjoyable activity; and increasing her confidence by praising her mothering and supporting and encouraging her to engage with the outside world.

Pattern 1 children's feelings about support

Pattern 1 children generally appeared to be experiencing their support for their mother in positive ways. Their supports were mainly low-stakes, because their mother was already experiencing relatively high levels of well-being. Although some of these mothers were still in the process of rebuilding their mental health, they generally expressed confidence in their ability to cope, enthusiasm about their current lives, and gratitude for their support networks (Sinko et al., 2021). In this positive emotional atmosphere, children's supports mainly appeared to be a spontaneous reflection of their love for their mother as opposed to a reaction to pressure or worry. Children's interviews indicated that they were supporting their mother not because they felt that they had to do so, but because they desired to do so.

Accordingly, children reported positive feelings about giving support. Katie (age 12) described how the support between herself and her mother was reciprocal, how giving support to her mother was enjoyable and beneficial, and also how she was benefiting from additional sources of support beyond her mother:

> KATIE: I think it used to help Mum [to have me to talk to], because my mum says I'm quite grown-up for my age because I've got a niece and I look after her quite a lot, and Mum says I'm grown-up and she just trusts me with stuff. It's the same with my gran; she trusts me with a lot of things, so yeah.

EMMA: What's that like for you; is it good *and* bad, good *or* bad?

KATIE: I feel like it's good, and I don't feel pressurized or anything that I've got this secret [her experiences of coercive control], and I'm not allowed to tell anyone or anything, 'cos my friend knows, because my mum told me to tell my friend. She's a really nice friend, and I could trust her with my life and she wouldn't tell anyone. But I feel quite grown-up about it, because I feel my mum could trust me with anything. I'm really proud about that.

EMMA: And how do you feel about telling things to your mum?

KATIE: I could tell my mum literally anything. I can trust my mum. However I feel, I could tell her and she'd be fine with it, and she'd help me out if it was a big problem. And I could also talk to my gran about it, because I'm really close to my gran and I can just tell her anything.

Katie's experiences illustrate that context is vital for understanding the extent to which taking on a supportive role is helpful or harmful for a child. Katie suggested that she felt no pressure or worry about supporting her mother. She described feeling strongly supported by her mother, her grandmother, and her own friend, being confident in sharing any information with them, and knowing that they would help her with any problems. She felt "really proud" and "grown-up" that her mother trusted and confided in her. Within this context, the child's role as her mother's confidant appeared to be benefiting her.

Other children also described the supports that they and their mother exchanged in positive terms. They suggested that the supports that they received from their mother were meeting their emotional needs:

(Happy tone of voice) We've helped to make each other feel better; we've given each other support throughout the whole thing. (Grace, age 14)

Mum's strong, intelligent, caring . . . She helps me; she knows how I'm feeling, like what moods I'm in. (Bob, age 12)

Findings around mutual supportiveness will be discussed in more detail in the next chapter. Here it is sufficient to note that the children quoted earlier described giving and receiving support, and this reciprocity was something that they appeared to value highly.

Overall, as the positive experiences of pattern 1 children show, child-to-mother support can take many forms. It is vital not to jump to the conclusion that children recovering from coercive control are burdened or parentified by supporting their mother (Katz, 2015a). Before conclusions are drawn about child-to-mother supports, the levels, contexts and impacts of the support, and children's and mothers' views about it, should be explored.

Pattern 1 mothers' feelings about support

Pattern 1 mothers expressed similarly positive attitudes about the supports that they were giving to, and receiving from, their children:

> Shannon always says she thinks I'm brave, which is really good, and she's so proud of me for going to court, and she's so proud of me for doing the stuff that I'm doing now with my volunteer work, and she obviously thinks I'm a very important person. I am [important] in her world; it's just lovely. (Ellie, mother)

> They're just there and we just do support each other. [. . . We support each other through] cuddles, cups of tea and chocolate. . . . We'll put a film on and just snuggle up together. . . . We just know we're going to be there for each other and we do help each other. We know that we love each other. (Lauren, mother)

These statements reflect the satisfaction and happiness that pattern 1 mothers expressed about their current relationships with their children. There is a sense within their words that these mothers' emotional needs were being met by the supports that they were receiving from their children. Rather than these child-to-mother supports being heavy or burdensome, they appeared to be light and enjoyable, such as the affirmation of saying, "I'm proud of you Mum," or watching a film and eating chocolate together. Nonetheless, by conveying love, closeness, and positive feelings, these "light" supports from children seemed to be powerful and effective.

Pattern 1 mothers were also usually positive about the supports that they were giving to their children. These mothers tended to demonstrate a high level of confidence in their parenting abilities and practices. This confidence was evident in the long and detailed descriptions that they provided when asked about their views and experiences around parenting:

> Trust, love, friendship, fun; and I do think you need to give boundaries to your child, and routine is so important. And just enjoy each other, you know? Being a parent should be fun; being a kid should be fun. Don't do what you think you "should" do; do what you and your child want to do. If your daughter wants you to play tea parties with her dollies, and you want to revert back to being a child, then do it, because I do, and it's great fun. (Ellie, mother)

> It's just a lot happier, calmer. I did the Triple P parenting course... and I've got like a toolkit for if anything does arise that I can put into place, like talking to the kids and stuff... So we just have a laugh, and they're being kids and I'm being a mum now, so, you know, they've got boundaries and stuff. (Isobel, mother)

> Lots of love, lots of praise to balance out any discipline you've got to do. Lots of silliness. Distraction instead of telling them off sometimes. Honesty, consistency, routine. Good boundaries, but fair boundaries. I think you've not got to sweat the small stuff. Manners: teach them to do the right thing, say sorry and to learn from their mistakes, and let them make mistakes. Lots of fresh air. Make the telly time special family time. And teamwork: stick together. (Ruby, mother)

In making these statements, pattern 1 mothers indicated that they were thoughtful and comfortable in their parenting. They were sufficiently confident to ignore "what you should do" and have childish fun with their children, and to allow their children to make mistakes. Their descriptions of their parenting were well-rounded, including discipline and boundaries as well as praise and laughter. They also often had strategies for avoiding conflicts and arguments with their children and for facilitating calmness in challenging situations.

As previously mentioned, these pattern 1 mother–child relationships were often being achieved within families that were still experiencing negative impacts from the coercive control they had experienced, particularly ongoing mental health issues. However, pattern 1 mothers were able to ensure that they had the emotional resources to continue parenting despite these ongoing impacts. One mother described how she was making sure that she was not always "in bits" in front of her daughter. Another mother explained how she had protected her mental health by initiating only the most winnable disputes with her ex-partner about contact between him and the children, and by accepting practical help from friends so that she had sufficient physical energy to look after the children. The presence or absence of mental health difficulties in mothers was therefore not a critical factor in whether mothers were able to positively support children and feel confident in parenting. Rather, what was important was whether or not mothers felt they were coping well with their mental health (and had formal and/or informal supports that were assisting them to cope well), enabling them to interact with their children in the ways that they wished.

As mentioned previously, the presence of informal supports often contributed to the high levels of well-being in pattern 1 families. Most pattern 1 families had access to assistance from friends and family. Maternal grandparents, especially, had often provided emotional and practical support at the beginning of families' recovery phases, giving mothers much-needed time to become emotionally stronger and more able to cope with the challenges of single-parenting. As we will discover in the next sections, families experiencing patterns 2, 3, and 4 tended to have fewer informal supports. Mothers in these families were much more likely to have been left to manage on their own.

Overall, pattern 1 mothers expressed positive attitudes toward their children, emphasizing how important their children were to them and the closeness of their mother–child relationships:

I just love her; I just love her to bits. She's my world, my absolute world. (Ellie, mother)

She's beautiful, talented, and she's a little star. (Lucy, mother)

We're very bonded, very happy, and very close. (Alison, mother)

Reflections on pattern 1

Pattern 1 represents the "success stories" of mother–child relationships thriving in the aftermath of coercive control. Such successes have rarely been the focus of research. In identifying pattern 1, this study highlights that mother–child relationships can heal, recover, and be a key source of strength and positivity for children and mothers with past experiences of coercive control. This study did not measure the "psychological adjustment" of the children who participated. However, the qualitative data gathered from children and mothers suggested that the children experiencing pattern 1 had achieved very good psychological adjustment and were well positioned to experience good outcomes as adults despite their experiences of coercive control. Further research into pattern 1 families is required to examine the extent to which this phenomenon may apply more widely.

Exploring pattern 1 deepens our understanding of the mother–child support that can take place in families with experiences of coercive control. Previous research has focused on the protective and supportive actions that take place while mothers and children are still living with coercive control. It has examined high-risk and dangerous actions, such as children attempting to protect their mother and siblings from violence, and children calling the police for help (Chanmugam, 2015; Mullender et al., 2002;

Øverlien and Hydén, 2009). However, this study's exploration of support-iveness after separation from perpetrators/fathers draws attention to very different types of support that have mostly gone unnoticed until now (for an exception, see Wuest et al., 2004). This study highlights a hidden world of mothers and children supporting each other in small, commonplace ways that are built into the fabric of their everyday lives. These supports are based on having a generally supportive and nurturing attitude toward each other, doing enjoyable activities together, exchanging compliments and encouragements, and having a sense of security that they will "be there" for one another to provide non-judgmental and friendly support should difficulties arise.

Routinely giving supports that are successful in assisting the person you are trying to help is very different from routinely giving supports to a person that do not have the impacts that you desire. While the former builds confidence, the latter tends to produce feelings of frustration and powerlessness. Given this distinction, a key reason why pattern 1 mothers and children felt positively about supporting each other may have been the effectiveness of their supports for one another. In pattern 1, the professional and informal help that mothers and children had received since separating from perpetrators/fathers had reduced their problems to manageable levels. A pattern 1 child therefore did not, for example, need to attempt single-handedly to build their mother's confidence up from nothing; rather, their mother's confidence had already improved considerably, and all that the child needed to do was to continue "topping it up" from time to time — something that they could do with ease and feel successful about. Tew et al. (2012, p. 452) argue that interpersonal relationships are beneficial to recovery when they situate the recovering person as "someone with abilities, and where interactions provide concrete experiences of being able to exert influence, offering opportunities to rediscover personal agency and efficacy." Pattern 1 mothers' and children's successes in giving support to one another may therefore have been increasing their personal "agency and efficacy" and building their sense of being skilled and powerful (the opposite of how perpetrators'/fathers' coercive control had made them feel).

Pattern 1 supportiveness is achievable when mothers and children are well recovered, and it also acts to further promote their recoveries. However, as we will now explore, when mothers and children were struggling more with the aftermath of coercive control and did not receive the help that they needed, they experienced different, less positive, patterns of support.

PATTERN 2: HIGH-STAKES SUPPORT, LIMITED RECOVERIES

Three families were experiencing pattern 2 at the time when they took part in the study. Like pattern 1, pattern 2 contained a high level of mother–child support. However, supports were experienced in a complex way, partly positive and partly negative. This mix of positive and negative experience had occurred because, in this pattern:

- Mothers were experiencing more mental health difficulties
- Child-to-mother support was high-stakes because the children were aware that mothers' mental health might deteriorate without their support
- Mothers' and children's feelings about the supports that they were exchanging tended to be more mixed

Furthermore, within these families:

- There were moderate-to-high levels of support, and mutual support was occurring between mothers and children
- Children were either supporting mothers slightly more than mothers were supporting children, or they were providing similar levels of support
- Mothers were struggling more with their mental health, so child-to-mother support was high-stakes, and not fully meeting the mother's emotional needs

- Children were often still experiencing emotional and behavioral impacts from the coercive control, and mothers' support was only partly meeting children's emotional needs
- Mothers and children were often struggling to connect with each other emotionally, and there were ongoing strains and tensions in mother–child relationships
- Mothers and children tended to have fewer outside sources of support

The three families experiencing pattern 2 were:

- Eloise and John
- Akeela, Brock, and Vince
- Violet, Angel, and Joe

Prior to separating from perpetrators/fathers, Eloise's relationship with her son had been very close and supportive, while Akeela's and Violet's relationships with their children had been mixed (see chapter 5).

Pattern 2 supportiveness

Pattern 2 mothers used many strategies to support their children. They were generally supportive of their children in their everyday lives, and expressed feelings of love for them. They were aware of their children's feelings, and attempted to be understanding and responsive to them. They also reported building their children's life-skills, such as cooking and paying bills, and supporting them to do things independently. These mothers were, however, sometimes overwhelmed by depression and other mental health difficulties, and these difficulties affected their everyday interactions with their children. One mother found her children's behavior difficult to cope with. She was therefore often upset, angry, or frustrated with them. Although many pattern 2 children identified their mother as an important source of support, there was only one family out of the three where the children said that their mother was always "there for" them.

Pattern 2 mothers made considerable efforts to help their children to recover from the coercive control they had experienced. They variously attempted to:

- Rebuild their children's confidence
- Reassure them, advising them not to allow the past to influence their present lives
- Encourage them to discuss or express their feelings and worries
- Enhance their feelings of safety (children were worried about the ongoing danger posed by their fathers)
- Secure professional help for them

Pattern 2 children supported their mothers as much as—perhaps even slightly more than—their mothers supported them. On a daily level, these children generally had supportive attitudes toward their mothers. The children described themselves as "being there" for their mothers. One mother, Eloise, stated that her son always listened to and understood her. These children also helped their mothers in practical ways, many of them typical of how children support parents in everyday life in "ordinary" families that have not experienced coercive control (Morrow, 2003). John (aged 20 at the time of interview) gave his mother money to help with bills. He sometimes cooked meals for her as a treat. Similarly, other pattern 2 children were helpful with housework and accompanied mothers to medical appointments. Brock and Vince showed understanding about their mother's financial limitations. At times they refrained from asking her to purchase items for them. Children also helped to rebuild their mother's confidence, lift her mood, and reassure her about the past.

However, some of pattern 2 children's supports were more problematic. Akeela said that her 15-year-old son, Ali (who did not participate in the study), was like a father to his younger brothers Brock (age 12) and Vince (age 13), and that she could not cope as a parent without his help. Such a high, adult-like level of support may have been having a detrimental impact on this 15-year-old. Brock and Vince themselves discussed in their interviews how they were trying to keep their mother safe from the perpetrator/father by telling her not to leave the house without them. This level of guarding, though possibly necessary given that the perpetrator still lived near to them, was not conducive to a healthy relationship of growing independence between this mother and her adolescent children. Finally, one child, John, mentioned that he sometimes withheld his negative thoughts or moods from his mother to avoid upsetting her, which may have been worsening his own well-being.

Pattern 2 mothers' mental health struggles

One significant feature of the pattern 2 families was that all of the mothers and children experiencing this pattern asked to be interviewed jointly rather than privately. As discussed in chapter 3, these joint interviews perhaps made it harder for children to discuss any negative feelings that they may have been experiencing about supporting their mothers. Wanting to be interviewed together reflected the fact that these mothers were—unlike pattern 1 mothers—very open with their children about how they were feeling, and therefore felt no need to be interviewed privately. Eloise and John were particularly adamant that they should be interviewed together, stating, "We don't have any secrets from each other." Pattern 2 mothers also described how they felt that it was correct and important to be always honest with their children. Akeela discussed the benefits of sharing her feelings with her children, something that she had only begun to do during their recoveries:

> With me talking to my children, and having that understanding, that's really helped us as a family—it's better. I needed them to know how upset I was, and that's really helped me. Mothers hide their emotions to protect their children, but to mothers it's a torture. After the boys got help, we all started sharing our emotions with each

other. Before, we kept our emotions locked up, I kept mine locked up, and we didn't understand each other like we do now. (Akeela, mother)

Although it may have been helpful for mothers and children to understand each other, the high level of openness between pattern 2 mothers and children meant that these children had been aware for many years that their mother struggled with mental health issues and sometimes felt suicidal.

Mothers discussed their mental health problems in their joint interviews. One mother and son shared a frank dialogue about it:

ELOISE: I get very, very depressed. When I feel depressed, like I can't go on, I tell him [son] that.

JOHN: (sighs)

ELOISE: Don't I? I say I can't go on anymore, life is too hard.

JOHN: So many times I've heard that. What a crush that is hearing your own mother saying she wants to kill herself, she wants to kill herself. It's horrible.

Experiencing his mother's suicidal feelings was clearly harming this child's well-being. Other interviews demonstrated the high-stakes nature of pattern 2 children's support, with children knowing that their support was critical to their mother's ability to cope:

To tell you the honest truth, if it wasn't for Ali I wouldn't be here today. I can't cope, I can't cope with the younger two. . . . With Ali being the oldest and having seen things and been part of it, he knows, he understands. . . . I would have had to put the youngest two in care, if it wasn't for Ali taking them aside and saying: "Why are you upsetting and stressing Mum?" (Akeela, mother)

Without the kids, I probably would've committed suicide. . . . We're very close, and as long as we're close things are okay. . . . I still have days when I feel like I can't cope. I just sit and cry. The kids ask me why, and I say I don't know. I usually try to just get on with things. (Violet, mother)

Pattern 2 children were placed in the position of being vital to their mothers' coping largely because of the inadequate responses that their mothers had received from services. For example, Joe explained that his mother depression was linked to the post-separation violence and stalking that the family had experienced from the perpetrator/father:

She'll be happy, and then something will happen, like she's told she has to move house [because of the ongoing threat from the perpetrator/father], and she'll be dead down. (Joe, age 14)

Rather than the perpetrator/father being punished for his violence, this mother and children had been forced to secure their own safety by fleeing the area, leaving behind their networks of support (Abrahams, 2010). It was these events that appeared to have triggered the mother's mental health struggles, and to still be negatively affecting the mother and her children years later when the study took place. This mother, Violet, also mentioned that she had received good professional support while she and her children had lived in a refuge, and that her well-being would have been better if this level of support had continued when she returned to the community.

Another mother, Eloise, described how the guilt that she felt about her son growing up with coercive control was harming her present-day mental health:

Everybody will say: "but you're not with him [the perpetrator/father] anymore; surely you should start feeling better?" but I don't. I feel bad about it, because I knew that it was my fault—me staying with him—that John's had problems. . . . I have flashbacks, like Post-Traumatic Stress, and I feel so bad that I allowed that man to put our child through what he did. (Eloise, mother)

Eloise believed that her ongoing depression was largely caused by these feelings of guilt and self-blame (see also Khan, 2020, and Sinko et al., 2021). Although she had been involved with multiple professionals because of the coercive control, it did not seem that she had received support around her relationship with her son or her feelings of guilt toward him. It is helpful to compare Eloise's words to that of a pattern 1 mother, Ellie. Ellie had once felt similar feelings of guilt, but had received effective professional supports to reduce them, enabling her to attain a higher level of well-being:

> My daughter and I are far more open with each other, and I think that's got a lot to do with the fact that we went to a post-abuse therapeutic course with the NSPCC [an Ontario-based program], which was absolutely fantastic. . . . I used to find it very difficult to tell Shannon off because she'd always say: "you don't love me," and I'd feel so guilty. But the whole program made me realize that there's nobody who's a perfect parent; you're gonna have your bad days sort of thing. . . . I'm able to be more comfortable now. . . . I do still feel guilty and know that I shouldn't, but I do, but nothing in comparison to how it crippled me before. So I'm able to answer painful questions that she puts to me about the past. (Ellie, mother)

Unlike the pattern 2 mothers, pattern 1 mother Ellie described receiving effective support that improved her mental health and enhanced her parenting skills. (For an evaluation of the program that helped Ellie, see Smith et al., 2015.) Effective support had allowed Ellie to introduce some discipline into her mother–child relationship, while also responding to her daughter's wish to communicate more openly about their past experiences. Such supports may have played a significant role in helping Ellie to experience pattern 1 rather than pattern 2. If the pattern 2 families had received such supports, then their mother–child relationships might have improved in the way that Ellie's did, and they may have transitioned into pattern 1. Increasing the commissioning and funding of such supports so that they can benefit more mothers and children may be very helpful for improving the long-term outcomes of domestic violence/coercive control survivors such as Eloise and John.

High-stakes support from pattern 2 children

Because of pattern 2 mothers' more substantial mental health difficulties, the supports provided by their children were more high-stakes than in pattern 1. It may have been that pattern 2 children were more worried than pattern 1 children about their mothers' well-being, and more concerned about the consequences of withdrawing (or providing less) support. These feelings were not expressed by children in their interviews, but may have been silenced because of the presence of mothers in the interviews. (As we have noted, pattern 2 families requested joint interviews.)

However, pattern 2 children generally used the same forms of support as pattern 1 children, rather than deploying forms of support that were specific to their mothers' suicidal thoughts or feelings of depression. For example, they increased their mother's confidence and lifted her mood:

Me and my brother [Brock] are a good support, because when Mum's crying we give her pep talks that bring her up and stuff. We say: "Oh, Mum, everything's going to be alright." (Vince, age 13)

He's very supportive and he's funny; he makes me laugh, and that's a really good quality. He's made me laugh a lot. . . . Any bad news brings me down; it brings it all back to me . . . so he'll make me laugh; he'll put a smile back on my face. . . . He'll say: "it would be good for you Mum," which is important because when you've had so many bad things happen, it does make you feel a "downer" and you do doubt. I doubt myself a lot, and what I'm capable of doing, but John gives me encouragement to do things . . . and how to dress; I always ask his opinion. He says I've turned him into a stylist! (Eloise, mother)

These forms of support seemed relatively light and positive. The closest that these children seemed to come to dealing directly with their mothers' mental health issues was in simple statements and actions; for example one child, Joe, spoke in his interview of warning his mother "not to do anything stupid" [i.e., commit suicide] and calling her at work to check whether she was feeling well.

However, there was a critical difference between patterns 1 and 2 in children's sense of "being there" for their mother. Whereas pattern 1 children tended to say in their interviews that they would be there for their mother *if* she needed them, pattern 2 children described how they *actually were* there for their mother:

> [What's helped Mum the most is] us *being there* for her, and taking care of her: If she ever needs help, we help her and if there's anything she wants done, we do it. . . . I've told Mum that I'll *always be there* for her, no matter what, and I'll help her if she needs help. (Angel, age 12, my italics)

There is a subtle difference in grammar here. The "I will" of pattern 2 children such as Angel is *not* a promise "to be there" if needed in the future, but a pledge to "always be there" in a *continual* state of "being there" for the mother.

In assisting their mothers, pattern 2 children were actively engaged in improving their mother's emotional well-being. This support was often successful in the short-term. For example, mothers found it helpful when their children encouraged them to undertake activities and used humor to raise their spirits. However, it was obvious that further supports were needed to meet these mothers' mental health needs (Khan, 2020). It was also uncertain what long-term impacts there could be if children continued to "be there" for their mothers in these ways. For example, looking into the future, John, Brock, Vince, Angel and Joe may be reluctant to relocate outside of their local area and be away from their family homes for education or employment opportunities in the years ahead. Furthermore, these children's experiences of trying to help their mother but not actually being able to resolve her problems may erode their sense of self-efficacy in the long term (Chanmugam, 2015; Tew et al., 2012).

Pattern 2 mothers' support for children

Pattern 2 mothers were still experiencing many negative impacts from the coercive control, and they therefore found it more challenging than pattern 1 mothers to help their children to recover. Their supports in this area were limited to verbal encouragements such as: "be strong"; "don't give up"; or "try not to think about the past and enjoy your life now." This strategy was perhaps the best available, given how much these mothers were struggling themselves. Yet, although these encouragements were well-meant, some may have had the unintended effect of suggesting to children that they should ignore their negative feelings, rather than address them.

Also, unlike pattern 1 mothers, mothers experiencing pattern 2 tended to frame their concern to build their children's independence in terms of equipping their children to cope without them:

> I've shown my boys how to pay bills. I tell them that they must be independent, and not rely on me, in case I'm not there anymore. (Akeela, mother)

> I tell them I'm not going to be around forever, so they need to know how to do things for themselves. . . I hate it when they argue. I say to them: "You should stick together because, if anything happens to me, you'll only have each other." (Violet, mother)

No pattern 2 children commented on how helpful this independence-building was for them. However, the way that this support was framed was possibly worrying for them, reminding them of their mother's mortality, and the possibility of her committing suicide.

Yet pattern 2 mothers did meet their children's emotional needs in other, potentially more effective ways, despite the difficulties that they were experiencing. For example, Violet described how she encouraged her children to turn to her, and also urged them to use other sources of support:

> I've always told the kids to tell me if they've got a problem, otherwise it won't get sorted out. I also encourage them to talk to teachers if they're having school problems. I tell them that there's people out there who can help them. (Violet, mother)

Such statements are potentially helpful, as they promote the idea that problems are there to be resolved, not endured. They frame the world as a place where support, when sought, is available. Of the pattern 2 families, Violet and her children had the most extensive circle of wider support. The other pattern 2 families appeared to have fewer sources of support, increasing their vulnerability (Beeble et al., 2009; Coker et al., 2003; Mburia-Mwalili et al., 2010).

Pattern 2 children's feelings about support

On the whole, pattern 2 children did not appear to feel negative about the supports that they were providing for their mother. These children were aware of their mother's mental health struggles, yet their supportive strategies often appeared to be light and positive (advising their mother on what clothes to wear, for example). No child reported that they were currently using more emotionally taxing strategies such as counseling their mother extensively about her depression. Children in other studies have described feeling resentful or concerned about assuming adult-like levels of responsibility for their parent's well-being (see, e.g., Chanmugam, 2014; Stanley et al., 2012). No child in this study discussed having such feelings (though this does not mean they never experienced them).

Furthermore, despite being aware of their mothers' mental health struggles, pattern 2 children described feeling well-supported by their mothers, and characterized their mothers in very positive terms:

[My relationship with Mum is] alright now. Mum talks to me now. She's kind, because she helps me out. She's just, like, so good, nice and generous, because, if I do something wrong, she doesn't shout at me or hit me like him [the perpetrator/father]. (Brock, age 12)

[If I could pick three words to describe my relationship with Mum, they would be:] nice, brilliant, fabulous. . . . We get on great. Mum tells us stuff, and it's been brilliant since he's been gone. (Vince, age 13)

[If I could pick three words to describe my relationship with Mum, they would be:] wonderful, fabulous, caring—because she always takes care of me, and whenever I want to talk to her she's there for me, and she's a wonderful person. (Angel, age 12)

Mum's lovely, caring, and just there all the time. [. . . Our relationship is] perfect, together all the time, loving, caring. I wouldn't change it for anything. Mum's the parent I can rely on. (Joe, age 14)

Although this positivity was perhaps encouraged by the context of the joint interviews, children's statements do highlight specific aspects of mothers' support that children found helpful. The children valued their mother having open conversations with them ("Mum talks to me now"; "Mum tells us stuff"; "whenever I want to talk to her she's there for me"), their mother's consistent support for them ("She's kind, because she helps me out"; "she always takes care of me"; "Mum's the parent I can rely on"), and their mother's "caring" approach to parenting. Furthermore, children valued their mother–child relationship partly by comparison with their relationship with perpetrators/fathers ("She's just, like, so good, nice, and generous, because, if I do something wrong, she doesn't shout at me or hit me like him"). It was perhaps this contrast, above all, that helped pattern 2 children to appreciate the positive aspects of their mothers' parenting. They may have been aware that, although these mother–child relationships were not perfect, they could have been much worse.

Children also spoke in broad, happy terms when discussing the help that they provided to their mother, and were proud of the actions that they were taking:

> What's helped Mum the most is us being there for her, and taking care of her. If she ever needs help, we help her, and if there's anything she wants done, we do it. (Angel, age 12)

> Me and [my brother] Vince get on really well, and we try to help our mum. (Brock, age 12)

When asked what he wanted for his mother in the future, Vince himself replied:

> I want her to have a good life, because she's made us have a good life, and I want her to have a good life. (Vince, age 13)

In expressing gratitude to his mother for providing a "good life" for him, Vince emphasized that he wanted her to "have a good life" in return. Reinforcing his brother Brock's assessment that "we try to help our mum," he was implying his devotion to taking actions to help Akeela, and his pride in doing so.

Only one pattern 2 child, John, reported experiencing negative impacts from his mother's ongoing depression. John felt that his own mental health was suffering as a result of living with a depressed parent:

JOHN: There are things in my head—this is what I told Mum the other day—there's always stuff you keep inside, and, yeah, it's messed my head up a little, but there's some things

> I won't say, and my mum's asked me before, but I won't tell her what goes through my head sometimes.
>
> EMMA: Is that sometimes because you don't want to upset or worry her or . . . ?
>
> JOHN: Yeah (pause).
>
> EMMA: Can I ask you a bit more about [Eloise's] depression, and how that affects the two of you?
>
> ELOISE: Greatly, I think if I didn't have my depression we'd have moved on a lot further wouldn't we?
>
> JOHN: Hm.

In Eloise and John's case, maternal depression was limiting the ability of both mother and child to recover (Fong et al., 2019; McFarlane et al., 2017). This example highlights how mothers and children experiencing pattern 2 mother–child relationships would benefit from mothers having access to appropriate professional supports for their mental health (Khan, 2020).

However, John and Eloise both spoke positively of their relationship with each other. John, like Vince (earlier), exemplified the gratitude that pattern 2 children tended to express for their mothers' efforts to support them. Although such support was constrained by mothers' mental health, pattern 2 children such as John and Vince still appeared to view it approvingly, and were aware of how it benefited their own well-being. John stated that he believed that his personal circumstances would be far more precarious without Eloise's guiding influence:

> EMMA: Of all the people or things in your life, what do you think's helped you the most?
>
> JOHN: Mum. If she wasn't here then I'd be off in the army now, or off the rails, in jail, dead, or whatever; I don't know.

Together, Eloise and John emphasized that, although they frequently argued, they felt affectionate and close to each other:

JOHN: I love my mum: You give me grief; I give you grief (Eloise laughs); we give each other a lot of grief, but I love her with all my heart.... Our relationship can be bumpy, but we always resolve it: We're always like a rock.

ELOISE: Solid.

JOHN: Yeah, solid.

ELOISE: We're close; we disagree; but we disagree in a nice way. We'll have heated arguments, but we get over them.

So, though Eloise and John acknowledged their "heated arguments," they were clear that these "bumpy" moments had not undermined the fundamental solidity of their relationship.

Pattern 2 mothers' feelings about support

Pattern 2 mothers expressed positive or mixed (both positive and negative) feelings about the levels and types of support in their mother–child relationships. For one mother, Akeela, negative feelings were based around (1) her children having to give her high levels of support; and (2) her inability to fully support her children in return because of her financial limitations. Both feelings were described by her as she discussed the help that her eldest child Ali had given to her since they had separated from the perpetrator/father eight years previously:

To me, overnight, Ali became an adult in those few months. Ali grew up for me, and sometimes I feel really upset. To tell you the truth, I think I deprived my son of his childhood; and [financially] things he wants and needs, I can't give him (crying). (Akeela, mother)

At this point in her interview, Akeela showed a double sense of guilt that she had needed to rely on Ali to such an extent, "depriv[ing] my son of his childhood," and was also depriving him of his material "wants and needs." However, at another part of her interview, her well-being seemed to increase as she spoke positively of the supportiveness of her older sons:

Vince is good. Vince understands; sometimes he has his tantrums [about me buying things for him], but then he says: "Mum, leave it," and Ali always works round me. You know, he does things for me and he understands. (Akeela, mother)

Pattern 2 mothers' feelings about their children's support could therefore be complex. At times they were greatly upset, but they were also grateful for their children's thoughtfulness and understanding.

Finally, pattern 2 mothers discussed positive feelings around the supportive relationships that they and their children had developed since separating from perpetrators/fathers. These supportive relationships included sharing each other's company and enjoying everyday activities together:

It's nice. John will cook for me, won't you? And he makes lovely little meals, don't you? And he said to me the other day: "Mum, will you teach me how to make pastry?," because he wants to learn. (Eloise, mother)

We're close, and, as long as we're close, things are okay. My kids are so funny, oh—they make me laugh. We have some crazy fun days together. I think my kids are amazing, and I love them to bits. (Violet, mother)

These examples—cookery and "crazy fun days"—serve to reiterate the often light and enjoyable nature of supports between pattern 2 mothers and their children.

Reflections on pattern 2

The relationship dynamics that are here termed "pattern 2" are very similar to those found in Chanmugam's (2014) research with 14 pairs of mothers and children (aged 12–14) residing in emergency domestic violence shelters in the US state of Texas. In Chanmugam's study, mothers and children described giving high levels of support to one another and feeling very emotionally close. Children's supports were high-stakes and mothers were reliant on their children to help them to function. Yet at the same time, those children expressed positivity about their mothers, and reported that their mothers were constantly looking after them. Chanmugam suggests that mother–child relationships with these dynamics are complex. They function protectively and positively for these mothers and children, and are adaptive and useful given the crises that these mothers and children are experiencing. However, the care-taking roles that children perform for their mothers also entail some losses and leave the child continually concerned about their mother. Chanmugam notes that such situations had not been chosen by mothers and children, but were created because of perpetrators'/fathers' abuse. Without the need to survive this abuse, these mothers and children would be able to "enjoy mutually supportive relational dynamics" (Chanmugam, 2014, p. 824) in low-stakes, low-pressure environments.

Pattern 2 mother–child relationships in some ways reflect findings of previous studies that children supporting mothers in domestic violence contexts are overburdened (see, e.g., Holt et al., 2008; Stanley et al., 2012). Giving support in a context where you do not believe that the person you are supporting could cope without you is high-stakes, worrisome, and stressful, especially when the support-giver is not yet an adult and is dependent on the person that they are supporting.

However, although pattern 2 families' supports were problematic in some ways, their circumstances tended to be distinctly different from the phenomenon of "parentification," where children are forced into assuming adult roles and adults become childlike. It would not be appropriate to apply the term "parentification" to pattern 2 families for a number of reasons. The children described themselves as willingly giving support to their mothers. Mothers reported continuing to support their children in ways that appeared to be at least partly meeting their children's emotional needs. Children also tended to describe their mother–child relationships as mutually supportive and beneficial.

Mothers and children discussed valuing each other's support. Finally, many of the types of supports that children were giving were consistent with their ages, such as making their mother laugh or participating with her in enjoyable activities.

There were therefore considerable strengths in these pattern 2 mother–child relationships. The main problematic issue, mothers' mental health, could have been addressed by professional supports, if such supports had been available (Khan, 2020). Through these professional supports, children would have been enabled to help their mothers in low-stakes, rather than high-stakes, ways. This analysis of pattern 2 therefore illustrates the value of making appropriate and specialized mental health supports available for adult victims/survivors of domestic violence/coercive control (see Khan 2020 for details of what such supports could involve). Such supports may have very positive impacts not only on adult victims/survivors, but also on their children.

PATTERN 3: STRUGGLING RELATIONSHIPS, STRUGGLING RECOVERIES

Four families were experiencing pattern 3 mother–child relationships at the time when they took part in the study. Pattern 3 families were different to pattern 1 and 2 families because:

- Mothers and children were supporting one another to a lesser extent. Although mothers did provide some limited support for children, children were not supporting mothers and seemed to be largely unaware of mothers' emotional needs. Mutual support was therefore not occurring.
- There were ongoing problems and conflicts between children and mothers. These problems were partly fueled by children's continued lack of understanding of the coercive control that they and their mothers had experienced.

Furthermore, within pattern 3 families:

- Mothers and children had problematic communication patterns and their relationships were often high in conflict
- Mothers were struggling with their mental health, and/or children were still experiencing emotional and behavioral impacts from the coercive control
- Mothers' supports were only partly meeting children's emotional needs
- Mothers and children were often without informal supports from family and friends
- Mothers were aware that their mother–child relationships were strained and they wanted to improve them
- Mothers and children were in need of high levels of support to help strengthen their mother–child relationships

The four families experiencing pattern 3 were:

- Kimberley and Elle
- Marie and Leah
- Charlie and Tanya
- Ria and Carly

Notably, these were the four families whose mother–child relationships had been very strained and distant while mothers were still in relationships with perpetrators/fathers (see chapter 5). The fact that these four families continued to experience extensive difficulties post-separation (and in three of these families, separation had occurred more than three years prior to the study) is an illustration of the long-term harms that coercive control can cause. As discussed earlier in this chapter, these mothers and children had accessed some professional supports to help them to recover from domestic violence. However, it seemed that these supports had been insufficient to meet the scale of their needs.

Pattern 3 supportiveness

Pattern 3 mothers expressed a wish to support their children. They were attempting, and struggling, to engage in the challenging and lengthy process of bringing about significant improvements in the behavioral problems that children had developed as a result of perpetrators'/fathers' coercive control:

> I just keep trying to reinforce it all the time: "We don't hit, we don't kick, we don't call names; that's wrong," and I just try to encourage all the kind behavior that you want, so, yeah, I've got a lot of work to do. (Marie, mother)

> When Tanya and her brother have an argument, he'll hit her and she'll hit him back—not a tap—she's bruised him and marked him. But it's very rare now; they don't fight so much. And that's sort of because I've had a rules list. (Charlie, mother)

These efforts by mothers are similar to the findings of Wuest et al. (2004) that mothers who have separated from perpetrators work hard to establish new standards for living together respectfully for their children and themselves.

One mother experiencing pattern 3, Kimberley, was making attempts to increase the confidence of her daughter Elle, who had become withdrawn, but seemed unsure how to do so. At times, Kimberley suggested that she attempted to compel Elle to interact and socialize more:

> Elle still doesn't venture out that much. She really just stays in the house. I try to force her to go. There's this carnival that I wanted her to help out with, and she was in the troop last year but she doesn't want to this year. I don't know why. (Kimberley, mother)

Kimberley's comment that she did not "know" or understand her daughter's feelings ("I don't know why") was echoed by another pattern 3 mother, Ria:

Obviously she's my world, and I hope she knows that. I do tell her, but whether it goes in or not, I don't know. But I'm sure it does in some way. (Ria, mother)

Ria was in a similar position to Charlie (see later), giving messages of love and support and hoping that "in some way" they were "go[ing] in"—but, as we will observe, not necessarily seeing evidence of this assimilation taking place in how their children were behaving toward them.

Overall, pattern 3 mothers were struggling to understand how to enable their children to move forward from the negative emotional and behavioral impacts of perpetrators'/fathers' coercive control. This difficulty was more pronounced because pattern 3 mothers often had fewer informal sources of practical assistance, emotional support, or advice about parenting. (They tended to report difficult relationships with their own mothers.) They therefore required additional professional supports, both to strengthen their relationships with their children and to develop their knowledge and skills in dealing with the challenging parenting situations that they faced.

Compared with pattern 1 mothers, pattern 3 mothers used fewer strategies to support their children. The supportive strategies that they *did* use included those mentioned earlier around reducing their children's withdrawn or aggressive behaviors, and also:

- Obtaining professional help for children, often through the UK charity Women's Aid
- Protecting children from having harmful post-separation contact with perpetrators/fathers, or, if protecting them from contact was impossible due a to family court order, then attempting to minimize its negative emotional and behavioral effects on children

And they lived happily ever after?

- Sometimes adopting everyday strategies to enhance children's confidence, to show affection for them, and to "be there" for them

Through these supports, pattern 3 mothers were helping to increase the well-being of their children.

The professional supports with which pattern 3 families had engaged had brought about some improvements, but had not produced significant transformations:

> She [daughter] still doesn't say much, but her communication is better than it was before . . . because she goes to counseling and [the Ontario-based program], that kind of helped her get her emotions out, what she was bottling up inside. (Kimberley, mother)

Professional supports could therefore have positive outcomes in some ways, such as helping children to express the emotions that they were "bottling up inside." However, they had not resolved the problems between pattern 3 mothers and children. (In this instance, the child was still not saying much to her mother.) To understand why professional supports that had been very successful for pattern 1 families had less impact on pattern 3 families, it is important to consider their different experiences. Pattern 3 mother–child relationships were the ones that were most severely undermined by the coercive control (see chapter 5), and this impact meant that they had begun their recovery phase with deeper and more entrenched problems that were harder to resolve.

Pattern 3 mothers were endeavoring to strengthen their mother–child relationships as much as possible, but they were swimming against the tide. Ria and Marie had not been able to bond with their newborn children while living with perpetrators/fathers (see also Buchanan, 2018). They were now attempting to become more openly affectionate with their children as part of moving forward with their lives. Ria appeared to be further ahead in this process; for Marie, "letting down my barriers and starting to have fun" still seemed a very difficult task:

I've struggled with giving her affection; I've struggled showing her love; I've struggled just cuddling her. It's been a gradual thing that I've started doing. At first, the only time we would cuddle is at bedtime—I would tell her I loved her—but now I'll just grab her and be like: "God, I love you," and you can see the [positive] difference it's had on her. (Ria, mother)

There's just so much distance between me and my kids, especially my oldest son, I've got to put my barriers down to feel like it's okay now, it's safe to love my kids and be emotionally attached to them. . . . I think, because I've sort of almost shut them out, I've got to . . . um . . . I just want us to all have fun. I'm still really struggling with that, because we haven't had fun for years, so it's about letting down my barriers and starting to have fun. (Marie, mother)

Marie and Charlie also discussed "being there" for their children. Charlie outlined how she attempted to do so by being open and communicative:

I've always told them: "If there's any problems, talk to me. I'm not gonna shout at you, or anything like that: we're just gonna talk things through." I let them know that I'm always there for them. I think that's the most important thing: that you can talk to your child, and they can talk to their parent, and showing them lots of love and care. (Charlie, mother)

Compared with the statement of confidence by Charlie that "I let them know that I'm always there for them," Marie was less assured:

I want the trust to build because I think that's been damaged, like they don't trust me and they don't believe in me I don't think, so I want to build that up so they feel safe and secure that they can trust me and that I'm there for them. (Marie, mother)

Marie here stressed that she "want[ed] the trust to build" but was aware that she was at an early stage of rebuilding her children's belief that she was "there for them."

Even for Charlie and Ria, the two mothers whose sense of self-efficacy appeared to be ahead of that of Marie, productive conversations were difficult to initiate. Both mothers acknowledged that interactions tended to take the form of irritable behavior, "bad attitude" from children, or "shouting at each other":

> We just have problems talking to each other. It's always, like, shouting at each other. It's the way she talks. . . . I have no patience with her anymore. . . . Bad attitude. . . . She doesn't understand about life; what we've got to do to have a life, money-wise. . . . Nothing's changed with my daughter. She said she'd change her attitude when we moved house, but she's gone back to her old self again, talking to me like a piece of dirt, things like that. So she's never changed. (Charlie, mother)

> We don't really talk. I think that's why I said we both need more support, because she's probably scared to talk to me, because I'm always ratty [irritable] and she probably thinks that I'll get upset. (Ria, mother)

What pattern 3 mothers had in common was that underlying, unresolved strains and problems in their families were undermining their efforts to "be there" for their children. Even where mothers felt that they were doing well in often talking supportively to their children, tensions were still surfacing in their interactional and conversational patterns.

Pattern 3 children's feelings about support

Only two children in pattern 3 families—Leah and Elle—were within the age-limit of the study and wished to be interviewed (and in the case of one child, Elle, daughter of Kimberley, the interview was concluded after about fifteen minutes as Elle appeared to be uncomfortable). It was therefore not possible to develop a detailed understanding of how pattern 3 children viewed their relationships with their mothers. However, when combined with their mothers' interviews, the limited data from pattern 3 children suggested that they had minimal understandings of their mother's feelings and emotions. The child who completed a full interview (Leah, age 11, daughter of Marie) described how she had only just begun to be aware of her mother's feelings when she realized that her mother had been "putting on a brave face" while living with her father to cover her unhappiness. She described how this realization had occurred through an activity that she had participated during an Ontario-based program:

LEAH: You got a mask, and you had to draw a happy face, but you had to pull a sad face and then put it on, so you're covering what you're feeling—so you're feeling really sad but you look happy. So we just talked about that, about what Mum was feeling with Dad—she was pretending she was happy with Dad, but she wasn't really happy.

EMMA: Um, yeah. Is that the first time that you'd sort of thought about that before?

LEAH: (nods.)

It was therefore possible that Leah's relationship with Marie would become more supportive in future as her understanding increased. Marie, in her own interview, similarly expressed a wish to become more open with her children now that she was living apart from the perpetrator/father.

However, most pattern 3 mothers and children were still having difficulty in being open with each other several years after separating from perpetrators/fathers. One mother, Charlie, expressed her belief that her children still did not understand how abusively their father had behaved:

Sometimes I feel my kids don't understand the way their dad's been to me. (Charlie, mother)

Pattern 3 children's lack of understanding tied into the conversational patterns of "shouting" detailed earlier, and the frequent conflicts that these children continued to have with their mothers.

Furthermore, some pattern 3 children had been, or were still being, encouraged by perpetrators/fathers to direct anger and blame toward their mothers. The "victim" persona used by some perpetrators/fathers was thus another ongoing problem that was fueling the mother–child conflicts that pattern 3 families were experiencing:

[My daughter] used to have it that it was me, I was stopping her dad from seeing her, because he would tell her that "Mummy doesn't love me anymore and she kicked me out," and things like that. Whereas I, I've never said anything bad about him. I've always tried to cocoon her, but for him it's always playing the victim kind of thing, and that's what's been drilled into her. (Ria, mother)

He's telling them things about me, bad things. When they come back [from seeing him] they're awful, their behavior's bad and normally I'm getting verbally attacked by my son who's having a go at me. (Marie, mother)

These experiences of victim-blaming demonstrate how perpetrators/fathers could continue to impact mother–child relationships in the post-separation period (Monk and Bowen, 2021; Thiara and Humphreys, 2017). The "bad things" that had been, or continued to be, "drilled" into children's perceptions of their mothers by perpetrators/fathers could cast an ongoing shadow, upsetting and disrupting children's and mother's abilities to support each other.

What pattern 3 children said that they wanted was simply to spend more time with their mothers:

I'd like us to spend more time together. (Elle, age 14)

I'd like us to spend more time and just, like, experience things and do things together that we haven't done before. (Leah, age 11)

Overall, it seemed that the pattern 3 children had little sense that they could, or might wish to, provide support to their mothers; it was not something that occurred to them in the context of their relationships. However, despite the problems in their mother–child relationships, they did wish to connect more closely and frequently with their mothers in future.

Pattern 3 mothers' feelings about support

Pattern 3 mothers described feeling saddened by the current state of their mother–child relationships. However, they were hopeful that these relationships could improve in the future. They particularly wished to communicate more effectively with their children:

I think if I change, and then they change, that's the only way we can move on: and that's why I've got them counseling now, to get things moved on. I've got a new house, [the kids have got] a new school, so that's the way I'm thinking about moving on and talking more. (Charlie, mother)

I think it's definitely a good time to start talking about it to her. Now she's got that bit of understanding of how it's impacted on me, she can hopefully talk to me about how it's impacted on her. (Ria, mother)

It's better than it was before. We're communicating better, and we're happier as well. . . . She still doesn't say much. . . . It's not going to change overnight, and there's a lot more work to do. (Kimberley, mother)

These mothers' recognition that substantial, difficult change was required is in line with the findings of previous research that mother–child communication is particularly harmed by domestic violence, and often requires professional support to recover (Humphreys et al., 2006; McManus et al., 2013).

It is notable that these mothers perceived improvements in their mother–child relationships as largely bilateral processes that required the input of their children, rather than an achievement that they could accomplish on their own (Kuczynski et al., 2003; Walton et al., 2017). Mothers viewed it as their responsibility to take the initial steps to create these improvements (by organizing counseling, or by opening conversations about the impacts of the coercive control); yet they were aware that their children would also need to respond (for example, Ria hoped that her daughter would begin to talk to her in return), and that they and their children needed to make reciprocal contributions to the improvement of their mother–child relationships.

Finally, in keeping with the long-established finding that mutual support between parents and children is a commonplace practice among families in general (e.g., Gillies et al., 2001; Arditti, 1999; Morrow, 2003), pattern 3 mothers stressed their desire to increase their and their children's level of mutual supportiveness. They described a good mother–child relationship as one in which there is two-way communication, the sharing of feelings, and a commitment to care for one another:

It's trusting each other and communicating—no matter what you're going through, I think it's best to communicate with each other and don't hide anything. If you hide certain things, and something's going off [happening], then how are you gonna know what that person's going through? So I think it's best if you communicate; it's really truly important. (Kimberley, mother)

What makes a good [mother–child] relationship? A relationship, I think, is when you feel at ease talking to each other. (Charlie, mother)

I just want us to be happy and, like, working together, because at the minute some of the kids are, like, working in the opposite way, and I'm hoping to build it up, because there's a lot of children and I want us to support each other, and be close, and be there for each other, and look after each other, and look out for each other. (Marie, mother)

These statements by pattern 3 mothers highlight how, for these mothers, mutual support was a key long-term goal. Kimberley wanted Elle to trust her, and reciprocally she wanted to trust Elle sufficiently to "open up" with her. Charlie believed that both she and her children needed to feel at ease talking to each other. Marie wished that every member of her family could work together to support and help one another. These issues of mutual supportiveness will be explored further in chapter 9.

Reflections on pattern 3

Pattern 3 represents the type of mother–child relationship that has been most often discussed in previous research—those with severe problems and high levels of strain caused by domestic violence (see, e.g., Humphreys et al., 2006; Thiara and Humphreys, 2017). For the pattern 3 mothers and children in this study, low levels of mother–child supportiveness and high levels of mother–child conflict were undermining their recoveries and well-being.

Pattern 3 mothers and children required intensive, long-term professional help to assist them in building stronger, more supportive mother–child relationships. Three out of the four pattern 3 families had completed Ontario-based programs. (Ria and Carly had not attended such a program.) Although they had tended to find these programs (involving an evening session on one day per week for ten weeks) slightly helpful, the scale of the strains and disconnections between pattern 3 mothers and their children meant that these programs were far from sufficient. These strains and disconnections were especially difficult to address when, as we have observed, they were being continually fueled by children's contact with the perpetrator/father, during which time he was saying "bad things" about the mother.

However, what was also of note was that pattern 3 mothers wished to develop a more positive type of relationship between themselves and their children. Their aspiration was for warm, respectful, mutually supportive mother–child relationships, where they and their children could pull together, be open, affectionate and trust in one another—in other words, they aspired toward the pattern 1 mother–child relationships described earlier. Therefore, looking to the future, there was an impetus on the part of these mothers for improvements in their mother–child relationships. It seemed likely, therefore, that these families would have been engaging with more extensive supports had such supports been offered to them.

PATTERN 4: BROKEN RELATIONSHIPS, BLOCKED RECOVERIES

Only one mother in the study was experiencing a pattern 4 mother–child relationship; so, as stated at the beginning of the chapter, pattern 4 is put forward more tentatively than patterns 1–3. In pattern 4:

- The mother was prevented by the perpetrator/father from supporting her child, and the child did not wish to support their mother
- The perpetrator's/father's coercive control had led to the child rejecting their mother, and the child was now assisting the perpetrator/father in his abuse of the mother

Furthermore, in pattern 4:

- The child could not recover from coercive control because they were still under the influence of the perpetrator/father, who was continuing his campaign of coercive control post-separation

- The mother was distressed by how her relationships with her child had been broken, and this distress was harming her mental health and limiting her recovery
- The mother and child were in need of very high levels of intervention and support to help them to undo the harms caused by the perpetrator/father and to build a positive mother–child relationship

Pattern 4 non-supportiveness

The one mother–child relationship in the study that had broken down to the extent that it had pattern 4 characteristics was the relationship between Marie and her 12 year-old daughter Louise. It was not possible to interview Louise, as she had continued to live with the perpetrator/father when her parents separated. (It was Louise's sister, Leah, who took part in this study. Marie's relationship with Leah is discussed under pattern 3, earlier.) Marie described how the situation between herself and Louise was very negative. Marie was afraid to talk to Louise because Louise had openly sided with the perpetrator/father and was acting on his behalf:

MARIE: He uses [Louise] to still control me, because he's sort of controlling her now. She's stolen keys, videoed my house so he could show children's services [to make a false report against the mother], she takes photographs. It sounds horrible, but basically I can't trust her because of what he's getting her to do. . . . He's doing it to still upset and get to me and control me through the kids and to still find out what I'm doing.

EMMA: Do you still see Louise?

MARIE: I do. At the moment it's only about once a week and it's not easy. God knows what he's been telling her. I just know that our relationship has got a massive crack though it. I'm scared to tell her anything or even speak to her because

> he's made it so it's [the information's going] straight back to him.

To begin analyzing this relationship, we can start with Marie's powerful metaphor of a relationship with a "massive crack through it." Marie and Louise were not living together. Marie was afraid to speak to Louise, as she knew that Louise was acting on the perpetrator's/father's behalf. Opportunities for mother–child supportiveness were therefore currently non-existent between Marie and Louise; the perpetrator's/father's control of Louise and Marie's knowledge of it was making it impossible for them to address the "massive crack" through their relationship. Marie's metaphor also points to the necessity, in a pattern 4 context, for a high level of professional supports. Like a window with a "massive crack through it," a mother–child relationship such as Marie and Louise's would require painstaking levels of expert care by appropriate specialists to reconstruct and repair.

This situation had not arisen recently, but was a continuation of dynamics that had existed for many years. Marie described how the perpetrator/father had made Louise his favored child within the family since her birth. He was uninterested and hostile toward his other children, but he had "spoilt" Louise, and regularly taken her to play her favorite sport, while preventing Louise from having any enjoyable time with her mother throughout her childhood (see chapter 5). This behavior from the perpetrator/father had contributed to Louise having an even more distant and strained relationship with her mother than the other children in the family, and this situation had continued after Marie and the other children had separated from the perpetrator/father.

Pattern 4 is therefore distinct from pattern 3 because it describes a situation where a perpetrator/father has not merely undermined and harmed a mother–child relationship, but has effectively destroyed it, succeeding in his goal of severing a child from their mother (see Bancroft et al., 2012; Monk and Bowen, 2021). Louise had, through many years of emotional abuse and manipulation from the perpetrator/father, sided with him and largely rejected her mother.

Although pattern 4 only occurred in one family in this study, it has been discussed in wider domestic violence research, particularly by Morris (2009) and Monk and Bowen (2021), whose research will now be drawn on. Morris (2009, p. 416) described what this study terms "pattern 4" through her examination of how coercive-control-perpetrating fathers "deliberately undermine and destroy" mother–child relationships through various tactics. Building on this research, Monk and Bowen (2021) identified a set of eight tactics used by perpetrators/fathers to cut children off from mothers. These were: (1) Lying to and manipulating children; (2) Sabotaging children's contact with their mothers; (3) Weaponizing children; (4) Conditioning children through reward and punishment; (5) Exploiting women's vulnerabilities, particularly as mothers; (6) Threatening mothers with taking their children from them; (7) Actively employing mother-blaming by exploiting mother-blaming institutions and practices; and (8) Denigrating mothers and elevating themselves in order to supplant mothers as children's primary caregivers and attachment figures.

In Marie's description of what she and Louise had experienced, at least six of these eight tactics (namely tactics 1, 3, 4, 5, 7, and 8) were present. The perpetrator/father manipulated (tactic 1), conditioned (tactic 4) and supplanted (tactic 8) by making Louise his favorite child, weaponized Louise against Marie to "control me through the kids" (tactic 5) by turning Louise into a surveillance operative in and around Marie's home (tactic 3) and, via Louise's creation of surveillance material to show social services, exploited institutional mother-blaming practices (tactic 7).

Responding to pattern 4

Morris's (2009) research suggests that, in order to respond to children and mothers whose relationships with each other have been sabotaged by domestically violent and abusive fathers, it is important to recognize that these children are being greatly influenced by perpetrators'/fathers' ongoing coercive control. Such children are usually living with the perpetrator/father, who has so discredited their mother and distorted their understanding of reality that they are unwilling to listen to her. For example, perpetrators/fathers use blame-shifting narratives to excuse, justify, minimize, and deny their abuse when they talk to their children, wider families, and communities, as well as to professionals within social services and justice systems (Bancroft et al., 2012; Cavanagh et al.; 2001; Harne, 2011; LeCouteur and Oxlad, 2011; Moulding et al., 2015; Towns and Adams, 2016). These narratives—which Monk and Bowen (2021) suggest perpetrators use as a way to "groom" the people around them—present the perpetrator/father as a victim, imply that the mother deserved to be treated badly and was responsible for the perpetrator's/father's treatment of her, and/or suggest that the mother is "mad," malicious, and inventing falsehoods (Bancroft et al., 2012; Monk, 2017; Monk and Bowen, 2021; Radford and Hester, 2006). Children may come to believe these narratives over their own lived experiences of their parents' behaviors (Bancroft et al., 2012; Monk and Bowen, 2021; Morris, 2009). If left unchecked, the lessons that children may ultimately learn from perpetrators/fathers—that abuse is justified or excusable, that power can be used negatively without consequence, and that abusers are good people—may have grave consequences for these children's outcomes as adults.

It is unlikely that children would be able to recover from their experiences of coercive control while they are still strongly under the influence of perpetrators. Mothers in these situations may effectively "lose" their children because they cannot safely maintain contact with them post-separation (Radford and Hester, 2006). Furthermore, it is an extremely difficult and painful task for a mother to attempt to recover from coercive control in the absence of one or more of her children, and little specialized support is currently available for mothers in these circumstances (one exception is the UK charity MATCH Mothers which supports mothers who live apart from their children).

The work of Morris (2009) suggests that the first step toward helping children experiencing such circumstances is to greatly reduce contact between child and perpetrator, ending it where possible. Protecting the child from further exposure in this way would initially be difficult, due to their attachments to the perpetrator/father. However Monk and Bowen (2021, p. 36), drawing on Radford and Hester (2006, p. 134), argue that doing so is important and justified, as "attachments made in such hostile environments, where children are essentially entrapped and dominated by their fathers," are not "secure attachment[s] based upon affection and security," but, instead, are "likely to be a response to trauma and fear." Efforts to reduce or end the child's contact with the perpetrator/father should be undertaken with the utmost care. The child's rights, wishes, and preferences should be taken into account as much as possible, and the child treated with respect and dignity, in order to minimize the risk of the child feeling unheard and disempowered. Alongside an extensive reduction or cessation of contact between perpetrator and child, a high-quality, lengthy intervention is needed to help children and mothers to understand their experiences of abuse at the hands of perpetrators/fathers and to begin to build positive relationships with each other. It is vital that such interventions are provided by professionals who understand the dynamics of coercive-control-based domestic violence, so that further victim-blaming and further coercion are avoided.

Intervening with children sensitively without using coercion or threats against them is vital. Doing so would represent a substantial shift away from the current coercive and authoritarian processes that children may be court-ordered into undergoing when they are refusing to see one of their parents and/or are labeled as "alienated" children. These court-ordered "remedies," especially popular in the United States, often involve forcing unwilling children into a "treatment program" with the parent whom they are refusing to see (Mercer, 2019). Taken away from their local area— often isolated from communication with the outside world, stripped of their money and phone, and forbidden to contact their liked parent and siblings—children may not be allowed to leave these programs until they have interacted positively over a sustained period of time with the parent whom they do not wish to see (Mercer, 2019). Subjecting children to such coercive processes renders them powerless, disregards their wishes, and carries high and foreseeable risks of harm (Dallam and Silberg, 2016). Even when "treatment programs" are not used, children who are refusing to see a parent may be subjected to other draconian measures: They may be forced or coerced into regular unwanted contact with the parent they do not want to see (Birchall and Choudhry, 2018; Thiara and Gill, 2012), or they may be forcibly removed from their accustomed home (often in great distress) and transferred against their will to live with a parent whom they dislike and possibly fear (Dispatches, 2021; Hill, 2020). All such practices violate children's rights as set out in the United Nations Convention on the Rights of the Child; especially Article 12, which gives children the right to have a say in matters that affect them, and for their views to be given due weight.

By contrast, Morris (2009) discusses ways of providing positive, non-coercive interventions for children and mothers whose relationships have been sabotaged by coercive control. These interventions could be carried out by organizations with long experience of supporting children in the aftermath of domestic violence (such as organizations that run the Ontario-based programs discussed in chapter 6). Morris (2009) suggests that such interventions should involve raising the awareness of both children and mothers about the abusive tactics that perpetrators use to cause confusion and to divide family members. Bringing these tactics into the light, by naming them and discussing them openly, breaks much of their destructive power. Mothers and children also need professional support to understand the similarities in each other's experiences of coercive control, and to identify and name the positive qualities in each other. Such work may have very beneficial outcomes:

> Interventions such as these enable women and children to evolve more positive behaviours towards one another, re-frame their identities, relationships and histories that were shaped by abuse, and step outside negative behaviours they adopted to survive such violence. Underpinned by integrated, consistent, non-blaming and supportive approaches by all services, women and children can develop a household . . . based on care and respect. (Morris, 2009, p. 424)

At present such positive interventions are not likely to be funded or available in many territories (if any). Making them available to the mothers and children who need them would be an important step forward in domestic violence/coercive control responses.

Finally, Monk and Bowen (2021) also advise that large-scale public awareness-raising and practitioner-training initiatives should be devised. The aim of such initiatives would be to help people to understand that when a coercive control perpetrator is sabotaging mother–child relationships, their doing so is part of their coercive control/domestic violence, and is in itself a serious form of abuse. This may assist mothers experiencing coercive control, the professionals involved with them, and the mother's own family and friends, to identify what is occurring and to take steps to counter it before the harms to children become entrenched. Further research is needed into the sabotaging of mother–child relationships in contexts of coercive control in order to illuminate this aspect of perpetrators' behavior and identify effective ways of responding to it.

Pattern 4 and "parental alienation"

Importantly, this book concurs with the recommendation of Monk and Bowen (2021) that it is unhelpful for researchers, professionals, policy-makers or activists to use the term "parental alienation" when describing cases where perpetrators have sabotaged mother–child relationships as part of their coercive control. Instead, this book recommends that the problem be framed as perpetrators sabotaging mother–child relationships as part of their campaign of coercive control. Though the use of the term "parental alienation" may be well intentioned, it in effect "buys into" and reinforces a highly controversial and contested concept that is frequently used *against* coercive control victims/survivors in family courts (Barnett, 2020; Birchall and Choudhry, 2021; Casas Vila, 2020; Elizabeth, 2020; Feresin, 2020; Hill, 2020; Hunter et al., 2020; Laing, 2017; Lapierre et al., 2020; Meier, 2020; Meier et al., 2019; Mercer and Drew, 2021; Rathus, 2020; Sheehy and Boyd, 2020; Zaccour, 2020).

As discussed earlier, within the actual framework of how "parental alienation" claims operate in practice (via the orders of family courts), the term is often used as a justification for subjecting children to aggressive and harmful processes. These processes involve courts forcing, coercing, and threatening the supposedly "alienated" child into having a relationship with the parent they do not wish to see (Dallam and Silberg, 2016; Hill, 2020; Kleinman, 2017). For instance, as mentioned before, family courts may order the police to "transfer" children from their accustomed home to the home of their disliked parent against their will. Police may carry out these removals during the night, taking children from their beds and transferring them to their disliked parent's home as the children beg, cry, protest, and scream in distress (Dispatches, 2021; Hill, 2020). Even if such processes are undertaken to transfer a child from an abusive parent to a safe one (i.e., framed as tackling "bad" coercive control with "good" coercive control by transferring an "alienated" child back to their safe parent against the child's will), such processes are still highly likely to be harmful for children. Such acts of forcing, coercing, and threatening a child overrides their rights and may leave the child feeling profoundly disempowered, unheard, and betrayed (Silberg and Dallam, 2019). Fundamentally, two wrongs do not make a right: One cannot remedy coercive control with yet more coercive control. Instead, as discussed before, interventions should be built on working sensitively with the child, while respecting their rights, dignity, wishes, and preferences as much as possible.

Because the vast majority of coercive control perpetrators are male (e.g., Barlow et al., 2020; Barnes and Aune, 2021; Hester et al., 2017; Johnson et al., 2014; Myhill, 2015; see chapter 1), the vast majority of parent–child relationships that are sabotaged as part of coercive control will be mother–child relationships, and fathers will be responsible for the sabotage. However, research on gender and coercive control suggests that there may also be a small minority of female coercive control perpetrators/mothers who sabotage father–child relationships as part of coercive control. There may also be cases where parent–child relationship sabotage is carried out by a LGBT+ perpetrator against an intimate partner with whom they are raising children (Hester et al., 2017; Johnson et al., 2014; Raghavan et al., 2019; Myhill, 2015).

Here, it is important to remain aware of what coercive control involves. A person cannot be viewed as a victim of coercive control purely on the basis that their partner or ex-partner has spoken negatively about them to their children, or that their children do not wish to see them. Nor can they be viewed as a coercive control victim on the basis that their partner has been violent toward them in self-defense or as an act of resistance against abuse; nor because their partner has spoken to them in an emotionally abusive manner. (Emotional abuse is harmful but, on its own, does not amount to coercive control.)

Rather, what adult victims/survivors of coercive control experience is a long-term campaign of being constrained, monitored, degraded, and isolated by the perpetrator. They will have had ordinary freedoms taken from them—causing a substantial adverse impact on their everyday lives—and they will have been routinely punished for non-compliance. It is likely that they will have been economically abused and sexually coerced by the perpetrator. It is probable too that they will have experienced chronic fear/distress, self-blame/self-doubt, trauma, exhaustion, and damage to their sense of self, i.e., their awareness of who they are, including for example their likes and dislikes. Adult victims/survivors may have maintained careers while experiencing coercive control and may not have *publicly* appeared to be suffering. However, in private, the perpetrator's campaign of coercive control will have been severely limiting their freedoms (Stark, 2007). (Chapter 1 includes a fuller discussion of all of these experiences.) These are among the core characteristics of coercive control; the experiences that we need to be mindful of when assessing whether a parent–child relationship has been sabotaged as part of a campaign of coercive control.

CONCLUSION

This chapter has explored the four patterns of mother–child relationships that developed after the mothers in the study had separated from perpetrators/fathers. In doing so, it has illustrated the different ways that mother–child relationships are experienced by mothers and children in the years after they separate from perpetrators/fathers. The "levels, contexts, impacts" framework developed in this chapter is designed to enable a more advanced understanding of these relationships; and, in particular, how mothers and children were supporting each other and the effects that these supports were having on their well-being and recoveries.

A critical factor in whether mothers and children were able to develop the most optimal relationship pattern during the post-separation phase was whether they received sufficient professional supports to help them to recover from their experiences. Increasing the supports that assist recovery for mothers and children is therefore vital. More resources and funding are required to make appropriate and suitable supports available to those who need them. The findings of this study suggest that such supports, when in place, are transformational, and lead to positive outcomes for both mothers and children.

Interestingly, most mothers and children in the study had the same ideal of mutually supportive, close mother–child relationships with high levels of trust, communication, and enjoyment. Some mothers and children had already developed these relationships, and spoke about them very positively. Others wished to develop such relationships in future. The importance of such mutual support, with children supporting mothers as well as mothers supporting children, is rarely considered in most domestic violence research. When domestic violence research has turned to mothering and mother–child relationships, emphasis has usually been placed on judging the damage that has been done to the quality of mothers' parenting (the overall framework being the misleading one that supportiveness should not be mutual; that the mother should be supporting the child without the child supporting the mother). The next chapter will explore mothers' and children's views and experiences of mutual supportiveness in more detail.

Future research can build on and further develop the four pattern typology presented here. It is possible that other patterns beyond these four are experienced by the wider population of coercive control victims and survivors. For instance, situations where children have become parentified, and are giving far more support to their mother than they are receiving in return, may constitute a pattern in their own right, as may situations where the mother and child are living apart from each other because of child protection interventions or family court decisions that have removed the child from the mother's care.

Furthermore, relationships between mothers and children did not always follow the same pattern. Rather, they evolved and changed over time and were influenced by the contexts around them. Few mothers and children were able to immediately achieve pattern 1, the most positive pattern, in the aftermath of separating from perpetrators/fathers. Instead, pattern 1 had usually been achieved gradually over a period of years as mothers and children had slowly recovered from their experiences of coercive control (see chapter 6). Most mothers' and children's relationships with each other had initially, at the beginning of the post-separation phase, resembled patterns 2 and 3, with high levels of mother–child conflict and more mental health and behavioral problems.

There was a gradual transition into pattern 1 for the mothers and children who had sufficient, appropriate, and timely professional supports to help them to recover, as their mental health, behaviors, communication patterns and understandings of coercive control had all improved. Whether or not mothers and children had access to sufficient supports seemed to depend partly on how severe their problems were (it was more difficult to find supports that were sufficiently sustained to deal with problems that were severe and deeply ingrained) and partly on the variability of what services were available in which area. The ages of the children were also important, as, for instance, some programs were not open to very young children or to older adolescents/young adults. In future, extending provision to cover the full range of children and young people from toddlers to 24-year-olds may be beneficial in preventing many victims/survivors of childhood coercive control from slipping through cracks in the system and not having their support and recovery needs met.

Given that mother–child relationships could change significantly in the months and years post-separation, it is possible for mother–child relationships to follow more than one pattern at certain points in time.

For example, a relationship that is transitioning from pattern 2 to pattern 1 as the mother and child progress in their recoveries might display characteristics from both patterns. In these cases, it is important for practitioners to explore the biographical history of the mother and child to understand what further help they might need to complete this transition.

Overall, further research is required into what happens to mother–child relationships post-separation. There are few studies on abused women's experiences of motherhood following divorce/separation from perpetrators/fathers (Goldblatt et al., 2014). Those which do exist focus mostly on what this study has termed "pattern 3," and occasionally also on patterns 2 and 4 (see, e.g., Humphreys et al., 2006; McManus et al., 2013; Monk and Bowen, 2021; Morris, 2009; Nolas et al., 2012; Sharp et al., 2011; Smith et al., 2015, Vergara et al., 2015). Researchers have focused on those more problematic mother–child relationships in order to develop knowledge and practical interventions to improve them. However, it is essential to take account of the full range of patterns, from the most negative to the most positive.

Indeed, it is particularly important for future research to focus on the more positive, pattern 1 mother–child relationships that can emerge several years after separating from perpetrators/fathers. Such relationships have received little or no attention to date. This chapter has provided some of the first knowledge of what these well-recovered mother–child relationships are like, and how they are experienced by mothers and children. Building detailed knowledge about the positive relationships that mothers and children can ultimately enjoy is necessary because it would provide policymakers, practitioners, and mothers and children themselves, with clearer understandings of the "end results" that can be achieved when sufficient supports are provided.

9

A new way of life

*Mutuality and closeness between
mothers and children*

INTRODUCTION

This chapter, the last of the chapters in which we introduce and analyze material from the interviews, explores the mutual supportiveness and reciprocal care that many mothers and children in the study experienced in the years after they had separated from perpetrators/fathers. It will highlight the views expressed by mothers and children about mutuality in their mother–child relationships. We will find that children, especially, described good mother–child relationships as ones that were actively maintained by both parents and children. Mothers expressed positive feelings about the mutuality in their relationships with their children, but also emphasized the actions that they performed exclusively as parents.

Assimilating insights from outside of the children and domestic violence field, this chapter draws on research on mutuality in the childhood and family studies fields (see also chapter 2). Specifically, there is research in these fields that explores how mutuality can be a normal and positive feature of "ordinary" parent–child relationships, and not a sign of dysfunction (Arditti, 1999; Kuczynski et al., 2016; Morrow, 2003; Oliphant and Kuczynski, 2011; Smart et al., 2001). This research indicates

Coercive Control in Children's and Mothers' Lives. Emma Katz, Oxford University Press. © Oxford University Press 2022.
DOI: 10.1093/oso/9780190922214.003.0009

that healthy parent–child relationships are bidirectional and are jointly maintained by parents and children (Burke et al., 2017; Harach and Kuczynski, 2005; Kuczynski et al., 1999, 2003, 2016; Kuczynski and De Mol, 2015; Lau Clayton, 2014; Marshall and Lambert, 2006; Oliphant and Kuczynski, 2011). Children are viewed in these studies not as passive beings but as agents who actively engage in reciprocal, age-appropriate caring relationships as part of their ordinary everyday lives (Eldén, 2016; Morrow, 2003). Employing this body of literature to illuminate the relationships between children and mothers who have survived coercive control-based domestic violence is an important, innovative way to finish the book's analysis of mothers' and children's experiences. To the best of the author's knowledge, it is the first academic research to have done so.

CHILDREN'S THOUGHTS AND FEELINGS ABOUT MUTUALITY IN THEIR MOTHER–CHILD RELATIONSHIPS

Children tended, in their interviews, to describe their mother–child relationships using collective pronouns such as "we," "us," and "our." When they spoke of what it means for a mother–child relationship to be "strong," they described relationships that are rich in shared interpersonal knowledge, and where both parties are responsible for protecting the relationship from outside interference:

> We have a strong relationship; we know lots about each other. (Bob, age 12)

> Our relationship is strong because we're really close, and we wouldn't let anything interfere with our relationship. (Katie, age 12)

Some children discussed the two directions of mutuality within their mother–child relationship at different stages of their interviews— suggesting the receiving of support in one answer ("Mum's a good source of support"), and, in another, the giving of it ("I think I help Mum by [doing this, this and this]"). Others referred to the reciprocity of their relationship more directly:

> We support each other. (Roxie, age 11)

> We've helped to make each other feel better; we've given each other support throughout the whole thing. (Grace, age 14)

Grace, who gave a particularly detailed account of the ways in which she and her mother supported each other during their recoveries, indicated that they had, when facing a problem, jointly shared their feelings with each other before agreeing how to respond:

> When Mum and my dad used to have [post-separation] arguments... Mum would tell me how she felt, and I'd tell her how I felt, and we'd just be able to help each other and tell each other what we should do. (Grace, age 14)

To summarize these quotes, children in their interviews were able to articulate a concept of strong mother–child relationships built around unity between mother and child. They also articulated the mutuality of such relationships in a very simple way: Apart from the collective "we," one phrase that occurs in almost all of these quotes is "each other." The children viewed a strong mother–child relationship as one that involved knowing each other well, supporting each other, helping each other to feel better, and advising each other on what to do in the future.

When they looked ahead to the future, the children who had close, mutually-supportive relationships with their mothers discussed how they wished for this mutuality to continue:

> When I'm older I want to be a success, thriving, with my jobs, whichever I have. And move to Ireland with Mum, and have my own horses and have loads of animals. (Shannon, age 10)

A new way of life

[In the future I want] to stay close with Mum. (Jane, age 11)

[Mum and I] have a strong relationship, and we'll have that forever. (Grace, age 14)

What was notable about statements such as these was that they were positive, ambitious, and emphatic. The children were able to dream about how the good state of their mother–child relationship would carry on "forever" into the future, and also, in the example of Shannon, how her mother would be part of her journey toward success and abundance in her future life.

Children's positive feelings about mutuality and reciprocity in mother–child relationships were also particularly evident in their responses to the question, "If you had to imagine a really good relationship between a child and a mother, what would it be like?" Children described relationships based on mutual friendship, trust, respect for each other's feelings and needs, and communication:

Spending time together, doing things, talking about what it was like before, and what might happen in the future. (Leah, age 11)

To be honest with each other, and to tell them everything. (Vince, age 13)

The mother is fun, firm but fair, and they trust each other, and most importantly they love each other. (Shannon, age 10)

You should always talk to each other, and if you need to say anything you should be able to say it to them. (Katie, age 12)

They share stuff with each other; they're nice to each other. (Jane, age 11)

Bonded—she's always there when you need her, and you're always there when she needs you. (Joe, age 14)

> It should be fun, close, and they need to talk to each other. (Roxie, age 11)

> Being able to talk to each other about stuff. (Zoe, age 12)

> Being able to trust them; being able to tell them what's going on in your life; being able to support each other through everything. (Grace, age 14)

These children's descriptions of "really good" mother–child relationships are interesting, because what they are describing is the *opposite* of the coercive control they had experienced. "Spending time together" and "talking"; being "honest," trusting, and open; being able to enjoy having a mother who was "fun" as well as authoritative; having a close and supportive mother–child bond—these were all aspects of good mother–child relationships that the children were acutely aware of because they had been deliberately narrowed or closed off completely by perpetrators'/fathers' coercive control.

It is striking too in this regard that, despite these children's experiences of coercive control, they were able to articulate what are quite "normal" and "average" conceptualizations of good family relationships. Descriptions of mutual supportiveness have been shown to be a characteristic feature of descriptions of good family relationships given by children who have not experienced coercive control. For example, Morrow (2003, p. 120) explored the family lives of a general community sample of nearly 200 British children aged 8–14 and found that: "Nearly half of the older children included elements of mutual support in their definitions of what families are for, using phrases such as 'caring for each other,' 'sharing' and 'looking after each other.'" Experiencing coercive control had not given the children in this study different or unusual perspectives on what makes a really good mother–child relationship. They were using phrases and sentiments that were similar to those of the children in Morrow's study.

It is also interesting that the extracts quoted earlier cover a wide range of children in the study. These included older and younger children, boys

A new way of life

and girls, and children experiencing patterns 1, 2, and 3 (that is, children with mothers with stronger mental health or much more fragile mental health, and children with high and low levels of conflict/closeness with their mothers, see chapter 8). Despite the differences in these children's actual mother–child relationships, they all described, as their ideal, mother–child relationships that were reciprocal and/or mutually supportive.

MOTHERS AND MUTUALITY

Mothers were less likely than children to discuss mutuality in their interviews, and focused more on their parenting. This was perhaps because "parenting" is the dominant discourse that shapes thinking about parent–child relationships. As Ambert (2013) argues, notions that parents are the ones who influence and shape parent–child relationships are deeply embedded in Western societies. The strength of this norm often means that people struggle to think in bidirectional terms about parent–child relationships, or to recognize the influence that children have on parents (De Mol and Buysse, 2008; Kuczynski et al., 2016).

However, as noted in the previous chapter, mutuality was discussed by mothers experiencing the most ongoing problems in their relationships with their children. These mothers expressed their wish for greater mutuality, especially when asked, "If you had to imagine a really good relationship between a child and a mother, what would it be like?" Here, both Charlie and Kimberley described relationships that are open and communicative, and where both parties are able to trust and confide in each other:

It's trusting each other and communicating. (Kimberley, mother)

What makes a good [mother–child] relationship? A relationship, I think, is when you feel at ease talking to each other. . . . I think the most important thing is that you can talk to your child, and they can talk to their parent, and showing them lots of love and care. (Charlie, mother)

This was in keeping with these two mothers expressing the wish, at other points in their interviews, that their relationship with their children would in future become more mutually communicative and supportive.

When other mothers were asked the question of what makes a good mother–child relationship, they placed emphasis on their abilities to look after their children. They explained their own roles—what the parent should do for, and with, their children—with a focus on "do's and don'ts":

Being honest—up to a point—protecting them from the bad things in life. Letting them be children, but giving them independence. Letting them make mistakes, and being there to pick up the pieces. (Lauren, mother)

You need to read between the lines, read their minds, and just be there. (Bella, mother)

Trust, love, friendship, fun; and I do think you need to give boundaries to your child, and routine is so important. And just enjoy each other, you know? Being a parent should be fun; being a kid should be fun. Don't do what you think you "should" do; do what you and your child want to do. (Ellie, mother)

Love and listening to them; doing stuff together like games; having fun; caring for them; putting them before you. (Sybil, mother)

Here, there are two direct contrasts with coercive control. The first is that the mothers discussed "trust, love, friendship, fun," "listening to [children]," and "read[ing] between the lines, read[ing] their minds." Under coercive control, mothers and children had often not been able to connect with each other as frequently or as closely as they had wished, because of the hyper-entitled mindsets and continual demands of perpetrators/fathers (Buchanan, 2018). Yet now, in these quotations, empathy with children and attunement to children's feelings was uppermost in mothers' minds.

The second contrast with coercive control in those quotations is found in the mention of, for example, "letting [children] be children, but giving them independence. Letting them make mistakes." Here, mothers showed awareness not only of the need for children to *have* freedom, but also of giving children *the right levels of* freedom ("and I do think you need to give boundaries to your child, and routine is so important"). That nuanced understanding of "independence," "routine," and "boundaries" is also collapsed under coercive control, where the perpetrator/father has freedom beyond reasonable limits, where routines and boundaries may be disrupted against the child's best interests by a perpetrator wishing to appear the "goody" in the child's eyes, and where mothers and children fear that the perpetrator/father will punish them for any perceived "independence." What these quotations show is that, in this new way of life, these mothers appreciated the importance of boundaries for their children, but boundaries balanced with freedom and "fun."

The importance of reciprocity and mutual supportiveness between mothers and their children, alluded to by Ellie and Sybil in those mentions of "friendship," "enjoying each other," and "doing stuff together," were also evident in the interviews with mothers:

> I'd say we are considerate of each other, we're sensitive to each other's feelings and emotions, and I'd say we have fun. (Isobel, mother)

> We all share our feelings now. It's better. (Akeela, mother)

> I enjoy my daughter; my daughter enjoys me. (Ellie, mother)

> We've been supportive of one another. We encourage each other: "you can do it." We try to bump each other's confidence up, you know, which is important.... We give each other space, and we don't judge one another. (Eloise, mother)

Overall, then, these mothers: (1) believed that there were some important actions within mother–child relationships that are taken exclusively by mothers, such as setting boundaries and guiding children's development;

and also (2) valued mutuality and reciprocity in their relationships with their children, seeing it as an important part—though not the only important part—of mother–child relationships.

MUTUALITY AS HEIGHTENED BY COERCIVE CONTROL?

As we have noted here, children and mothers in this study viewed mutual support and reciprocity as important in mother–child relationships, a view that has also frequently been found among parents and children who have not experienced coercive control (Arditti, 1999; Morrow, 2003; Oliphant and Kuczynski, 2011). This raises the question of whether it was the experiences of adversity that created the mutual supportiveness between the mothers and children in this study, whether this mutuality would have been present regardless of the adversity, or whether it was a combination of the two. Definite answers are not possible here, as this question only became apparent during the data analysis phase of the study, and data was not purposefully collected about the issue.

However, one mother, Ruby, did suggest that the closeness and interdependence in "normal" families is heightened in families with experiences of coercive control. In difficult times, she said, families naturally respond by becoming stronger and more united:

> Definitely there is an interdependence between us, but I think there would be in a normal family without domestic violence anyway— but perhaps not at such a critical level. . . . I think you come together as a unit because of the domestic violence, so our unit was me, Katie [daughter] and Thomas [son] . . . so we probably came together and strengthened up, like families do in a time of crisis. (Ruby, mother)

Similarly, Lapierre et al.'s (2018) research found that adversity could increase levels of closeness between some children and mothers. Ruby's discussion of "com[ing] together as a unit" suggests a way of understanding close and supportive mother–child relationships in contexts of coercive control. Such relationships may form partly as a coping strategy that helps mothers and children to survive "in a time of crisis."

MUTUALITY, INTERDEPENDENCE, AND INDEPENDENCE

Two notable themes that emerged during families' discussions of mutuality and closeness were interdependence (being close and relying on each other) and independence (being comfortable doing activities separately). Mothers and children commonly discussed how, in positive ways, children's independence and peer friendships was starting to develop alongside their close interdependence with their mothers:

> Katie goes into town now with her friends, because she wants more independence. I think generally our relationship has shifted more towards Katie being independent, but she's still around a lot. (Ruby, mother)

> [Jane and I] are very close. . . . Jane is massively grown up, mature and independent. . . . The children are happy in everything they do, they're well rounded, they do lots of sports and other clubs, they have lots of friends. (Alison, mother)

> [Mum and I] have a strong relationship; we know lots about each other. . . . I think I have a lot more freedom now because I'm older. . . . I've been working harder in school. I've got better friends. They help me; let me have a laugh and things; we go places. (Bob, age 12)

As these comments suggest, many mothers' and children's recoveries had reached a stage where they could function happily without each other, as well as enjoying close relationships with each other.

There was only one mother, Ellie, who expressed concerns about the interdependence between her and her daughter (10-year-old Shannon). Ellie felt that their closeness was positive, but that it would be healthier for them to also become more independent and able to function separately:

> Things that are good are: we have a very close relationship, and a very open relationship. I think the things that aren't so good would be that we are both very dependent upon each other, really. To a large extent, we're like sort of one person, and if we spend a long time away from each other then we both get quite anxious and miss each other. I think that's because we've been together more or less constantly through all the domestic violence, and then moving to different addresses and whatever, so we are hypersensitive to each other's feelings and needs and probably, well definitely, very over-protective of one another. I think that's good, but it's also bad, you know, for Shannon. I think that she needs for me to maybe let her go a little bit more, and let her start growing up, but it's very difficult. (Ellie, mother)

Elsewhere in her interview, Ellie mentioned that Shannon was still so affected by her experiences of coercive control that, at home, she refused to be on a different floor of the house to Ellie, did not like to be left alone in a room, and was sharing a bed with her mother.

This interdependence may have reflected the extreme violence and prolonged fear that Ellie and Shannon had experienced during the coercive control and post-separation period. After leaving, there were occasions when they believed that they were safe, only to be brutally re-attacked by the perpetrator/father (see chapter 6). They had been in a position to recover for only one year prior to their interviews, and were still at a relatively early stage of the process. It seemed likely, then, that their interdependence would decrease over time.

This process may have already begun at the time of interview. Ellie mentioned that Shannon had recently attended a school trip that involved an overnight stay, and had started to walk home from school independently. Ellie also described how, over the last year, she and Shannon had progressed from having little engagement with their community to having a joint social life:

> We've started to have our own social life together. We've started going to storytelling events at the library, we've been to the hairdressers together, [and] we've been out for a meal a couple of times, which is really, really nice. (Ellie, mother)

At Ellie's and Shannon's early stage of recovery, attending events together was a positive step. It may have been too difficult at this stage to engage with the outside world separately. By engaging with it together, they appeared to be helping each other to recover from the traumas that they had faced in a manageable way.

BEYOND PARENT AND CHILD? "FRIENDS" AND "SISTERS"

A final theme in the data was that some mothers and children referred to their relationships as being akin to those of friends or sisters. In line with the findings of Arditti (1999) and Wuest et al. (2004), this was usually discussed positively, either as being better than a straightforward parent–child relationship or as a normal aspect of children growing older:

Eloise and John (age 20)—

ELOISE: We'd go shopping together. It was just nice. He's my son, but he once said: "Mum you're more than my mum, you're my best friend." And that's how he was to me too—my friend.

JOHN: [If I could pick three words to describe Mum, they would be:] loving; considerate; a friend.

EMMA: Could you tell me a bit more about the ways that you're friends as well as mum and son?

ELOISE: I think we can tell each other anything.

JOHN: Yeah we can tell each other anything.

Ellie and Shannon (age 10)—

We've started going to storytelling events at the library, we've been to the hairdressers together, [and] we've been out for a meal a couple of times, which is really, really nice, so we're like best friends. (Ellie, mother)

Ruby and Katie (age 12)—

EMMA: You said that you and Katie are kind of like sisters and like friends. Could you tell me a little bit more about that?

RUBY: Well, going shopping for clothes or make-up, or doing face masks. Even if she goes into town with her friends, she always brings me a 99p [inexpensive] present. Until very recently, it was like our cord had never been cut. She didn't know there was a difference between me and her, and she used to struggle with going to school—she wanted to be home with me. So now it's nice that she's got that independence, but she's not disappeared altogether. We're like sisters.

These extracts suggest that friend- and sister-like qualities in mother–child relationships came partly from enjoying activities together as a pair. Beyond this, the meaning of having friend- and sister-like relationships appeared to differ in different families. Eloise and John indicated that they felt like friends because they could be more open with each other than traditional parents and children (particularly around issues such as sex and relationships). For Ruby, developing a sisterly parent–child relationship with her adolescent daughter was associated with moving away from being connected umbilically to each other ("until very recently, it was like our cord had never been cut") and with moving toward a greater balance between independence and connection.

There was a strong association between friend- and sister-like relationships and children's increasing maturity. This was expressed especially when mothers talked about how they envisaged their future relationships with their children:

It's nice that she's got that independence, but she's not disappeared altogether. We're like sisters, and I suppose that will carry on the older she gets. (Ruby, mother)

I want things to carry on as they are—for us to keep communicating, [to] keep that friendship that we've got. I see me and my mum as best friends, and can see that kind of relationship developing between me and Grace, and me and Zoe, in the future. (Lauren, mother)

Overall, then, the mothers and children in this study appeared to regard these friend- or sister-like aspects of their relationships as enhancements, and hoped that they would continue in the future.

There was only one mother, Ria, who used the term "sisterly" in a negative way. She indicated her own struggle to use parental authority by discussing her and her daughter Carly's "sisterly" tendency to argue with each other:

We've not really got that mother–daughter relationship; it's more like a sisters' relationship. We clash quite a lot. It's just a constant battle, mine and Carly's relationship. Like I say, we're very sisterly. We shout all the time, she's even started shouting [back], and I think one time she actually said she hates me and that hurt. She acts so much older than what she is. She's only 7 but she acts like a 15-year-old. She's very grown up. (Ria, mother)

As discussed in chapter 8, Ria and Carly's relationship had a high level of ongoing conflict, was not mutually supportive, and would have benefited from professional supports to help both mother and child to recover further from coercive control. Ria's comments imply that their relationship was sisterly in the negative sense that they were reacting to each other in similar, adolescent ways.

By contrast, the mothers who described having positive sister-like relationships with their daughters were also clear about their ongoing roles as mothers. As we saw in the previous chapter, Ruby described the multiple ways that she guided her children:

> Lots of love, lots of praise to balance out any discipline you've got to do. Lots of silliness. Distraction instead of telling them off sometimes. Honesty, consistency, routine. Good boundaries, but fair boundaries. I think you've not got to sweat the small stuff. Manners: teach them to do the right thing, say sorry and to learn from their mistakes, and let them make mistakes. Lots of fresh air. Make the telly time special family time. And teamwork: stick together. (Ruby, mother)

This extract indicates Ruby's high levels of parenting confidence and skill. The differences between Ria's and Ruby's experiences suggests that friend- and sister-like relationships within this study may have been positive when they existed *alongside* strong parent–child relationships. It was when friend- and sister-like relationships were occurring *instead* of parent–child relationships that they became problematic.

CONCLUSION

Most of the mothers and children in the study expressed positive feelings about mutual supportiveness. Some reported seeing one another not only as a parent or child, but as a "friend" or "sister" too. This was discussed by most mothers and children as an enhancement of the conventional parent–child relationship. Mothers and children often associated these friend- or sister-like relationships with closeness and trust, or with healthy development and children's progress toward maturity and independence in adulthood.

Mothers' and children's discussions of good mother–child relationships centered on ideas of mutuality and reciprocity. Children discussed "doing things together," "talking together," and "supporting each other through everything." Where children had such relationships with their mothers, they often expressed a hope that this mother–child relationship would continue into the future. Mothers associated togetherness with "having fun," sharing feelings rather than "bottling them up," and meeting each other's emotional needs. Mothers' and children's views about what made a good mother–child relationship were notably similar to views expressed by parents and children who had not experienced coercive control (Arditti, 1999; Gillies et al., 2001; Morrow, 2003).

There was no evidence that mutual support was undermining mothers' parenting abilities. On the contrary, the interviews suggested that mothers were often engaged in relationships of mutual support while setting boundaries for their children and guiding their development. Mutuality also usually coexisted with children being more independent, increasingly engaged with the outside world, and having friendships with peers besides being close with their mother.

In this final chapter of interview analysis, this book has broken new ground in the domestic violence field by identifying and exploring positive aspects of mutuality and reciprocity between mothers and children. The convention in previous research was for focus to be placed on negative aspects of children giving emotional support to mothers. Several studies explore how this can be burdensome to children, and apply the concept of "parentification" (Holden, 2003; Holt et al., 2008; Stanley et al., 2012). Giving care and support can certainly be burdensome to children in some contexts, especially when they are called on to give high-stakes support in frightening circumstances. However, this chapter has shown us that, in other contexts, giving care and support can also be mutually beneficial.

For many of the children and mothers in this study, practices of care and support were low-stakes and ordinary, built into their everyday lives through routine events. These could include, for example, expressions of affection such as offering a cup of tea, or shared activities such as watching films together on the sofa (Marshall and Lambert, 2006; Oliphant and Kuczynski, 2011). These routine events were not only pleasant; they may also have been playing important roles in children's development. As Burke et al. (2017, p. 9) remark, "[parent–child] experiences that build close connection, mutual positivity and responsiveness are not a "frill" but are critical to [...] the foundations of children's [...] positive social development."

At the time of interview, several of the mothers and children in the study were enjoying warm, caring relationships with one another. This was indicative of the effective formal and informal supports that some of these families had benefited from during their recoveries. But it can also be viewed as a testament to these mothers' and children's determination to replace the destruction of coercive control with new family lives based on positivity and nurturance.

Most of the mothers and children in this study had been separated from perpetrators/fathers for several years, and most of the children were no longer having contact with perpetrators/fathers. It was during these post-separation years that their mother–child relationships had evolved into their current forms. Professionals working with mothers and children at earlier stages of their recoveries may find it useful to talk with them about how they would like their mother-child relationships to develop over time. It may also be productive for professionals to give encouragement to mothers and children at those earlier stages—to convey that, as they move forward, it may well be possible for them to build stronger and more mutually supportive relationships with each other.

10

Ways ahead

INTRODUCTION

This book advances the "coercive control revolution" that is currently taking place in the wider fields of research, policy, and practice on domestic violence. In that shifting landscape, there is a pressing need for research in the children and domestic violence field to take a bold step forward. The first part of this chapter breaks down that bold step into five precise recommendations. The first two recommendations concern the issue of making perpetrators of coercive control more visible as the persons responsible for the harms experienced by children, both in the foci of studies and in the language we use. The third recommendation concerns the need to consider the similarities in mothers' and children's experiences of coercive control, and to determine how children and mothers may best be supported, together, to recover and thrive after breaking free from it. The fourth recommendation involves the importance of recognizing not only the dramatic incidents of physical violence that mothers and children may suffer, but also the many different, usually unremarked-upon acts in their everyday lives through which they may pursue agentic resistance and attempt to protect and support one another. The last recommendation concerns the need to pay attention to the complexities and nuances of children's relational agency and mother–child supportiveness in contexts of coercive control.

Coercive Control in Children's and Mothers' Lives. Emma Katz, Oxford University Press. © Oxford University Press 2022.
DOI: 10.1093/oso/9780190922214.003.0010

Following those five recommendations for research, this concluding chapter then sets out five recommendations for policy and practice. The first recommendation is for the introduction of interventions that help children to break free from distorted ways of thinking that perpetrators/fathers have imposed on them. The second recommendation is for the reform of family courts, with the pro-contact culture of the courts being superseded by recognition of the needs and rights of children to be free from domestic violence/coercive control. The third recommendation is for greater availability of mother–child abuse-recovery programs, including both Ontario-based programs and—for the mother–child relationships most severely harmed by perpetrators'/fathers' coercive control—more lengthy and extensive packages of support. The fourth recommendation is for practitioners to implement approaches that help victims/survivors to recognize and reflect on their own strengths and power. Finally, the fifth recommendation is for interventions with child victims/survivors to be shaped around giving children opportunities to make choices and express preferences, and around giving children freedoms to explore the world around them and socialize with supportive peers.

FIVE RECOMMENDATIONS FOR RESEARCH

Research recommendation 1: A greater visibility of perpetrators in the foci of studies

Embarking on a new phase of studies on coercive control presents an opportunity to correct a central problem that we observed in chapter 1: the tendency in the children and domestic violence field for perpetrators (usually the children's father or father-figure) to be ignored and left invisible, and for the victim/survivor parent (usually the children's mother) to be overscrutinized and portrayed as responsible for how children are affected (see, e.g., Bair-Merritt et al. 2015; Fong et al., 2019; Holmes et al., 2017; Huth-Bocks and Hughes, 2008; Johnson and Lieberman, 2007; Lamela et al., 2018; Letourneau et al., 2007; Levendosky et al., 2006;

Rosser-Limiñana et al., 2020; Samuelson et al., 2012; Sturge-Apple et al., 2010). As we noted in chapter 1, Callaghan's analysis of the terms most frequently used in children and domestic violence studies published from 2002–2015 found that "mothers" was the 5th most frequently occurring term, "women" was the 24th, and "maternal" was the 38th. By contrast, "fathers" was the 147th most frequent, while the terms "men," "stepfather," and "paternal" were so little used that they did not appear in Callaghan's results at all.

There is a need for substantially more research into how perpetrators'/fathers' coercive control affects children, including the impacts on children's emotional, psychological, mental, and physical health, and on children's development, behavior, learning, economic well-being, and educational achievements. For instance, as mentioned in chapter 1, there is a need for research to examine whether children's behavioral problems are associated with the extent to which perpetrators/fathers employ tactics to split the family by undermining children's relationships with their mother and siblings. Another important inquiry would be whether there is an association between reduced positive functioning in children and perpetrators/fathers preventing mothers and children from spending time with each other as part of their everyday lives, or if there are associations between children's functioning and the extent to which perpetrators/fathers perceive their children as owned objects. These are just a few examples; there are dozens, perhaps hundreds more issues pertaining to perpetrators'/fathers' effects on children that require further scrutiny.

Research recommendation 2: A greater visibility of perpetrators in the language we use

On a linguistic level, we should be attentive, in the ways that we write, to how we can actively make clearer and more visible the roles played by perpetrators/fathers in harming children. Even where studies focus on mothers, it would be helpful to ensure that perpetrators/fathers are mentioned throughout the work, in recognition of their causal responsibility for the coercive control taking place. For instance, rather than stating that children became socially isolated "when mothers were prevented from seeing family and friends," a better phrasing would be to state that children became socially isolated "when perpetrators/fathers prevented mothers from seeing family and friends." If we can lift the "invisibility" of perpetrators/fathers in this way, we could be more incisive, constantly reinforcing in readers' minds that it is the perpetrator/father who is responsible for the harm caused to the children and the victimized adult. In the domains of policy and practice, too, we cannot help to tackle the problem at its source without naming the source of the problem: the perpetrator/father.

The need for linguistic emphasis on perpetrators applies whether the perpetrator is male or female. The use of the term "perpetrator/father" throughout this book (and throughout this chapter with the exception of this paragraph) is based on the understanding, emphasized in chapter 1, that coercive control is perpetrated by men in far greater numbers than by women (Barlow et al., 2020; Hester et al., 2017; Johnson et al., 2014; Myhill, 2015), and that, in families with children, the perpetrator is usually, though not always, the child's father or father-figure. Yet, as was also stressed in chapter 1, there are cases where it is the woman/mother who perpetrates against the man/father and/or the children. These much rarer instances of female-perpetrated coercive control require further research in their own right (as do other contexts in which coercive control can occur, see chapter 1), in addition to the continuing research that is needed on male-perpetrated coercive control.

Research recommendation 3: Highlighting the similarities of mothers' and children's experiences

Another key direction for future research that this book signposts is to explore the similarities in mothers' and children's experiences of coercive control. Each child and mother in this study had been entrapped in a perpetrator's/father's "world" of coercive control. Perpetrators/fathers used the same emotionally manipulative tactics against children as they use against mothers, such as crying, apologizing for abuse, gift-giving, and sometimes behaving in a "fun" way. Children, as well as mothers, had to habitually constrain and modify their behavior to avoid angering perpetrators/fathers. Several perpetrators/fathers seemed to expect the same constant obedience from their children as they did from mothers.

The related objective of further research here should be to determine how children and mothers may best be supported, together, to recover and thrive after breaking free from coercive control. This book has illustrated how the roads to recovery after separating from perpetrators/fathers may be strikingly similar for children and mothers. For the mothers and children in this study, these roads ran in parallel and tended to involve many of the same twists and turns: replacing the harmful ideas that perpetrators/fathers had instilled in them with more accurate and truthful understandings; strengthening their mental health, confidence, and self-esteem; increasing their abilities to relax and to express themselves and share feelings in positive ways; feeling sufficiently secure to attempt new activities/learn new skills; and developing new family relationships based on mutual respect and reciprocal care.

Research recommendation 4: Focusing on everyday life in a way that transcends the focus on visible happenings and events

As this book has demonstrated, in order to "see" coercive control, researchers need to focus not just on the realm of the dramatic incident of physical violence, but also on the realm of child and adult survivors' everyday lives. We need to ask: "What is it that the adult and child survivors have to do, or are unable to do, because of how the perpetrator/father would react?" Or, put another way, researchers need to focus on what is *not* happening, as well as what is happening. For instance, a child may be experiencing harm because the perpetrator/father has not allowed them to visit their maternal grandparents for the last several years. They may miss their grandparents and yearn to see them. Yet this is a form of harm that is "invisible"—being based on something not happening, it is an absence, a missing dimension in the child's life, rather than a bruise or other obvious sign of harm.

Furthermore, by observing coercive control through this "infra-red lens" that sees beyond recorded happenings, researchers would be able to recognize not just the wider harms, but also the many different, usually unremarked-upon acts in their everyday lives in which children and mothers often pursue agentic resistance and attempt to protect and support one another. Thus, it may well be incorrect to view children and mothers simply as passive or to view mothers as "failing to protect" if they are unable to stop the perpetrator's/father's most recent use of violence. They may actually be continually resisting and attempting to maintain each other's well-being through everyday acts such as cuddles, reassurance, and brief moments of attention and enjoyment shared when the perpetrator/father is not present. They may be doing what they *actually can do* at this everyday level, within the (very narrow) space for action left for them by the perpetrator/father.

Research recommendation 5: Highlighting the complexities of children's relational agency and mother–child supportiveness

Finally, this book also suggests a need to research the ways in which children influence and actively contribute to their relationships with others. Children use their agency relationally. Supporting, caring for, and influencing others are *not* activities that are exclusive to adulthood; they are part of normal, positive childhoods (see, e.g., Arditti, 1999; Eldén, 2016; James, 2013; Kuczynski et al., 1999, 2003, 2016; Marshall and Lambert, 2006; Morrow, 2003; Oliphant and Kuczynski, 2011). Yet, at the same time, it is possible for children to give care and support in contexts that are worryingly "high-stakes" and to extents that are excessive for their age (though perhaps necessary in the circumstances).

Carefully crafted, nuanced explorations are therefore needed. Coercive control creates unique complications and challenges for mother–child relationships, especially because perpetrators/fathers often prevent expressions of support or affection between those they are attempting to control, and because of the mental health and behavioral impacts that perpetrators/fathers can have on children and mothers. There are therefore diverse ways that mother–child supportiveness can function in situations where children and mothers are experiencing, or have formerly experienced, coercive control.

FIVE RECOMMENDATIONS FOR POLICY AND PRACTICE

Policy and practice recommendation 1: Enabling children to break free from distorted ways of thinking

An important way of helping victims/survivors of coercive control is to support them to break free from victim-blaming or perpetrator/father-excusing ideas that have been planted in their thought-processes by perpetrators/fathers (see Cavanagh et al., 2001; Towns and Adams, 2016; Williamson, 2010). Professional supports can be necessary to help victims/survivors in the often-extremely difficult challenge of overcoming these distorted ways of thinking—and this study, like other relevant studies (e.g., Monk and Bowen, 2021; Moulding et al., 2015; Radford and Hester, 2006; Thiara and Gill, 2012), has pointed to the need for such help to be much more widely available to *child* victims/survivors. We are currently more accustomed to the idea of helping adults to break free from such ways of thinking. For instance, many adult female survivors in the United Kingdom attend the Freedom Programme, a group program designed to educate survivors about the tactics used by perpetrators/fathers and to help them to make sense of their experiences. For mothers, the distorted ways of thinking are often self-blaming ideas, such as "it's mostly my fault" or "he's a great person really, he just has a short temper." Yet far less thought has been given to equipping *child* victims/survivors with an equivalent education.

For children, the problem is sometimes one of self-blame, and sometimes one of blame being redirected by the perpetrator/father toward the mother, via statements such as "everything would be okay if she'd let me come home," "she's stopping us being a family," or "your mother doesn't love me anymore and she's kicked me out." These victim-blaming or perpetrator/father-excusing ideas can leave children feeling confused and uncertain. Given that children depend on being able to trust adults, especially their parents, it is especially upsetting for children to hear different, conflicting accounts from adults that present an incoherent picture of reality. To overcome this issue, children may need to be given age-appropriate knowledge of coercive control/domestic violence, and, more specifically, may require particular professional assistance in breaking free from the distorted ideas imposed upon them by perpetrators/fathers.

A case study in how to break free from distorted ways of thinking: The experiences of Grace and Bob

Two child participants in this study, 14-year-old Grace and 12-year-old Bob, children of Lauren and Isobel, respectively, had received such help via counseling sessions that they had undertaken. Around the time that these children's mothers had separated from perpetrators/fathers, both Grace and Bob had been highly influenced by their fathers' narratives that the domestic violence and also the separation was the fault of the mother, and that he was the real sufferer (see also Monk and Bowen, 2021). Both children had been determined to see their fathers; Grace had contemplated leaving her mother's care and going to live with her father, and Bob had suffered from memory blocks that left him unable to remember times when his father had been highly abusive.

Due to their engagement with counseling over a period of several months, it seemed that Grace's and Bob's mental health, confidence, and general well-being had significantly improved. It was unclear from the children's accounts whether this counseling had occurred through a specialist domestic violence organization, or through the United Kingdom's National Health Service (NHS), or been given by a counselor in private practice. Yet, wherever these counseling sessions had occurred, they appeared to have assisted Grace and Bob in psychologically breaking free from their fathers' coercive control. Ultimately, both children had made the decision to not have any further contact with their fathers, and both had not had any such contact for 2–4 years prior to taking part in the study. Grace explained the circumstances that led her to make this decision:

> Everything that went badly in his life, he'd blame my mum and he'd blame us [me and my sister] and it just made me feel awful, so I decided, I said to him on the phone, I said: "I don't want to come and see you anymore." (Grace, age 14)

Grace outlined the improvements that she had experienced since she had chosen to stop contact:

> [After I stopped contact] I could just be, I suppose, *me* again, because before I had really low confidence and stuff. So I suppose I've come out of my shell a lot more and I can talk to people more. (Grace, age 14)

The counseling sessions had benefited Grace and Bob by encouraging them to focus on their own memories of what had occurred and to prioritize their own lived experiences over their fathers' false narratives. Grace suggested that her counselor had also educated her about manipulative behavior and how to recognize it, which, in her words, "basically showed me what my dad was trying to do and what he was trying to gain from it." Understanding the manipulation techniques used by perpetrators/fathers had given Grace the tools to break free—to make the informed choice to say, in her words, "I don't want to come and see you anymore" and to be "*me* again" instead.

Although Bob did not choose to discuss this aspect of his experiences in his interview, his mother Isobel described how counseling had helped Bob to come to terms with "what was going on" with his father. Once Bob had received support to psychologically process the difficult truths of how his father had behaved, he, like Grace, was able to decide that he no longer wanted contact with his father:

> Bob had to have loads of counseling. He went through a stage where he put his dad on a pedestal and he had memory blocks and [he'd say]: "When my dad comes out [of prison] we're gonna go fishing." ... He wanted to write to him and everything. But then when he'd had his counselling and realized, you know, what was going on, he doesn't want anything to do with him now. (Isobel, mother)

Bob's own interview suggested he was thriving in the absence of the perpetrator/father: "I've been working harder and I can be more focused in school. I feel safer. I've got better friends; they help me; let me have a laugh and things." Bob also described how he was now making positive use of his own experiences by actively supporting other children with their difficulties:

> There's this activity club and there's children who go there who've had mentors and stuff and I'm a helper there and I go there and ask how their week's been and I try and help them feel better about themselves, because I know what it's like to feel bullied and left out and isolated and everything. I like the feeling I get when I've helped someone. People get really down, they're being bullied, teased, things like that. I don't want them to turn into people who are all hard and everything. (Bob, age 12)

Moving forward in this way by supporting peers who had experienced adversity (Sinko et al., 2021), Bob was practicing a positive form of masculinity, showing care and empathy for others. Indeed, by embarking on this path, he was perhaps becoming the opposite type of man from his self-centred and abusive father.

Breaking free from distorted ways of thinking: Applying the "Five Factor Framework"

The Five Factor Framework discussed in chapter 5 may be of use in identifying when professional interventions such as those that helped Grace and Bob are needed. Listing in turn factors 1–4 (we will leave out factor 5, the child's view of mother and father, as it is in part a culmination of influences from the first four factors), we can say that children may be particularly in need of professional assistance to break free from distorted ways of thinking when they have been subjected to: (1) a perpetrator/father whose behavior toward the children alternates between hostility, disinterestedness, and seemingly more "positive" behaviors; (2) a perpetrator/father who uses coercive control in subtle ways that children struggle to understand as abusive behavior; (3) a perpetrator/father who is determined to undermine the children's relationships with their mother; and (4) situations where a perpetrator's/father's coercive control has had such negative impacts on the mother that she has been largely unable to emotionally connect with the children.

When children experience a number of these four factors (even sometimes just one or two), they may be highly vulnerable to perpetrators/fathers manipulating them to further their coercive control. This vulnerability was apparent in the study with regard to a number of children for whom the factors were experienced in this manner. Those children were Bob, Leah, Louise (see also chapter 8), Zoe and Grace, Tanya, and Carly. It was apparent—either from the children's own interviews or from their mother's interviews—that these children had in the past suffered (or, in some cases, were still suffering) from distorted ways of thinking. These ways of thinking had sometimes involved the child adoring the perpetrator/father and/or being profoundly confused about what had happened.

One recommendation for professional practice here is that children in these circumstances may benefit from interventions—delivered via group work and/or one-to-one sessions—that are focused on helping such children to break free from these distorted ideas. Such interventions would show children, in age-appropriate ways, how to recognize healthy and unhealthy parenting behaviors, healthy and unhealthy behavior toward a romantic partner, and coercive control dynamics. These interventions may help children to reject beliefs such as, for example, that a loving and faultless parent could be one who upsets them during each contact visit, or that the parent who loves them the most is the one who buys them the most gifts. Such interventions may also help children who have been brought up to put the needs of the abusive parent before their own. Children could be supported to realize that always prioritizing someone else above themselves is unhealthy and that their own needs *are* important. Armed with the knowledge from these interventions, children would be more able to make sound, well-informed judgments about how the people around them are behaving, and how they themselves wish to behave.

In terms of the practicalities of implementation, specialist domestic violence organizations would be ideally placed to develop and deliver such interventions, provided they were given the additional funding required to do so. Meanwhile, the reform of family courts also has a role to play here, and it is this issue to which we will now turn.

Policy and practice recommendation 2: Reforming family courts

We have just discussed how children such as Grace and Bob can benefit from receiving help to break free from the confusions and distorted ways of thinking that were being created by perpetrators/fathers as part of their coercive control. However, alongside helping children to break free, it is vital that the door be open for them to exit their relationship with their perpetrator parent, or to reduce their contact with them, if they so wish. Unfortunately, at present, if family courts are involved then the door is usually pulled shut; children are not allowed to exit, and are compelled to continue contact with the perpetrator parent. The reason why the door is so often closed by the family courts is because of the particular ways in which they currently operate.

At present, across multiple countries, family courts are a major weakpoint in the systems that deal with domestic violence. Often, indeed, family courts are the means through which perpetrators/fathers maintain coercive control post-separation. The recent history of family courts across Western countries is one of ordering post-separation contact between children and domestically violent fathers; even when such orders contradict children's clearly expressed wishes that they do not want and/ or are terrified by contact. Family courts do not always act in this way, but it is a pronounced tendency (see, e.g., Bancroft et al., 2012; Coy et al., 2015; Coy et al., 2012; Elizabeth, 2017; Galántai et al., 2019; Harne, 2011; Harrison, 2008; Hill, 2020; Hunter et al., 2020; Laing, 2017; Macdonald, 2016; Mackay, 2018; Radford and Hester, 2006; Stark, 2009; Thiara and Gill, 2012; Varcoe & Irwin, 2004). One reason for the strength of this tendency is the increasing prevalence in family courts of the theory of parental alienation/parental alienation syndrome: a theory in which the child's wish not to see a parent is viewed as being caused by the other parent manipulating the child (see Meier, 2009).

Disbelieving mothers and parental alienation

Parental alienation/parental alienation syndrome is a theory that is often used by domestically violent fathers during family court cases to discredit mothers' and children's reports of the father's history of abuse, and to claim that the mother is the real abuser due to her "alienating" behavior. Fathers whose children are unwilling to see them do not need to have any evidence to make this claim that the mother is an "alienator"; all they need to do is make the allegation, and the court's attention tends to switch away from considering whether or not he is an abuser, and onto the mother, who is now viewed with extreme suspicion and is perceived to be "the problem" (Barnett, 2020; Birchall and Choudhry, 2021; Casas Vila, 2020; Elizabeth, 2020; Feresin, 2020; Hill, 2020; Hunter et al., 2020; Meier et al., 2019; Meier, 2020; Mercer and Drew, 2021; Laing, 2017; Lapierre et al., 2020; Rathus, 2020; Sheehy and Boyd, 2020; Zaccour, 2020).

Meier et al.'s (2019) research into nationwide family court outcomes, discussed more fully in chapter 4, shows how alienation claims are being used in this way by domestically violent and abusive fathers in the United States. As noted in that chapter, when fathers make a claim of "alienation," they are often successful. The courts are likely not only to disbelieve reports by mothers that the father is abusive (an outcome that occurred in almost four-fifths of such cases); they also, in half of such cases, go so far as to put the child(ren) into the father's custody. We also observed in chapter 4 how there was a gender bias here. When roles were reversed and it was fathers who were claiming that mothers were abusive and mothers were claiming that fathers were engaging in parental alienation, mothers received custody from the courts about half as often, in only around 30% of cases (Meier, 2020; Meier et al., 2019). Meier's comprehensive data showed how serious the problem of alienation claims by abusive fathers is in the United States; and such claims are also a major problem in the family courts of other countries including, among others, the United Kingdom, Australia, Canada, Italy, Spain, and New Zealand (see, e.g., Barnett, 2020; Birchall and Choudhry, 2021; Casas Vila, 2020; Elizabeth, 2020; Feresin, 2020; Hill, 2020; Hunter et al., 2020; Mercer and Drew, 2021; Laing, 2017; Lapierre et al., 2020; Rathus, 2020; Sheehy and Boyd, 2020; Zaccour, 2020).

Even when fathers do *not* accuse mothers of parental alienation, mothers and children are still likely to experience negative outcomes in family courts if they inform the court about the father's history of abuse and raise concerns that contact would be unsafe. Meier et al. (2019) found that mothers were disbelieved by family courts in 59% of cases where they told the court that the father had been abusive. Courts were especially unlikely to believe that fathers had been sexually abusing their children. When mothers reported to the family court that fathers had sexually abused their children, 85% of mothers were disbelieved (Meier et al., 2019; see also Webb et al., 2021). This is despite research suggesting that false accusations from mothers in these circumstances are rare (Trocmé and Bala, 2005). Summarizing these findings, Meier et al. (2019, p. 26) concluded that courts are "excessively skeptical" of reports that fathers have been abusive or domestically violent (see also Hunter et al., 2020).

The necessity of reform: Pro-contact culture versus the needs and rights of children to be free from domestic violence/ coercive control

Family courts therefore require fundamental reform in their treatment of cases where mothers and/or children state that child-father contact would be unsafe. In the United Kingdom, a 2020 report authored for the Government's Ministry of Justice recommended reform of the "pro-contact culture" of the courts and professionals involved in child arrangement cases. It found:

> Concerns . . . that abuse is systematically minimized, ranging from children's voices not being heard, allegations being ignored, dismissed or disbelieved, to inadequate assessment of risk, traumatic court processes, perceived unsafe child arrangements, and abusers exercising continued control through repeat litigation and the threat of repeat litigation. (Hunter et al., 2020, p. 4)

A reformed family court system would consistently safeguard the needs and rights of children to be free of domestic violence/coercive control: but in its current form, the family court system instead tends to act as a roadblock to these children's safety. When child victims/survivors of coercive control are faced with this roadblock, they have little chance of escaping from coercive control; and nor do their victim/survivor parents. As Stanley and Humphreys (2017, p. 112) state, "extensive unsupervised, court-ordered contact with fathers who use violence has often placed children in the situation where they are [. . .] *unable to leave an abusive relationship* [my emphasis]." This book, alongside the research of others, points to the necessity of game-changing reform in this area.

Policy and practice recommendation 3: Greater availability of mother–child domestic violence recovery programs

Some of the mothers and children in the study were also in need of longer-term supports to rebuild their mother–child relationships. For child survivors in particular, there were innumerable benefits to having a stronger relationship with their mother. Strengthening their mother–child relationship made children feel more secure, loved, and cared for. It also meant, in practical terms, that they had somebody to whom they could turn for guidance when they were experiencing difficulties, for instance at school or with peers in the community.

ONTARIO-BASED PROGRAMS

For many of the mothers and children in the study, the key resources for rebuilding their mother–child relationships were found in Ontario-based programs run by specialist domestic violence services. (For evaluations of these programs, see McManus et al., 2013; Nolas et al., 2012; Sharp et al., 2011; Smith, 2016; Smith et al., 2015, Smith et al., 2020.) As mentioned in chapter 6, Ontario-based programs are constructed on a child-centered, psychoeducational model where children work with a group of peers and adult facilitators over approximately 12 weeks to discuss their experiences of domestic violence, find healthy ways of expressing feelings, overcome feelings of self-blame, and develop safety plans. Meanwhile, as part of such programs, a concurrent group is also held for the children's mothers, to help mothers to support their children's engagement in the sessions.

The findings of this study indicate that families would benefit from the scaling-up of these resources (see also Howarth et al., 2015; Howarth et al., 2016). Access to Ontario-based programs and other community-based interventions is sometimes restricted to children in middle childhood and early adolescence. For instance, in the United Kingdom, the NSPCC's DART program is only open to children aged 7–14, which would have excluded survivors from this study such as Eloise and her son John (who was aged 16 when he and Eloise broke free from the perpetrator/father), and Ria and her daughter Carly (who was aged 3 when she and Ria broke free). Ria and Carly in particular had been in need of immediate age-appropriate support when they broke free from the perpetrator/father, to repair the damage that he had caused to their mother–child relationship. Unfortunately, they did not receive this support. It would be helpful, therefore, to extend such programs and interventions to a wider age-range of children.

MORE LENGTHY AND EXTENSIVE PACKAGES OF SUPPORT

Moreover, the findings presented in this book suggest not only the need to adapt and extend these programs to children of different ages but also to provide customized support for families with greater levels of need. In chapter 8, we distinguished that Ontario-based programs were most effective for mothers and children whose mother–child relationships were *somewhat or moderately* harmed by perpetrators'/fathers' coercive control: the ones that fitted into the "very close and supportive" and the "mixed" categories of mother–child relationship established in chapter 5. Ontario-based programs helped to bring these mother–child relationships to the point where these mothers and children seemed to be enhancing each other's resilience and well-being.

However, the Ontario-based programs in their current form were insufficient to produce a substantial "turnaround" for the mother–child relationships that were most severely harmed by perpetrators'/fathers' coercive control; the ones categorized in chapter 5 as "very strained and distant." For this category, the programs were somewhat helpful; but these mothers and children seemed to require more lengthy and extensive packages of support to help them to heal the deeper wounds that perpetrators/fathers had left in their mother–child relationships (see also Monk and Bowen, 2021 and Morris, 2009).

Mothers receiving help to strengthen their mental health

As we observed in chapter 8, another aspect of support that was usually necessary, post-separation, was for mothers to receive help to strengthen their mental health, which had been undermined by perpetrators'/fathers' coercive control. A small number of mothers in this study had needed, but had not been offered, this support. These mothers were left struggling with high levels of mental ill-health several years into their post-separation lives (see the discussion of pattern 2 in chapter 8). These mothers' children were also living with the knowledge that their mother—the person on whom they depended—was in emotional distress and sometimes felt suicidal. These children were regularly attempting to help their mother to feel positive and to alleviate her distress; yet giving support in such high-stakes contexts (where you feel that your mother may commit suicide if your support is ineffective) is stressful and worrying for the giver.

To prevent children from being put in these positions, it is vital that mothers be provided with the mental health supports that they need. In the United Kingdom, the National Health Service (NHS) does not currently provide appropriate services to facilitate the long-term mental health recoveries of domestic violence survivors. Khan (2020), writing about the UK context, suggests that such services are urgently needed, and that these services could potentially be based on Herman's (1992) model of recovering from complex trauma.

Policy and practice recommendation 4: Practitioners using strengths-based and empowering approaches

Coercive control perpetrators undermine victims'/survivors' strength and power. They do so by attacking victims'/survivors' confidence, self-esteem, and sense of self-efficacy. They also attempt to persuade victims/survivors that their experiences are not real and that their feelings are unimportant or wrong. These actions may include the perpetrator/father making remarks to their partner such as "you're so stupid, you could never cope without me," or "you're way too sensitive" (Matheson et al., 2015; SafeLives, 2019). Moreover, perpetrators/fathers not only disempower their adult partner in these ways; they may also disempower the children in the family in ways that undermine children's confidence, self-esteem, and sense of self-efficacy. For instance, a perpetrator/father may criticize a child harshly for making trivial mistakes, while punishing them if they show signs of budding independence or if they question the perpetrator's/father's authority. A child's confidence may be undermined to the extent that they are afraid to use their voice within the family in case they say the "wrong thing."

Yet, as this study has shown, victims/survivors do have strength and power. In chapters 4 and 5, we observed the efforts made by mothers in their everyday lives to maintain their children's physical and emotional well-being during the period when they were entrapped in relationships with perpetrators/fathers; efforts that were being made by mothers even as perpetrators/fathers had left them living in fear, suffering with depression and PTSD, and with shattered self-esteem (see also Wendt et al., 2015). We also observed children's and mother's active strategies of resistance to coercive control. Later, in chapter 7, we explored how some of the mothers and children in this study were helping one another to recover from coercive control. (Not all of the mothers and children were at a stage where they could provide each other with this mutual support, and it depended to an extent on their access to wider networks of support such as helpful wider family, friends, and practitioners.) As part of their everyday interactions with one another, the mothers and children who could support each other were increasing each other's confidence, encouraging each other to "try new things," praising each other's skills and achievements, and conveying respect and care for one another's feelings and needs.

HELPING VICTIMS/SURVIVORS TO RECOGNIZE AND REFLECT ON THEIR STRENGTH AND POWER

It is therefore not necessarily the case that practitioners need to *give* strength and power to victims/survivors, or that they can "will" it into existence. In many instances it may be that practitioners can help victims/survivors to *recognize* and *reflect on* the strengths and power that they already possess. Lauren made an apt comment at the end of her interview; an interview where she had, seemingly for the first time, been given a space to articulate the ways in which she had helped her daughters during the years of their recoveries:

> It's just strange, you know, it's strange after all these years to think about it like a process. I never thought about it that way, about supporting the children. I just did it [supported them] automatically, it was just life. (Lauren)

It was notable in the study that participants such as Lauren did not necessarily "put the pieces together" and realize the full importance of how they had been supporting their children in everyday life or how extensively they had helped their children to recover: "it was just life." Raising this self-knowledge—especially around how mothers and children have positively helped each other's recoveries—could be very powerful.

So, practitioners working with mothers and children in families such as Lauren's have opportunities to: (1) ask friendly questions about the ways that they have tried to help each other, and (2) guide children and mothers toward perceiving their actions as powerful and important. Such an approach may be beneficial because, as Tew et al. (2012, p. 452) suggest, it encourages mothers and children to view themselves as "someone with abilities" and assists them in becoming more aware of their "personal agency and efficacy"; that is, their ability to positively influence the course of events and take successful actions. This approach can be understood as helping the survivor to build, with the support of others, a more positive self-identity post-coercive control (Kong, 2021; Sinko et al., 2021). Such positive self-identities can empower mothers and children, as they develop increased awareness of the skills and capabilities that they already have, and gather greater confidence and self-esteem as they work to overcome their experiences of coercive control.

Policy and practice recommendation 5: Child-centered approaches for interacting with child victims/survivors of coercive control

More generally, this study (alongside other research—see, e.g., Callaghan et al., 2018; Øverlien, 2013) points toward a potentially beneficial set of approaches for how practitioners should interact with child victims/survivors of coercive control. (These practitioners may include teachers, police officers, social workers, counselors/therapists, nurses/doctors, and specialist domestic violence workers.) These approaches might include, for example, giving such children opportunities to make a choice or express a preference (developing their "voice"), and reassuring them about anything that they might have done less than perfectly in their everyday lives (to demonstrate that it is permissible, and admirable, to develop skills gradually and go through processes of trial and error, and that it is okay to make mistakes). It is also helpful for practitioners to interact with such children in ways that help them to feel *important, worthwhile,* and *intelligent*—the opposite of how they have probably been made to feel by the perpetrator/father under his regime of coercive control.

There are further possible approaches that might be added here. For example, child victims/survivors may benefit from opportunities that practitioners can give them to explore the world around them and to socialize with supportive peers—the perpetrator/father may have deprived the child of those freedoms—and to express their emotions in safe settings. It can also be helpful for such children to see adults in authority respond in a fair, calm, and open manner (that is, not become defensive or aggressive in the way that the perpetrator/father would have done) when their authority is challenged. Finally, child victims/survivors of coercive control would benefit from being allowed and encouraged to participate in decisions being made about their lives. These decisions need not only be major ones; they might include letting the child decide what activity they would like to do next, or where they would like to travel to on a day out: anything that shows the child that their views are important, that their decisions are respected, and that they have some freedom of choice.

FINAL THOUGHTS

Before you put down this book, I would like to leave you, the reader, with three key points.

Mothers and children are co-victims and co-survivors

This book has demonstrated the similarity of children's and mothers' experiences of coercive control, and has suggested that children and mothers who have been subjected to this form of abuse should be understood as "co-victims" and "co-survivors."

Stopping domestic violence means stopping perpetrators

Any efforts that societies make to reduce or eliminate domestic violence must focus on stopping perpetrators. Supporting existing child and adult victims to break free and recover is absolutely vital, but this must also be accompanied by separately funded, ambitious strategies to tackle perpetrators and the social norms and structural inequalities that enable their abuse (see, e.g., Drive Project, 2020; Hill, 2020; Kuskoff and Parsell, 2020). There is a need for more preventative work with boys and young men that diverts them onto more positive paths before they start perpetrating domestic violence/coercive control.

According to the children and mothers in this study, at least six perpetrators/fathers—the ex-partners of Eloise, Kimberley, Violet, Lauren, Ria, and Bella—were now in new relationships. They were abusing their new partners and had, in some cases, fathered new children whom they were also abusing. Thus, even as the mothers and children in this study were making tremendous efforts to recover and build new lives, often with the assistance of numerous practitioners and services, perpetrators/ fathers were elsewhere and were actively harming new people. This is a cycle that must be stopped.

Coercive control is an issue of freedom

Ultimately, coercive control is about perpetrators/fathers taking away victims'/survivors' freedom to make choices about how they want to live and how they want to express themselves. It is about perpetrators/fathers attempting to force, threaten, and confuse victims/survivors into redirecting their lives, shifting away from meeting their own needs and shifting toward continually serving and pleasing someone else: the perpetrator/father.

To live exclusively to please somebody else is to be less than half alive, and being made to live this way is similarly harmful for children as it is for adults. Nowhere in this study was this better described than by 12-year-old Katie, who explained the transformation that she, her brother, and her mother had collectively experienced from dullness to joyful engagement with life after they had escaped from coercive control and gained their freedom. Let's finish with her words:

> We just love life at the moment because then we were all dull and didn't like life much and now we're all happy. We feel we can do anything we want. (Katie, 12)

REFERENCES

Abrahams, H. (2010). *Rebuilding Lives After Domestic Violence: Understanding Long-Term Outcomes*. London: Jessica Kingsley.

Addae, E.A., & Tang, L. (2021). "How can I feel safe at home"? Adolescents' experiences of family violence in Ghana. *Frontiers in Public Health*, *9*, article number 672061.

Aghtaie, N., & Gangoli, G. (Eds.). (2014). *Understanding Gender Based Violence: National and International Contexts*. Abingdon: Routledge.

Aghtaie, N., Larkins, C., Barter, C., Stanley, N., Wood, M., & Øverlien, C. (2018). Interpersonal violence and abuse in young people's relationships in five European countries: Online and offline normalisation of heteronormativity. *Journal of Gender-Based Violence*, *2*(2), 293–310.

Åkerlund, N., & Sandberg, L. (2016). Children and violence interactions: Exploring children's experiences of responses. *Child Abuse Review*, *26*(1), 51–62.

Alderson, P. (2005). Designing ethical research with children. In A. Farrell (Ed.), *Ethical Research with Children* (pp. 27–36). Maidenhead: Open University Press.

Alderson, P., & Morrow, V. (2011). *The Ethics of Research with Children and Young People: A Practical Handbook*. London: Sage.

Alexander, J., Callaghan, J., Sixsmith, J., & Fellin, L. (2016). Children's corporeal agency and use of space in situations of domestic violence. In B. Evans, J. Horton, & T. Skelton (Eds.), *Play and Recreation, Health and Wellbeing* (pp. 523–543). Singapore: Springer.

Ambert, A.-M. (2013). *The Effect of Children on Parents* (2nd ed.). London: Routledge.

Anderson, D.K., & Saunders, D.G. (2003). Leaving an abusive partner: An empirical review of predictors, the process of leaving, and psychological well-being. *Trauma, Violence, & Abuse*, *4*(2), 163–191.

Anderson, K.M., & Danis, F.S. (2006). Adult daughters of battered women: Resistance and resilience in the face of danger. *Affilia*, *21*(4), 419–432.

Anderson, K.M., Danis, F.S., & Havig, K. (2011). Adult daughters of battered women: Recovery and posttraumatic growth following childhood adversity. *Families in Society*, *92*(2), 154–160.

Anderson, K.M., Renner, L.M., & Bloom, T.L. (2017). Exploring protective strategies among rural women in an abusive relationship. *Issues in Mental Health Nursing*, *38*(8), 610–618.

Appel, A.E., & Holden, G.W. (1998). The co-occurrence of spouse and physical child abuse: A review and appraisal. *Journal of Family Psychology, 12*(4), 578–599.

Arai, L., Heawood, A., Feder, G., Howarth, E., MacMillan, H., Moore, T.H.M., Stanley, N., & Gregory, A. (2021). Hope, agency, and the lived experience of violence: A qualitative systematic review of children's perspectives on domestic violence and abuse. *Trauma, Violence, & Abuse, 22*(3), 427–438.

Arditti, J.A. (1999). Rethinking relationships between divorced mothers and their children: Capitalizing on family strengths. *Family Relations, 48*(2), 109–119.

Arnull, E., & Stewart, S. (2021). Developing a theoretical framework to discuss mothers experiencing domestic violence and being subject to interventions: A cross-national perspective. *International Journal for Crime, Justice and Social Democracy, 10*(2), 113–126.

Artz, S., Jackson, M.A., Rossiter, K.R., Nijdam-Jones, A., Géczy, I., & Porteous, S. (2014). A comprehensive review of the literature on the impact of exposure to intimate partner violence on children and youth. *International Journal of Child, Youth and Family Studies, 5*(4), 493–587.

Bair-Merritt, M.H., Ghazarian, S.R., Burrell, L., Crowne, S.S., McFarlane, E., & Duggan, A.K. (2015). Understanding how intimate partner violence impacts school age children's internalizing and externalizing problem behaviors: A secondary analysis of Hawaii Healthy Start Program evaluation data. *Journal of Child & Adolescent Trauma, 8*(4), 245–251.

Baker, H. (2005). Involving children and young people in research on domestic violence and housing. *Journal of Social Welfare and Family Law, 27*(3), 281–297.

Bancroft, L. (2002). *Why Does He Do That? Inside the Minds of Angry and Controlling Men.* New York, NY: G.P. Putnam's Sons.

Bancroft, L., & Silverman, J.G. (2002). *The Batterer as Parent: Addressing the Impacts of Domestic Violence on Family Dynamics.* London: Sage.

Bancroft, L., Silverman, J.G., & Ritchie, D. (2012). *The Batterer as Parent: Addressing the Impacts of Domestic Violence on Family Dynamics* (2nd ed.). London: Sage.

Barlow, C., Johnson, K., Walklate, S., & Humphreys, L. (2020). Putting coercive control into practice: Problems and possibilities. *British Journal of Criminology, 60*(1), 160–179.

Barnard, M. (2012). Critical qualitative theory and "framework" analysis. In S. Becker, A. Bryman, & H. Ferguson (Eds.), *Understanding Research for Social Policy and Social Work: Themes, Methods and Approaches* (2nd ed.) (pp. 334–337). Bristol: Policy Press.

Barnes, R., & Aune, K. (2021). Gender and domestic abuse victimisation among churchgoers in north west England: Breaking the Church's gendered silence. *Journal of Gender-Based Violence, 5*(2), 271–288.

Barnett, A. (2014). Contact at all costs? Domestic violence and children's welfare. *Child & Family Law Quarterly, 26*, 439–462.

Barnett, A. (2020). A genealogy of hostility: Parental alienation in England and Wales. *Journal of Social Welfare and Family Law, 42*(1), 18–29.

Barter, C., Lanau, A., Stanley, N., Aghtaie, N., & Øverlien, C. (2021). Factors associated with the perpetration of interpersonal violence and abuse in young people's intimate relationships. *Journal of Youth Studies.* Advanced online publication.

Barter, C., McCarry, M., Berridge, D., & Evans, K. (2009). *Partner Exploitation and Violence in Teenage Intimate Relationships*. London: NSPCC.

Beeble, M.L., Bybee, D., & Sullivan, C.M. (2007). Abusive men's use of children to control their partners and ex-partners. *European Psychologist, 12*(1), 54–61.

Beeble, M.L., Bybee, D., Sullivan, C.M., & Adams, A.E. (2009). Main, mediating, and moderating effects of social support on the well-being of survivors of intimate partner violence across 2 years. *Journal of Consulting and Clinical Psychology, 77*(4), 718–729.

Beetham, T., Gabriel, L., & James, H. (2019). Young children's narrations of relational recovery: A school-based group for children who have experienced domestic violence. *Journal of Family Violence, 34*(6), 565–575.

Berns, N. (2004). *Framing the Victim: Domestic Violence, Media and Social Problems*. New Brunswick, NJ: AldineTransaction.

Bidarra, Z.S., Lessard, G., & Dumont, A. (2016). Co-occurrence of intimate partner violence and child sexual abuse: Prevalence, risk factors and related issues. *Child Abuse & Neglect, 55*, 10–21.

Birchall, J., & Choudhry, S. (2018). *What About My Right Not to Be Abused? Domestic Abuse, Human Rights and the Family Courts*. Bristol: Women's Aid.

Birchall, J., & Choudhry, S. (2021). "I was punished for telling the truth": How allegations of parental alienation are used to silence, sideline and disempower survivors of domestic abuse in family law proceedings. *Journal of Gender-Based Violence*. Advanced online publication.

Bishop, C., & Bettinson, V. (2018). Evidencing domestic violence, including behaviour that falls under the new offence of "controlling or coercive behaviour." *International Journal of Evidence & Proof, 22*(1), 3–29.

Bomsta, H., & Sullivan, C.M. (2018). IPV survivors' perceptions of how a flexible funding housing intervention impacted their children. *Journal of Family Violence, 33*(6), 371–380.

Brown, L., Callahan, M., Strega, S., Walmsley, C., & Dominelli, L. (2009). Manufacturing ghost fathers: The paradox of father presence and absence in child welfare. *Child & Family Social Work, 14*(1), 25–34.

Buchanan, F. (2018). *Mothering Babies in Domestic Violence: Beyond Attachment*. London: Routledge.

Buchanan, F., Power, C., & Verity, F. (2013). Domestic violence and the place of fear in mother/baby relationships: "What was I afraid of? Of making it worse." *Journal of Interpersonal Violence, 28*(9), 1817–1838.

Buckley, H., Holt, S., & Whelan, S. (2007). Listen to me! Children's experiences of domestic violence. *Child Abuse Review, 16*(5), 296–310.

Budgeon, S. (2016). The "problem" with single women: Choice, accountability and social change. *Journal of Social and Personal Relationships, 33*(3), 401–418.

Burke, T., Kuczynski, L., & Perren, S. (2017). An exploration of Jamaican mothers' perceptions of closeness and intimacy in the mother–child relationship during middle childhood. *Frontiers in Psychology, 8*, article number 2148.

Burnette, C.E., Ferreira, R.J., & Buttell, F. (2017). Male parenting attitudes and batterer intervention: Assessing child maltreatment risk. *Research on Social Work Practice, 27*(4), 468–477.

Bushin, N. (2007). Interviewing with children in their homes: Putting ethical principles into practice and developing flexible techniques. *Children's Geographies, 5*(3), 235–251.

CAFCASS & Women's Aid (2017). *Allegations of Domestic Abuse in Child Contact Cases: Joint Research by CAFCASS and Women's Aid.* London/Bristol: CAFCASS/ Women's Aid.

Cairns, K., & Johnston, J. (2015). *Food and Femininity.* London: Bloomsbury.

Callaghan, J. (2015). Mothers and children? Representations of mothers in research on children's outcomes in domestic violence. *Psychology of Women Section Review, 17,* 13–20.

Callaghan, J.E.M., & Alexander, J.H. (2015). *Understanding Agency and Resistance Strategies (UNARS): Children's Experiences of Domestic Violence.* European Commission Project JUST/2012/DAP/AG/3461. University of Northampton.

Callaghan, J., Alexander, J., & Fellin, L.C. (2016a). Children's embodied experience of living with domestic violence: "I'd go into my panic, and shake, really bad." *Subjectivity, 9*(4), 399–419.

Callaghan, J., Alexander, J., Sixsmith, J., & Fellin, L.C. (2016b). Children's experiences of domestic violence and abuse: Siblings' accounts of relational coping. *Clinical Child Psychology and Psychiatry, 22*(4), 649–668.

Callaghan, J.E.M., Alexander, J.H., Sixsmith, J., & Fellin, L.C. (2018). Beyond "witnessing": Children's experiences of coercive control in domestic violence and abuse. *Journal of Interpersonal Violence, 33*(10), 1551–1581.

Callaghan, J., Fellin, L., Alexander, J., Mavrou, S., & Papathanassiou, M. (2017a). Children and domestic violence: Emotional competencies in embodied and relational contexts. *Psychology of Violence, 7*(3), 333–342.

Callaghan, J.E.M., Fellin, L.C., Mavrou, S., Alexander, J., & Sixsmith, J. (2017b). The management of disclosure in children's accounts of domestic violence: Practices of telling and not telling. *Journal of Child and Family Studies, 26*(12), 3370–3387.

Cameranesi, M., Piotrowski, C.C., & Brownridge, D.A. (2020). Profiles of adjustment in children and adolescents exposed to intimate partner violence: A scoping review investigating resilience processes. *Journal of Positive School Psychology, 4*(1, sup. 1), 117–136.

Campbell, E. (2017). How domestic violence batterers use custody proceedings in family courts to abuse victims, and how courts can put a stop to it. *UCLA Women's Law Journal, 24*(1), 41–66.

Campbell, R., Adams, A.E., Wasco, S.M., Ahrens, C.E., & Sefi, E. (2010). "What has it been like for you to talk with me today?": The impact of participating in interview research on rape survivors. *Violence Against Women, 16*(1), 60–83.

Carlson, J., Voith, L., Brown, J.C., & Holmes, M. (2019). Viewing children's exposure to intimate partner violence through a developmental, social-ecological, and survivor lens: The current state of the field, challenges, and future direction. *Violence Against Women, 25*(1), 6–28.

Casas Vila, G. (2020). Parental Alienation Syndrome in Spain: Opposed by the Government but accepted in the Courts. *Journal of Social Welfare and Family Law, 42*(1), 45–55.

REFERENCES

Castro Sandúa, M., & Mara, L.C. (2014). The social nature of attractiveness: How to shift attraction from the dominant traditional to alternative masculinities. *International and Multidisciplinary Journal of Social Sciences, 3*(2), 182–206.

Cater, A., & Forssell, A.M. (2014). Descriptions of fathers' care by children exposed to intimate partner violence (IPV): Relative neglect and children's needs. *Child & Family Social Work, 19*(2), 185–193.

Cavanagh, K. (2003). Understanding women's responses to domestic violence. *Qualitative Social Work, 2*(3), 229–249.

Cavanagh, K., Dobash, R.E., Dobash, R.P., & Lewis, R. (2001). "Remedial work": Men's strategic responses to their violence against intimate female partners. *Sociology, 35*(3), 695–714.

Chan, K.L. (2011). Children exposed to child maltreatment and intimate partner violence: A study of co-occurrence among Hong Kong Chinese families. *Child Abuse & Neglect, 35*(7), 532–542.

Chanmugam, A. (2014). Got one another's backs: Mother–teen relationships in families escaping intimate partner violence. *Journal of Human Behavior in the Social Environment, 24*(7), 811–827.

Chanmugam, A. (2015). Young adolescents' situational coping during adult intimate partner violence. *Child & Youth Services, 36*(2), 98–123.

Chantler, K., & McCarry, M. (2020). Forced marriage, coercive control, and conducive contexts: The experiences of women in Scotland. *Violence Against Women, 26*(1), 89–109.

Christensen, P., & James, A. (Eds.). (2008). *Research with Children: Perspectives and Practices* (2nd ed.). London: Routledge.

Christensen, P., & Prout, A. (2002). Working with ethical symmetry in social research with children. *Childhood, 9*(4), 477–497.

Clements, K.A., Sprecher, M., Modica, S., Terrones, M., Gregory, K., & Sullivan, C.M. (2021). The use of children as a tactic of intimate partner violence and its relationship to survivors' mental health. *Journal of Family Violence*. Advanced online publication.

Coker, A.L., Watkins, K.W., Smith, P.H., & Brandt, H.M. (2003). Social support reduces the impact of partner violence on health: Application of structural equation models. *Preventive Medicine, 37*(3), 259–267.

Coy, M., Perks, K., Scott, E., & Tweedale, R. (2012). *Picking Up the Pieces: Domestic Violence and Child Contact*. London: Rights of Women.

Coy, M., Scott, E., Tweedale, R., & Perks, K. (2015). "It's like going through the abuse again": Domestic violence and women and children's (un) safety in private law contact proceedings. *Journal of Social Welfare and Family Law, 37*(1), 53–69.

Coyne, C. (2010). Research with children and young people: The issue of parental (proxy) consent. *Children & Society, 24*(3), 227–237.

Crossman, K.A., Hardesty, J.L., & Raffaelli, M. (2016). "He could scare me without laying a hand on me": Mothers' experiences of nonviolent coercive control during marriage and after separation. *Violence Against Women, 22*(4), 454–473.

Cully, L., Wu, Q., & Slesnick, N. (2021). The role of maternal acceptance in mediating child outcomes among substance using women experiencing intimate partner violence. *Journal of Interpersonal Violence, 36*(7–8), 3191–3208.

Curtice, J., Clery, E., Perry, J., Phillips, M., & Rahim, N. (Eds.). (2019). *British Social Attitudes: The 36th Report*. London: National Centre for Social Research.

Dallam, S., & Silberg, J.L. (2016). Recommended treatments for "parental alienation syndrome" (PAS) may cause children foreseeable and lasting psychological harm. *Journal of Child Custody, 13*(2–3), 134–143.

Damant, D., Lapierre, S., Lebossé, C., Thibault, S., Lessard, G., Hamelin-Brabant, L., Lavergne, C., & Fortin, A. (2010). Women's abuse of their children in the context of domestic violence: Reflection from women's accounts. *Child & Family Social Work, 15*(1), 12–21.

Davies, C.T. (2019). This is abuse? Young women's perspectives of what's "OK" and "not OK" in their intimate relationships. *Journal of Family Violence, 34*(5), 479–491.

Day, A., & Bowen, E. (2015). Offending competency and coercive control in intimate partner violence. *Aggression and Violent Behavior, 20*, 62–71.

De Mol, J., & Buysse, A. (2008). The phenomenology of children's influence on parents. *Journal of Family Therapy, 30*(2), 163–193.

De Puy, J., Radford, L., Le Fort, V., & Romain-Glassey, N. (2019). Developing assessments for child exposure to intimate partner violence in Switzerland: A study of medico-legal reports in clinical settings. *Journal of Family Violence, 34*(5), 371–383.

De Simone, T., & Heward-Belle, S. (2020). Evidencing better child protection practice: Why representations of domestic violence matter. *Current Issues in Criminal Justice, 32*(4), 403–419.

Dispatches. (2021). *Torn Apart: Family Courts Uncovered* [TV program]. Channel 4 (UK), July 20, 22:00.

Dobash, R.E., & Dobash, R. (1979). *Violence Against Wives: A Case Against the Patriarchy*. New York, NY: Free Press.

Dobash, R.P., Dobash, R.E., Wilson, M., & Daly, M. (1992). The myth of sexual symmetry in marital violence. *Social Problems, 39*(1), 71–91.

Douglas, H. (2018). Legal systems abuse and coercive control. *Criminology & Criminal Justice, 18*(1), 84–99.

Douglas, H., & Fell, E. (2020). Malicious reports of child maltreatment as coercive control: Mothers and domestic and family violence. *Journal of Family Violence, 35*(8), 827–837.

Douglas, H., & Walsh, T. (2010). Mothers, domestic violence, and child protection. *Violence Against Women, 16*(5), 489–508.

Downes, J., Kelly, L., & Westmarland, N. (2019). "It's a work in progress": Men's accounts of gender and change in their use of coercive control. *Journal of Gender-Based Violence, 3*(3), 267–282.

Dragiewicz, M., Harris, B., Woodlock, D., & Salter, M. (2021a). Digital media and domestic violence in Australia: Essential contexts. *Journal of Gender-Based Violence, 5*(3), 377–393.

Dragiewicz, M., Woodlock, D., Salter, M., & Harris, B. (2021b). "What's Mum's password?": Australian mothers' perceptions of children's involvement in technology-facilitated coercive control. *Journal of Family Violence*. Advanced online publication.

Drive Project. (2020). *A Domestic Abuse Perpetrator Strategy for England and Wales*. London: Drive Partnership (Respect/SafeLives/Social Finance).

Dutton, M.A., & Goodman, L.A. (2005). Coercion in intimate partner violence: Toward a new conceptualization. *Sex Roles, 52*(11–12), 743–756.

Edleson, J.L. (1998). Responsible mothers and invisible men: Child protection in the case of adult domestic violence. *Journal of Interpersonal Violence, 13*(2), 294–298.

Edleson, J.L. (1999a). Children's witnessing of adult domestic violence. *Journal of Interpersonal Violence, 14*(8), 839–870.

Edleson, J.L. (1999b). The overlap between child maltreatment and woman battering. *Violence Against Women, 5*(2), 134–154.

Edleson, J.L. (2006). *Emerging Responses to Children Exposed to Domestic Violence.* Harrisburg, PA: National Resource Center on Domestic Violence.

Edwards, R., & Mauthner, M. (2012). Ethics in feminist research: Theory and practice. In T. Miller, M. Birch, M. Mauthner, & J. Jessop (Eds.), *Ethics in Qualitative Research* (2nd ed.) (pp. 14–28). London: Sage.

Eldén, S. (2016). An ordinary complexity of care: Moving beyond "the family" in research with children. *Families, Relationships and Societies, 5*(2), 175–192.

Elizabeth, V. (2017). Custody stalking: A mechanism of coercively controlling mothers following separation. *Feminist Legal Studies, 25*(2), 185–201.

Elizabeth, V. (2020). The affective burden of separated mothers in PA (S) inflected custody law systems: A New Zealand case study. *Journal of Social Welfare and Family Law, 42*(1), 118–129.

Elizabeth, V., Gavey, N., & Tolmie, J. (2012). " . . . He's just swapped his fists for the system": The governance of gender through custody law. *Gender & Society, 26*(2), 239–260.

Enander, V. (2011). Leaving Jekyll and Hyde: Emotion work in the context of intimate partner violence. *Feminism and Psychology, 21*(1), 29–48.

Eriksson, M. (2012). Participation for children exposed to domestic violence? Social workers' approaches and children's strategies. *European Journal of Social Work, 15*(2), 205–221.

Eriksson, M., Hester, M., Keskinen, S., & Pringle, K. (2005). *Tackling Men's Violence in Families: Nordic Issues and Dilemmas.* Bristol: Policy Press.

Eriksson, M., & Näsman, E. (2008). Participation in family law proceedings for children whose father is violent to their mother. *Childhood, 15*(2), 259–275.

Eriksson, M., & Näsman, E. (2012). Interviews with children exposed to violence. *Children & Society, 26*(1), 63–73.

Esterberg, G.K. (2002). *Qualitative Methods in Social Research.* New York, NY: McGraw-Hill.

Ewen, B.M. (2007). Failure to protect laws: Protecting children or punishing mothers? *Journal of Forensic Nursing, 3*(2), 84–86.

Fairchild, R., & McFerran, K.S. (2018). Understanding children's resources in the context of family violence through a collaborative songwriting method. *Children Australia, 43*(4), 255–266.

Fellin, L.C., Callaghan, J.E.M., Alexander, J.H., Harrison-Breed, C., Mavrou, S., & Papathanasiou, M. (2019). Empowering young people who experienced domestic violence and abuse: The development of a group therapy intervention. *Clinical Child Psychology and Psychiatry, 24*(1), 170–189.

Fellin, L.C., Callaghan, J.E.M., Alexander, J.H., Mavrou, S., & Harrison-Breed, C. (2018). Child's play? Children and young people's resistances to domestic violence and abuse. *Children & Society, 33*(2), 126–141.

Feresin, M. (2020). Parental alienation (syndrome) in child custody cases: Survivors' experiences and the logic of psychosocial and legal services in Italy. *Journal of Social Welfare and Family Law, 42*(1), 56–67.

Feresin, M., Bastiani, F., Beltramini, L., & Romito, P. (2019). The involvement of children in postseparation intimate partner violence in Italy: A strategy to maintain coercive control? *Affilia, 34*(4), 481–497.

Finkelhor, D., Ormrod, R.K., & Turner, H.A. (2007). Poly-victimization: A neglected component in child victimization. *Child Abuse & Neglect, 31*(1), 7–26.

Finkelhor, D., Turner, H.A., Ormrod, R.K., & Hamby, S.L. (2009). Violence, crime, and exposure in a national sample of children and youth. *Pediatrics, 124*(5), 1411–1423.

Fleury, R.E., Sullivan, C.M., & Bybee, D.I. (2000). When ending the relationship does not end the violence: Women's experiences of violence by former partners. *Violence Against Women, 6*(12), 1363–1383.

Fogarty, A., Woolhouse, H., Giallo, R., Wood, C., Kaufman, J., & Brown, S. (2021). Mothers' experiences of parenting within the context of intimate partner violence: Unique challenges and resilience. *Journal of Interpersonal Violence, 36*(21–22), 10564–10587.

Fong, V.C., Hawes, D., & Allen, J.L. (2019). A systematic review of risk and protective factors for externalizing problems in children exposed to intimate partner violence. *Trauma, Violence, & Abuse, 20*(2), 149–167.

Fontes, L.A. (2015). *Invisible Chains: Overcoming Coercive Control in Your Intimate Relationship*. London: Guilford.

Ford-Gilboe, M., Wuest, J., & Merritt-Gray, M. (2005). Strengthening capacity to limit intrusion: Theorizing family health promotion in the aftermath of woman abuse. *Qualitative Health Research, 15*(4), 477–501.

Galántai, J., Ligeti, A.S., & Wirth, J. (2019). Children exposed to violence: Child custody and its effects on children in intimate partner violence related cases in Hungary. *Journal of Family Violence, 34*(5), 399–409.

Gillett-Swan, J.K., & Sargeant, J. (2018). Unintentional power plays: Interpersonal contextual impacts in child-centred participatory research. *Educational Research, 60*(1), 1–16.

Gillies, V., Ribbens McCarthy, J., & Holland, J. (2001). *Pulling Together, Pulling Apart: The Family Lives of Young People*. London: Family Policy Studies Centre/Joseph Rowntree Foundation.

Goldblatt, H., Buchbinder, E., & Cohen, R. (2014). Re-experiencing motherhood: Transformation of relationships between formerly abused women and their children. *Violence Against Women, 20*(5), 561–580.

Gorin, S., Hooper, C.-A., Dyson, C., & Cabral, C. (2008). Ethical challenges in conducting research with hard to reach families. *Child Abuse Review, 17*(4), 275–287.

Guille, L. (2004). Men who batter and their children: An integrated review. *Aggression and Violent Behavior, 9*(2), 129–163.

REFERENCES

Haight, W.L., Shim, W.S., Linn, L.M., & Swinford, L. (2007). Mothers' strategies for protecting children from batterers: The perspectives of battered women involved in child protective services. *Child Welfare, 86*(4), 41–62.

Halliwell, G., Daw, J., Hay, S., Dheensa, S., & Jacob, S. (2021). "A life barely half lived": Domestic abuse and sexual violence practitioners' experiences and perceptions of providing care to survivors of non-physical abuse within intimate partner relationships. *Journal of Gender-Based Violence, 5*(2), 249–269.

Hamby, S., Finkelhor, D., Turner, H., & Ormrod, R. (2010). The overlap of witnessing partner violence with child maltreatment and other victimizations in a nationally representative survey of youth. *Child Abuse & Neglect, 34*(10), 734–741.

Harach, L.D., & Kuczynski, L.J. (2005). Construction and maintenance of parent–child relationships: Bidirectional contributions from the perspective of parents. *Infant and Child Development: An International Journal of Research and Practice, 14*(4), 327–343.

Hardesty, J.L., Khaw, L., Ridgway, M.D., Weber, C., & Miles, T. (2013). Coercive control and abused women's decisions about their pets when seeking shelter. *Journal of Interpersonal Violence, 28*(13), 2617–2639.

Hardesty, J.L., Crossman, K.A., Haselschwerdt, M.L., Raffaelli, M., Ogolsky, B.G., & Johnson, M.P. (2015). Toward a standard approach to operationalizing coercive control and classifying violence types. *Journal of Marriage and Family, 77*(4), 833–843.

Harne, L. (2011). *Violent Fathering and the Risks to Children: The Need for Change.* Bristol: Policy Press.

Harrison, C. (2008). Implacably hostile or appropriately protective? Women managing child contact in the context of domestic violence. *Violence Against Women, 14*(4), 381–405.

Haselschwerdt, M.L. (2014). Theorizing children's exposure to intimate partner violence using Johnson's typology. *Journal of Family Theory & Review, 6*(3), 199–221.

Haselschwerdt, M.L., Hlavaty, K., Carlson, C., Schneider, M., Maddox, L., & Skipper, M. (2019a). Heterogeneity within domestic violence exposure: Young adults' retrospective experiences. *Journal of Interpersonal Violence, 34*(7), 1512–1538.

Haselschwerdt, M.L., Savasuk-Luxton, R., & Hlavaty, K. (2019b). A methodological review and critique of the "intergenerational transmission of violence" literature. *Trauma, Violence, & Abuse, 20*(2), 168–182.

Haselschwerdt, M.L., Maddox, L., & Hlavaty, K. (2020). Young adult women's perceptions of their maritally violent fathers. *Family Relations, 69*(2), 335–350.

Havard, T.E., & Lefevre, M. (2020). Beyond the power and control wheel: How abusive men manipulate mobile phone technologies to facilitate coercive control. *Journal of Gender-Based Violence, 4*(2), 223–239.

Hayes, B.E. (2017). Indirect abuse involving children during the separation process. *Journal of Interpersonal Violence, 32*(19), 2975–2997.

Heilman, B., Barker, G., & Harrison, A. (2017). *The Man Box: A Study on Being a Young Man in the US, UK, and Mexico.* London: Promundo.

Herman, J.L. (1992). *Trauma and Recovery: The Aftermath of Violence—From Domestic Abuse to Political Terror.* New York, NY: Basic Books.

Hester, M. (2006). Making it through the criminal justice system: Attrition and domestic violence. *Social Policy and Society, 5*(1), 79–90.

Hester, M. (2011). The three planet model: Towards an understanding of contradictions in approaches to women and children's safety in contexts of domestic violence. *British Journal of Social Work, 41*(5), 837–853.

Hester, M. (2012). Portrayal of women as intimate partner domestic violence perpetrators. *Violence Against Women, 18*(9), 1067–1082.

Hester, M., Jones, C., Williamson, E., Fahmy, E., & Feder, G. (2017). Is it coercive controlling violence? A cross-sectional domestic violence and abuse survey of men attending general practice in England. *Psychology of Violence, 7*(3), 417–427.

Heward-Belle, S. (2016). The diverse fathering practices of men who perpetrate domestic violence. *Australian Social Work, 69*(3), 323–337.

Heward-Belle, S. (2017). Exploiting the "good mother" as a tactic of coercive control: Domestically violent men's assaults on women as mothers. *Affilia, 32*(3), 374–389.

Heward-Belle, S., Humphreys, C., Healey, L., Toivonen, C., & Tsantefski, M. (2019). Invisible practices: Interventions with men who use violence and control. *Affilia, 34*(3), 369–382.

Heward-Belle, S., Laing, L., Humphreys, C., & Toivonen, C. (2018). Intervening with children living with domestic violence: Is the system safe? *Australian Social Work, 71*(2), 135–147.

Hill, J. (2020). *See What You Made Me Do: Power, Control and Domestic Abuse.* London: Hurst.

HM Government. (2018). *Regional Ethnic Diversity.* London: HMSO.

Holden, G.W. (2003). Children exposed to domestic violence and child abuse: Terminology and taxonomy. *Clinical Child and Family Psychology Review, 6*(3), 151–160.

Holmes, M.R. (2013). Aggressive behavior of children exposed to intimate partner violence: An examination of maternal mental health, maternal warmth and child maltreatment. *Child Abuse & Neglect, 37*(8), 520–530.

Holmes, M.R., Richter, F.G.C., Votruba, M.E., Berg, K.A., & Bender, A.E. (2018). Economic burden of child exposure to intimate partner violence in the United States. *Journal of Family Violence, 33*(4), 239–249.

Holmes, M.R., Yoon, S., & Berg, K. (2017). Maternal depression and intimate partner violence exposure: Longitudinal analyses of the development of aggressive behavior. *Aggressive Behavior, 43*(4), 375–385.

Holt, S. (2017). Domestic violence and the paradox of post-separation mothering. *British Journal of Social Work, 47*(7), 2049–2067.

Holt, S., Buckley, H., & Whelan, S. (2008). The impact of exposure to domestic violence on children and young people: A review of the literature. *Child Abuse & Neglect, 32*(8), 797–810.

Holtzworth-Munroe, A., Smutzler, N., & Sandin, E. (1997). A brief review of the research on husband violence: Part II: The psychological effects of husband violence on battered women and their children. *Aggression and Violent Behavior, 2*(2), 179–213.

Hooper, L.M. (2007). The application of attachment theory and family systems theory to the phenomena of parentification. *Family Journal, 15*(3), 217–223.

Houghton, C. (2015). Young people's perspectives on participatory ethics: Agency, power and impact in domestic abuse research and policy-making. *Child Abuse Review, 24*(4), 235–248.

Howarth, E., Moore, T.H.M., Shaw, A.R.G., Welton, N.J., Feder, G.S., Hester, M., MacMillan, H.L., & Stanley, N. (2015). The effectiveness of targeted interventions for children exposed to domestic violence: Measuring success in ways that matter to children, parents and professionals. *Child Abuse Review*, 24(4), 297–310.

Howarth, E., Moore, T.H.M., Welton, N.J., Lewis, N., Stanley, N., MacMillan, H., Shaw, A., Hester, M., Bryden, P., & Feder, G. (2016). IMPRoving Outcomes for children exposed to domestic ViolencE (IMPROVE): An evidence synthesis. *Public Health Research*, 4(10), 1–341.

Humphreys, C. (1999). Avoidance and confrontation: Social work practice in relation to domestic violence and child abuse. *Child and Family Social Work*, 4, 77–87.

Humphreys, C., Lowe, P., & Williams, S. (2009). Sleep disruption and domestic violence: Exploring the interconnections between mothers and children. *Child & Family Social Work*, 14(1), 6–14.

Humphreys, C., & Absler, D. (2011). History repeating: Child protection responses to domestic violence. *Child & Family Social Work*, 16(4), 464–473.

Humphreys, C., Diemer, K., Bornemisza, A., Spiteri-Staines, A., Kaspiew, R., & Horsfall, B. (2019). More present than absent: Men who use domestic violence and their fathering. *Child & Family Social Work*, 24(2), 321–329.

Humphreys, C., Healey, L., & Heward-Belle, S. (2020). Fathers who use domestic violence: Organisational capacity building and practice development. *Child & Family Social Work*, 25(sup. 1), 18–27.

Humphreys, C., Mullender, A., Thiara, R., & Skamballis, A. (2006). "Talking to my mum": Developing communication between mothers and children in the aftermath of domestic violence. *Aggressive Behavior*, 6(1), 53–63.

Humphreys, C., & Thiara, R. (2003). Mental health and domestic violence: "I call it symptoms of abuse." *British Journal of Social Work*, 33(2), 209–226.

Humphreys, C., Thiara, R.K., & Skamballis, A. (2011). Readiness to change: Mother–child relationship and domestic violence intervention. *British Journal of Social Work*, 41(1), 166–184.

Hungerford, A., Wait, S.K., Fritz, A.M., Clements, C.M. (2012). Exposure to intimate partner violence and children's psychological adjustment, cognitive functioning, and social competence: A review. *Aggression and Violent Behaviour*, 17(4), 373–382.

Hunter, R., Burton, M., & Trinder, L. (2020). *Assessing Risk of Harm to Children and Parents in Private Law Children Cases: Final Reports*. London: HM Government.

Huth-Bocks, A.C., & Hughes, H.M. (2008). Parenting stress, parenting behavior, and children's adjustment in families experiencing intimate partner violence. *Journal of Family Violence*, 23(4), 243–251.

Jaffe, P., Wolfe, D.A., & Campbell, M. (2012). *Growing Up with Domestic Violence*. Boston, MA: Hogrefe.

James, A. (2013). *Socialising Children*. Basingstoke: Palgrave Macmillan.

Johansen, A.-K., & Sundet, R. (2018). Stepchildren's judicial interview narratives of experiencing domestic violence. *Qualitative Research in Psychology*, 18(2), 183–203.

Johnson, M.P. (2008). *A Typology of Domestic Violence: Intimate Terrorism, Violent Resistance, and Situational Couple Violence*. Boston, MA: Northeastern University Press.

Johnson, M.P., Leone, J.M., & Xu, Y. (2014). Intimate terrorism and situational couple violence in general surveys: Ex-spouses required. *Violence Against Women*, *20*(2), 186–207.

Johnson, S.P., & Sullivan, C.M. (2008). How child protection workers support or further victimize battered mothers. *Affilia*, *23*(3), 242–258.

Johnson, V.K., & Lieberman, A.F. (2007). Variations in behaviour problems of preschoolers exposed to domestic violence: The role of mothers' attunement to children's emotional experiences. *Journal of Family Violence*, *22*(5), 297–308.

Jouriles, E.N., & McDonald, R. (2015). Intimate partner violence, coercive control, and child adjustment problems. *Journal of Interpersonal Violence*, *30*(3), 459–474.

Jouriles, E.N., McDonald, R., Slep, A.M.S., Heyman, R.E., & Garrido, E. (2008). Child abuse in the context of domestic violence: Prevalence, explanations, and practice implications. *Violence and Victims*, *23*(2), 221–235.

Jouriles, E.N., Rosenfield, D., McDonald, R., Vu, N.L., Rancher, C., & Mueller, V. (2018). Children exposed to intimate partner violence: Conduct problems, interventions, and partner contact with the child. *Journal of Clinical Child & Adolescent Psychology*, *47*(3), 397–409.

Jurkovic, G.J., Thirkield, A., & Morrell, R. (2001). Parentification of adult children of divorce: A multidimensional analysis. *Journal of Youth and Adolescence*, *30*(2), 245–257.

Källström, Å., & Thunberg, S. (2019). "Like an equal, somehow"—What young people exposed to family violence value in counseling. *Journal of Family Violence*, *34*(6), 553–563.

Katz, E. (2015a). Domestic violence, children's agency and mother-child relationships: Towards a more advanced model. *Children & Society*, *29*(1), 69–79.

Katz, E. (2015b). Recovery-promoters: Ways that mothers and children support one another's recoveries from domestic violence. *British Journal of Social Work*, *45*(sup. 1), i153–i169.

Katz, E. (2016). Beyond the physical incident model: How children living with domestic violence are harmed by and resist regimes of coercive control. *Child Abuse Review*, *25*(1), 46–59.

Katz, E. (2019). Coercive control, domestic violence and a five-factor framework: Five factors that influence closeness, distance and strain in mother–child relationships. *Violence Against Women*, *25*(15), 1829–1853.

Katz, E., Nikupeteri, A., & Laitinen, M. (2020). When coercive control continues to harm children: Post-separation fathering, stalking, and domestic violence. *Child Abuse Review*, *29*(4), 310–324.

Kellett, M. (2010). *Rethinking Children and Research: Attitudes in Contemporary Society*. London: Continuum.

Kelly, L. (2007). A conducive context: Trafficking of persons in Central Asia. In M. Lee (Ed.), *Human Trafficking* (pp. 73–91). Cullompton: Willan.

Kelly, L., Sharp, N., & Klein, R. (2014). *Finding the Costs of Freedom: How Women and Children Rebuild Their Lives After Domestic Violence*. London: Solace/Women's Aid.

Kelly, L., & Westmarland, N. (2015). *Domestic Violence Perpetrator Programmes: Steps Towards Change*. Durham: Durham University.

Kelton, K., Elrod, N., Kaylor, L., Copeland, M., & Weaver, T.L. (2020). "She's just a bad mother": Perceptions of failure to protect children in relationships with intimate partner violence. *Journal of Family Trauma, Child Custody & Child Development, 17*(4), 295–316.

Khan, S. (2020). *Growth After Intimate Partner Violence: A Mixed Methods Study* (Unpublished PhD thesis). City, University of London, London.

Kirk, S. (2007). Methodological and ethical issues in conducting qualitative research with children and young people: A literature review. *International Journal of Nursing Studies, 44*(7), 1250–1260.

Kitzinger, J. (2015). Who are you kidding? Children, power, and the struggle against sexual abuse. In A. James & A. Prout (Eds.), *Constructing and Reconstructing Childhood: Contemporary Issues in the Sociological Study of Childhood* (pp. 145–166). London: Routledge.

Kitzmann, K.M., Gaylord, N.K., Holt, A.R., & Kenny, E.D. (2003). Child witnesses to domestic violence: A meta-analytic review. *Journal of Consulting and Clinical Psychology, 71*(2), 339–352.

Kleinman, T. (2017). Family court ordered "reunification therapy": Junk science in the guise of helping parent/child relationships? *Journal of Child Custody, 14*(4), 295–300.

Knezevic, Z., Nikupeteri, A., Laitinen, M., & Kallinen, K. (2021). Gender-and power sensitivity, securitisation and social peace: Rethinking protection for children exposed to post-separation violence. *Journal of Gender-Based Violence.* Advanced online publication.

Kong, S.-T. (2021). Beyond "safeguarding" and "empowerment" in Hong Kong: Towards a relational model for supporting women who have left their abusive partners. *Journal of Family Violence, 36*(6), 683–694.

Kong, S.-T., & Hooper, C.-A. (2018). Building a community of practice for transforming "mothering" of abused women into a "mutual care project": A new focus on partnership and mutuality. *British Journal of Social Work, 48*(3), 633–655.

Kuczynski, L., & De Mol, J. (2015). Dialectical models of socialization. In W.F. Overton & P.C.M. Molenaar (Eds.), *Handbook of Child Psychology and Developmental Science, Volume 1: Theory and Method* (7th ed.) (pp. 323–368). Hoboken, NJ: Wiley.

Kuczynski, L., Harach, L., & Bernardini, S.C. (1999). Psychology's child meets sociology's child: Agency, influence and power in parent–child relationships. In S. Shehan (Ed.), *Through the Eyes of the Child: Revisioning Children as Active Agents of Family Life* (pp. 21–51). Bingley: Emerald.

Kuczynski, L., Lollis, S., & Koguchi, T. (2003). Reconstructing common sense: Metaphors of bidirectionality in parent–child relations. In L. Kuczynski (Ed.), *Handbook of Dynamics in Parent-Child Relations* (pp. 421–438). London: Sage.

Kuczynski, L., Pitman, R., Ta-Young, L., & Harach, L. (2016). Children's influence on their parent's adult development: Mothers' and fathers' receptivity to children's requests for change. *Journal of Adult Development, 23*(4), 193–203.

Kuczynski, L., Pitman, R., & Twigger, K. (2018). Flirting with resistance: Children's expressions of autonomy during middle childhood. *International Journal of Qualitative Studies on Health and Well-being, 13*(sup. 1), article number 1564519.

Kuskoff, E., & Parsell, C. (2020). Preventing domestic violence by changing Australian gender relations: Issues and considerations. *Australian Social Work, 73*(2), 227–235.

Laing, L. (2017). Secondary victimization: Domestic violence survivors navigating the family law system. *Violence Against Women, 23*(11), 1314–1335.

Lamb, K., Humphreys, C., & Hegarty, K. (2018). "Your behaviour has consequences": Children and young people's perspectives on reparation with their fathers after domestic violence. *Children and Youth Services Review, 88,* 164–169.

Lamela, D., Jongenelen, I., Pinto, R., & Levendosky, A. (2018). Typologies of intimate partner violence-maternal parenting and children's externalizing problems: The moderating effect of the exposure to other forms of family violence. *Child Abuse & Neglect, 81,* 60–73.

Lapierre, S. (2008). Mothering in the context of domestic violence: The pervasiveness of a deficit model of mothering. *Child & Family Social Work, 13*(4), 454–463.

Lapierre, S. (2010a). More responsibilities, less control: Understanding the challenges and difficulties involved in mothering in the context of domestic violence. *British Journal of Social Work, 40*(5), 1434–1451.

Lapierre, S. (2010b). Striving to be "good" mothers: Abused women's experiences of mothering. *Child Abuse Review, 19*(5), 342–357.

Lapierre, S., Côté, I., Lambert, A., Buetti, D., Lavergne, C., Damant, D., & Couturier, V. (2018). Difficult but close relationships: Children's perspectives on relationships with their mothers in the context of domestic violence. *Violence Against Women, 24*(9), 1023–1038.

Lapierre, S., Ladouceur, P., Frenette, M., & Côté, I. (2020). The legitimization and institutionalization of "parental alienation" in the Province of Quebec. *Journal of Social Welfare and Family Law, 42*(1), 30–44.

Lau Clayton, C. (2014). "With my parents I can tell them anything": Intimacy levels within British Chinese families. *International Journal of Adolescence and Youth, 19*(1), 22–36.

LeCouteur, A., & Oxlad, M. (2011). Managing accountability for domestic violence: Identities, membership categories and morality in perpetrators' talk. *Feminism & Psychology, 21*(1), 5–28.

Lehmann, P., Simmons, C.A., & Pillai, V.K. (2012). The validation of the checklist of controlling behaviors (CCB): Assessing coercive control in abusive relationships. *Violence Against Women, 18*(8), 913–933.

Letourneau, N.L., Fedick, C.B., & Willms, J.D. (2007). Mothering and domestic violence: A longitudinal analysis. *Journal of Family Violence, 22*(8), 649–659.

Levendosky, A.A., Leahy, K.L., Bogat, G.A., Davidson, W.S., & von Eye, A. (2006). Domestic violence, maternal parenting, maternal mental health, and infant externalizing behaviour. *Journal of Family Psychology, 20*(4), 544–552.

Lewis, R. (2009). Recruiting parents and children into a research project: A qualitative exploration of families' decision-making processes. *International Journal of Social Research Methodology, 12*(5), 405–419.

Lombard, N. (2015). *Young People's Understandings of Men's Violence Against Women.* London: Routledge.

REFERENCES

Lombard, N. (2016). "Because they're a couple she should do what he says": Young people's justifications of violence: Heterosexuality, gender and adulthood. *Journal of Gender Studies, 25*(3), 241–253.

Loveland, J.E., & Raghavan, C. (2017). Coercive control, physical violence, and masculinity. *Violence and Gender, 4*(1), 5–10.

Lux, G., & Gill, S. (2021). Identifying coercive control in Canadian family law: A required analysis in determining the best interests of the child. *Family Court Review, 59*(4), 810–827.

Macdonald, G.S. (2016). Domestic violence and private family court proceedings: Promoting child welfare or promoting contact? *Violence Against Women, 22*(7), 832–852.

Macdonald, G.S. (2017). Hearing children's voices?: Including children's perspectives on their experiences of domestic violence in welfare reports prepared for the English courts in private family law proceedings. *Child Abuse & Neglect, 65*, 1–13.

Mackay, K. (2018). Child contact as a weapon of control. In N. Lombard (Ed.), *The Routledge Handbook of Gender and Violence* (pp. 145–157). London: Routledge.

Maher, J., Fitz-Gibbon, K., Meyer, S., Roberts, S., & Pfitzner, N. (2021). Mothering through and in violence: Discourses of the "good mother." *Sociology, 55*(4), 659–676.

Mandel, D., Mitchell, A., & Stearns Mandel, R. (2021). *How Domestic Violence Perpetrators Manipulate Systems: Why Systems & Professionals Are So Vulnerable & 5 Steps to Perpetrator-Proof Your System*. Canton, CT: Safe & Together Institute.

Marshall, S.K., & Lambert, J.D. (2006). Parental mattering: A qualitative inquiry into the tendency to evaluate the self as significant to one's children. *Journal of Family Issues, 27*(11), 1561–1582.

Mason, J., & Hood, S. (2011). Exploring issues of children as actors in social research. *Children and Youth Services Review, 33*(4), 490–495.

Matheson, F.I., Daoud, N., Hamilton-Wright, S., Borenstein, H., Pedersen, C., & O'Campo, P. (2015). Where did she go?: The transformation of self-esteem, self-identity, and mental well-being among women who have experienced intimate partner violence. *Women's Health Issues, 25*(5), 561–569.

Matolcsi, A. (2020). Unwanted sex with third parties in domestic abuse relationships and its impact on help-seeking and justice. *Journal of Gender-Based Violence, 4*(1), 107–121.

Maynard, M. (1994). Methods, practices and epistemology: The debates about feminism and research. In M. Maynard & J. Purvis (Eds.), *Researching Women's Lives from a Feminist Perspective* (pp. 10–26). London: Taylor & Francis.

Mburia-Mwalili, A., Clements-Nolle, K., Lee, W., Shadley, M., & Yang, W. (2010). Intimate partner violence and depression in a population-based sample of women: Can social support help? *Journal of Interpersonal Violence, 25*(12), 2258–2278.

McCarry, M., Radford, L., & Baker, V. (2021). What helps? Mothers' and children's experiences of community-based early intervention programmes for domestic violence. *Child Abuse Review, 30*(2), 114–129.

McDonald, S.E., Collins, E.A., Maternick, A., Nicotera, N., Graham-Bermann, S., Ascione, F.R., & Williams, J.H. (2019). Intimate partner violence survivors' reports of their children's exposure to companion animal maltreatment: A qualitative study. *Journal of Interpersonal Violence, 34*(13), 2627–2652.

McDonald-Harker, C. (2016). *Mothering in Marginalized Contexts: Narratives of Women Who Mother in and Through Domestic Violence*. Toronto, ON: Demeter.

McFarlane, J., Fredland, N.M., Symes, L., Zhou, W., Jouriles, E.N., Dutton, M.A., & Greeley, C.S. (2017). The intergenerational impact of intimate partner violence against mothers on child functioning over four years. *Journal of Family Violence, 32*(7), 645–655.

McGee, C. (2000). *Childhood Experiences of Domestic Violence*. London: Jessica Kingsley.

McLeod, D. (2018). *Coercive Control: Impacts on Children and Young People in the Family Environment*. Totnes: Research in Practice.

McManus, E., Belton, E., Barnard, M., Cotmore, R., & Taylor, J. (2013). Recovering from domestic abuse, strengthening the mother–child relationship: Mothers' and children's perspectives of a new intervention. *Child Care in Practice, 19*(3), 291–310.

Meier, J.S. (2009). A historical perspective on parental alienation syndrome and parental alienation. *Journal of Child Custody, 6*(3–4), 232–257.

Meier, J.S. (2017). Dangerous liaisons: A domestic violence typology in custody litigation. *Rutgers University Law Review, 70*(1), 115–174.

Meier, J.S. (2020). US child custody outcomes in cases involving parental alienation and abuse allegations: What do the data show? *Journal of Social Welfare and Family Law, 42*(1), 92–105.

Meier, J.S., Dickson, S., O'Sullivan, C., Rosen, L., & Hayes, J. (2019). Child custody outcomes in cases involving parental alienation and abuse allegations. GWU Law School Public Law Research Paper (2019–56).

Mercer, J. (2019). Examining parental alienation treatments: Problems of principles and practices. *Child and Adolescent Social Work Journal, 36*(4), 351–363.

Mercer, J., & Drew, M. (Eds.). (2021). *Challenging Parental Alienation: New Directions for Professionals and Parents*. Abingdon: Routledge.

Meyer, S. (2011). "Acting in the children's best interest?": Examining victims' responses to intimate partner violence. *Journal of Child and Family Studies, 20*(4), 436–443.

Miller, E., Decker, M.R., McCauley, H.L., Tancredi, D.J., Levenson, R.R., Waldman, J., Schoenwald, P., & Silverman, J.G. (2010). Pregnancy coercion, intimate partner violence and unintended pregnancy. *Contraception, 81*(4), 316–322.

Miller, L.E., Howell, K.H., & Graham-Bermann, S.A. (2014). Developmental changes in threat and self-blame for preschoolers exposed to intimate partner violence (IPV). *Journal of Interpersonal Violence, 29*(9), 1535–1553.

Miller, T., Birch, M., Mauthner, M., & Jessop, J. (Eds.). (2012). *Ethics in Qualitative Research* (2nd ed.). London: Sage.

Mohaupt, H., Duckert, F., & Askeland, I.R. (2020). How do men in treatment for intimate partner violence experience parenting their young child? A descriptive phenomenological analysis. *Journal of Family Violence, 35*(8), 863–875.

Monckton Smith, J. (2012). *Murder, Gender and the Media: Narratives of Dangerous Love*. Basingstoke: Palgrave Macmillan.

Monckton Smith, J. (2020a). *In Control: Dangerous Relationships and How They End in Murder*. London: Bloomsbury.

Monckton Smith, J. (2020b). Intimate partner femicide: Using Foucauldian analysis to track an eight stage progression to homicide. *Violence Against Women, 26*(11), 1267–1285.

Monk, L. (2017). *Improving Professionals' Responses to Mothers Who Become, or Are at Risk of Becoming, Separated from Their Children, in Contexts of Violence and Abuse* (Unpublished PhD thesis). Coventry University, Coventry.

Monk, L., & Bowen, E. (2021). Coercive control of women as mothers via strategic mother–child separation. *Journal of Gender-Based Violence, 5*(1), 23–42.

Morris, A. (2008). *Optimising the "Spaces In-Between": The Maternal Alienation Project and the Politics of Gender in Macro and Micro Contexts* (Unpublished PhD thesis). University of Adelaide, Adelaide.

Morris, A. (2009). Gendered dynamics of abuse and violence in families: Considering the abusive household gender regime. *Child Abuse Review, 18*(6), 414–427.

Morris, A., Hegarty, K., & Humphreys, C. (2012). Ethical and safe: Research with children about domestic violence. *Research Ethics, 8*(2), 125–139.

Morris, A., Humphreys, C., & Hegarty, K. (2015). Children's views of safety and adversity when living with domestic violence. In N. Stanley & C. Humphreys (Eds.), *Domestic Violence and Protecting Children: New Thinking and Approaches* (pp. 18–33). London: Jessica Kingsley.

Morrow, V. (2003). Perspectives on children's agency within families: A view from the sociology of childhood. In L. Kuczynski (Ed.), *Handbook of Dynamics in Parent-Child Relations* (pp. 109–129). London: Sage.

Moulding, N.T., Buchanan, F., & Wendt, S. (2015). Untangling self-blame and mother-blame in women's and children's perspectives on maternal protectiveness in domestic violence: Implications for practice. *Child Abuse Review, 24*(4), 249–260.

Moulding, N., Franzway, S., Wendt, S., Zufferey, C., & Chung, D. (2021). Rethinking women's mental health after intimate partner violence. *Violence Against Women, 27*(8), 1064–1090.

Mullender, A., Hague, G., Imam, U., Kelly, L., Malos, E., & Regan, L. (2002). *Children's Perspectives on Domestic Violence*. London: Sage.

Münger, A.-C., & Markström, A.-M. (2018). Recognition and identification of children in preschool and school who are exposed to domestic violence. *Education Inquiry, 9*(3), 299–315.

Myhill, A. (2015). Measuring coercive control: What can we learn from national population surveys? *Violence Against Women, 21*(3), 355–375.

Namy, S., Carlson, C., O'Hara, K., Nakuti, J., Bukuluki, P., Lwanyaaga, J., Namakula, S., Nanyunja, B., Wainberg, M.L., Naker, D., & Michau, L. (2017). Towards a feminist understanding of intersecting violence against women and children in the family. *Social Science & Medicine, 184*, 40–48.

Naughton, C.M., O'Donnell, A.T., Greenwood, R.M., & Muldoon, O.T. (2015). "Ordinary decent domestic violence": A discursive analysis of family law judges' interviews. *Discourse & Society, 26*(3), 349–365.

Naughton, C.M., O'Donnell, A.T., & Muldoon, O.T. (2019). Young people's constructions of their experiences of parental domestic violence: A discursive analysis. *Journal of Family Violence, 34*(4), 345–355.

Nevala, S. (2017). Coercive control and its impact on intimate partner violence through the lens of an EU-wide survey on violence against women. *Journal of Interpersonal Violence, 32*(12), 1792–1820.

Niemi, L., & Young, L. (2016). When and why we see victims as responsible: The impact of ideology on attitudes toward victims. *Personality and Social Psychology Bulletin, 42*(9), 1227–1242.

Nikupeteri, A., Katz, E., & Laitinen, M. (2021). Coercive control and technology-facilitated parental stalking in children and young people's lives. *Journal of Gender-Based Violence, 5*(3), 395–412.

Nikupeteri, A., & Laitinen, M. (2015). Children's everyday lives shadowed by stalking: Postseparation stalking narratives of Finnish children and women. *Violence and Victims, 30*(5), 830–845.

Nolas, S.-M., Neville, L., & Sanders-McDonagh, E. (2012). *Evaluation of the Community Group Programme for Children & Young People: Final Report.* London: Middlesex University/University of Sussex/AVA Community Groups Project.

Nolsoe, E. (2021). One in three women in relationships are financially dependent on their partner. YouGov. Available from: www.yougov.com.

O'Dell, L. (2008). Representations of the "damaged" child: "Child saving" in a British children's charity ad campaign. *Children & Society, 22*(5), 383–392.

Oliphant, A.E., & Kuczynski, L. (2011). Mothers' and fathers' perceptions of mutuality in middle childhood: The domain of intimacy. *Journal of Family Issues, 32*(8), 1104–1124.

Osofsky, J.D. (2003). Prevalence of children's exposure to domestic violence and child maltreatment: Implications for prevention and intervention. *Clinical Child and Family Psychology Review, 6*(3), 161–170.

Øverlien, C. (2010). Children exposed to domestic violence: Conclusions from the literature and challenges ahead. *Journal of Social Work, 10*(1), 80–97.

Øverlien, C. (2013). The children of patriarchal terrorism. *Journal of Family Violence, 28*(3), 277–287.

Øverlien, C., & Hydén, M. (2009). Children's actions when experiencing domestic violence. *Childhood, 16*(4), 479–496.

Peled, E. (1993). *The Experience of Living with Violence for Preadolescent Witnesses of Woman Abuse* (Unpublished PhD thesis). University of Minnesota, Minneapolis.

Pence, E., & Paymar, M. (1986). *Power and Control: Tactics of Men Who Batter.* Duluth: Minnesota Program Development.

Pence, E., & Paymar, M. (1993). *Education Groups for Men Who Batter: The Duluth Model.* New York, NY: Springer.

Pitman, T. (2017). Living with coercive control: Trapped within a complex web of double standards, double binds and boundary violations. *British Journal of Social Work, 47*(1), 143–161.

Pomerantz, J.B., Cohen, S.J., Doychak, K., & Raghavan, C. (2021). Linguistic indicators of coercive control: Evidenced in sex trafficking narratives. *Violence and Gender.* Advanced online publication.

Radford, L. (2013). Domestic violence, safety and child contact in England: Hiding violent men in the shadows of parenting. In N. Lombard & L. McMillan (Ed.), *Violence Against Women: Current Theory and Practice in Domestic Abuse, Sexual Violence and Exploitation* (pp. 53–69). London: Jessica Kingsley.

REFERENCES

Radford, L., Aitken, R., Miller, P., Ellis, J., Roberts, J., & Firkic, A. (2011a). *Meeting the Needs of Children Living with Domestic Violence in London*. London: Refuge/NSPCC.

Radford, L., Corral, S., Bradley, C., Fisher, H., Bassett, C., Howat, N., & Collishaw, S. (2011b). *Child Abuse and Neglect in the UK Today*. London: NSPCC.

Radford, L., & Hester, M. (2006). *Mothering Through Domestic Violence*. London: Jessica Kingsley.

Radford, L., Lombard, N., Meinck, F., Katz, E., & Mahati, S.T. (2017). Researching violence with children: Experiences and lessons from the UK and South Africa. *Families, Relationships and Societies, 6*(2), 239–256.

Raghavan, C., Beck, C.J., Menke, J.M., & Loveland, J.E. (2019). Coercive controlling behaviors in intimate partner violence in male same-sex relationships: A mixed-methods study. *Journal of Gay & Lesbian Social Services, 31*(3), 370–395.

Randell, M. (2010). Sexual assault law, credibility, and "ideal victims": Consent, resistance, and victim blaming. *Canadian Journal of Women and the Law/Revue Femmes et Droit, 22*(2), 397–433.

Rathus, Z. (2020). A history of the use of the concept of parental alienation in the Australian family law system: Contradictions, collisions and their consequences. *Journal of Social Welfare and Family Law, 42*(1), 5–17.

Rhodes, K.V., Cerulli, C., Dichter, M.E., Kothari, C.L., & Barg, F.K. (2010). "I didn't want to put them through that": The influence of children on victim decision-making in intimate partner violence cases. *Journal of Family Violence, 25*(5), 485–493.

Richards, C.M. (2019). Looking back in anger: The impact of domestic violence and abuse on the mother and child relationship. In A. Salamon & A. Chng (Eds.), *Multiple Early Childhood Identities* (pp. 172–184). London: Routledge.

Ritchie, J., & Spencer, L. (2002). Qualitative data analysis for applied policy research. In M.A. Huberman & M.B. Miles (Eds.), *The Qualitative Researcher's Companion* (pp. 305–329). London: Sage.

Rivera, E.A., Sullivan, C.M., Zeoli, A.M., & Bybee, D. (2018). A longitudinal examination of mothers' depression and PTSD symptoms as impacted by partner-abusive men's harm to their children. *Journal of Interpersonal Violence, 33*(18), 2779–2801.

Rivera, E.A., Zeoli, A.M., & Sullivan, C.M. (2012). Abused mothers' safety concerns and court mediators' custody recommendations. *Journal of Family Violence, 27*(4), 321–332.

Rosser-Limiñana, A., Suriá-Martínez, R., & Mateo Pérez, M.Á. (2020). Children exposed to intimate partner violence: Association among battered mothers' parenting competences and children's behavior. *International Journal of Environmental Research and Public Health, 17*(4), article number 1134.

SafeLives. (2019). *Psychological Violence*. London: SafeLives.

Salisbury, E.J., Henning, K., & Holdford, R. (2009). Fathering by partner-abusive men: Attitudes on children's exposure to interparental conflict and risk factors for child abuse. *Child Maltreatment, 14*(3), 232–242.

Saltmarsh, S., Tualaulelei, E., & Ayre, K. (2021). "I'm trying to tell you this man is dangerous . . . and no one's listening": Family violence, parent–school engagement and school complicity. *Australian Educational Researcher, 48*(4), 771–794.

Samuelson, K.W., Krueger, C.E., & Wilson, C. (2012). Relationships between maternal emotion regulation, parenting, and children's executive functioning in families exposed to intimate partner violence. *Journal of Interpersonal Violence, 27*(17), 3532–3550.

Sanders, C.K. (2015). Economic abuse in the lives of women abused by an intimate partner: A qualitative study. *Violence Against Women, 21*(1), 3–29.

Saunders, D.G., & Oglesby, K.H. (2016). No way to turn: Traps encountered by many battered women with negative child custody experiences. *Journal of Child Custody, 13*(2–3), 154–177.

Sharp, C., Jones, J., Netto, G., & Humphreys, C. (2011). *We Thought They Didn't See: Cedar in Scotland: Children and Mothers Experiencing Domestic Abuse Recovery Evaluation Report.* Edinburgh: Research for Real.

Sharp, N. (2008). *"What's Yours Is Mine": The Different Forms of Economic Abuse and Its Impact on Women and Children Experiencing Domestic Violence.* London: Refuge.

Sharp, S. (2014). Resisting religious coercive control. *Violence Against Women, 20*(12), 1407–1427.

Sharp-Jeffs, N., Kelly, L., & Klein, R. (2018). Long journeys toward freedom: The relationship between coercive control and space for action—Measurement and emerging evidence. *Violence Against Women, 24*(2), 163–185.

Sheehy, E., & Boyd, S.B. (2020). Penalizing women's fear: Intimate partner violence and parental alienation in Canadian child custody cases. *Journal of Social Welfare and Family Law, 42*(1), 80–91.

Sijtsema, J.J., Stolz, E.A., & Bogaerts, S. (2020). Unique risk factors of the co-occurrence between child maltreatment and intimate partner violence perpetration. *European Psychologist.* Advanced online publication.

Silberg, J., & Dallam, S. (2019). Abusers gaining custody in family courts: A case series of over turned decisions. *Journal of Child Custody, 16*(2), 140–169.

Silberg, J., Dallam, S., & Samson, E. (2013). *Crisis in Family Court: Lessons From Turned Around Cases. Final Report submitted to the Office of Violence Against Women, Department of Justice.* Washington, DC: U.S. Department of Justice.

Sinko, L., James, R., & Hughesdon, K. (2021). Healing after gender-based violence: A qualitative metasynthesis using meta-ethnography. *Trauma, Violence, & Abuse.* Advanced online publication.

Skamballis, A., Mullender, A., Humphreys, C., & Thiara, R.K. (2006a). *Talking About Domestic Abuse: A Photo Activity Workbook to Develop Communication Between Mothers and Young People.* London: Jessica Kingsley.

Skamballis, A., Mullender, A., Humphreys, C., & Thiara, R.K. (2006b). *Talking to My Mum: A Picture Workbook for Workers, Mothers and Children Affected by Domestic Abuse.* London: Jessica Kingsley.

Skinner, T., Hester, M., & Malos, E. (Eds.). (2005). *Researching Gender Violence: Feminist Methodology in Action.* Cullompton: Willan.

Smart, C., Neale, B., & Wade, A. (2001). *The Changing Experience of Childhood: Families and Divorce.* Cambridge: Polity.

Smith, E. (2016). *Domestic Abuse, Recovering Together (DART): Evaluation Report.* London: NSPCC.

Smith, E., Belton, E., Barnard, M., Fisher, H.L., & Taylor, J. (2015). Strengthening the mother–child relationship following domestic abuse: Service evaluation. *Child Abuse Review, 24*(4), 261–273.

Smith, E., Belton, E., & Cooke, S. (2020). *Impact Evaluation of the Scale-Up of Domestic Abuse, Recovering Together*. London: NSPCC.

Smith, J., & Humphreys, C. (2019). Child protection and fathering where there is domestic violence: Contradictions and consequences. *Child & Family Social Work, 24*(1), 156–163.

Solace/Women's Aid. (2021). *Supporting Older Survivors*. London: Solace/Women's Aid.

Staf, A.G., & Almqvist, K. (2015). How children with experiences of intimate partner violence towards the mother understand and relate to their father. *Clinical Child Psychology and Psychiatry, 20*(1), 148–163.

Stanley, N. (2011). *Children Experiencing Domestic Violence: A Research Review*. Dartington: Research in Practice.

Stanley, N., & Humphreys, C. (2017). Identifying the key components of a 'whole family' intervention for families experiencing domestic violence and abuse. *Journal of Gender-Based Violence, 1*(1), 99–115.

Stanley, N., Miller, P., & Richardson Foster, H. (2012). Engaging with children's and parents' perspectives on domestic violence. *Child & Family Social Work, 17*(2), 192–201.

Stansfield, R., & Williams, K.R. (2021). Coercive control between intimate partners: An application to nonfatal strangulation. *Journal of Interpersonal Violence, 36*(9–10), NP5105–NP5124.

Stanziani, M., & Cox, J. (2021). The failure of all mothers or the mother of all failures? Juror perceptions of failure to protect laws. *Journal of Interpersonal Violence, 36*(1–2), NP690–NP711.

Stark, E. (2007). *Coercive Control: The Entrapment of Women in Personal Life*. Oxford: Oxford University Press.

Stark, E. (2009). Rethinking custody evaluation in cases involving domestic violence. *Journal of Child Custody, 6*(3–4), 287–321.

Stark, E. (2012). Looking beyond domestic violence: Policing coercive control. *Journal of Police Crisis Negotiations, 12*(2), 199–217.

Stark, E. (2018). Coercive control as a framework for responding to male partner abuse in the UK: Opportunities and challenges. In N. Lombard (Ed.), *The Routledge Handbook of Gender and Violence* (pp. 15–27). London: Routledge.

Stark, E., & Flitcraft, A. (1995). Killing the beast within: Woman battering and female suicidality. *International Journal of Health Services, 25*(1), 43–64.

Stark, E., & Hester, M. (2019). Coercive control: Update and review. *Violence Against Women, 25*(1), 81–104.

Stewart, L.-L., & Scott, K. (2014). Who are these guys? An exploration of patterns of parenting problems among fathers who have maltreated their children. *Canadian Journal of Community Mental Health, 33*(2), 67–83.

Sturge-Apple, M.L., Davies, P.T., Cicchetti, D., & Manning, L.G. (2010). Mother's parenting practices as explanatory mechanisms in associations between interparental violence and child adjustment. *Partner Abuse, 1*(1), 45–60.

Swanston, J., Bowyer, L., & Vetere, A. (2014). Towards a richer understanding of school-age children's experiences of domestic violence: The voices of children and their mothers. *Clinical Child Psychology and Psychiatry, 19*(2), 184–201.

Tarzia, L. (2021). "It went to the very heart of who I was as a woman": The invisible impacts of intimate partner sexual violence. *Qualitative Health Research, 31*(2), 287–297.

Tarzia, L., Wellington, M., Marino, J., & Hegarty, K. (2019). "A huge, hidden problem": Australian health practitioners' views and understandings of reproductive coercion. *Qualitative Health Research, 29*(10), 1395–1407.

Taylor, A. (2012). *Single Women in Popular Culture: The Limits of Postfeminism.* Basingstoke: Palgrave Macmillan.

Tew, J., Ramon, S., Slade, M., Bird, V., Melton, J., & Le Boutillier, C. (2012). Social factors and recovery from mental health difficulties: A review of the evidence. *British Journal of Social Work, 42*(3), 443–460.

Thiara, R.K., & Gill, A.K. (2012). *Domestic Violence, Child Contact and Post-Separation Violence Issues for South Asian and African-Caribbean Women and Children: A Report of Findings.* NSPCC: London.

Thiara, R.K., & Hague, G. (2014). Double jeopardy: Disabled women's experiences of domestic violence. In N. Aghtaie & G. Gangoli (Eds.), *Understanding Gender Based Violence: National and International Contexts* (pp. 130–146). Abingdon: Routledge.

Thiara, R.K., & Humphreys, C. (2017). Absent presence: The ongoing impact of men's violence on the mother–child relationship. *Child & Family Social Work, 22*(1), 137–145.

Thiara, R.K., & Roy, S. (2020). *Reclaiming Voice: Minoritised Women and Sexual Violence—Key Findings.* London: Imkaan.

Thomas, K.A., Joshi, M., & Sorenson, S.B. (2014). "Do you know what it feels like to drown?": Strangulation as coercive control in intimate relationships. *Psychology of Women Quarterly, 38*(1), 124–137.

Thompson-Walsh, C., Scott, K.L., Lishak, V., & Dyson, A. (2021). How domestically violent fathers impact children's social-emotional development: Fathers' psychological functioning, parenting, and coparenting. *Child Abuse & Neglect.* Advanced online publication.

Towns, A.J., & Adams, P.J. (2016). "I didn't know whether I was right or wrong or just bewildered": Ambiguity, responsibility, and silencing women's talk of men's domestic violence. *Violence Against Women, 22*(4), 496–520.

Trocmé, N., & Bala, N. (2005). False allegations of abuse and neglect when parents separate. *Child Abuse & Neglect, 29*(12), 1333–1345.

Valls, R., Puigvert, L., & Duque, E. (2008). Gender violence among teenagers: Socialization and prevention. *Violence Against Women, 14*(7), 759–785.

Van den Bulck, J., Custers, K., & Nelissen, S. (2016). The child-effect in the new media environment: Challenges and opportunities for communication research. *Journal of Children and Media, 10*(1), 30–38.

Varcoe, C., & Irwin, L.G. (2004). "If I killed you, I'd get the kids": Women's survival and protection work with child custody and access in the context of woman abuse. *Qualitative Sociology, 27*(1), 77–99.

Vergara, M., Comas, E., Gautam, I., & Koirala, U. (2015). Supporting the relationship between mother and child within the context of domestic violence: A pilot parenting programme in Surkhet, Midwestern Nepal. *Intervention, 13*(2), 110–120.

Walton, K., Kuczynski, L., Haycraft, E., Breen, A., & Haines, J. (2017). Time to re-think picky eating? A relational approach to understanding picky eating. *International Journal of Behavioral Nutrition and Physical Activity, 14*(1), article number 62.

Wate, R. (2018). *Safer Lincolnshire Partnership Domestic Homicide Review: The Homicides of Claire and Charlotte Hart July 19th 2016.* Lincoln: Safer Lincolnshire Partnership, Lincolnshire County Council.

Watson, L.B., & Ancis, J.R. (2013). Power and control in the legal system: From marriage/relationship to divorce and custody. *Violence Against Women, 19*(2), 166–186.

Webb, N., Moloney, L.J., Smyth, B.M., & Murphy, R.L. (2021). Allegations of child sexual abuse: An empirical analysis of published judgements from the Family Court of Australia 2012–2019. *Australian Journal of Social Issues, 56*(3), 322–343.

Wendt, S. (2008). Christianity and domestic violence: Feminist poststructuralist perspectives. *Affilia, 23*(2), 144–155.

Wendt, S., Buchanan, F., & Moulding, N. (2015). Mothering and domestic violence: Situating maternal protectiveness in gender. *Affilia, 30*(4), 533–545.

Westmarland, N., & Kelly, L. (2013). Why extending measurements of "success" in domestic violence perpetrator programmes matters for social work. *British Journal of Social Work, 43*(6), 1092–1110.

Wiles, R., Crow, G., Heath, S., & Charles, V. (2008). The management of confidentiality and anonymity in social research. *International Journal of Social Research Methodology, 11*(5), 417–428.

Williams, F. (2004). *Rethinking Families.* London: Calouste Gulbenkian Foundation.

Williamson, E. (2010). Living in the world of the domestic violence perpetrator: Negotiating the unreality of coercive control. *Violence Against Women, 16*(12), 1412–1423.

Williamson, E. (2014). Heterosexual men as victims of domestic violence and abuse: Prevalence, help-seeking, and challenges to feminist theoretical frameworks. In N. Aghtaie & G. Gangoli (Eds.), *Understanding Gender Based Violence: National and International Contexts* (pp. 147–161). Abingdon: Routledge.

Women's Aid (2016). *Nineteen Child Homicides: What Must Change So Children Are Put First in Child Contact Arrangements and the Family Courts.* Bristol: Women's Aid.

Women's Aid, Hester, M., Walker, S.-J., & Williamson, E. (2021). *Gendered Experiences of Justice and Domestic Abuse: Evidence for Policy and Practice.* Bristol: Women's Aid.

Woodlock, D. (2017). The abuse of technology in domestic violence and stalking. *Violence Against Women, 23*(5), 584–602.

Woodlock, D., McKenzie, M., Western, D., & Harris, B. (2020). Technology as a weapon in domestic violence: Responding to digital coercive control. *Australian Social Work, 73*(3), 368–380.

Wuest, J., Ford-Gilboe, M., Merritt-Gray, M., & Berman, H. (2003). Intrusion: The central problem for family health promotion among children and single mothers after leaving an abusive partner. *Qualitative Health Research, 13*(5), 597–622.

Wuest, J., Merritt-Gray, M., & Ford-Gilboe, M. (2004). Regenerating family: Strengthening the emotional health of mothers and children in the context of intimate partner violence. *Advances in Nursing Science, 27*(4), 257–274.

Yule, K., Houston, J., & Grych, J. (2019). Resilience in children exposed to violence: A meta-analysis of protective factors across ecological contexts. *Clinical Child and Family Psychology Review, 22*(3), 406–431.

Zaccour, S. (2020). Does domestic violence disappear from parental alienation cases? Five lessons from Quebec for judges, scholars, and policymakers. *Canadian Journal of Family Law, 33*(2), 301–358.

INDEX

For the benefit of digital users, indexed terms that span two pages (e.g., 52–53) may, on occasion, appear on only one of those pages.

Tables and figures and boxes are indicated by *t* and *f* following the page number

abuse. *See also* child abuse and neglect; domestic violence; economic abuse; sexual abuse; violence
 cycles of, 344
 emotional (*see* emotional abuse)
 faith-based, 6
 mothers' attempts to conceal from children, 166, 171–72
 perpetration by child victims/survivors, 247
 perpetrators' justifications of, 20–21
 physical (*see* physical abuse)
 post-separation (*see* post-separation abuse)
 psychological (*see* psychological abuse)
 spiritual, 6
 verbal (*see* verbal abuse)
academic discourse, mutualizing language in, 35–37
adversity, and mother–child relationship, 314–15
affection, mother–child, post-separation increase in, 215, 233–34
age, of perpetrator, 37–38
age-limits
 for children included in research on coercive control, 58–59
 of recovery programs, 338–39

agency
 bilateral, in recovery, 214–15
 children's, 40–4, 214–15 (*see also* relational agency, children's)
 in experiences of coercive control, 45–46
 in parent–child relationships, 49–54
 recognition of, 46–49
 definition of, 40
 equal, in bilateral model of parent–child relationships, 51–52
 expression of, power and resources for, 52
 as inherent human quality, 52
aggressive behavior, in child victim/survivor, 86
 mothers' help in overcoming, 225–27, 283
anger
 in child victim/survivor, mothers' help in overcoming, 225–27
 in mother–child relationship, 154
anxiety, in mothers, 142–43
arguments, in context of coercive control, 20
attacks
 post-separation, 189, 190–91, 316
 used in coercive control, 23–24
attention, mother's, perpetrator's demands for, 85–86, 100–1, 140

INDEX

behavior(s), of perpetrator/
    father, 3, 15–22. *See also*
        tactics (of coercive control)
    cataloging of, in reports, 107
    childlike, 164–65
    courts' views of, 21–22
    "cultural authorization" of, 28
    disguised as socially normal, 26–27
    media portrayals of, 21–22
    perpetrators' warped versions of, 20–21
    "positive"-seeming, 15–17
    toward children, 32
        "Jekyll and Hyde," 133–35
        and mother–child relationship, 126,
            130–36, 132*t*, 161–62 (*see also*
            Five Factor Framework)
        unpredictability of, 133–35
behavioral problems, in child victims/
        survivors of coercive control, 86,
        192–200, 283–87
    mothers' help in overcoming, 225–27
    research needs, 325
"being there"
    and high-stakes support from pattern
        2 children, 271–73
    in pattern 3 families, 286–87
    as valued mother–child support,
        216, 240–42
belief-systems, traditional,
        perpetrator's, 84, 85
blame. *See also* self-blame; victim-blaming
    in victims/survivors, 146
boundaries, mothers' thoughts and
        feelings about, 312–14

"campaigns of coercive control," 9, 79
    victims of, 105–7
CEDAR (Children Experiencing Domestic
        Abuse Recovery), 201
child abuse and neglect. *See also*
        child sexual abuse
    coercive control and, 78–79, 98–111
        as intertwined, 105–7
    and domestic violence, conceptual
        approach to, 98–99, 121–22
    false accusations of, 119

mothers' reports to family court about,
        court's disbelief of, 116–19
    as part of coercive control, 78–79
    by women, in context of perpetrator's/
        father's coercive control, 113–14
child-centered approaches, for interacting
        with child victims/survivors,
        recommendations for, 343
child-centered research, 57, 58, 62
    power hierarchy and, 58, 62, 63
child-to-parent influence, positive, 245,
        256–57, 259–60
child-to-parent violence, 141
children. *See also* children in research for
        this volume
    agency of, 40–4, 214–15
        in engaging with mother's
            support, 226–27
        in experiences of coercive
            control, 45–46
        individual, 214–15
        in parent–child relationships, 49–54
        recognition of, 46–49
        regarding contact with perpetrator/
            father, 222–23, 243–44, 297–98
        relational (*see* relational agency)
    breaking free from perpetrators'/fathers'
        distorted versions of reality,
        204–7, 324, 329–34
    care and support from (*see* support,
        child-to-mother)
    as co-victims/co-survivors, 79, 80–81,
        92, 103–4, 114, 344
    coercive control of, 18, 42–45
        effects of, research needs, 325
    conceptualization as victims as well as
        copers/survivors, 54–55
    confidence-building in, mother's
        support for, 227–30
    constraints on, created by coercive
        control, 87–88
    coping strategies of, 46–49
    in custody of abuser, numbers of, 120
    data collection from, 46–47
    disclosure by, 48–49
    distorted images of, 39–3

education, perpetrator's undermining of, 82–83

emotional and behavioral impacts of coercive control, mothers' help with, 225–27

experience of coercive control, similarity to mothers' experience, 45, 323, 326–27

experience of domestic violence
damage caused by, 46–47
distorted images of, 39–3
outcomes with, 247
prevalence of (numbers of), 11–12

experiences under coercive control, similarity to adults' experiences, 45, 323, 326–27

"exposure" to domestic violence (*see* "exposure" to domestic violence)

false accusations of child abuse made by, 119

family courts and, 116–17

favorite/favored, of perpetrator/father, 148, 177, 294–96

harms to, by perpetrator's coercive control, 78, 79–81, 121–22
deliberate, as part of control of mother, 101–5
direct, 79–92, 99–101, 103–4
family courts' responses to, 121–22
female victims'/survivors' accountability for, 29–33 (*see also* failure to protect)
indirect (as byproduct), 79–81, 100–1
"invisible," 327–28
parallels with harms to adult victims, 104–5

inclusion in coercive control revolution, 40–46

and independent perspectives on perpetrator/father, 223–24

indirect support for mothers' recoveries, 215, 234–37

as informants on mother, 82, 101–2

as means of controlling mother, 82, 101–2

mother's emotional support for, 237

ownership of, perpetrators' belief in, 85, 325

parentification of, 53–54

perpetrator's/father's behavior toward, 32
"Jekyll and Hyde," 133–35
and mother–child relationship, 126, 130–36, 132*t*, 161–62 (*see also* Five Factor Framework)
unpredictability of, 133–35

perpetrators' tactics used on, 8–9, 42–45

as positive focus to mothers' lives, 236–37, 262

positive views of their mothers
factors affecting, 144–46
post-separation support and, 206–7

post-separation contact with perpetrator/father, 192–200, 222–23, 243–44, 284
reducing/ending, 297–98

post-traumatic growth of, 247

practical support for mothers, in post-separation/recovery, 216, 237, 239

as primary targets of perpetrator, 108–9

punishment of
perpetrator's creation of opportunities for, 88–90, 103–4
for resistance to coercive control, 88–90, 104

resources used by, 48–49

strategies for assisting their mothers' recoveries, 214–15

supports for, in dealing with negative parenting, 135–36

understanding of coercive control, mothers helping with, 215, 219–24

understanding of perpetrator's behavior as wrong, 174–75

used as tools of abuse, 101–2, 110–11

variance in mother's relationships with, 148

views of mother and perpetrator/father, and mother–child relationship, 127, 130–33, 132*t*, 135, 138, 139, 144–46 (*see also* Five Factor Framework)

children in research for this volume, 58–59
  ages of, 66
  contact with perpetrators, 67, 192–200,
    222–23, 243–44, 284
  interviewing, 61–64, 68–69
  nonverbal cues from, 63–64
  perpetrator's relationship to, 67
  responses to being interviewed, 63
  sex distribution of, 66
  strengths of, 47
  viewed as passive bystanders/silent
    witnesses, 46–50
Children's Perspectives on Domestic Violence
    (Mullender et al.), 47–48
"co-occurrence" (of domestic violence and
    child abuse), 98–99
co-victims/survivors, 121–22, 344. *See also*
    children
  adult and child/ren as, 114, 344
coercive control
  age of perpetrator and, 37–38
  alternative contexts for, 37–38
  carer as perpetrator of, 37–38
  and child abuse, as intertwined, 105–7
  child as perpetrator of, 37–38
  child as target of, 37–38
  children's understanding of, mothers
    helping with, 215, 219–24
  context and, 12–15
  core characteristics of, 302
  criminalization of, in United
    Kingdom, 40–41
  by cult leaders, 38
  as dictatorship, 1, 18–19, 164–65
  dynamics of, 15–22
  effects on victims/survivors, 2
  escalation of, 136, 155–56
  everyday aspects of, as research focus,
    323, 327–28
  as gendered form of abuse, 24–28
  harms to both adults and
    children, 105–7
  by hostage-takers, 38
  impacts of, 15–22
  as issue of freedom, 345

by kidnappers, 38
mothers' and children's experiences of,
    similarities in, 45, 323, 326–27
multiple perpetrators and, 37–38
as multi-stranded form of abuse, 78–79,
    105–7, 122–24
mutualizing language about, 35–37
nonviolent
  children's experience of, 11–12, 44–45
  prevalence of, 22, 44
numbers of victims experiencing, 11–12
in other than intimate/caring
    contexts, 37–38
by pimps/sex traffickers, 38
post-separation (*see* post-separation
    coercive control)
prevalence of, 11
research on (*see* research on coercive
    control)
and situational couple violence, 9–12
tactics (*see* tactics)
unique situations created by, 105–7
victims' responses to, 10
and violence, 22–24
violent, children's experience of, 43–44
woman/mother as perpetrator of, 37–38
coercive control model, of domestic
    violence, 1–2
coercive control revolution, 323
  children's inclusion in, 40–46
communication. *See* mother–child
    communication
  in mother–child supportiveness
    children's thoughts and feelings
      about, 309–10
    mothers' thoughts and feelings
      about, 311–12
Community Group Programme, 201
community services, and recovery from
    coercive control, 213
competency, in use of coercive
    control, 22–23
compulsive behavior, in child victim/
    survivor, mothers' help in
    overcoming, 225–27

INDEX

conducive contexts, 25
confidence-building, 215, 227–32, 260–61, 341
consent. *See also* informed consent
  ongoing, children's, in research for this
    volume, 62–64
consent forms, 70
"conspiracy of silence," between abused
    mothers and children, 127
constraint, created by coercive control,
    78–79, 87–88
control. *See also* coercive control
  extent and depth of, in coercive control,
    12, 13–14
    combined with credible threat, 14–15
  of family, perpetrators', 18, 79–81
  of time
    space, and movement, 4–5
    children's experience of, 44, 81–82
counseling
  of child victims/survivors, 205–6
  and children's breaking free from
    perpetrator's distorted
    thinking, 330–33
credible threat, presence of, 12–13, 14
  combined with extent and depth of
    control, 14–15
criminal activity, coercion of, 7
criminal justice system, 1–2, 7
  perpetrators and, 187
  perpetrator's response to, 108–9
cult leaders, coercive control by, 38

DART (Domestic Abuse: Recovery
    Together), 201, 338–39
daughters
  perpetrators' control of, 18
  perpetrators' sexual abuse of, 85
death threats, 7, 16–17
  post-separation, 191
denial, perpetrators'/fathers' use of,
    204–7, 212
depression, maternal, 142–43, 151,
    265–66, 269–70
  negative effects of, in pattern 2
    families, 276–77

developmental delay, in children living
    with coercive control, 87–88
digital technology, and monitoring/
    stalking of victims/survivors, 5
discipline, mother's, perpetrator's/
    father's overriding of, 140, 165–
    66, 176–77
domestic violence
  and child abuse, conceptual approach
    to, 98–99, 121–22
  child protective services' views
    of, 114–15
  children's resistance to, 92
  coercive control model of, 1–2
  distorted images of, 39–3
  family recovery from, outcomes in, 247
  male-against-female, mutualizing
    language for, 35–37
  numbers of children exposed to, 11–12
  perpetrator's/father's use of, and
    mother–child relationship, 127,
    132*t*, 136–39 (*see also* Five Factor
    Framework)
  as physical violence, 1–2
  prevalence of, 11
  prevention of, 344
  reconceptualization of, 54–55
  stopping, means stopping
    perpetrators, 344
  typology of, family courts and, 21–22
drug abuse
  by mothers, 151
  perpetrator's/father's, 156–57
"dual exposure" (to domestic violence and
    child abuse), 98–99

economic abuse, 5–6, 16–17, 111–12, 138,
    155–56, 175–76
  children's experience of, 44, 101
  resistance to, 93–94
education, children's, perpetrator's
    undermining of, 82–83
emotional abuse, 3–4, 15–17, 175–76, 302
emotional attentiveness, mother's and
    child's, and recovery, 215, 238–39

emotional manipulation, perpetrators'/
    fathers', 326–27
  children's resistance to, 96–97
emotions, dealing with, post-
    separation, 207–10
entitlement, perpetrators' sense of, 17,
    27–28, 80–81
  and child sexual abuse, 85
  and distortion of family dynamics,
    91–92, 312
entrapment, 16–17, 22, 78–79, 111–12
ethics, feminist, 57
"exposure" to domestic violence,
    children's, 46–49, 98–99
  questioning the concept of, 99–101

failure to protect, 79, 113–14, 328
  mothers' punishments for, 120
false narratives, perpetrators' creation of,
    6–7, 109–10, 111–12
family
  bilateral model of parent–child
    relationships and, 52–53
  children's definitions of, 52–53
  everyday activities that support and
    sustain, 242
  perpetrators' control of, 18
  recovering from domestic violence,
    outcomes in, 247
  role-reversal in, 53–54
family court, 114–22
  judgments, aftermath of, for mothers
    and children, 120
  manipulation of, by perpetrator/
    father, 116–17
  mothers disbelieved in, 335–37
  mothers' struggle to be believed
    by, 116–20
  and parental alienation claims, 335–37
  "pro-contact culture" of, 79, 114–15
    reforms needed in, 121–22, 337–38
  reform of, recommendations for,
    121–22, 334–35
  responses to coercive control, reforms
    needed in, 121–22

as road-block to child safety, 337–38
and split identities of father and
    perpetrator, 34–35
and typology of domestic
    violence, 21–22
family dynamics, distortion
    of, by perpetrator's
    hyper-entitlement, 91–92, 312
family law system
  and post-separation coercive
    control, 198–99
  and recovery possibility, 198–99
family relationships. *See also* mother–
    child relationship; parent–child
    relationships
  "good," descriptions of, by children who
    had and had not experienced
    coercive control, 310, 320–21
father/father figure. *See also* perpetrator/
    father
  abuse of children and young people,
    8–9, 42–45
  children's expectations of, 34
  domestically violent, invisibility of, 29–
    37, 324–26
  emotionally abusive, but not coercively
    controlling, 105–7
  false accusations of child abuse made
    by, 119
  "good enough," 34–35
  held accountable by children, 33–
    34, 48–49
  identity as, split from identity as
    perpetrator, 34–35
  neglectful, but not coercively
    controlling, 105–7, 108
  violent
    but not coercively controlling, 105–7
    policy gap around, 35
father–child relationship, 125
  sabotaged by female coercive
    control, 301
fear, victims'/survivors', 14–15
feelings
  dealing with, post-separation, 207–10

mother's and child's attentiveness/
consideration of, 215, 238–39
female(s), as perpetrators of coercive
control, 24–25, 37–38, 76, 326
femicide, by perpetrators, 108
feminine gender roles, 26
femininity, stereotypes of, 26–27
feminist ethic of care, 57
filicide, by perpetrators, 108
finances, post-separation constraints on,
children's practical responses
to, 239
Five Factor Framework, 126–27, 130–48,
131f, 132t
applied to breaking free from distorted
ways of thinking, 333–34
and interventions, 148
food, deprivation of, 83–84, 101
freedom
coercive control as issue of, 345
curtailed by post-separation abuse, 188
lack of
experienced by mothers and
children, 100
resistance to, 93–94
mothers' thoughts and feelings
about, 312–14
perpetrator's/father's, post-
separation, 192
victims'/survivors', restriction of, 19
Freedom Programme, 329–30
friend-like qualities, in mother–child
relationship, 317–20
friendship, in mother–child
supportiveness, children's
thoughts and feelings
about, 309–10

gaslighting, 3–4, 204–7, 212
gender bias, in family court
outcomes, 117–18
gender roles
as platform for coercive control, 26–27
and victim-blaming, 34
gendered nature of coercive control, 24–28

gifts, from perpetrator/father, child's
destruction of, as form
of resistance to coercive
control, 96–95
grooming of others, 6–7
guilt
maternal, 137, 140, 154–55, 210, 218,
269–70, 278
in victims/survivors, 146

harassment, post-separation, 187–92
head of household belief-system, 84,
85, 104
hoarding, by child victim/
survivor, mother's help in
overcoming, 226–27
homicide
threats of (*see* death threats)
of victim, 7–8, 24
hostage-takers, coercive control by, 38
hostile contexts, 25
housing, post-separation
problems with, 189–90
role in recovery, 203
safety of, 201–4
hyperentitlement, and distortion of family
dynamics, 91–92

imprisonment, in home, perpetrator's use
of, 83–84, 103–4, 189
incest, 85
"incipient intimate terrorism," 136,
149, 155–59
independence-building, for children
mothers' thoughts and feelings
about, 312–14
mutuality and interdependence,
315–17
in pattern 2 families, 273
informed consent, children's, in research
for this volume, 62
institutions, perpetrators' exploitation of,
to discredit victims, 7
interdependence, in mother–child
relationship, 315–17

interventions
  Five Factor Framework and, 148
  for helping children break free
          from perpetrator's distorted
          thinking, 334
  for mother–child relationship sabotaged
          by coercive control, 296–300
  perpetrators' response to, 110, 115
interview(s) [for research reported in this
          volume], 56
  of children, 61–64
  children's responses to, 63
  and confidentiality, 69–70
  ethical considerations, 69–71
  joint/separate, 69–70, 267
  length of, 68–69
  logistics of, 67–69
  nonverbal cues in, 63–64
  perspectives represented in, 76
  questions in
      order of, 71–72
      sequencing of, to minimize
          distress, 72
      similar, to allow comparisons
          of mothers' and childrens'
          experiences, 73
  rapport in, 71
  refocusing of, based on children's
          preferences, 63
  strengths-based approach for, 72–73
  structure and design of, 71–73
  venue for, 67–68
  who was interviewed first in, 68
intimate partner violence, mutualizing
          language used about, 35–37
isolation, 111–12
  children's experience of, 81–82, 100
  overlap with other tactics, 9
  from sources of support, 6, 16–17
  children's experience of, 44

jealousy, perpetrator's, of mother–child
          relationship, 85–86, 100–1, 177
"Jekyll and Hyde" behavior, of
          perpetrators/fathers, 133–35

justification, perpetrators'/fathers' use of,
          204–7, 212

kidnappers, coercive control by, 38
killing(s). *See also* homicide
  by perpetrators, 108

love, girls' and women's beliefs
          about, 26–27

male(s). *See also* perpetrator/father
  as perpetrators of coercive
          control, 24–25
manipulation of others, 6–7
manipulative behavior
  child victim's understanding of, 331
  perpetrators'/fathers', 326–27
    children's resistance to, 96–97
masculinity
  hegemonic, perpetrators' identification
          with, 17, 27–28
  stereotypes of, 26–27
MATCH Mothers, 297
mental health, maternal, 142–43,
          151, 167–69
  children's awareness of, 267–69, 271
  children's post-separation contact with
          perpetrator/father and, 194
  and high-stakes support from pattern 2
          children, 271–73, 281
  in pattern 1 families, 261
  in pattern 2 families, 264, 265–66,
          267–71, 281
  post-separation, 190, 255–56
  and post-separation mother–child
          relationship, 250*t*, 251
  supports for, 281
    recommendations for, 340
micromanagement, of victims/survivors, 4–5
minimization, perpetrators'/fathers' use of,
          204–7, 212
mistakes, mothers' messages to children
          about, 90–91, 226, 243, 261, 341, 343
monitoring, 5
  of children, 42–43

of mother, 138
children used in, 82, 102, 294–96
mood-lifting, childrens' attempts at, and recovery, 215, 224–25
mother(s). *See also* participants in research for this volume
accountability for perpetrators' harms to children, 29–33 (*see also* failure to protect)
attempts to protect children, 163–64
autonomy over parenting, 136, 156
child abuse by, in context of perpetrator's/father's coercive control, 113–14
children's efforts to support (*see* support, child-to-mother)
children's expectations of, 34
children's loss of respect for, 140
children's negative opinions of, 167
children's practical support for, in post-separation/recovery, 216, 237, 239
children's preference for, 144–46
confidence as parents, and recovery, 211–12
confidence-building in, children's support for, 230–32
constructed as "the problem," 30–33, 335–37
emotional connection to children, 151
and mother–child relationship, 127, 132*t*, 139, 142–44, 162–63, 173–74, 178–79 (*see also* Five Factor Framework)
emotionally shut down ("robotic," "on autopilot"), 142, 167–69, 178–79
experience of coercive control, similarity to children's experience, 45, 323, 326–27
false accusations of child abuse made by, 119
family courts and, 116–17, 118–20, 335–37
loss of custody of children, 117–18, 119–20, 336

micro-level strategies for protecting children, 112–13
numbness/disconnection/disassociation experienced by, 142–43, 172–73
perpetrator's/father's disrespect for, 166–67, 193, 195–96
validation of, by children, 230–32
victim-blaming directed at, 33–34, 113–14
mother–child communication
harms to, by domestic violence, 291
in pattern 3 families, 285–87, 290–92
post-separation, 202, 207–10
in recovery, 215, 232–33
workbooks for, 209–10
mother–child interactions
enjoyable, 144, 146
in post-separation period and recovery, 215, 233–34
prevention of, by perpetrator, 85–86
mother–child relationship, 125
addressing feelings and, 207–10
adversity and, 314–15
anger in, 154
bilateral model of, 51*f*, 51–53, 56–57, 218
categories of, 126, 128, 129*t*
children's agency in, 49–54
children's positive evaluation of, in pattern 2 families, 274–78
close/supportive, 126, 146–48, 246
closeness in
benefits of, 146
as resistance to coercive control, 94–96
complexity of, 127–28
destroyed by perpetrator/father, 250*t*, 252–53, 294–96
distant/strained, 126, 146–48, 246
everyday, and opportunities for resistance, 93
five factors affecting, 126–27, 180–82 (*see also* Five Factor Framework)
impacts of, 146–48
as "friends" and "sisters," 317–20
harm to, by coercive control, 126, 246

mother–child relationship (*cont.*)
improvement post-separation, 255
and independence, 315–17
interdependence in, 315–17
joint maintenance by mothers and
children, 146
"mixed" category, 126, 128, 129*t*, 147,
160–70, 255
closeness and supportiveness
in, 161–65
strains and distance in, 165–69
in mother–teen pairs escaping domestic
violence, 279–81
as obstacle to perpetrators'
control, 125–26
only-children and, 154
outcomes for, 246–47
in pattern 3 families, 285–87, 292–93
pattern 3 mothers' feelings
about, 290–92
perpetrator's/father's undermining of,
127, 130, 132*t*, 139–42, 165, 166–
67, 176, 285, 294–96 (*see also*
Five Factor Framework)
protection from, 158
perpetrator's jealousy of, 85–86, 100–1,
177
post-separation (*see* post-separation
mother–child relationship)
post-separation abuse and, 187–92
post-separation evolution of, 322
"really good," children's descriptions of,
as opposite of coercive control,
310, 320–21
and recovery from coercive control,
185–86, 212–13, 214
sabotaged by coercive control, 250*t*,
252–53, 293–302
awareness-raising about, 300
interventions for, 296–300
strains in, 158–59
strengthening, benefits to child victims/
survivors, 338
variance in, among children, 148

"very close" category, 126, 128, 129*t*, 146,
149–60, 255
closeness and supportiveness
in, 149–59
factors affecting, 144–46
severe coercive control and, 149–55
"very distant and strained" category,
126, 128, 129*t*, 147–48, 170–80,
251–52, 282
factors affecting, 144–46
recovery programs needed for, 339
mother–child separation, perpetrator's
strategic use of ("goody" versus
"baddy"), 82–83, 102–3, 139–42,
165–66, 176
mother–child supportiveness
and attentiveness/consideration of each
other's feelings, 215, 238–39
children's practical support for mothers
and, 216, 237, 239
and children's understanding of coercive
control, 215, 219–24
and communication, 215, 232–33
complexity of, 247
contexts of, 248
directed toward recovery from coercive
control, 215, 217–37
framework for ("levels, contexts, and
impacts"), 247–49, 302–5
general, 215–16, 237–44
as heightened by coercive
control, 314–15
impacts of, 248–49
and increased affection, 215, 233–34
lack of, in pattern 4 family, 294–96
levels of, 248
and mood-lifting, 224–27
mothers' thoughts and feelings
about, contrasts with coercive
control, 312–14
mutuality in, 231, 257–59, 302–5, 306–
7, 320–22
children's thoughts and feelings
about, 307–11

INDEX

mothers' thoughts and feelings
about, 311–14
and pattern 3 families, 291–92
ordinary and routine events in, 321
and overcoming emotional and
behavioral impacts of coercive
control, 215, 225–27
pattern 1, 253–54, 255–57
pattern 2, 265–67
pattern 3, 283–87
and positive outcomes, 244–45
and reassurance (about past, present,
and future), 215, 217–19
in rebuilding each other's confidence,
215, 227–32
reciprocity in, children's thoughts
and feelings about, 307–8,
309, 320–22
research on, recommendations for,
323, 328–29
through upsets and tiredness,
215, 237–38
types of, 215–16
as mutually reinforcing, 216
variance in, 216
MPOWER intervention, 45
murder. *See* homicide
mutuality
as heightened by coercive
control, 314–15
in mother–child supportiveness, 231,
257–59, 302–5, 306–7, 320–22
children's thoughts and feelings
about, 307–11
mothers' thoughts and feelings
about, 311–14
and pattern 3 families, 291–92
in parent–child relationships, 51–54,
306–7, 311–14, 320–22
in situational couple violence, 36–37
mutualizing language, 35–37

noncommunication, between abused
mothers and children, 127

Ontario model, 200–1, 213, 338–39
ownership, of girlfriends/wives, social
normalization of, 27–28

parent(s). *See also* father/father figure;
mother(s); victim/survivor parent
custodial, false accusations of child
abuse made by, 119
mothers as, constructed as "the
problem," 30–33, 335–37
noncustodial, false accusations of child
abuse made by, 119
parental alienation/parental alienation
syndrome
claims of, family courts' handling
of, 335–37
mothers accused of, 116–17, 335–37
pattern 4 and, 300–2
processes applied to, 300–2
successful allegations of, by perpetrators/
fathers, 117–18, 335–37
parent–child relationships. *See also*
mother–child relationship
bilateral model of, 51f, 51–53, 218
children's agency in, 49–54
friend- and sister-like relationships
existing within/along
with, 317–20
healthy, as bidirectional, 306–7
mothers' focus on parenting in, 311–
14, 321
contrasts with coercive control, 312–14
mutuality in, 51–54, 306–7, 311–
14, 320–22
sabotage of, in LGBT+ relationship, 301
unilateral model of, 50f, 50–51
parentification, 53–54, 198, 214–15, 280–
81, 321
parenting
of domestically violent fathers, 135
mothers'
positive, post-separation, 260–61
and resilience/recovery of
children, 225–27

parenting (*cont.*)
  mothers' autonomy over, 136, 156
  mothers' confidence in,
      improving, 211–12
  mothers' focus on, 311–14, 321
  negative, by perpetrator/father, 135–36
  permissive, perpetrator's/father's, 140, 165
  perpetrators' style of, 18
  positive, children's distorted beliefs
      about, 141
participants in research for this volume,
      64–65, 65*t*
  ages, 66
  anonymity of, 70
  consent forms for, 70
  data security for, 70
  demographics of, 66–67, 75
  ethnicity of, 66
  experience with refuge services, 66
  information sheets for, 70
  power imbalances with, reducing, 71
  rapport with, 71
  recruitment via support services, 61, 75
  remuneration for, 69
  sex distribution, 66
  time since separating from
      perpetrator, 67
perpetrator/father. *See also* father/
      father figure
  blame-shifting narratives used by, 195–
      98, 204–7, 289, 296–97, 329–33
  characteristics of, 38
  child siding with, 293–302
  children's post-separation contact with,
      192–200, 222–23, 243–44, 284
    reducing/ending, 297–98
  children's preference for, 144–46
  and cycles of abuse, 344
  dangerousness of, 107–11
    and mothers' decision to
      leave, 183–84
  as dictator, 1, 18–19, 164–65
  distorted reality of, 18–19
    children's breaking free from, 18–19,
      204–7, 324, 329–34

identification of, in reports, 107
invisibility of, 29–37, 324–26
manipulation of family court
    systems, 116–17
in new relationships, 344
nonviolent, dangers posed by, 23–24
persistence of, 107–11, 115
as person responsible for harms
  linguistic emphasis on, 323, 325–26
  visibility in foci of studies,
      323, 324–25
post-separation abuse by, 107–11
presenting himself as victim, 197–98
and professionals involved with
    family, 109–10
public persona of, 22–23
relationship with children, 80
resistance to change, 107–11, 115
single-mindedness of, 107–11
skill in escaping detection, 22–23
stopping, to stop domestic violence, 344
unaccountability of, 29–37, 191–92
"victim" persona used by, 289, 296–
      97, 330–33
and violence, 22–24
physical abuse, 7–8
  children's awareness of, and mother–
      child relationship, 137–38, 145
  perpetrators' cessation of, 110–11
  threats of, 7, 16–17
physical ill-health, in mothers, 142–43,
      167–69, 171
  children's practical responses to, 239
pimps/sex traffickers, coercive
    control by, 38
plan, perpetrator's
  to control partner, 80
  to control partner and children, 80–81
police, response to post-separation
    coercive control, 191–92
policy and practice, recommendations for,
      324, 329–43
  recommendation 1: enabling children to
      break free from distorted ways
      of thinking, 324, 329–34

recommendation 2: reforming family courts, 324, 334–35
recommendation 3: greater availability of mother–child recovery programs, 324, 338–40
recommendation 4: practitioners' use of strengths-based and empowering approaches, 324, 340–42
recommendation 5: child-centered approaches for interacting with child victims/survivors, 324, 343
policy discourse, mutualizing language in, 35–37
polyvictimization, 98–99
post-separation abuse, 107–11, 187–92
post-separation coercive control, 107–11, 112–13, 184, 186, 187–92
children's contact with perpetrator/ father and, 192–200, 222–23, 243–44, 289, 296–98
family courts and, 116–17, 335–37
ongoing campaigns of, 198–99
reduction in
benefits of, 199–200
timing of, 199–200, 203–4
post-separation mother–child relationship, 212–13
children's contact with perpetrator/ father and, 192–200, 222–23, 243–44, 296–300
pattern 1: positive supportiveness, positive recoveries, 249–51, 250t, 253–64
factors affecting, 262–64
research on, future directions for, 302–5
pattern 2: high-stakes support, limited recoveries, 250t, 251, 264–81
factors affecting, 279–81
pattern 3: struggling relationships, struggling recoveries, 250t, 251–52, 281–93
factors affecting, 292–93

pattern 4: broken relationships, blocked recoveries, 250t, 252–53, 293–302
interventions for, 296–300
nonsupportiveness in, 294–96
and parental alienation, 300–2
responding to, 296–300
patterns of, 246–47, 249, 250t, 302–5
changes in, 253, 302–5
links to professional support, 249–53
research on, future directions for, 302–5
supports for, 302–5
power
in families and intimate relationships, social and cultural expectations about, 27
victims'/survivors'
approaches based on, practitioners' use of, recommendations for, 340–42
helping victims/survivors to recognize, 341–42
power hierarchy(ies)
with research participants, reducing, 71
and research with child participants, 58, 62, 63
practitioner discourse, mutualizing language in, 35–37
pregnancy, abuse during, perpetrator's/ father's targeting of, 142–43, 172
professionals
control/manipulation by perpetrators, 109–10, 117–18, 335–36
use of Five Factor Framework, 148
prostitution/unwanted sexual activity, coercion of victims/survivors into, 5
psychological abuse, 3–4, 15–16, 84, 111–12, 138
of children, 42–43
PTSD, complex, in mothers, 142–43

qualitative research, with mothers and children, about coercive control, 56–57

rape, 5, 110, 149. *See also* sexual abuse
post-separation, 189, 218–19
reassurance (about past, present, and
future), and recovery, 215,
217–19, 255, 256
reciprocity, in mother–child
supportiveness, 320–22
children's thoughts and feelings about,
307–8, 309
recovery from coercive control. *See also*
mother–child supportiveness;
post-separation mother–child
relationship
beginning of, 200–12
children's, mothers' support of, benefits
to mother from, 215, 234–37
difficulties of, 184
elements needed for, 185, 186, 200–13
mother and child, intertwining of, 212–
13, 242–45
mothers', children indirectly supporting,
215, 234–37
obstacles to, 184–85, 186–200
reassurance (about past, present, and
future) and, 215, 217–19
state's actions and, 198–99
strategies and techniques for
emergence/development of, 242–45
types of, 243
supports for, for mothers and children
together, 327
recovery programs
benefits of, 213
and children's understanding of coercive
control, 219–24, 287–88
funding of, 213
greater availability of, recommendations
for, 338–40
and help dealing with feelings, 207–10
for mothers and children, research
recommendations on,
323, 326–27
Ontario-based, 200–1, 213, 338–39
for pattern 3 families, 292–93
for pattern 4 families, 299–300

relational agency, children's, 40, 49–54, 214–15
research on, recommendations for,
323, 328–29
research. *See also* child-centered research;
research on coercive control;
research recommendations
agency-focused, with children, 47–48
bilateral model of parent–child
relationships in, 52–53
on children and domestic
violence, 41–42
mutualizing language in, 35–37
unilateral model of parent–child
relationships and, 51
research on coercive control [for this
volume], 3. *See also* interview(s)
access to child participants for, 61–62
access to participants for, 61
age-limits for children included in, 58–59
children's informed consent and, 62
cultural situatedness of, 74–75
data analysis, 73–74
ethical considerations in, 57–58
ethical rationale for, 60–61
fieldwork location, 60
focus on most frequent type/context of
coercive control, 76
inclusion criteria for, 58–59
interviewing children in, 61–64
limitations of, 74–76
perpetrator-focused, 32–33
perpetrators' invisibility/
unaccountability in, 29–32
recruitment for, 61–62
safety considerations in, 59
sample used for, 64–65, 65t (*see also*
children in research for this
volume; participants in research
for this volume)
size of, 75
sampling methods, 60
research recommendations, 323, 324–29
recommendation 1: greater visibility of
perpetrators in foci of studies,
323, 324–25

INDEX

recommendation 2: greater visibility of perpetrators in language, 323, 325–26

recommendation 3: highlighting similarities of mothers' and children's experiences, 323, 326–27

recommendation 4: focusing on everyday life, 323, 327–28

recommendation 5: highlighting complexities of children's relational agency and mother–child supportiveness, 323, 328–29

resilience, of child victims/survivors, 45–47, 247

development of, 81–82

mothers' contributions to, 244–45

resistance to coercive control, 121–22, 327–28

by adult victims/survivors, 19–20, 92–97, 341

by child victims/survivors, 45–46, 78–79, 92–97, 104–5, 341

perpetrators' punishment of children for, 88–90, 104

to perpetrators' undermining tactics, 141–42

significance of, 97

respect, in mother–child supportiveness, children's thoughts and feelings about, 309–10

risk-averse behavior, in child victim/survivor, mothers' help in overcoming, 225–27

safety

of home, post-separation, 201–4

post-separation, 201–4, 316

reassurances about, 218–19

undermining of, post-separation, 189–90

sampling

purposive, 60

snowball, 60

self-blame

in child victims/survivors, 217–18, 330

maternal, 329–30

self-centeredness, perpetrators', 17

and child sexual abuse, 85

self-defense, victims'/survivors', 19–20

self-determination, victims', 93

self-identity, positive, in victims/survivors, 342

"self-policing," 14–15

separation from perpetrator/father, mothers' decision-making about, 183–84

Serious Crime Act 2015 s. 76

children left behind by, 40–41

victims/survivors defined in, 40–41

services, perpetrators' exploitation of, to discredit victims, 7

sexual abuse, 5, 85, 138, 175–76. *See also* rape

child's recovery from, mother's help with confidence-building and, 229

mothers' reports to family court about, court's disbelief of, 118–19, 336–37

perpetrators' cessation of, 110–11

sexual coercion, 5

overlap with other tactics, 9

shame, overcoming, confidence-building and, 228–29

sister-like qualities, in mother–child relationship, 317–20

situational couple violence

children's experience of, 43–44

coercive control and, 9–12, 43–44

as "lesser offense", 21–22

male vs. female rates of, 24–25

mutuality in, 36–37

prevalence of, 11

society/socialization, messages/ narratives in, and coercive control, 26–28

space for action, victims'/survivors', restriction of, 19

speech, delayed, in child living with
 coercive control, 87–88
stalking, 5
 of children, by perpetrator, 86–87
 post-separation, 187–92
Stark, Evan, *Coercive Control: How Men
 Entrap Women in Personal Life*,
 1–2, 41
state systems
 and post-separation coercive
 control, 198–99
 and recovery possibility, 198–99
strength(s), victims'/survivors'
 approaches based on, practitioners' use
 of, recommendations for, 340–42
 helping victims/survivors to
 recognize, 341–42
suicide
 mothers' decisions about, children's
 presence and, 215, 234–37
 mothers' feelings about, children's
 awareness of, 267–69, 273
 by perpetrators, 108
 by victim, 7–8
support(s). *See also* mother–child
 supportiveness
 child-to-mother, 95–96, 152–54, 159,
 163, 256–57, 259–60
 children's positive evaluation of,
 in pattern 2 mother–child
 relationship, 276
 healthy versus unhealthy, 52–54
 high-stakes, 264, 271–73, 280
 in pattern 2 mother–child
 relationship, 265–67, 271–73
 as resistance to coercive control, 94–96
 for children, in dealing with negative
 parenting, 135–36
 formal (*see also* recovery programs)
 sources of, 200–1
 improving, recommendations for, 339
 informal
 lack of, in pattern 3 families, 284

 in pattern 1 mother–child
 relationships, 261
 mother-to-child, 151, 152
 emotional, as resistance to coercive
 control, 94–96
 in pattern 2 mother–child
 relationship, 265–67, 273–74
 for mothers and children, research
 recommendations on,
 323, 326–27
 networks of, post-separation, 256, 341
 pattern 1 children's feelings
 about, 257–59
 pattern 2 children's feelings
 about, 274–78
 pattern 3 children's feelings
 about, 287–90
 for pattern 3 families, 292–93
 in pattern 1 families, 261, 262–64,
 270–71
 pattern 1 mothers' feelings
 about, 259–62
 pattern 2 mothers' feelings
 about, 278–79
 pattern 3 mothers' feelings
 about, 290–92
 post-separation
 inadequate, effects on outcomes,
 251–52, 282
 and positive outcomes, 249–51
 sources of, 256, 274
 professional
 for children, 284
 and children's breaking free
 from perpetrator's distorted
 thinking, 330–34
 effects of, in pattern 3 families, 285
 and mother–child relationship
 patterns post-separation, 249–
 53, 269, 277, 282
 in pattern 4 families, 299–300
 sources of, isolation from, 6, 16–17
 children's experience of, 44

INDEX

supportiveness. *See* mother–child
   supportiveness
surveillance, 111–12
   perpetrator's, children used in, 82, 102,
      294–96
system(s), perpetrators' exploitation of, to
   discredit victims, 7

tactics (of coercive control), 1–2, 3–9, 13,
      16–17, 121–22, 302
   nonviolent versus violent, 22–24
   as not hard to "read," 181
   overlap of, 9
   targeted at children and young people,
      8–9, 42–45
   for undermining mother–child
      relationship, 139–40
   used to destroy mother–child
      relationship, 296
*Talking about Domestic Abuse: A
   Photo Activity Workbook
   to Develop Communication
   between Mothers and Young
   People*, 209–10
*Talking to My Mum: A Picture Workbook
   for Workers, Mothers and
   Children Affected by Domestic
   Abuse*, 209–10
tantrums, perpetrator's, 164–65
threat, 7, 16–17. *See also* credible threat;
      death threats
   perpetrator's use of, 111–12
   post-separation, 187–92
time together, mother and child
   enjoyable, 144
   increased, in recovery, 215, 233–34
   in pattern 2 families, 279
   in pattern 3 families, 289–90
   perpetrator's/father's prevention of,
      140, 177–78
   post-separation abuse and, 188
   as resistance to coercive control, 94–96,
      151–52

as supportive, 157
trust, in mother–child supportiveness
   children's thoughts and feelings
      about, 309–10
   mothers' thoughts and feelings
      about, 311–12

unfreedom, 16–17
United Nations Convention on the Rights
   of the Child, 298–99

verbal abuse, 16–17
   of mother, by perpetrator/father,
      167, 176
   mother's protection of children
      from, 157
victim-blaming, 33–34, 113–14, 329–30
   and children's post-separation recovery,
      195–98, 204–7, 289
   mutualizing language and, 36–37
victim/survivor parent
   attempts to extricate themselves from
      coercive control, 112–13
   gendered perceptions of, 29–37
   limited space for action, recognition
      of, 111–12
   micro-level strategies for protecting
      children, 112–13
   understanding the position of, 111–14
victims/survivors
   child and adult, similarity of
      experiences, 45, 323, 326–27
   male to female ratios of, 24–25
   overfocus on parenting by, damage
      done by, 31–32
violence. *See also* domestic violence;
      intimate partner violence;
      situational couple violence
   child-to-parent, 141
   gender-based, 38
   overlap with other tactics, 9
   perpetrators and, 22–24
   physical (*see* physical abuse)

violence (*cont.*)
    post-separation, 187–92
    threats of, 7, 16–17
    against victim, 7–8
    victims'/survivors' use of, 19–20

withdrawn behavior, in child victim/
    survivor, 86
    mothers' help in overcoming,
        225–27, 283

women
    child abuse by, in context of
        perpetrator's/father's coercive
        control, 113–14
    dependence on partners, 25–26
    as perpetrators of coercive control,
        24–25, 37–38, 76, 326
workbooks
    as aids for recovery, 209–10
    for mother–child communication, 209–10